Helen Laurence
William Miller
Editors

Academic Research on the Internet: Options for Scholars and Libraries

Academic Research on the Internet: Options for Scholars and Libraries has been co-published simultaneously as *Journal of Library Adminisration,* Volume 30, Numbers 1/2 and 3/4 2000.

Pre-publication
REVIEWS,
COMMENTARIES,
EVALUATIONS . . .

"This work emphasizes quality over quantity. Each chapter presents the reader with best research-oriented web sites in the field, including both fee and free sources. *Academic Research on the Internet* serves as both a state-of-the-art review of academic use of the Internet as well as guide to the best Internet sites and services. It will be a useful addition for any academic library."

David A. Tyckoson, MLS
Head of Reference
California State University-Fresno

"It is ironic that the most thorough and systematic treatment of the utility of the World Wide Web for scholarly research is found in a book, and one written by librarians as well. This book will help all of us get a better handle on the solid research material that is available on the Web without relying on traditional search engines.

This book demonstrates the power that libraries can and must have to organize and make more accessible the resources that form the raw material for the scholar. That has been our role in the past and I am confident that it will continue to be our role. This volume is a testament to the ability of librarians (perhaps uniquely) to make sense of the chaotic state of the Internet.

This is an essential book for all librarians and most scholars. It is the best guide to the Internet available today. And it should continue to be useful in the future, particularly if it is updated regularly."

Rush G. Miller
University Librarian
University of Pittsburgh

"In this book, Helen Laurence and William Miller have compiled contributed highlights of some of the best academic research resources available on the Internet. The book does not attempt to measure the Internet resources against the print. Its benefit is in each contributor's assessment of the real value of the extent to which the Internet can support scholarly research in 14 disciplines. Most striking were the comments on the roles the librarian must command in sharing Internet resources information with discipline faculty and assisting them in discovery, in knowledge building, and in integrating Internet resources in cources and publications.

The contributors give an overview of each discipline, explaining how the researchers of the field do their research and how the Internet may or may not enhance a particular discipline, and giving the cautions and pitfalls librarians should be aware of in assisting researchers. The chapters are in alphabetical order (how else!) and in that way the book will be most useful as a reference tool and a textbook."

Derrie Roark Perez, EdD, MLS
Interim Director
University of South Florida Library
Tampa, FL

Academic Research on the Internet: Options for Scholars and Libraries

Academic Research on the Internet: Options for Scholars and Libraries has been co-published simultaneously as *Journal of Library Administration,* Volume 30, Numbers 1/2 and 3/4 2000.

The *Journal of Library Administration* Monographic "Separates"

Below is a list of "separates," which in serials librarianship means a special issue simultaneously published as a special journal issue or double-issue *and* as a "separate" hardbound monograph. (This is a format which we also call a "DocuSerial.")

"Separates" are published because specialized libraries or professionals may wish to purchase a specific thematic issue by itself in a format which can be separately cataloged and shelved, as opposed to purchasing the journal on an on-going basis. Faculty members may also more easily consider a "separate" for classroom adoption.

"Separates" are carefully classified separately with the major book jobbers so that the journal tie-in can be noted on new book order slips to avoid duplicate purchasing.

You may wish to visit Haworth's website at . . .

http://www.HaworthPress.com

. . . to search our online catalog for complete tables of contents of these separates and related publications.

You may also call 1-800-HAWORTH (outside US/Canada: 607-722-5857), or Fax 1-800-895-0582 (outside US/Canada: 607-771-0012), or e-mail at:

getinfo@haworthpressinc.com

Academic Research on the Internet: Options for Scholars and Libraries, edited by Helen Laurence, MLS, EdD, and William Miller, MLS, PhD (Vol. 30, No. 1/2/3/4, 2000). *"Emphasizes quality over quantity. . . . Presents the reader with the best research-oriented Web sites in the field. A state-of-the-art review of academic use of the Internet as well as a guide to the best Internet sites and services. . . . A useful addition for any academic library."* (David A. Tyckoson, MLS, Head of Reference, California State University, Fresno)

Management for Research Libraries Cooperation, edited by Sul H. Lee, PhD (Vol. 29. No. 3/4, 2000). *Delivers sound advice, models, and strategies for increasing sharing between institutions to maximize the amount of printed and electronic research material you can make available in your library while keeping costs under control.*

Integration in the Library Organization, edited by Christine E. Thompson, PhD (Vol. 29, No. 2 1999). *Provides librarians with the necessary tools to help libraries balance and integrate public and technical services and to improve the capability of libraries to offer patrons quality services and large amounts of information.*

Library Training for Staff and Customers, edited by Sara Ramser Beck, MLS, MBA (Vol. 29, No. 1, 1999). *This comprehensive book is designed to assist library professionals involved in presenting or planning training for library staff members and customers. You will explore ideas for effective general reference training, training on automated systems, training in specialized subjects such as African American history and biography, and training for areas such as patents and trademarks, and business subjects.* Library Training for Staff and Customers *answers numerous training questions and is an excellent guide for planning staff development.*

Collection Development in the Electronic Environment: Shifting Priorities, edited by Sul H. Lee (Vol. 28, No. 4, 1999). *Through case studies and firsthand experiences, this volume discusses meeting the needs of scholars at universities, budgeting issues, user education, staffing in the electronic age, collaborating libraries and resources, and how vendors meet the needs of different customers.*

The Age Demographics of Academic Librarians: A Profession Apart, by Stanley J. Wilder (Vol. 28, No. 3, 1999). *The average age of librarians has been increasing dramatically since 1990. This unique book will provide insights on how this demographic issue can impact a library and what can be done to make the effects positive.*

Collection Development in a Digital Environment, edited by Sul H. Lee (Vol. 28, No. 1, 1999). *Explores ethical and technological dilemmas of collection development and gives several suggestions on how a library can successfully deal with these challenges and provide patrons with the information they need.*

Scholarship, Research Libraries, and Global Publishing, by Jutta Reed-Scott (Vol. 27, No. 3/4, 1999). *This book documents a research project in conjunction with the Association of Research Libraries (ARL) that explores the issue of foreign acquisition and how it affects collection in international studies, area studies, collection development, and practices of international research libraries.*

Managing Multicultural Diversity in the Library: Principles and Issues for Administrators, edited by Mark Winston (Vol. 27, No. 1/2, 1999). *Defines diversity, clarifies why it is important to address issues of diversity, and identifies goals related to diversity and how to go about achieving those goals.*

Information Technology Planning, edited by Lori A. Goetsch (Vol. 26, No. 3/4, 1999). *Offers innovative approaches and strategies useful in your library and provides some food for thought about information technology as we approach the millennium.*

The Economics of Information in the Networked Environment, edited by Meredith A. Butler, MLS, and Bruce R. Kingma, PhD (Vol. 26, No. 1/2, 1998). *"A book that should be read both by information professionals and by administrators, faculty and others who share a collective concern to provide the most information to the greatest number at the lowest cost in the networked environment." (Thomas J. Galvin, PhD, Professor of Information Science and Policy, University at Albany, State University of New York)*

OCLC 1967-1997: Thirty Years of Furthering Access to the World's Information, edited by K. Wayne Smith (Vol. 25, No. 2/3/4, 1998). *"A rich–and poignantly personal, at times–historical account of what is surely one of this century's most important developments in librarianship." (Deanna B. Marcum, PhD, President, Council on Library and Information Resources, Washington, DC)*

Management of Library and Archival Security: From the Outside Looking In, edited by Robert K. O'Neill, PhD (Vol. 25, No. 1, 1998). *"Provides useful advice and on-target insights for professionals caring for valuable documents and artifacts." (Menzi L Behrnd-Klodt, JD, Attorney/Archivist, Klodt and Associates, Madison, WI)*

Economics of Digital Information: Collection, Storage, and Delivery, edited by Sul H. Lee (Vol. 24, No. 4, 1997). *Highlights key concepts and issues vital to a library's successful venture into the digital environment and helps you understand why the transition from the printed page to the digital packet has been problematic for both creators of proprietary materials and users of those materials.*

The Academic Library Director: Reflections on a Position in Transition, edited by Frank D'Andraia, MLS (Vol. 24, No. 3, 1997). *"A useful collection to have whether you are seeking a position as director or conducting a search for one." (College & Research Libraries News)*

Emerging Patterns of Collection Development in Expanding Resource Sharing, Electronic Information, and Network Environment, edited by Sul H. Lee (Vol. 24, No. 1/2, 1997). *"The issues it deals with are common to us all. We all need to make our finds go further and our resources work harder, and there are ideas here which we can all develop." (The Library Association Record)*

Interlibrary Loan/Document Delivery and Customer Satisfaction: Strategies for Redesigning Services, edited by Pat L. Weaver-Meyers, Wilbur A. Stolt, Yem S. Fong (Vol. 23, No. 1/2, 1997). *"No interlibrary loan department supervisor at any mid-sized to large college or university library can afford not to read this book." (Gregg Sapp, MLS, MEd, Head of Access Services, University of Miami, Richter Library, Coral Gables, Florida)*

Access, Resource Sharing and Collection Development, edited by Sul H. Lee (Vol. 22, No. 4, 1996). *Features continuing investigation and discussion of important library issues, specifically the role of libraries in acquiring, storing, and disseminating information in different formats.*

Managing Change in Academic Libraries, edited by Joseph J. Branin (Vol. 22, No. 2/3, 1996). *"Touches on several aspects of academic library management, emphasizing the changes that are occurring at the present time. . . . Recommended this title for individuals or libraries interested in management aspects of academic libraries." (RQ American Library Association)*

Libraries and Student Assistants: Critical Links, edited by William K. Black, MLS (Vol. 21, No. 3/4, 1995). *"A handy reference work on many important aspects of managing student assistants. . . . Solid, useful information on basic management issues in this work and several chapters are useful for experienced managers." (The Journal of Academic Librarianship)*

The Future of Resource Sharing, edited by Shirley K. Baker and Mary E. Jackson, MLS (Vol. 21, No. 1/2, 1995). *"Recommended for library and information science schools because of its balanced presentation of the ILL/document delivery issues." (Library Acquisitions: Practice and Theory)*

The Future of Information Services, edited by Virginia Steel, MA, and C. Brigid Welch, MLS (Vol. 20, No. 3/4, 1995). *"The leadership discussions will be useful for library managers as will the discussions of how library structures and services might work in the next century." (Australian Special Libraries)*

The Dynamic Library Organizations in a Changing Environment, edited by Joan Giesecke, MLS, DPA (Vol. 20, No. 2, 1995). *"Provides a significant look at potential changes in the library world and presents its readers with possible ways to address the negative results of such changes. . . . Covers the key issues facing today's libraries . . . Two thumbs up!" (Marketing Library Resources)*

Access, Ownership, and Resource Sharing, edited by Sul H. Lee, PhD (Vol. 20, No. 1, 1995). *The contributing authors present a useful and informative look at the current status of information provision and some of the challenges the subject presents.*

Planning for Library Services: A Guide to Utilizing Planning Methods for Library Management, edited by Charles R. McClure, PhD (Vol. 2, No. 3/4, 1982). *"Should be read by anyone who is involved in planning processes of libraries–certainly by every administrator of a library or system." (American Reference Books Annual)*

Libraries as User-Centered Organizations: Imperatives for Organizational Change, edited by Meredith A. Butler (Vol. 19, No. 3/4, 1994). *"Presents a very timely and well-organized discussion of major trends and influences causing organizational changes." (Science Books & Films)*

Declining Acquisitions Budgets: Allocation, Collection Development and Impact Communication, edited by Sul H. Lee (Vol. 19, No. 2, 1994). *"Expert and provocative. . . . Presents many ways of looking at library budget deterioration and responses to it . . . There is much food for thought here. "(Library Resources & Technical Services)*

The Role and Future of Special Collections in Research Libraries: British and American Perspectives, edited by Sul H. Lee (Vol. 19, No. 1, 1993). *"A provocative but informative read for library users, academic administrators, and private sponsors." (International Journal of Information and Library Research)*

Catalysts for Change: Managing Libraries in the 1990s, edited by Gisela M. von Dran, DPA, MLS, and Jennifer Cargill, MSLS, MSed (Vol. 18, No. 3/4, 1994). *"A useful collection of articles which focuses on the need for librarians to employ enlightened management practices in order to adapt to and thrive in the rapidly changing information environment." (Australian Library Review)*

Integrating Total Quality Management in a Library Setting, edited by Susan Jurow, MLS, and Susan B. Barnard, MLS (Vol. 18, No. 1/2, 1993). *"Especially valuable are the librarian experiences that directly relate to real concerns about TQM. Recommended for all professional reading collections." (Library Journal)*

Monographic "Separates" list continued at the back

Academic Research
on the Internet:
Options for Scholars and Libraries

Helen Laurence
William Miller
Editors

Academic Research on the Internet: Options for Scholars and Libraries has been co-published simultaneously as *Journal of Library Administration,* Volume 30, Numbers 1/2 and 3/4 2000.

The Haworth Information Press
An Imprint of
The Haworth Press, Inc.
New York • London • Oxford

Published by

The Haworth Information Press, 10 Alice Street, Binghamton, NY 13904-1580 USA

The Haworth Information Press is an imprint of the The Haworth Press, Inc., 10 Alice Street, Binghamton, NY 13904-1580 USA.

Academic Research on the Internet: Options for Scholars and Libraries has been co-published simultaneously as *Journal of Library Administration,* Volume 30, Numbers 1/2 and 3/4 2000.

The development, preparation, and publication of this work has been undertaken with great care. However, the publisher, employees, editors, and agents of The Haworth Press and all imprints of The Haworth Press, Inc., including The Haworth Medical Press® and Pharmaceutical Products Press®, are not responsible for any errors contained herein or for consequences that may ensue from use of materials or information contained in this work. Opinions expressed by the author(s) are not necessarily those of The Haworth Press, Inc.

Cover design by Thomas J. Mayshock Jr.

Library of Congress Cataloging-in-Publication Data

Academic research on the Internet : options for scholars & libraries / Helen Laurence, William Miller, editors.
     p. cm.
     Published also as v.30, no. 1/2 and 3/4, 2000 of the Journal of Library Administration.
     Includes bibliographical references and index.
     ISBN 0-7890-1176-X (alk. paper)–ISBN 0-7890-1177-8 (alk. paper)
     1. Computer network resources. 2. Computer network resources–United States. 3. Scholarly Web sites. 4. Scholarly Web sites–United States. I. Laurence, Helen. II. MIller, William, 1947- III. Journal of library administration.
ZA4201 .A216 2000
025.04–dc21
                                                      00-057557

INDEXING & ABSTRACTING

Contributions to this publication are selectively indexed or abstracted in print, electronic, online, or CD-ROM version(s) of the reference tools and information services listed below. This list is current as of the copyright date of this publication. See the end of this section for additional notes.

- *Academic Abstracts/CD-ROM*
- *Academic Search: data base of 2,000 selected academic serials, updated monthly*
- *AGRICOLA Database*
- *BUBL Information Service, an Internet-based Information Service for the UK higher education community <URL: http://bubl.ac.uk/>*
- *CNPIEC Reference Guide: Chinese National Directory of Foreign Periodicals*
- *Current Articles on Library Literature and Services (CALLS)*
- *Current Awareness Abstracts of Library & Information Management Literature, ASLIB (UK)*
- *Current Index to Journals in Education*
- *Educational Administration Abstracts (EAA)*
- *FINDEX <www.publist.com>*
- *Higher Education Abstracts*
- *IBZ International Bibliography of Periodical Literature*
- *Index to Periodical Articles Related to Law*
- *Information Reports & Bibliographies*
- *Information Science Abstracts*
- *Informed Librarian, The <http://www.infosourcespub.com>*
- *INSPEC*
- *Journal of Academic Librarianship: Guide to Professional Literature, The*
- *Konyvtari Figyelo-Library Review*
- *Library & Information Science Abstracts (LISA)*

(continued)

- *Library and Information Science Annual (LISCA)* *<www.lu.com/arba>*
- *Library Literature*
- *MasterFILE: updated database from EBSCO Publishing*
- *Newsletter of Library and Information Services*
- *OCLC Public Affairs Information Service <www.pais.org>*
- *OT BibSys*
- *PASCAL, c/o Institute de L'Information Scientifique et Technique*
- *Referativnyi Zhurnal (Abstracts Journal of the All-Russian Institute of Scientific and Technical Information–in Russian)*
- *Trade & Industry Index*

Special Bibliographic Notes related to special journal issues (separates) and indexing/abstracting:

- indexing/abstracting services in this list will also cover material in any "separate" that is co-published simultaneously with Haworth's special thematic journal issue or DocuSerial. Indexing/abstracting usually covers material at the article/chapter level.
- monographic co-editions are intended for either non-subscribers or libraries which intend to purchase a second copy for their circulating collections.
- monographic co-editions are reported to all jobbers/wholesalers/approval plans. The source journal is listed as the "series" to assist the prevention of duplicate purchasing in the same manner utilized for books-in-series.
- to facilitate user/access services all indexing/abstracting services are encouraged to utilize the co-indexing entry note indicated at the bottom of the first page of each article/chapter/contribution.
- this is intended to assist a library user of any reference tool (whether print, electronic, online, or CD-ROM) to locate the monographic version if the library has purchased this version but not a subscription to the source journal.
- individual articles/chapters in any Haworth publication are also available through the Haworth Document Delivery Service (HDDS).

Academic Research on the Internet: Options for Scholars and Libraries

CONTENTS

ABOUT THE EDITORS

Helen Laurence, MLS, EdD, graduated from Harvard University, received the MEd from Harvard Graduate School of Education and the EdD from the University Massachusetts–Amherst. After ten years as a Librarian with the Division of Libraries, Museums and Archaeological Services in St. Croix, U.S. Virgin Islands, she earned the MLS from University of South Florida and went to work as a Reference Librarian at Florida Atlantic University. She began teaching Internet classes in 1994. Dr. Laurence now serves as Systems and Honors College Librarian and co-manages the Florida Atlantic University Libraries Web site.

William Miller, PhD, MLS, is Director of Libraries at Florida Atlantic University. He formerly served as Head of Reference at Michigan State University, and as Associate Dean of Libraries at Bowling Green State University (Ohio). Dr. Miller has a PhD from the University of Rochester and an MLS from the University of Toronto. He is Past-President of the Association of College and Research Libraries, has served as Chair of the *Choice* Editorial Board, and is a frequent contributor to professional journals, as well as being a contributing editor of *Library Issues.* Dr. Miller also teaches English Literature courses.

Introduction

Helen Laurence

Purveyors of electronic commerce, shaping the look and feel of the Web, vigorously promote the notion that the answers to all our questions are only a keystroke away. As a result, library patrons expect to find it all in cyberspace. Many library patrons probably can satisfy all their information needs in cyberspace, but for the purposes of academic research, such expectations are unrealistic and even dangerous. Library administration have been under increasing pressure to cancel print products in the face of the conventional wisdom telling us that "everything's on the Web for free." Library decision makers, who at first might have rejoiced that digitization technology would liberate them from the upward spiral of subscription prices, have quickly learned that the putative cost-savings associated with electronic products are as ephemeral as Web-based resources themselves.[1]

This volume seeks to assess the real value of the Internet for scholarly research. We begin with Carol Tenopir's analysis of fee-based vs. free online resources. In "Getting What You Pay For?" Tenopir cites the results of Susan Feldman's 1998 "Internet Search-Off" contest in which expert searchers were asked to run the same searches on the free Web and in commercial online services. The winning searches (mine among them) produced results consistent with Tenopir's conclusions: both methodologies are useful tools with differing strengths and weaknesses; both tools should be utilized for a complete job of research.

The utility of propriety indexes and full-text databases for scholarly research is well-established; the free Internet is more problematic.

[Haworth co-indexing entry note]: "Introduction." Laurence, Helen. Co-published simultaneously in *Journal of Library Administration* (The Haworth Information Press, an imprint of The Haworth Press, Inc.) Vol. 30, No. 1/2, 2000, pp. 1-8; and: *Academic Research on the Internet: Options for Scholars & Libraries* (ed: Helen Laurence, and William Miller) The Haworth Information Press, an imprint of The Haworth Press, Inc., 2000, pp. 1-8. Single or multiple copies of this article are available for a fee from The Haworth Document Delivery Service [1-800-342-9678, 9:00 a.m. - 5:00 p.m. (EST). E-mail address: getinfo@haworthpressinc.com].

Although the Internet was conceived as a vehicle for scientific communication, for collaboration among scientists, and for presenting the results of scientific inquiry, today's commodity Internet is confusing, disorganized, huge, and growing. In late 1997, there were 320 million searchable Web pages, according to a widely-reported study conducted by a team of computer scientists at the NEC Research Institute.[2] By February of 1999, the same team determined that the searchable Web consisted of 800 million pages, a growth rate of about 250% per year.[3]

Sheer size alone, however, is insufficient to explain the frustrating unreliability of the Internet for serious research. Compare the estimated 6 trillion characters in those 800 million Web pages with the 20 trillion characters calculated to comprise the collections of the Library of Congress. Yet every item in the Library of Congress can be accurately identified and located, while Web documents are unreliably retrieved with significantly less efficiency by relatively primitive search engines. Even the search engine with the most comprehensive index of Web resources (Northern Light at <http://www.northernlight. com/>) covers only about 16% of the 800 million indexable Web pages. Northern Light is followed by Snap and AltaVista at 15.5%. HotBot, which, according to the earlier study, led the pack at 34% coverage of the then 320 million available Web pages, now trails at 11.3%.[4]

ORGANIZING FOR ACCESS

What distinguishes access to information in the Library of Congress from access to information on the Internet, aside from the fact that the entire LC database is indexed, is a standardized classification system, which the Library of Congress has and which the Internet still needs. Indeed, a growing number of projects are using standard library classification schemes and/or controlled vocabularies to organize Web resources. One of the most well-established is OCLC's NetFirst. Another is CyberStacks, a demonstration project at Iowa State University limited to scholarly resources in selected fields of Science and Technology.[5] Gerry McKiernan, the architect of CyberStacks, also maintains "Beyond Bookmarks," a clearinghouse of Web sites which have applied standard controlled vocabularies and/or classifications to organize Web resources.[6] The Finnish Virtual Library[7] represents the most comprehensive application of controlled vocabularies for this purpose to date.[8] This approach, which requires human intervention to identify, select and describe significant resources, is our best current strategy for overcoming the problems of search inefficiency and lack of quality control which have characterized the performance of search engines.

Services that began as simple search engines have now developed into portals with value-added directories of selected links to impose structure upon the random serendipity of search results. Lycos, for example, licensed the Open Directory, with volunteer subject specialists selecting quality Web sites and assigning them to categories.[9] Many search engines now incorporate information retrieval enhancements such as ranking and relevance ratings but still fall short of the level of specificity provided by a standard classification scheme.[10]

A parallel development that should improve resource discovery in the distributed, networked environment is the use of intelligent agents to filter and rank Internet resources based on specific criteria. Intelligent Web tools typically create individual user profiles by such techniques as linguistic analysis and then make recommendations of Web resources that match the inferred information needs. Increasingly sophisticated algorithms are being developed to imbue agents with more learning capability.[11] Even after this technology matures, however, the quality of search results will still depend on the quality of the target database–a variation on the theme of "garbage in: garbage out," and the Internet, as we know, is full of garbage.

An early (1995-96) attempt at quality control was Argos, a limited area search engine developed by the Internet Applications (IA) Lab at the University of Evansville. Argos used a Web crawler to search a dataset of 14,000 established sites in ancient and medieval studies. Human intervention was required to ensure that any Web page found through Argos was hand-picked by a subject specialist. URL: <http://argos.evansville.edu/>. The GOLIATH Project, an interdisciplinary joint venture by the IA Lab and the International Consortium for Alternative Academic Publication (ICAAP) combines the use of agent software with human peer-review.[12] URL: <http://www.icaap.org/standards.html>. The GOLIATH search engine is based on DAVID (Dedicated Accrediting Variable Indexing Device). The developers of DAVID explain that it is "accrediting" because it guarantees that "any item appearing in a return set has undergone a procedure of true peer-review." "Variable" refers to its use of a "database requiring human intervention" for Web resources without metadata, and "automatically defaults to a meta-tag system" for Web sites with metadata, regardless of the metadata standard used.[13]

In a felicitous application of traditional library collection development principles to Web-based resources, *Choice*, the monthly review service published by the Association of College and Research Libraries, now issues a special supplement of Web reviews. The reviews are arranged in the standard *Choice* subject categories and evaluate "sites that most closely match *Choice*'s three principal selection criteria for Internet resources: (1) subject matter appropriate for undergraduate use; (2) content that complements the undergraduate curriculum and is relevant to academic libraries; and (3) materials that reflect high quality and authoritative producers."[14] The 1999 supplement contains nearly 600 signed reviews, 496 of them reprinted from previous Web supplements or regular issues of *Choice*. Although the supplement is issued only in paper format, a subject-based list of links to all reviewed resources is maintained at the *Choice* Web site. URL: <http://www.ala.org/acrl/choice>.

THE CURRENT STATE OF THE NET

The combination of a dataset, or many datasets created and indexed by human expert knowledge and mediated by software agents, promises to shape the future of academic research on the Internet. That future is still far from realization, however, and until then, researchers need expert guidance about Internet resources in the various disciplines. Therefore, we asked librarians and other subject specialists to assess the extent to which Internet resources can currently support scholarly research in a representative sample of fields.

We asked them to develop a snapshot of the state of the Net for academic research in their respective disciplines at this moment in time. We asked them to limit their attention to scholarly, rather than popular resources. Finally, we asked them to consider fee-based as well as free information.

COMMON THEMES

As the "snapshots" began to develop, we observed the recurrence of common themes from field to field. We discovered that the mass migration of government documents to the Web has created a relatively stable and reliable repository of extremely valuable data across the disciplines. We were impressed by the degree to which professional associations, organizations, and individual scholars have created and maintained collections of primary and secondary materials, often unavailable in any other formats.

For example, Dittemore and McMillan, in their brilliant article on Anthropology and Sociology, highlight the leading roles that libraries, archives, museums and government agencies play by creating online resources based on their own specialized collections. Here too, a familiar theme emerges: In addition to the uneven and even haphazard representation of important scholarly works on the Internet, the "chaotic shelving" of those resources contributes to the "unexpected rewards" as well as the "puzzling gaps" in Internet search results. "It is especially here that the guidance of respected organizations, such as the professional associations or libraries (which enter this arena with considerable expertise) is needed."

Similarly, when Bruce Pencek, for his extraordinarily comprehensive article on Political Science, polled academic colleagues on their use of Internet resources, he found that U.S. government publications are the "conspicuous exception" to the common complaint that "Internet counterparts to . . . established reference resources tend at best to be approximations: very strong on current affairs but lacking historical depth, heavily hyperlinked but of unknown staying power. . . ." Pencek suggests that the Internet is peerless for current events, news and analysis, and basic directory information. For archival information, however, "the Web remains problematic in point of storage, indexing, and retrieval."

QUALITY CONTROL

We were not surprised to find that all the authors in this volume address the issue of quality control. Steven Bell characterizes his effort to identify useful business resources as "finding gems among the rocks." He articulates what every librarian on the front line knows: that even though the quality of Internet resources is uneven at best, the average student "will almost always initially consult the Internet for information before seeking out other sources . . . [and] these students will also be completely unconvinced that most library resources are of any value." Proprietary, Web-based full text journal databases, published by such established vendors as Elsevier and the Johns Hopkins University Press, were at first universally hailed by librarians as a means to restore a measure of quality control to student bibliographies. Such resources are costly, however, and can ironically circumscribe rather than enhance scholarship. Scott Stebelman, in his definitive analysis of English and American literature Internet resources, issues an important caveat concerning the exclusive reliance on these tools:

> The result was indeed the citing of reputable scholarship, but at a cost; students, instead of trying to identify the best literature on a topic, increasingly defer to the path of least resistance, which is to incorporate *only* those articles that can be downloaded from a full-text database. . . . The library, which may still expend hundreds of thousands of dollars on its print subscriptions, may find that money wasted as print titles languish on the shelf. As for the students, they acquire negative research skills, believing that a self-contained database of articles can substitute for the diversity of opinion that is more likely to come from a multitude of publishers and information formats.

In general, however, the tendency in the articles included in this volume is not to measure Internet resources against their print counterparts. Stebelman refers to his own bibliography on hypertext and hypermedia "that nullifies traditional format boundaries." Michael Seadle, in particular, in his elegant treatment of history resources, seeks to "discard . . . traditional taxonomies and build . . . instead on the new capabilities that separate digital publishing from its paper-based predecessor."

This means that Seadle organizes resources by format in order to highlight the unique and unprecedented capabilities of the Internet that enable the creation of multimedia history. He abandons the "easy and obvious" classification of Web sites by country, period, or methodology and instead focuses on six groupings which seem significant now, including discussion groups, multimedia collections, photographic image collections, searchable text collections, indexes and reviews, and maps, data and transformative systems.

Finally, everyone mentions copyright. As Dittemore and McMillan put it, "where content on the Internet is concerned, the operant word in the phrase 'intellectual property' is property." Reliance on materials in the public domain must be tempered by the understanding that most of the seminal literature in all fields will remain under copyright for many years, and will accordingly be costly to access. Students in particular will usually prefer to use what is free, rather than what is good, although as Stebelman points out, public domain editions may be "the most spurious; an example are some of the editions made available through Project Gutenberg."

Unquestionably, the Internet can now support significant research in many fields, but in most circumstances the researcher must still consult traditional library resources and use a mix of online and print materials. Much of the best research material identified in this volume is only available for a fee; this will be a real barrier to the independent researcher, and, to a lesser extent, to those using the resources paid for by all but the most well-heeled libraries.

All these issues–archiving, quality control, indexing, storage and retrieval, ownership and especially cost–will figure prominently in ongoing conversations about the usefulness of the Internet as a vehicle for scholarly enterprise. The creation of a parallel Internet, in the high-speed networks under construction as part of the Internet2 project, will surely be a significant factor in this continuing debate, and perhaps in time, the Internet will become the predominant resource for scholarship. Until such time, the articles in this volume will help the student and scholar assess the current state of the Internet and determine the degree to which it can be used today for academic research.

Note: All URLs in this volume were accurate as of August 31, 1999.

NOTES

1. Majka, David R. "The Seven Deadly Sins of Digitization." *Online* 23 (March 1999):44. URL: *http://www.onlineinc.com/onlinemag/OL1999/majka3.html*

2. Lawrence, Steve and C. Lee Giles. "Searching the World Wide Web," *Science* 280 (April 3, 1998): 98-100.

3. Lawrence, Steve and C. Lee Giles. "Accessibility of information on the web," *Nature* 400 (July 8, 1999): 107-109.

4. Ibid.

5. CyberStacks. URL: *http://www2.iastate.edu/~CYBERSTACKS/homepage.html*. Retrieved July 29, 1999.

6. Beyond Bookmarks. URL: *http://www.public/iastate.edu/~CYBERSTACKS/CTW.htm*. Retrieved August 1, 1999.

7. Finnish Virtual Library. URL: *http://www.jyu.fi/library/virtuaalikirjasto/engvirli. htm*. Retrieved August 1, 1999.

8. McKiernan, Gerry. Posting to LITA-L. Subject: "New Items for *Journal of Internet Cataloging*." July 28, 1999.

9. Rappoport, Avi. "Racing the Engines: The Infonortics Search Engines Meeting, 1999." *Searcher* 7 (July-August 1999): 46.

10. McKiernan, Gerry. "Beyond Bookmarks: A Review of Frameworks, Features, and Functionalities of Schemes for Organizing the Web." *Internet Reference Services Quarterly* 3 (1998): 69-82.

11. Cheung, David W., Ben Kao, Joseph Lee. "Discovering user access patterns on the World Wide Web." *Knowledge-Based Systems* 10 (1998): 463-470.

12. Beavers, Anthony F. "Evaluating Search Engine Models for Scholarly Purposes." *D-Lib Magazine*, December, 1998. URL: *http://www.dlib.org/dlib/december98/12beavers. html*. Retrieved July 23, 1999.

13. Ibid, p. 6 of 7.

14. Graf, Francine. "About Web III," *Choice* 36 Supplement (1999): 18.

Getting What You Pay For?

Carol Tenopir

SUMMARY. What can we tell library funders who believe subscriptions can be cancelled because everything is on the Web for free? Specifically, how does the open Internet compare with proprietary online services as a research tool? Tenopir presents answers offered by representatives of Lexis-Nexis and Factiva (Dow Jones & Reuters), and cites the results of the "Internet Search-Off." She concludes that both Internet and traditional online services must be used to offer complete information services.

KEYWORDS. Internet-evaluation, Internet-research, online databases-evaluation, online databases-research, Lexis-Nexis, Factiva, Bates, Mary Ellen

The old adage, "you get what you pay for," doesn't always apply to the World Wide Web. Certainly, you frequently encounter worthless information (or wrong information, which is worse), but there's a wealth of very useful and valuable free information. Many government agencies, professional societies, medical support groups, museums, and libraries create content-rich free Web sites.

Still, although the number of authoritative sites grows daily, not

Carol Tenopir (E-mail: tenopir@utknx.utk.edu) is Professor at the School of Library and Information Science, University of Tennessee at Knoxville.

Reprinted from Library Journal February 1, 2000. Copyright© 2000 by Reed Elsevier, USA. Used by permission.

[Haworth co-indexing entry note]: "Getting What You Pay For?" Tenopir, Carol. Co-published simultaneously in *Journal of Library Administration* (The Haworth Information Press, an imprint of The Haworth Press, Inc.) Vol. 30, No. 1/2, 2000, pp. 9-14; and: *Academic Research on the Internet: Options for Scholars & Libraries* (ed: Helen Laurence, and William Miller) The Haworth Information Press, an imprint of The Haworth Press, Inc., 2000, pp. 9-14.

every topic is successfully or best searched on the Web. Library funders, however, may not understand why libraries also continue to pay for a variety of electronic information sources. Isn't everything needed, they ask, available for free on the Web?

Commercial online services and fee-based Web sites, of course, have a vested interest in the answers. Recently I asked representatives from Lexis-Nexis and Factiva, a Dow Jones & Reuters Company (formerly Dow Jones/Reuters Business Interactive) what they suggest librarians tell questioning funders. Although their answers often relate specifically to their own online systems, the arguments are broadly applicable.

LEXIS-NEXIS VS. THE WEB

Jill Konieczko, a regional representative for Lexis-Nexis, points out that L-N surpasses the Web in several ways. I've grouped her points into six themes:

Size. A new Web page is put up every four seconds, but L-N puts up 15.7 documents per second; L-N includes approximately one billion documents, the Web just 40 million.

Organization. L-N information is grouped into easily accessible and logical libraries or group files, while information is scattered on the Web. Similar information resources are grouped together on L-N for easier access (such as caselaw and filings or Investext and Dun & Bradstreet information), but Web sites from different providers are maintained separately.

Archives. L-N maintains deep archives, usually from the time a resource was added to the system, while there is little or no archive on much of the Web.

Searching. L-N includes powerful search tools in both its Boolean logic search engine and its relevance ranking/statistical search engine (FreeStyle). These tools include the capacity to improve precision with features such as focus, segments (fields), and proximity connectors. Advanced search features on many Web search engines are often limited to Boolean and/or adjacency.

Response time. L-N claims 99.84 percent reliability and less than six second response times on searches, while response time on the Web is highly variable, not to mention dependent on local conditions.

Customer service. L-N (and other online services) offers 24-hour customer service for technical and search assistance. On the Web, well, you're on your own.

While people may quibble about statistics used for size and that response time can be improved locally, organization of resources and efficiency of searching almost always clearly favor fee-based online aggregator services.

FACTIVA VS. THE WEB

Perhaps the best way to compare the relative merits of Web resources with fee-based services is to conduct head-to-head tests, so Factiva commissioned a "White Paper" by writer and information entrepreneur Mary Ellen Bates: "Selecting Business Intelligence Sources: The Public Web vs. Value-Added Online Services." (Dow Jones Interactive subscribers can find the paper in PDF format.)

Bates tested three common ways to access information: the free Web, fee based Web sites (such as Northern Light and the Electric Library), and value-added business information services (like Dow Jones Interactive).

Bates's six business queries ranged from the straightforward ("we need a copy of the article that appeared in yesterday's *Washington Post* about the EPA's rules . . ." and "a company profile of Genentech") to the more complex ("market analysis of nicotine patches" and "product development of in-seat power supplies for airline passengers"). The paper includes in-depth analysis for every search, including cost, completeness of answers, time needed, and depth of archives.

When comprehensive or complete answers to complex information are required, searchers must access a variety of sources. Bates found that "at least part of every business question could be answered using Web resources alone or in conjunction with fee-based sources. However, in almost every case, complete answers were only available through the value-added service."

The Web compared well on very simple searches, such as finding a recent newspaper article, but, as the questions became more complex, the Web took longer to search and retrieved less useful information. Because most commercial online services aggregate different types of sources–including indexes and abstracts, full texts of journals, and statistical sources–and because they have deeper archives, users find complete answers faster.

Research time, or cost-efficiency, is another important area where commercial online services compare well (at least for an experienced online searcher). In Bates's study, every question (except retrieving a current *Washington Post* article) took longer on the Web, while yielding a less complete answer.

She also calculated "true research costs" by adding in personnel costs. In many cases, these actual costs came out lower for Dow Jones Interactive than for the Web or fee-based Web sites because of time saved. In one question, the searcher spent 33 minutes on the Web (calculated at a personnel cost of $25.74) and found no useful material. Although the cost was $76.47 on Dow Jones Interactive, it took the experienced searcher only 14 minutes to get a complete answer. For some but not all of the other questions, the "true research costs" were actually higher on the Web.

If asked to assemble a presentation listing relative strengths and weaknesses of the free Web vs. commercial online services, you might include the following points that are detailed in Bates's White Paper.

STRENGTHS AND LIMITATIONS

For the free Web, the strengths are: many expert sites, maintained by experts on a particular topic; links to other resources; government Web sites that offer reliable information; information available at little cost for good searchers; cheap access to newspapers and other current information.

The limitations are: no capacity to aggregate or integrate searches; limited archives; instability of sites; limited power searching features; questionable reliability and accuracy of sites. Another limitation of Web search engines is the growing practice of adjusting relevance rankings if a site pays a premium to the search engine (or Web sites may just manipulate the relevance ranking of search engines by "spam-indexing").

For fee-based Web sites (such as Northern Light or Electric Library), the strengths include: usually provide an archive as well as current information; allow power searching; provide copyrighted materials such as journal and magazine articles for a relatively low fee; provide collections by topic.

The limitations are: usually require credit cards for purchase; encourage impulse buying of articles when the same source may already be available (from the library) to the person doing the ordering; usually limited to one type of information.

For commercial online services, Bates highlights five main strengths of services such as Dow Jones Interactive, Lexis-Nexis, and Dialog. They provide aggregation of hundreds of sources that can be searched simultaneously: extensive archives; a wide variety of types of sources; powerful search and output features; and automatic alert or current awareness search services.

Bates does not summarize limitations of value-added online services, but some should be mentioned. High out-of-pocket costs are the most obvious drawback. Another is the need to have someone trained to get the most out of the many power-searching features. Reliability is always cited as a strength of fee-based publications, but sometimes resources such as directories are inaccurate because they are not kept up-to-date by the publishers. Online aggregators make no claims as to the accuracy or reliability of the sources they provide, although, unlike with the Web, there is always a publisher for these resources with a reputation to uphold. Also, Web sources usually include graphics and links.

OTHER COMPARISONS

Bates was not the first expert searcher to run tests to compare the Web with commercial online services. In a 1998 column ("Online Meetings of Minds," *LJ* 10/1/98, p. 38, 40), I mentioned Susan Feldman's "Internet Search-Off," results of which were presented at the 1998 National Online Meeting (a preliminary description was published in *Searcher*, 2/98 [p. 28-35]). Her findings remain valid today.

Feldman challenged experienced searchers to run the same searches in Dialog, Dow Jones Interactive, and on the free Web. Like Bates, Feldman found that Web searching takes much more time to get the same or less complete results for many topics. She found the Web to be better for current information about specific small companies; locating pictures and illustrations; product information directly from a company; and current medical statistics.

Most often, users must search both the Web and traditional online sources for complete information. Feldman reported they complement each other, especially when searches seek a range of items: standards; general interest articles; popular subjects; organizations or directory information; reviews, evaluations, and how-to information; government regulations; competitive intelligence; and information about "obscure topics."

Traditional online services alone were found to give better results for more specific items: archival or longitudinal information; chemical or electrical engineering; history; market or industry reports; current drug studies; industry newsletters and journals; financial industry coverage; scholarly journal articles; high-quality information; and quick searches when the user knows the information is likely to be there and time is a factor.

Like Bates, Feldman reminds fellow-searchers to "always remember–time is money. Free information that takes too long to find and format is expensive information."

In 1998 *Online* magazine began a feature called "Head-to-Head," which compared the results of searching on traditional online services and the Web for different questions. The results varied with the type of information needed. The expert searchers who participated show remarkable variations in strategies. Almost all came to the conclusion that both resources are needed.

Nancy Garman of *Online* suggests instead of viewing the question as the Internet vs. traditional online, "why not think in terms of ORing the Internet with the traditional online services for many of our searches."

As studies repeatedly show, comparisons should not be used to choose one type of online resource over another. To offer complete information services, every library needs to offer Web access and a variety of fee-based online services, not to mention CD-ROM and print.

Anthropology and Sociology
On and About the Internet

Margaret R. Dittemore
Gary A. McMillan

SUMMARY. Especially with the appearance of the World Wide Web, the Internet has had a major impact on scholarly activity in the fields of Anthropology and Sociology, although their principal scholarly records remain largely print-bound and continued access to and use of these print materials is crucial for study, teaching, research, and publication. However, the potential both to provide substantial resources in support of networked scholarship and to influence the shaping of these disciplines themselves is now acknowledged. Who and which organizations are taking the leadership in bringing these disciplines to the Internet, what reference and research resources are currently available, and what the prospects and consequences for research are if the current trends continue are all discussed. The focus is on discipline-specific resources and on the situation in the United States. *[Article copies available for a fee from The Haworth Document Delivery Service: 1-800-342-9678. E-mail address: <getinfo@haworthpressinc.com> Website: <http://www.HaworthPress.com>]*

KEYWORDS. Anthropology and sociology, Internet research in, Internet resources in, online research in, online resources in

---

Margaret R. Dittemore is Head of the John Wesley Powell Library of Anthropology, Smithsonian Institution Libraries.

Gary A. McMillan is Head of the Social Work Library and Bibliographer for anthropology and sociology at Howard University Libraries.

[Haworth co-indexing entry note]: "Anthropology and Sociology On and About the Internet." Dittemore, Margaret R., and Gary A. McMillan. Co-published simultaneously in *Journal of Library Administration* (The Haworth Information Press, an imprint of The Haworth Press, Inc.) Vol. 30, No. 1/2, 2000, pp. 15-37; and: *Academic Research on the Internet: Options for Scholars & Libraries* (ed: Helen Laurence, and William Miller) The Haworth Information Press, an imprint of The Haworth Press, Inc., 2000, pp. 15-37. Single or multiple copies of this article are available for a fee from The Haworth Document Delivery Service [1-800-342-9678, 9:00 a.m. - 5:00 p.m. (EST). E-mail address: getinfo@haworthpressinc.com].

15

INTRODUCTION

It has been roughly a decade since the first articles concerning the Internet and its applications (e.g., Anderson and Brent 1989) appeared in scholarly and professional journals in the fields of anthropology and sociology. Viewed by many even today as a large and shifting landscape, the Internet was initially avoided by some as an unreliable or simply too popular environment in which to work while others set about to explore the benefits of this new terrain for scholarship. Certainly more sociologists were probably in the latter camp than anthropologists given the quantitative emphasis within some subfields of that discipline. In fact, as late as 1996, Schwimmer (1996: 561) in his evaluative review of anthropology on the Internet bemoaned the overall lack of resources and the fact that those "under construction" (were proceeding) "at a very slow pace."[1]

Most of these "under construction" efforts have now come to fruition. A host of academic departments, museums, professional associations, and the like are now represented on the Web. Scholars are using computers in new and exciting ways, and a myriad of online resources are available in both fields with new ones appearing almost every day. Especially with the appearance of the World Wide Web, the potential of the Internet to provide substantial resources in support of networked scholarship is now acknowledged by many scholars as is its impact on shaping the disciplines themselves (as print-technology did). Three issues of critical importance to be discussed here are who or which organizations are taking the leadership in bringing these disciplines to the Internet, what reference and research resources are currently available, and what are the prospects and the consequences for researchers if the current trends continue into the future. The focus here will be on the situation of these disciplines in the United States and on discipline-specific resources. (The interests of both anthropologists and sociologists take them into many other disciplines. For those resources, see other articles in this volume.)

THE DISCIPLINES ON THE INTERNET

One key concern regarding the representation of any discipline, especially on the Internet, is its credibility. While one would normally rely upon structured review by peers or scholarly organizations for quality assurance, to date, neither the major U.S. professional associations in anthropology and sociology nor those other organizations, such as the **National Science Foundation** (URL: http://www.nsf.gov/home/sbe/start.htm) or **WennerGren** (URL: http://www.wennergren.org) that have also supported these fields over the years, have played a significant role in the development of networked scholarship in these disciplines. Their Web sites primarily convey the basic business of their organizations–directory and membership information, governance activities, registration and programs for annual meetings, funding opportunities, etc. In some cases, they also include excellent educational material and/or lists of links to other relevant sites.[2] Nevertheless, this stands in contrast to the **American Psychological Association** which has long sought to preserve "the record" and promote "the image" of the discipline with the early creation of a peer-reviewed e-journal and electronic access tools to its literature dating to the late 1800s. It remains to be seen if these organizations, which have supported and guided these fields for so long, will eventually take a leadership role (either themselves or through their funding) in bringing these disciplines into this new environment. The **American Anthropological Association** Advisory Group on Electronic Communication made its recommendations in early 1999. URL: <http://www.aaanet.org>. Although not in the report, it seems likely that over the next three to five years the Association will also become an important gateway to scholarly resources through its own Web site and those of its sections. Encouragingly, the **American Sociological Association** (URL: http://www.asanet.org) did contribute financially to the development of **Dead Sociologists' Society**, an excellent reference site. URL: <http://www.runet.edu/~lridener/DSS/DEADSOC.HTML>.

A substantial part of current activity on the Internet in these two disciplines appears to be led by energetic, computer-savvy individuals or small groups, often in college or university environments, sometimes working independently and sometimes as part of a loose confederation of consultants/volunteers. Within the field of anthropology, archaeologists have been the most active, with cultural anthropologists being somewhat less so, and physical anthropologists and linguists probably the least. Within sociology, progressives (e.g., **Progressive Sociologists Network**), social activists, and Marxists/leftist scholars early on embraced the possibilities of the Internet. URL <gopher://csf.colorado.edu:70/11/psn>.

Organizations–especially, but not exclusively, libraries, archives, government agencies, and increasingly, museums–are also playing an essential role through the creation of online resources based on their own holdings. The two major indexing tools in anthropology, **Anthropological Literature** and **Anthropological Index Online**, are products of important anthropological libraries in the United States and England, respectively. The U.S. government must be credited with making available major cross-disciplinary indexes, such as **Medline**, vast storehouses of primary data through its agencies or subject-specialized clearinghouses (e.g., **ICPSR**), and online, interactive tools, such as the **General Social Survey**. Finally, within museums such as the Smithsonian Institution (SI), both its Libraries and its National Anthropological Archives (Department of Anthropology) are making an important part of its history (and thus of anthropology) available through the creation of Internet-accessible publications, indices, and images related to the study of the American Indian (see below).

Beyond these, there is the commercial sector. Sociology in particular has deferred to private interests (profit and nonprofit) to produce the major indexing and abstracting tools for its literature and most of these have migrated to the Internet to protect their market share. The concern of this sector with retaining its broad customer base risks biasing its selection away from those resources with smaller audiences and/or less visibility, such as alternative or small presses, non-English language publications, etc. At the same time, sociology and anthropology remain a soft market for many full-text ventures (as compared to fields like medicine, law, or business with their inherent ability to recover information costs) and thus are vulnerable to exclusion by database producers. Fortunately, lobbying efforts by library groups such as ACRL's Anthropology and Sociology Section have been effective in producing positive results.

In sum, Internet representation for both disciplines has been rapidly, but somewhat haphazardly growing with some major figures and seminal works represented and others not; some subdisciplines taking off and others lagging behind; some resources associated with institutions and others seemingly free-floating in cyberspace. As a result, Internet searching yields both unexpected rewards and puzzling gaps. In addition, this situation is made more complex by the somewhat "chaotic shelving" of resources, making it difficult at times to identify what is related to the serious study of anthropology or sociology and what is not. It is here especially that the guidance of respected organizations, such as the professional associations or libraries (which enter this arena with considerable expertise), is needed.

THE INTERNET AS A FORUM FOR COMMUNICATION AND EXCHANGE

As with scholars in most disciplines, both anthropologists and sociologists have enjoyed the benefits of new mechanisms for communication and exchange: from communication between scholars via e-mail or real-time conferencing to participation in subject-oriented discussion groups (Kling 1997; Iscan and King 1997). The wider, more rapid exchange of ideas and information has created closer, more immediate relationships among individuals as well as enlarged their overall network of colleagues, in many cases to include people sharing similar interests throughout the world. This is particularly true in the case of listservs or discussion groups which provide a forum where information can be distributed, opinions exchanged, and assistance sought. Some of these forums, such as ANTHRO-L or SOCIOLOGY, are broadly based and others are more subject specific. Says one scholar about *AegeaNet*, the leading electronic forum for pre-classical Aegean archaeology:

> Three and a half years ago 'AegeaNet' promised merely to be a useful research tool; I thought I would find it convenient only for acquiring bibliography, facts and learned opinions. I never thought I'd find friends, fresh ideas, and an electronic extension of my imagination in cyberspace. (Younger 1997: 1054)

Examples of the large number of anthropology-related newsgroups, listservs and other discussion groups are available through **WWW Virtual Library: Anthropology** (URL: http://anthrotech.com/resources/) or **ArchNet** (URL: http://archnet.uconn.edu). **Sociological Mailing Lists** (URL: http://www.pscw.uva.nl/sociosite/mailinglists.html) and **Discussion: Newsgroups, Listservs, Chats** on the **WWW Virtual Library: Sociology** (URL: http://www.mcmaster.ca/socscidocs/w3virtsoclib/discuss.htm) identify nearly 200 such forums.

The mixed constituencies these forums allow have meant that the exchange of ideas and information is no longer limited to a few professionals, but often includes a broader audience of scholars, students and the general public. For librarians on **ANSS-L**, ACRL's **Anthropology and Sociology Section** listserv (URL: http://www.lib.odu.edu/anss/anssweb.html), the inclusion of scholars and students in these fields has been very fruitful. For some other listservs and discussion groups, this wider participation has received mixed reviews. Some welcome this as inclusiveness, insisting that, for example, "(a)rchaeology cannot afford to be elitist; in order to survive, it needs to be recognized as worthwhile by the public at large. The new technology provides the opportunity for this public to gain access to archaeological data and to interact with it" (Allason-Jones 1995: 42). Others describe it as a "decentering" of the fields of study. They express concern that such inclusiveness often discourages candor and the free flow of data, ideas, and opinion among scholars and has the potential of "framing" many discussions or issues in ways that would not otherwise have been and even of politicizing them.

Certainly with respect to electronic communication and exchange, both disciplines are firmly entrenched on the Internet. With broader interaction, and often collaboration, among scholars and increased ability to use or distribute scholarly resources, the Internet has created a unique environment that is having a substantial impact. It has also provided a means for anyone with Internet access to explore these disciplines and interact with their members in a way that was not possible in the past.

THE INTERNET AS AN ENVIRONMENT FOR RESEARCH AND DISSEMINATION

To date, the overwhelming body of scholarly literature for both of these fields is in print. In his article "From Print Culture to Electronic Culture," Chippindale (1997: 1070) reminds us that "(f)or centuries, scholarship in the western tradition has centered on printed books as the defining medium by which it expresses and preserves knowledge." The rewards of such have been "steadfastly tied" to print publications as well. To a large extent, the quality of electronic resources on the Internet to date reinforces the preeminence of print.

ONLINE CATALOGS

Libraries committed early to making their catalogs available over the Internet, and some archives were not far behind with both their holdings and finding aids to them. Many, if not most, libraries' holdings are now online, including those of Research Libraries' Group (RLIN) and OCLC which contain the collective records of many libraries around the world. Online catalogs rank among the very important front line research tools for all scholars. For example, demographers often consult the **University of Pennsylvania's Population Studies Center Library**'s online catalog because of the strength of its collection. URL: <http://www.pop.upenn.edu>. Some institutions are even beginning to integrate other, non-standard types of information into their catalog as well. The inclusion of analytic records relating to African art, history and culture directly into the Smithsonian Institution Libraries OPAC is an example. Created by African Art librarian Janet Stanley, they extend access to related information in a host of serials for researchers and librarians alike.[3] Likewise, the linking of images to archival catalog records, such as the National Anthropological Archives (Smithsonian Institution) is now doing, is also extremely useful to researchers. As for archives and museums, the Internet has enabled both to improve accessibility to their collections. The growing number of archival online catalogs and finding aids provide important information on manuscripts, correspondence, photos, fieldnotes, etc.–primary data for anthropology. Online access to museum collections for researchers is also improving. Finally, other online catalogs bring together materials which are physically scattered over some distance–an excellent example being that of the **HADDON Project**, a catalog of archival ethnographic film footage shot outside the U.S. and Europe from 1895 to 1945 and physically located in archives, museums, and other institutions around the world. URL: <http://www.bodley.ox.ac.uk/isca/haddon/>.

INDEXES AND ABSTRACTS

There are a variety of ways of accessing the mainstream social science literature in scholarly journals, conference papers, book reviews, and some edited volumes, as most of the traditional indexing and abstracting sources have migrated to electronic format to retain their market shares. As the interests of both anthropology and sociology are very broad, both cross-disciplinary and area studies tools remain a real need as does more retrospective access.

One of the most widely available for sociology is Cambridge Scientific Abstracts' **Sociofile**[4] which covers over 2,600 journals in sociology and related fields, many dated back to the 1960s. URL: <http://www.socabs.org>. Public and community college libraries may opt for the more limited H.W. Wilson's **Social Sciences Index/Abstracts** which covers roughly 400 core behavior and social sciences titles. URL: <http://www.hwwilson.com/databases/socsci.html>. A select group of institutions are also able to afford the Institute for **Scientific Information's Social Sciences Citation Index** which covers more than 1,700 journals. URL: <http://www.isinet.com/products/citation/citssci.html>. For retrospective access to the journal literature, most libraries use printed indexes; however, for those who can afford it, *Periodicals Contents* from Chadwyk-Healey includes selected social sciences journals from their first volume to 1990/1991. URL: <http://pci.chadwyck.com>.

Although many anthropologists, especially those with social and cultural interests, rely on the above resources as well, anthropology also has two English-language bibliographic indexes devoted exclusively to anthropological literature. They are **Anthropological Literature** (URL: http://www.rlg.org/cit-anl.html), published by the Tozzer Library at Harvard University and available as an online database through the Research Library Group's CitaDel service; and **Anthropological Index Online** (URL: http://lucy.ukc.ac.uk/AIO.html), an index to periodicals in the Museum of Mankind Library (incorporating the former Royal Anthropological Institute Library) in England. The former now includes nearly half a million entries from the 19th century to the present. The latter reaches back to 1970, but is still in the process of filling in and building its back files. Both are based on the serials and edited volumes received by these exceptional anthropology libraries.

As to subdisciplinary and cross-disciplinary research, the following databases are among those available that are relevant to either or both sociologists and anthropologists. Among the fee-based databases are **PAIS** for economic/political issues, **PsycINFO** for social psychology, **GeoRef** for geology and geosciences, **LLBA** for linguistics and language behavior, **Biosis** for life sciences, and **America: History and Life**. A fairly new development has been the free availability of government-produced or subsidized data bases such as **ERIC**/Educational Resources Information Clearinghouse (URL: http://ericae.net/search. htm), **MEDLINE** (URL: http://igm.nlm.nih.gov), **NCJSR**/National Criminal Justice Reference Service (URL: http://www.ncjrs.org), **Child Abuse &**

Neglect Abstracts (URL: http://www.calib.com/nccanch/index.htm), and the **National Clearinghouse for Alcohol and Drug Information** (URL: http://www.health.org/DBarea/index.htm).

FULL TEXT VERSIONS OF PRINT PUBLICATIONS

Although the lion's share of the online indexes and abstracts currently point to print serial publications, increasingly electronic full-text products are being offered as well. In some respects, this phenomenon has complicated librarians' lives as they help patrons interpret and navigate such a variety of formats. Selected anthropology and sociology journals now appear full-text in omnibus online databases (e.g., EbscoHost, SearchBank, ProQuest Direct, and Lexis/Nexis Universe), in more subject-focused database products (e.g., Ethnic News Watch and SIRS Researcher), in JSTOR (a consortium-based program providing access to journal backruns), and in publisher-created Web sites (e.g., Wiley, Project Muse, and Project Ideal) as a print subscription bonus or a print subscription surcharge. Institutions with the requisite technology and financial resources can have distributed, desk-top access to a wide if somewhat random selection of the latest scholarly journal articles.

Publishers desiring to stay solely in print but with a Web presence for publicity and/or access purposes have created sites ranging from a page on the Internet with subscription information, to one including the table of contents for at least recent volumes published with or without abstracting, and finally to one which also includes a selection of articles. **Anthropological Linguistics** offers via the Web a table of contents and abstracts for the last decade. URL: <http://www.indiana.edu/~anthling/>. The British journal *Antiquity*'s Web presence includes the only full index of the journal (none exists in print) plus the first page or so of chosen articles as "highlights or teasers." The American Sociological Association's quarterly publication, *Teaching Sociology,* includes a table of contents for the last several years and abstracts for some articles.

To explore what's available, consult the sources above (most have Web pages) or sample the following lists. For sociology, see the **WWW Virtual Library: Sociology**'s list of **Electronic Journals and Newsletters** (URL: http://www.mcmaster.ca/socscidocs/w3virtsoclib/journals.htm) with its nearly 50 listings or its broader-based **Social**

Sciences Electronic Journals (URL: http://www.clas.ufl.edu/users/gthursby/socsci/ejournal.htm). For anthropology, look at **Journals and Bulletins** (URL: http://anthro.org/journals.htm), part of Seeking Sites Afar's **Point of Reference-Anthropology, Archaeology and History**. Also try **ArchNet's Electronic Journals in Anthropology and Archaeology**. URL: <http://archnet.uconn.edu/archnet/other/journals.html>.

Among the other print publications which have full-text electronic counterparts, reference works dominate, and some believe that "paper-based book publishing technology cannot survive as a reference medium for much longer" (Lock and Peters 1996). However, the current paucity of sociology and anthropology discipline-based reference works leaves their role ill defined at present. The **Annual Reviews** of both sociology and anthropology are available online with articles from 1993 to present and abstracts and/or tables of contents going back to 1984. URL: <http://social.annualreviews.org>. Other examples include valuable linguistic works such as **Ethnologue** (URL: http://www.sil.org/ethnologue/) now in its 13th print edition; different bibliographies and directories; and indexes such as the one granting access to the Smithsonian's historic **Bureau of American Ethnology Publications**. URL: <http://www.sil.si.edu/DigitalCollections/BAE/Bulletin200/200title.htm>.

As for monographs, their numbers currently remain small; the "comfort factor" (in part as described below) remains a very significant issue in both disciplines. The **Centre for Social Anthropology and Computing's Ethnographics Gallery** offers an *Anthropology Intermedia Library*, an experimental section for books which are out of print or under author copyright. Its success is dependent upon contributors and volunteers. URL: <http://lucy.ukc.ac.uk/library.html>. In a discipline where monographs, including older publications, remain as important as serials, this is telling. Among **CSAC**'s offerings is **Forty-Five Years in the Turkish Village** with a hypertext version of Stirling's 1965 *Turkish Village* supplemented with his fieldnotes from 1949-1986, photographs, and a Turkish villagers' database. URL: <http://lucy.ukc.ac.uk/TVillage/index.html>. The 1994 hypertext version of Robert Dunnel's 1971 text **Systematics in Prehistory** provides another example of the available educational materials. URL: <http://weber.u.washington.edu/~anthro/BOOK/book.html>.

Finally, there are a number of important scholarly papers on the Internet published by organizations (including journal publishers) or individuals. The **Marx and Engels WWW Library** includes some of their seminal works. URL: <http://csf.Colorado.EDU/psn/marx/Archive/>. As part of its pilot project in electronic publishing, the Smithsonian Institution Libraries republished John Ewers' 1957 **Hairpipes in Plains Indian Adornment**, replacing its previously published black-and-white photos with their color originals. URL: <http://sil.si.edu/DigitalCollections/BAE/Bulletin164>.

WEB DIRECTORIES

Important gateways primarily to online resources are the Web directories or virtual libraries that exist in large numbers on the Internet. As the following examples show, there is a wide range of criteria for including a site and of experience among those maintaining these directories.

Among the better known gateways are the **WWW Virtual Library: Sociology** by Carl Cuneo, a faculty member in the Department of Sociology, McMaster University (URL: http://www.mcmaster.ca/socscidocs/w3virtsoclib/index.htm) and **WWW Virtual Library: Anthropology** (URL: http://anthrotech.com/resources/). The latter is maintained by Anthro TECH, a consulting firm founded by Eliott Lee, who sought to combine his Masters in Applied Cultural Anthropology with an interest in computers, graphic design, and Web technology. Together with other consultants like himself, he reviews, selects, and promotes resources through this directory and other projects. Casting a somewhat broader, less evaluative net, the search engine Yahoo indexes and points to a much larger number of related Internet resources through **Yahoo! Sociology** (URL: http://dir.yahoo.com/Social_Science/Sociology/) and Yahoo! **Anthropology and Archaeology** (URL: http://dir.yahoo.com/Social_Science/Anthropology_and_Archaeology). Other examples include **Socioweb** (URL: http://www.socioweb.com/~markbl/socioweb/), **A Sociological Tour through Cyberspace** (URL: http://www.trinity.edu/~mkearl/) and **Sociology Ring Home Page** (URL: http://www.markfoster.net/sociology/socring.html), a free service which allows any Web site owners to join an existing or start a new ring and to travel easily from any ring site to other sites in that ring. Finally, **Anthropology Resources on the Internet** is an example of an excellent privately-constructed and maintained site that has recently changed hands, its creator falling victim to the substantial burden of regularly updating such directories. URL: <http://home.worldnet.fr/clist/Anthro/index.html>.

Library Web sites are also excellent directories to scholarly resources. As Dvorak (1997) stated in "Online Libraries as Great Research Tools," his *New York Times on the Web* article, "(l)ibrary webmasters have the same addiction to posting favorite links (as others); since these people are professional librarians, their links tend to be quite impressive." Carefully selected for reliability and content, "many library sites are better jumping-off points for broad research than common search engines." The **University of Pennsylvania Library Home Page** is an excellent example with Web sites for 57 different subjects ranging from African-American Studies to Women's Studies, and equally rich lists of e-journals and databases (including major indexes, abstracts, and full-text). URL: <http://www.library.upenn.edu>. A reference shelf with information about or access to print and online dictionaries, encyclopedias, and directories is also included. The University's academic strength in both anthropology and sociology make this a good resource. Another library/archive gateway is **ABZU**, an excellent guide to resources for the study of the ancient Near East by Charles E. Jones, archivist of the University of Chicago Oriental Institute Research Archives. URL: <http://www-oi.uchicago.edu/OI/DEPT/RA/ABZU/ABZU.HTML>.

There are numerous other directories smaller in scope, focusing on directly or primarily relevant resources which allow relatively easy movement through the Web's maze.[5] Among them are **Dead Sociologists' Society, Human-Languages Page** (URL: http://www.june29.com/HLP/), **Enter Evolution: Theory and History** (URL: http://www.ucmp.berkeley.edu/history/evolution.html), and University of Connecticut's ArchNet (URL: http://archnet.uconn.edu/) devoted primarily to online archaeology. Finally, there is the University of Kent (England) **Centre for Social Anthropology and Computing's (CSAC) Ethnographics Gallery** (URL: http://lucy.ukc.ac.uk/), which is not only a gateway but also a producer and contributor to quality scholarly resources on the Internet.

PRIMARY MATERIALS

Both anthropology and sociology make use of quantitative and documentary materials, and, especially for the quantitative materials, the Internet has succeeded as an alternative to print publishing for the their storage, manipulation, and dissemination. Not only are the print costs prohibitively expensive where the publishing of large data sets has occurred (as with the decennial census), but also the format is not readily conducive to secondary analysis. A good portion of the data used by both disciplines is produced by U.S. government agencies. Many data sets now and in the future may never exist outside the electronic medium.

For sociologists and many other social scientists the International Association for Social Science Information Service & Technology (**IASSIST**) is just one of the organizations helping producers and users of social sciences data grapple with these new mechanisms of storing and sharing data. URL: <http://datalib.library.ualberta.ca/iassist/index.html>. In the United States, the **ICPSR** (Inter-University Consortium for Political and Social Research) at the University of Michigan has long been synonymous with data archiving and distribution. URL: <http://www.icpsr.umich.edu/contents.html>. This role has dramatically increased as the Consortium provides access to several subject-specialized data clearinghouses and provides links to data resources around the world. Two other useful gateways to global information resources are the **Online Survey Research/Public Opinion Centers: A Worldwide Listing** (URL: http://www.ukans.edu/cwis/units/coms2/po/index.html) and the **Social Science Data Collection, University of California, San Diego** (URL: http://ssdc.ucsd.edu). The private sector has also risen to social scientists' increasing demands for data sets useful for research and teaching. For example, **Sociometrics Corporation** distributes research data sets to subscribers via CD-ROM and the Internet, providing collections of data sets packaged around important social issues and problems. URL: <http://www.socio.com/overview.htm>.

The types of primary material that anthropologists use range from government-produced soil surveys, infectious disease statistics and the census to actual fieldnotes, including interviews, word lists, measurements, and the like. Much of the latter material (i.e., fieldnotes, word lists, etc.) which exists in different formats is only beginning to become Internet-accessible through online catalogs, finding aids, etc., and groups such as CoPAR (Council for the Preservation of the Anthropological Record) are working towards proper disposition and preservation.

A few examples of other databases used by anthropologists (often as part of cooperative ventures) follow. Among the better known is **Electronic HRAF**, a full-text database that provides primarily descriptive information on selected cultures to paying members, and is produced by the Human Relations Area Files, an internationally recognized consortium of research institutions in the field of cultural anthropology. URL: <http://www.yale.edu/hraf/>. Originally a print product, it is being both converted to electronic format and enlarged with annual installations of approximately 50,000 pages of text on 15 or more cultures. Another, the **Mayan Epigraphic Database**, refers to itself as an "experiment in networked scholarship with the purpose of enhancing Classic Mayan epigraphic research" and thoughtfully compares the experience of a student researching a glyph both with and without Internet-accessible resources. URL: <http://jefferson.village.virginia.edu/med/home.html>. Included are an archive of digitally transcribed Mayan texts, and relational databases of glyphs, images, and phonetics as well as semantic values. For archaeologists, the **National Archeological DataBase** is a computerized communications network containing the NADB-Reports, NADB-NAGPRA, and NADB-maps for the archaeological and historic preservation community. URL: <http://www.cast.uark.edu/products/NADB>. It is maintained through a cooperative agreement between the National Park Service and the Center for Advanced Spatial Technologies (CAST) at the University of Arkansas.

Finally, the **Anthropology Department at the University of Tennessee, Knoxville** manages a number of databases of primary data, including the Forensic Anthropology Data Bank, Franz Boas' century-old anthropometrics from North American Indians and Siberians, and W.W. Howells' large collection of craniometric data compiled from 1965 to 1980. URL: <http://web.utk.edu/~anthrop/>. Early on Howells knew he "could hardly exhaust the possibilities of the material" (Howells 1996: 441) and began sharing it with others, initially on punch cards. The Internet, however, has greatly facilitated this sharing, and as Howells states, he ". . . has been both surprised and certainly gratified, by what others have been able to do with it" (Howells 1996: 441).

ELECTRONIC PUBLICATION

Both fields are experimenting with the idea of electronic-only journals or e-journals. Some see them as a solution to the current problems of scholarly publishing as well as an escape from the expensive print runs and distribution costs that increasing specialization in both fields, and resulting smaller readership, have caused. However, to date the "comfort factor" with e-journals as journals of record simply does not compare with that of print. The concerns for archiving, quality control of both content and form, issues of peer-review before publication vs. post-publication commentary, copyright, and the like are all very real and will need to be resolved before scholarly publishing in this format can be fully accepted.

The experiences of several early unsuccessful ventures in anthropology made by individuals without peer review or an editorial board illustrate this problem clearly.[6] A substantially more successful e-journal, **Internet Archaeology**, created by a consortium of British archaeological organizations, has published 6 issues since the fall of 1996 and is now indexed by two major sources. URL: <http://intarch.ac.uk>. Its last issue is a special theme issue entitled "Digital Publication." Examples in sociology include **Sociological Research Online** (URL: http://www.socresonline.org.uk/socresonline/) and **Electronic Journal of Sociology** (URL: http://www.sociology.org/frametoc.html), the latter considered by its editors as a model for a new publishing paradigm where scholars retain control of scholarly communication. Freely available, peer reviewed (in most cases), scholarly **Full Text Electronic Journals in Sociology** is a list derived from the International Consortium for Alternative Academic Publications (ICAAP) database. URL: <http://www.sociology.org/journals.shtml>.

Despite the aforementioned issues which all electronic-only publications must deal with, electronic publishing remains especially attractive to some anthropologists and sociologists whose work can only be partially published in print form. Hypertext publication allows for the integration of sounds and images with text and the inclusion of far greater amounts of data. Archaeologists especially, have experimented with e-publishing excavation reports, at present primarily on CD ROM, but with the Internet not far away. *Excavating Occaneechi Town: Archaeology of an Eighteenth-Century Indian Village in North Carolina* is an excellent example which integrates and presents the various types of information (text, photos, data) and allows complete access to the excavation records, including data in an easily analysable form. The latter fact may well mean that fieldwork publication may no longer be the final product, but may become the beginning of a dialogue with others who want to explore the data, either for comparative purposes, solutions to other problems, or because of alternative views.

THE STUDY OF CYBERCULTURE

Anthropologists and sociologists are intrigued by the Internet as a democratizing social forum and cyberspace as an alternative "but not quite" community (e.g., Calhoun 1998; Cushing 1996). They are also exploring cyberspace as a research environment and Internet utilities as mechanisms for collecting research data (e.g., Brent 1996; Fisher, Margolis, & Resnik 1996; Miskevich 1996; and Hewson, Laurent, & Vogel 1996). However, there is not yet a substantial body of literature grappling with these theoretical and methodological issues and little of it appears in the "core" anthropology or sociology journals.

THE INTERNET AS AN EDUCATIONAL ENVIRONMENT

The Internet has provided exceptional educational opportunities at all levels, and an explosion of activity is occurring in this arena, especially with the appearance of the World Wide Web. Most academic departments now have online course listings and schedules, and more recently have begun adding course outlines, reading lists, course reserves, exercises, and even some lectures and workshops. Content and quality vary with no particular pedagogic model seeming to predominate. For sociology, see the **WWW Virtual Library: Sociology's Institutions and Departments** (URL: http://www.mcmaster.ca/socscidocs/w3virtsoclib/ institut.htm) with listings by continent and by country and the **American Sociological Association's Directory of Departments** (URL: http://www.asanet.org/Pubs/DOD.htm). See also **SOCNET: Courses and Curricular Resources** offering access to a world of ideas and exercises for use in the classroom. URL: <http://www.mcmaster.ca/ socscidocs/w3virtsoclib/socnet.htm>. For anthropology, see **ArchNet's Educational Resources for Anthropology & Archaeology.** URL: <http://www.archnet.uconn.edu/archnet/topical/educat/>.

Online course material or supplements created by professors are increasingly common, and more communication and coordination with libraries would be beneficial. **Biological Anthropology Links** is a list organized by a professor around the chapter readings in the required text of his introductory course. URL: <http://www.oneonta. edu/~anthro/anth130/links.html>. Interactive Web tutorials such as **OsteoInteractive** (URL: http://medstat.med.utah.edu/kw/osteo) and **Kinship and Social Organization** (URL: http://www.umanitoba.ca/ faculties/arts/anthropology/kintitle.html) are also available. The latter investigates the instructional use of hypertext to link ethnographic examples and analytical concepts. **Introduction to Archaeology** offered at the University of Texas serves as an example of a course requiring students to use Web resources to construct their own syntheses of prehistoric topics as new Web pages. URL: <http://www.dla.utexas.edu/depts/ anthro/courses/97spring/wilsonarch97/>.

Finally, there exists at least one hypermedia Ph.D. thesis which is discussed by its author, Cornelius Holtorf, in his article, "Is History Going to be on My Side?" (Holtorf 1999).

There is a plethora of other educational resources on the Internet for both disciplines. Again, evaluation is necessary as there can be a substantial difference between the site of an enthusiastic student and a mature scholar or institution. For sociology, sites such as **Sociologists–Dead and Very Much Alive** (URL: http://www.pscw.uva.nl/ sociosite/TOPICS/Sociologists.html) and **A Sociology Timeline from 1600** (URL: http://www.ac.wwu.edu/~stephan/timeline.html) are rich supplements to an introduction or historical study. The much-heralded **French Cave Paintings** demonstrated the reach and immediacy of the Web, appearing shortly after their discovery and allowing the wide interest in them to be satisfied before the much later final publication appears. URL: <http://www.culture.fr/culture/arcnat/chauvet/fr/grsites.htm>. The upcoming **AsiaQuest** and its predecessors amply demonstrate the Internet's interactive ability and appeal, allowing teachers and students to join researchers in the field thousands of miles away and interact with, even advise them in the daily problems they encounter in their work. URL: <http://quest.classroom.com/>. For those seeking career information, the Smithsonian Institution Libraries' **Anthropology on the Internet for K-12** is both a gateway to other excellent sources about anthropology as a profession and an inside look at what museum anthropologists do. URL: <http://www.sil.si.edu/SILPublications/ Anthropology-K12>. With regard to the latter, the Internet has enabled museums to take on a more far-ranging and proactive educational role. See **Anthropology Museums on the Web** for examples of virtual exhibits, tours, image databases, and the like. URL: <http://luna. cas.usf.edu/~curtis/antmus.html>.

CONCLUSION

There is no question that the Internet has had a major impact on scholarly communication and libraries, especially since the appearance of the World Wide Web, and will continue to do so no matter what form the Web or its replacement takes. New forms of communication are facilitated and their costs redistributed, bringing together a far-flung and diverse community of participants and offering nearly everyone the ability to be a contributor and/or a user of primary and secondary research materials. Efficiencies have been introduced in the transmission of information, and libraries can provide end-user access to a growing pool of reference and research sources. The Internet has become an essential component of every library, allowing it to function as a gateway to vast storehouses of dispersed information, and thus transforming the way students, scholars, and librarians think about collections and service.

However, in spite of all this, the perception by some that print materials are being replaced by electronic is not globally true, nor is it so, to date, for anthropology and sociology. The principal scholarly records of both disciplines remain largely print-bound, and continued access to and use of these materials is crucial for study, teaching, research, and publication. Although it is encouraging to see efforts to put freely available, full-text classic anthropology and sociology works on the Internet, the storehouse of public domain works has its limits. Much of the foundational literature of these two disciplines will remain under copyright for some time.

Certainly, the government, and to some extent the professions themselves (especially anthropology), are to be credited for their substantial contributions in the area of electronic indexing, abstracting, full-text publications, and primary data. However, electronic access as a whole remains heavily dependent upon the political economy of the publishing and commercial database industry. Where content on the Internet is concerned, the operant word in the phrase "intellectual property" is property. This industry will remain a major force for at least some time to come. Finally, the overwhelming amount of current scholarly publishing continues to take place with well-established print journals and monograph publishers. Concerns with archiving/security of information, quality control of both content and form, academic respectability, etc., are very real and must all be settled before electronic literature can truly be considered the literature of record.

So what can anthropologists, sociologists, and librarians expect to find on the Internet ten years (or more?) from now? Certainly the future of scholarly publishing will depend upon what form the Internet takes and who the participants are. That said, with the effective lobbying of librarians and faculty, they may find greater inclusion of scholarly journals (both indexing and full-text) in the mainstream, commercially available electronic databases. Anthropologists and sociologists routinely make excursions into other literatures; better representation of both in widely accessible databases will encourage cross-disciplinary research in both directions. Some benevolent foundation or institution will have supported a retrospective indexing project for sociology-related journals (as now exists with anthropology), and JSTOR will provide full backruns for *at least* one hundred titles in each discipline, ensuring that a substantial proportion of their historical records are highly accessible **and** electronically preserved. This must occur if student research, in particular, is to reflect more than just a superficial foray into the "convenience sample"[7] of articles currently accessible electronically.

Finally, after a "shaking out" period, anthropology and sociology librarians and archivists, working through academic institutions, professional associations, and the like, will have "institutionalized" their roles in identifying, vetting, and conceptually organizing links to the vast amounts of free-floating "grey literature" in cyberspace. Thus, the major discipline-sanctioned gateways to these disciplines on the Web will have permanent organizational homes. Moreover, they may take advocacy and instrumental roles in archiving the work of those industrious information entrepreneurs whose Web sites burn brightly until research interests and/or career trajectories cause them to move on. Indeed, there are great things to anticipate and opportunities for discovery ahead.

NOTES

1. It is important to note that Joyce Ogburn (1997: 286-287), then chair of the Association of College and Research Libraries' Anthropology and Sociology Section, took Schwimmer to task for what he forgot to mention–primarily the considerable amount of work being done by libraries in the creation of online resources.

2. Many of the professional associations have very good essays on education and professional work in these disciplines. For anthropology, see the *What about a Career?* section of the Smithsonian Institution Libraries' *Anthropology on the Internet for K-12*. URL: <http://www.sil.Si.edu/SILPublications/Anthropology-K12>.

3. Janet Stanley, librarian at the Smithsonian Institution Libraries' National Museum of African Art branch, began the indexing in 1980 in card catalog form. In 1995 the conversion of this information and its transfer into the Libraries' online database was begun funded by the Getty Grant Program. The recon phase includes 30,000 to 35,000 records with current indexing at approximately 3,000 to 4,000 new records a year. Each analytic bib record is enriched with a generous assignment of subject headings to capture all topics using vocabulary from the Art and Architecture Thesaurus, in addition to Library of Congress Subject headings.

4. **Sociofile** mirrors *Sociological Abstracts* from 1963 (the print version began in 1952) as well as including the full coverage of *Social Planning/Policy & Development Abstracts* from 1980 (the latter of which is available exclusively electronically since 1997). For most libraries retrospective access to the journal literature requires the use of printed indexes (e.g., *CRIS: Combined Retrospective Index to Journals in Sociology, 1874-1975* or the *Social Sciences Index* which, combined with its predecessors, covers core scholarly journals back to the late nineteenth century).

5. Two examples from the host of area studies directories useful to both disciplines are the University of Texas's **Latin American Network Information Center** or **LANIC** (URL: http://lanic.utexas.edu/) and the **Asian Studies WWW Virtual Library** edited by T.M. Ciolek and 45 co-editors (URL: http://coombs.anu.edu.au/WWWVL-AsianStudies.html).

6. One of them, the **Journal of World Anthropology**, folded in 1997 after producing four issues, their University of Buffalo editors having encountered "all the problems and frustrations of a print journal." URL: http://wings.buffalo.edu/academic/department/anthropology/jwa>. They have redirected their efforts to **Anthropological Review Database** URL: <http://wings.buffalo.edu/anthropology/ARD/>.

7. Online indexes and abstracts, for example, are now preferred by many students and the reluctance of some to use print tools (in order to include those journals not indexed electronically, for example) has librarians and professors alike concerned about the possible resultant bias in learning and subsequent scholarship.

WEBLIOGRAPHY

Association of College and Research Libraries/Anthropology and Sociology Section. *Resources for Anthropology & Sociology Librarians & Information Specialists* [Online]. Retrieved May 12, 1999. URL: <http://www.lib.odu.edu/anss/resources.htm>.

American Anthropological Association [Online]. Retrieved May 11, 1999. URL: <http://www.aaanet.org/>.

Centre for Social Anthropology and Computing. *CSAC's Ethnographics Gallery* [Online]. Canterbury: University of Kent. Retrieved May 17, 1999. URL: <http://lucy.ukc.ac.uk/>.

Clist, B. *Anthropology Resources on the Internet* [Online]. Retrieved May 11, 1999. URL: <http://home.worldnet.fr/clist/Anthro/index.html>.

Cuneo, C. *WWW Virtual Library: Sociology* [Online]. Hamilton, Ontario: McMaster University. Retrieved May 24, 1999. URL: <http://www.mcmaster.ca/socscidocs/w3virtsoclib/index.htm>.

Inter-University Consortium for Political and Social Research. *ICPSR Website Contents* [Online]. Ann Arbor: University of Michigan. Retrieved May 24, 1999. URL: <http://www.icpsr.umich.edu/contents.html>.

Plunkett, T. and Lizee, J. ArchNet: WWW Virtual Library-Archaeology. [Online]. Storrs, CT: University of Connecticut. Retrieved May 8, 1999. URL: <http://archnet.uconn.edu/>.

Ridener, L. *Dead Sociologists' Society* [Online]. Radford, VA: Radford University. Retrieved May 24, 1999. URL: <http://www.runet.edu/~lridener/DSS/DEADSOC.HTML>.

SocioWeb. *Your Independent Guide to Sociological Resources on the Internet* [Online]. Retrieved May 24, 1999. URL: <http://www.socioweb.com/~markbl/socioweb>.

University of Michigan Documents Center. *Statistical Resources on the Web* [Online]. Ann Arbor: University of Michigan. Retrieved May 26, 1999. URL: <http://www.lib.umich.edu/libhome/Documents.center/stats.html>.

Yahoo! *Social Science: Sociology* [Online]. Retrieved May 24, 1999. URL: <http://dir.yahoo.com/social_science/sociology/>.

Yahoo! *Social Science: Social Research Data Collections* [Online]. Retrieved May 24, 1999. URL: <http://dir.yahoo.com/social_science/social_research/data_collections/>.

REFERENCES

Allason-Jones, Lindsay, Colm O'Brien, and Glyn Goodrick. 1995. "Archaeology, Museums, and the World Wide Web." *Journal of European Archeology* 3 (2): 33-42.

Anderson, R.E., and E.E. Brent. 1989. "Computing in Sociology: Promise and Practice." *Social Science Computer Review* 7 (4): 487-502.

Brent, E. 1996. "Electronic Computing and Sociology: Looking Backward, Thinking Ahead, Careening toward the Next Millennium." *American Sociologist* 27 (1): 4-10.

Calhoun, C. 1998. "Community without Propinquity Revisited: Communications Technology and the Transformation of the Urban Public Sphere." *Sociological Inquiry* 68 (3): 373-397.

Carlson, David L. 1997. "Electronic Communications and Communities." *Antiquity* 71 (274): 1049-1051. [Also Online] Retrieved March 12, 1999. URL: <http://intarch.ac.uk/antiquity/electronics/index.html>.

Champion, Sara. 1997. "Archaeology on the World Wide Web: a User's Field-Guide." *Antiquity* 71 (274): 1027-1038. [Also Online] Retrieved March 12, 1999. URL: <http://intarch.ac.uk/antiquity/electronics/champion.html>.

Champion, Sara, and Christopher Chippindale. 1997. "Electronic Archaeology/Special Review Section." *Antiquity*. [Online] Retrieved March 12, 1999. URL: <http://intarch.ac.uk/antiquity/electronics/index.html>.

Chippindale, Christopher. 1997. "From Print Culture to Electronic Culture." *Antiq-

uity 71 (274): 1070-1073. [Also Online] Retrieved March 12, 1999. URL: <http://intarch.ac.uk/antiquity/electronics/chippindale.html>.

Clausen, C. 1996. "Welcome to Post-Culturalism." *American Scholar* 65 (3): 379-388.

Cohen Williams, Anita, and Julia A. Herndon. 1995. "Internet Resources for Anthropology." *College and Research Libraries News* 56 (2): 87-90, 113.

Cushing, Pamela J. 1996. "Gendered Conversational Rituals on the Internet." *Anthropologica* 38 (1): 47-80.

Davis, Jr., R. P. Stephen, Patrick C. Livingood, H. Trawick Ward, and Vincas P. Steponaitis, eds. 1998. *Occaneechi Town: Archaeology of an Eighteenth-Century Indian Village in North Carolina.* [CD-Rom] Chapel Hill: University of North Carolina Press.

Dvorak, John C. 1997. "Online Libraries are Great Research Tools." From the November 3, 1997, column "Taking in the Sites." *New York Times on the Web.* [Online] Retrieved on April 28, 1999. URL: <http://www.nytimes.com/library/cyber/sites/110397sites.html>.

Fisher, B., M. Margolis, and D. Resnik. 1996. "Breaking Ground on the Virtual Frontier: Surveying Civic Life on the Internet." *American Sociologist* 27 (1): 11-29.

Gaffney, Vince, and Sally Exon. 1997. "From Order to Chaos: Publication, Synthesis and the Dissemination of Data in a Digital Age." Special Theme Issue: Digital Publication. *Internet Archaeology* 6. [Online] Retrieved May 8, 1999. URL: <http://intarch.ac.uk/journal/issue6/gaffney/index.html>.

Handler, Mark. 1989. "Sociology, Anthropology." In: *Information Needs in the Social Sciences: An Assessment.* Prepared for the Program for Research Information Management of The Research Libraries Group, Inc. pp. 27-31; 41-49. Mountain View: RLG.

Harnad, Stevan. 1997. "Learned Inquiry and the Net: the Role of Peer Review, Peer Commentary and Copyright." *Antiquity* 71 (274): 1042-1048. [Also Online] Retrieved March 12, 1999. URL: <http://intarch.ac.uk/antiquity/electronics/harnad.html>.

Hewson, C.M., D. Laurent, and C.M. Vogel. 1996. "Proper Methodologies for Psychological and Sociological Studies Conducted via the Internet." *Behavior Research Methods, Instruments, and Computers* 28 (2): 186-191.

Heyworth, Mike, Julian Richards, Alan Vince, and Sandra Garside-Neville. 1997. "Internet Archaeology: A Quality Electronic Journal." *Antiquity* 71 (274): 1039-1042. [Also Online] Retrieved March 12, 1999. URL: <http://intarch.ac.uk/antiquity/electronics/heyworth.html>.

Holtorf, Cornelius. 1999. "Is History Going to be on My Side? On the Experience of Writing and Submitting a Hypermedia Ph.D. Thesis. Special Theme Issue: Digital Publication." *Internet Archaeology* 6. [Online]. Retrieved May 8, 1999. URL: <http://intarch.ac.uk/journal/issue6/holtorf/biblio.html>.

Howells, W.W. 1996. "Howells' Craniometric Data on the Internet." *American Journal of Physical Anthropology* 101 (3): 441-442.

Iscan, M. Yasar, and William R. King. 1997. "Electronic Communication for Biological Anthropologists." In: *Biological Anthropology: the State of the Science.*

Edited by Noel T. Boaz and Linda D. Wolfe. pp. 195-206. Bend: International Institute for Human Evolutionary Research.

Kling, R. 1997. "The Internet for Sociologists." *Contemporary Sociology* 26 (4): 434-444.

Lock, Andrew, and Charles R. Peters. 1996. *Handbook of Human Symbolic Evolution*. [Online] Oxford: Clarendon Press. Retrieved May 24, 1999. URL: <http://www.massey.ac.nz/~ALock/hbook/frontis.htm>.

McMillan, Gary A., Margaret R. Dittemore, and Carol Ritzen Kem. 1995. "Internet Resources for Sociology." *College and Research Libraries News* 56 (9): 639-643.

Miskevich, S.L. 1996. "Killing the Goose that Laid the Golden Eggs: Ethical Issues in Social Sciences Research on the Internet." *Science and Engineering Ethics* 2 (2): 241-242.

Ogburn, Joyce L. 1997. "On Anthropology and the Internet." *Current Anthropology* 38 (2): 286-287.

Peachey, Elizabeth, and Christopher Chippindale. 1997. "Antiquity's Experience in Adding an Electronic Element to a Printed Journal." *Antiquity* 71 (274): 1060-1061. [Also Online] Retrieved March 12, 1999. URL: <http://intarch.ac.uk/antiquity/electronics/peachey.html>.

Ryan, A. 1997. "Exaggerated Hopes and Baseless Fears." *Social Research* 64 (3): 1167-1190.

Schwimmer, Brian. 1996. "Anthropology on the Internet: A Review and Evaluation of Networked Resources." *Current Anthropology* 37 (3): 561-568. [Also Online] Retrieved March 12, 1999. URL: <http://ascc.artsci.wustl.edu/~anthro/ca/papers/schwimmer/intro.html>.

Vince, Alan. 1997. "Publishing Archaeology on the Web: Who Reads this Stuff Anyway?" *Internet Archaeology* 3 (Autumn 1997). [Online] Retrieved May 8, 1999. URL: <http://intarch.ac.uk/journal/issue3/vince_toc.html>.

Younger, John G. 1997. "Managing AegeaNet" *Antiquity* 71 (274): 1052-1054.

Zeitlyn, David, and Gustaaf Houtman. 1996. "Information Technology and Anthropology." *Anthropology Today* 12 (3): 1-3.

Art on the 'Net:
Enhanced Research
for Art and Architecture

Roberto C. Ferrari

SUMMARY. Researchers in the fields of art and architecture can now find a wealth of information to complement traditional print resources in the humanities. The evolution of visual imagery technology on the Internet and the gradual development of a controlled vocabulary, namely the *Art and Architecture Thesaurus,* have made this possible. This article highlights some of the best resources for art and architecture, from subject directories and periodical indexes to image sites and auction information. Scholars researching art and architecture on the Internet will find these resources useful. *[Article copies available for a fee from The Haworth Document Delivery Service: 1-800-342-9678. E-mail address: <getinfo@haworthpressinc.com> Website: <http://www.HaworthPress.com>]*

KEYWORDS. Art and architecture, Internet research in, Internet resources in, online research in, online resources in

Roberto C. Ferrari is Arts and Humanities Reference Librarian and Assistant University Librarian at the S. E. Wimberly Library at Florida Atlantic University in Boca Raton, FL. Prior to joining the library faculty at FAU, he was Associate Dean of the Nevin C. Meinhardt Memorial Library at The Art Institute of Fort Lauderdale. He is the author of "Simeon Solomon: A Bibliographic Study," recently published in *The Journal of Pre-Raphaelite Studies*. He is a member of the ARLIS/NA Web Site Administrative Board and Webmaster for the Southeast Chapter of ARLIS/NA. He earned both his Master of Library Science and Master of Liberal Arts in Humanities degrees from the University of South Florida in Tampa.

[Haworth co-indexing entry note]: "Art on the 'Net: Enhanced Research for Art and Architecture." Ferrari, Roberto C. Co-published simultaneously in *Journal of Library Administration* (The Haworth Information Press, an imprint of The Haworth Press, Inc.) Vol. 30, No. 1/2, 2000, pp. 39-62; and: *Academic Research on the Internet: Options for Scholars & Libraries* (ed: Helen Laurence, and William Miller) The Haworth Information Press, an imprint of The Haworth Press, Inc., 2000, pp. 39-62. Single or multiple copies of this article are available for a fee from The Haworth Document Delivery Service [1-800-342-9678, 9:00 a.m. - 5:00 p.m. (EST). E-mail address: getinfo@haworthpressinc.com].

It is through Art, and through Art only, that we can realise our perfection . . .

–Oscar Wilde, *The Critic as Artist*, 1891

There is no end to our researches; our end is in the other world.

–Michel de Montaigne, *Essays* III.13, 1588

Art and architecture information is now conveniently available on the Internet, although this wasn't always true. Because visual imagery is important for art and architecture research, the DOS and LYNX computer world had to evolve to address this demand for visual imagery. Graphically based operating systems such as Windows, software like Adobe Photoshop and 3D Studio Max, and interactive Internet browsers such as Netscape and Internet Explorer have all helped transform this once text-only arcane environment. As a result these new computer applications have made the Internet more appealing to art and architecture users because now they can create and interact through visual imagery. For the first time, museums invite users to visit their galleries in a virtual environment. Databases provide scholars with full-text and graphical information resulting from a query performed by a search engine. Professors digitize slides for online courses. Architectural firms post building schematics for others to preview and comment. Artists make their paintings and sculptures instantly accessible to an international audience, providing them with a new venue for creativity and marketing. Yet, there are still concerns regarding the Internet and art-related information.

One of these concerns is the identification and retrieval of images on the Internet. For instance, when using a popular search engine such as AltaVista, typing in "picture of Starry Night" does not guarantee that you will retrieve an image of Vincent van Gogh's famous painting. Unless a Web site designer has used the word "picture" in his/her meta-tags or in the content of an "ALT" HTML tag, chances are the search will be unsuccessful. This problem of image identification has begun to be rectified as Web site designers learn how to draw people to their sites with meta-tags and SGML-encoded images, not to mention the ever-increasing number of image databases that are now available on the Internet, some of which are discussed below.

The second concern relates to research itself and the ability to identify the most accurate art and architecture information available on a topic. Art-related research is often convoluted in its goals. Consider a prospective arts-related research topic: aspects of the goddess Venus as depicted in fifteenth-century Northern Italian oil paintings. Problems are encountered here. The first is the choice of which database to search. Information on this topic would obviously be found in a database such as the *Art Index,* but it is also likely that additional material will be found in religion and history databases or perhaps even in an encyclopedia on iconography, mythology, or semiotics. Compare this kind of search to one in the social sciences in which a psychology researcher, for instance, knows where to search for his/her information: *PsychLit.* The reality is that arts research has been and continues to be characterized by the need for a more multidisciplinary approach and database.

Researchers in the arts are also impeded by the lack of a controlled language. Ron Blazek and Elizabeth Aversa have pointed out that humanities research is complicated by "the relative lack of standard or controlled vocabularies of the sort that are common in the pure and applied sciences" (Blazek, 1994:3). A study of online searching by humanities scholars performed by the Getty Information Institute demonstrated that in the humanities "thesauri probably should be designed on different principles from conventional thesauri" (Bates, 1995:520). The *Library of Congress Subject Headings* or subject thesauri such as those designed for *ERIC* or *Sociological Abstracts* were created for access to collections of material based on common terms. Research in art and architecture is usually multi-faceted; it does not focus on one single topic, which makes it difficult to work with a controlled vocabulary of common subject headings. Instead, search terms often include concepts related to specific people or works, chronology or history, geography, and/or medium, components which typically are not a part of the design structure of the *Library of Congress Subject Headings* or traditional subject thesauri. The search given above exemplifies this: aspects of the goddess Venus (person or topic) as depicted in fifteenth-century (historical) Northern Italian (geographical) oil paintings (medium).

Fortunately, the *Art and Architecture Thesaurus* (AAT), a controlled vocabulary designed for the multi-faceted, arts-related search, has made this kind of research easier. The *AAT* allows a cataloger to describe an art monograph, art reproduction, architectural model, slide, or other work by supplying key concepts to seven different subject areas that are faceted and hierarchical. These seven facets are: associated concepts (i.e., abstract ideas); physical attributes (i.e., descriptions); styles and periods (i.e., historical and ethno-cultural); agents (i.e., related persons and groups); activities (i.e., related actions), materials (i.e., medium), and objects (i.e., inanimate entities) (*Art & Architecture Thesaurus,* 1990, p. 26-28). By using these concepts, a researcher is more likely to generate the specific, accurate hits which he/she is seeking. The *AAT* has also been made available free on the World Wide Web as *The Art & Architecture Thesaurus Browser* by the Getty Research Institute. URL: <http://shiva.pub.getty.edu/aat_browser/>. The site is fully searchable for hierarchical terms and scope notes related to the controlled vocabulary.

As Internet tools continue to become more responsive to the needs of arts and architecture research, one question remains: are art and architecture researchers using the Internet for their research? No studies have been published analyzing the use of the World Wide Web by scholars in the fields of art and architecture; therefore, one cannot know for sure.[1] However, one may surmise that these scholars have not fully integrated the Internet into their research, based on the traditional information-seeking strategies of these and other humanities scholars, as compared to social and "hard" scientists. These strategies include some of the following points:

1. Humanities scholarship is based on questions of value rather than collected scientific data. For instance, a researcher may explore the aesthetics of Frank Lloyd Wright and the Prairie school of architectural design.
2. Humanities scholars typically work alone with ideas and opinions and generate a school of thought, such as in the cases of cultural critics such as Derrida and Foucault, unlike the scientific group approach where two or more scholars may conduct a collaborative study.
3. Humanities scholars consider library resources to be the center of their research, whereas scientists whose primary work is done in a laboratory use the library in a supporting role.
4. Humanities scholars often work with source material and items that are based on creativity, and then with age, medium, and theories related to these creative examples, such as in Leonardo da Vinci's *Mona Lisa.*

5. Humanities scholars usually choose monographs as primary resources with journal articles as secondary sources for critical support, while scientists count on current journal articles for the most up-to-date information (Blazek, 1994, p. 2-7).

Perhaps these last few points best clarify the basis of humanities research. Art and architecture researchers usually work first with three-dimensional forms (e.g., works of art or architecture) and then apply ideas to them. They need to "see" the work which they are discussing, and thus often visit museums or landmarks. When personal visits are not possible, they rely on monographs, from catalogues raisonnes to "coffee table books," to provide the detailed information (i.e., visual images) they need for study.

This reliance on monographs and site visits would seem to negate the use of the Internet as a research tool. This assumption, however, is a mistake. While electronic books are not currently the trend for art and architecture research, there is a wealth of resources on the World Wide Web that complement, not replace, the traditional print resources of humanities scholars. Lois Swan Jones has pointed out that researchers "need to learn how Internet material compares to information provided in other formats–print resources, CD-ROMs, documentary videos, and microfiche sets–and how it can be complemented with these additional resources" (Jones, 1999: xiii).

This complementary relationship of the Internet to traditional print resources, and vice-versa, is the crux of mastering art and architecture research today. The humanities scholar should not be afraid to use the Internet, but rather should explore the Internet's possibilities. The resources discussed here have been chosen because they reflect this notion of complementarity.

The first part, "Getting Started," focuses on resources that will enable art and architecture scholars to begin their Internet research. "Image Sites," the second section, provides sites where researchers can locate visual images on the Internet. Lastly, "Research Databases" describes World Wide Web databases where scholars can find everything from auction information to journal citations. Some of these resources are available both in print and on the Internet. All resources cited were available, and all prices quoted were accurate as of June 1, 1999.

GETTING STARTED

Jones, L. S. (1999). *Art information and the Internet.* Phoenix: Oryx.

Jones, L. S. *Art Information and the Internet Update* [Online]. Phoenix: Oryx. Retrieved June 17, 1999. URL: <http://www.oryxpress. com/artupdate/>.

> This work is the best resource currently available on using the Internet for art and architecture research. Author Lois Swan Jones, professor emeritus in the School of Visual Arts at the University of North Texas, has been recognized as one of the leaders in art research since at least the 1970s with the publication of her first book on art research.[2] Her latest work is truly a guide to art and architecture literature in many formats. While focusing on the Internet, Jones has not excluded print sources, which reflects her intention of complementing traditional sources with the Internet. As she writes in the introduction, "This book shows how to locate visual and text data on the Internet and how to evaluate and supplement that data with material from other information formats to produce quality research results" (Jones, 1999: xiii).
>
> Jones starts her discussion with background on using the Internet for research, covering topics from explaining uniform resource locators to evaluating Web sites. She focuses on specific types of Web sites, from art museums and academic institutions to professional organizations and libraries. Jones approaches research topics by providing selective examples, from the lives of artists to Asian cultural studies, and then evaluates databases and various print and Internet resources that would be useful. She also discusses style manuals, copyright, and conservation.
>
> In the course of nearly 280 pages, she covers the spectrum of information on the use of the Internet for art research as a complementary tool to art research in general. In a world where Web site directories published over the past few years are almost immediately out of date, Jones maintains currency by providing a Web site to accompany the book. URL: <http://www.oryxpress. com/artupdate/>. This Web site provides updates to links discussed in the book, adds new links, and provides news clippings

of information related to the arts. The book is priced at $45, an investment that is well worth the cost.

Brown, J. *Architecture and Building* [Online]. Las Vegas: University of Nevada. Retrieved April 28, 1999. URL: <http://library.nevada. edu/arch/rsrce/webrsrce/contents.html>.

One of the oldest Web site directories for architecture is *Architecture and Building* by Jeanne Brown, head of the University of Nevada Las Vegas Architecture Studies Library. URL: <http://library. nevada.edu/arch/rsrce/webrsrce/contents.html>. Updated regularly, this directory includes related areas, such as design, planning, and energy and the environment. Brown's site is a selective list of links, including some meta-sites. Although she does not state her criteria for selectivity, she does include sites which, in her words, "show promise" of becoming quality sites.

The subject directory is broken down into two parts: Reference Tools (e.g., bibliographies, dictionaries, etc.) and Resources (e.g., Architectural Archives, Discussion Groups, Libraries, Virtual Galleries, etc.). In a separate page, she provides a complete alphabetical list of all of the links. Every link is annotated and also includes the hyperlink from the written-out URL instead of the site name, enabling those who might print out the directory to retrieve the URL from a printed page. One pleasant feature is the ability to go from page to page and browse the index as if it were a printed book. All those researching architecture will find this site most useful as Brown continues to update this site.

Witcombe, C. L. C. E. *Art History Resources on the Web* [Online]. Sweet Briar, VA: Sweet Briar College. Retrieved April 28, 1999. URL: <http://witcombe.sbc.edu/ARTHLinks.html>.

One of the most frequently used textbooks for introductory art history courses is *Gardiner's Art Through the Ages,* the 11th edition scheduled for publication by Harcourt Brace in 2000. To accompany this standard work, Christopher Witcombe, Professor of Art History at Sweet Briar College, designed this massive list of annotated art history Web links. URL: <http://witcombe.sbc.edu/ ARTHLinks.html>.

His logo, found on each page, is the *Venus of Willendorf,* one of the best known examples of prehistoric art. The site is broken down into the following easy-to-use titled categories: Prehistoric Art; Ancient Art (including Egyptian, Greek, and Roman); Art of the Middle Ages; Renaissance Art; Baroque; 18th-Century Art; 19th-Century Art; 20th-Century Art; Non-European Art (including Asia and Africa); Research Resources (including Image Finders, Research and Methodology, etc.); Museums and Galleries; and Prints and Photography. He provides links to major sites and specific related pages within these Web sites. The series of links on each page occasionally seems scattered and is not always well organized, but the pages are updated on a regular basis, with Witcombe encouraging people to contribute links. While he does not cite criteria for selecting links, it seems to be one of the most comprehensive Web site directories for art history.

Molinaro, M. *ArtSource* [Online]. Lexington: University of Kentucky. Retrieved September 21, 1999. URL: <http://www.ilpi.com/artsource/>.

Mary Molinaro, a librarian at the University of Kentucky and listserv moderator for ARLIS-L (the electronic discussion list for ARLIS/NA, the Art Libraries Society of North America), is the author of *ArtSource*. URL: <http://www.ilpi.com/artsource/>. This fast-loading, text-based, beginners' Web site directory for art is quick and easy to use. The home page explains that the site provides "selective, rather than comprehensive" Internet links related to art and architecture research. *ArtSource* has been considered one of the Internet's best art subject directories. In a recent article on citation analysis of links to art-related Web sites, *ArtSource* was the most popular link from a list of approximately 900.[3]

The "Table of Contents" gives a breakdown of the various subject areas: Architecture Resources; Art and Architecture Programs; Art and Architecture Libraries; Art Journals Online; Artist's Projects; Electronic Exhibitions; Events; General Resources and Bibliographies; Image Collections; Museum Information; New Media; Organizations; and Vendor Information. Each section contains an alphabetical list of links, and each link is annotated, although some of the annotations are taken from the linked site and not written by the author.

The "Search Services" page features the ability to search the *ArtSource* site or to use any of the linked search engine tools to search the Internet directly from Molinaro's site. The "ArtSource Gift Shop" provides links to art books which can be purchased from Amazon.com, ultimately helping to support *ArtSource* through this partnership.

As a subject directory of resources on the World Wide Web and some Newsgroups, the site is superb. While there may be more comprehensive subject directories, this one provides a good summary to some of the best available information and will not overwhelm an Internet novice.

Midkiff, A. *Mother of All Art History Links Pages* [Online]. Ann Arbor: University of Michigan. Retrieved June 21, 1999. URL: <http://www.umich.cdu/~hartspc/histart/mother/>.

> The *Mother of All Art History Links Pages* is another well-designed comprehensive directory that focuses on art history, but also includes peripheral information. URL: <http://www.umich.edu/~hartspc/histart/mother/>. The site's logo is a beautiful painting by Bouguereau from the University of Michigan Museum of Art. The site is divided into various sections with all links annotated in detail. The sections are "A Sampling of Art History Departments," "Research Resources," "Image Collections and Online Art," "A Sampling of Online Exhibits," "Sites of the Sacred," "Art Museums," and "Textual and Linguistic Resources."

Liu, A. *Voice of the Shuttle* [Online]. Santa Barbara: University of California. Retrieved June 21, 1999. URL: <http://humanitas.ucsb.edu>.

> Perhaps one of the most famous Web site directories for the humanities has been *Voice of the Shuttle*. Created by Alan Liu (English Department, University of California, Santa Barbara), this site has been a long-standing Web site directory since it premiered on the Internet in 1995. *Voice of the Shuttle* is broken up into specific subject pages. There are pages for Art and Art History as well as Architecture. On the Art and Art History page, sections include links on Art Theory and Politics, Design, and

Image Copyright and Intellectual Property Issues. The Architecture page includes sections on Architectural Historical Preservation, Journals, and Departments and Programs. Related subject pages include Archaeology, Cultural Studies, and Photography. Each section of each subject page has an alphabetical list of mostly-annotated links to relevant Web pages. There is also a search engine for the entire site.

World Wide Arts Resources [Online]. Retrieved June 22, 1999. URL: <http://wwwar.com>.

World Wide Arts Resources (WWAR) is a large arts-related site that indexes Web sites. While most of the information is geared towards the general audience, art researchers may find some useful information here. There is a master search engine, but the site also allows for categorical browsing. For instance, the link for "Art Museums" provides a choice of geographical locations and then listings with links to museum pages. Related services such as "Arts News" includes information on exhibits worldwide. Other features include an arts chat room and a section for posting or searching resumes. WWAR is certainly one of the most comprehensive arts-related Web directories.

IMAGE SITES

Berinstein, P. (1996). *Finding images online*. Wilton, CT.

Berinstein, P. *Berinstein Research* [Online]. Woodland Hills, CA: Berinstein Research. Retrieved June 22, 1999. URL: <http://www. berinsteinresearch.com/>.

Berinstein's book is one of the best works on the identification of images online, and the accompanying Web site makes the work even more useful. The author's definition of "online" consists of four general areas: consumer services (ISPs such as America Online and CompuServe); systems for visually-oriented professionals (e.g., Kodak Picture Exchange); Internet (including World Wide Web, FTP, Gopher, and Usenet); and databases (e.g., DIALOG).

The chapter on digital image basics gives an excellent overview to understanding the digitization process, from explaining pixels and DPIs to file compression and conversion. In chapters six and seven Berinstein offers insightful suggestions and advice for searching and browsing online sources for images, such as useful keywords and Boolean techniques. She also highlights search strategies that are most beneficial for identifying specific types of images, such as works of art, clip art, historical costumes, and news photos. Her brief chapter on copyright is also enlightening in terms of the use of images taken from online sources, although readers should cross-reference her information with the recent changes in copyright law. Among her appendices is an extensive 70-page "Subject Index to Online Resources" that focuses on Web sites and other online sources to find pictures. The bibliography provides additional reading about online visual resources.

Berinstein recognizes that online resources in print may be outdated rather quickly, so her accompanying Web site provides extensive revised information from the text. Berinstein updates this site quarterly. The Web site, its URL different from the one originally published in the book, advertises her company but includes links directly related to *Finding Images Online*. The section "Picture Resources" includes links to special search engines that can identify online images, such as the Image Surfer from Yahoo! (URL: http://ipix.yahoo.com/) and Scour.Net (URL: http://www.scour.net/); the latter also searches for audio and multimedia files. Berinstein also includes an updated and more extensive subject index than the one found in the original print edition. Another section, "Updates to *Finding Images Online*," provides full-text supplements or complements to chapters in the original print edition. This Web site is a great accompaniment to the book itself. Together they will provide art and architecture researchers with effective tools to find the images they need.

Center for Cultural Technology. *Arthur Image Search System* [Online]. Los Angeles: Information Sciences Institute. Retrieved July 21, 1999. URL: <http://www.isi.edu/cct/arthur/>.

Until recently it has been very difficult to search specifically for visual images on the World Wide Web. The development of

Arthur (ART media and text HUb and Retrieval system) has begun to make this task less difficult. Arthur is powered by AMORE (Advanced Multimedia Oriented Retrieval Engine), a search engine specifically designed for finding visual images on the World Wide Web. In actuality, Arthur acts like an indexing system for visual images on the World Wide Web, providing links and information about visual images. The site uses frames to display graphical images on the left while providing search options on the right.

One can browse by choosing a specific database (Selected Art/Art History Websites; Art Museum Network Websites; and Greek/Roman Websites) and select one of the sample images and browse through similar images. To identify specific images or components of images, one can use the search engine. Use of the Visual option finds other images that are similar in size or color. The Contextual option allows searching for other images based on their context within its host Web site. The general Keyword option performs a random search of text surrounding the image on Web sites. For instance, a search on "Michelangelo" using the "Selected Art/Art History Websites" database resulted in 47 hits, displayed as thumbnails on the left with the ability to click on each image or the button for similar works visually or contextually.

Each page of information includes a thumbnail graphic, detailed information regarding the location of the image, any ALT tag information, captions, and links to the actual Web site where the image can be found. The keyword search engine looks for keywords in the hypertext, nearby text, and captions. The Arthur database is critical for art and architecture researchers and should be one of the first places to look for visual images of art and architecture on the World Wide Web.

Kohl, A. T. *AICT: Art Images for College Teaching* [Online]. Minneapolis: Minneapolis College of Art and Design. Retrieved July 6, 1999. URL: <http://www.mcad.edu/AICT/>.

One of the most useful aspects of images on the Internet is their potential incorporation in both traditional and distance education classroom lessons, as slides have always been used in standard art history classes. The ease with which images may be downloaded from the Internet, however, raises the issue of copyright. Allan Kohl, Visual Resources Librarian and Lecturer for Art History at the Minneapolis College of Art and Design, has generated a Web site that eliminates this problem. All of the images on his site are copyright-free for use by anyone for educational or personal non-profit use. URL: <http://www.mcad.edu/AICT/>.

The images on *AICT* are predominantly photographs taken by Kohl of works of art and architecture in the public domain. The Web site itself is a sampler of images that Kohl has made available on Kodak Photo-CDs which are available free to institutions for downloading and manipulating for projects under the same agreements as the images on the Web site. The page with the image provides detailed information on the work of art or architecture itself and directions for downloading for PC or Mac. One of the best parts of the site is the textbook concordance, with page references to discussion of the image in major art history textbooks.

Malyon, J. *Artcyclopedia: The Guide to Museum-Quality Art on the Internet* [Online]. Calgary, Canada: Artcyclopedia. Retrieved July 6, 1999. URL: <http://www.artcyclopedia.com>.

Artcyclopedia bills itself as the guide for finding "museum-quality art on the Internet." URL: <http://www.artcyclopedia.com>. From the home page one can browse an alphabetical list of artists or use the search engine of nearly 5,500 artists' pages, all of which include both the masters and contemporary artists. There are special monthly featured artists, museums, art books, and art prints. The site focuses primarily on fine art painting and sculpture but includes links to information on other forms of visual art (e.g., decorative art). Each page on an artist provides a list of links to digital images on the World Wide Web, sometimes accompanied by a digital image itself. The links are arranged by kind of sites, such as artists' Web pages, museum listings, and online articles. The site is updated regularly.

Harden, M. *Mark Harden's Artchive* [Online]. Retrieved July 6, 1999. URL: <http://www.artchive.com/>.

Mark Harden's Artchive is a wonderful collection of digitized works of art and a continuous work in progress. After following the link to the "Artchive" itself, the well-designed use of frames facilitates the selection of over 230 artists and/or time periods. A list of works by title appears in the main frame. In some cases Harden provides a paragraph-length entry on the artist and links to all of the available digital images. Each image can be viewed in the main frame with information about the work itself. However, many of the images can also be viewed using the Image Viewer, which allows one's browser to alter the size of the image to fit one's screen and to zoom in on details. Harden provides these works to the public under the claim of public domain and fair use for copyrighted works. He provides stipulations for use of these images, which should be consulted by potential users. From the home page one can also visit the virtual galleries he has designed and browse through other art information.

RESEARCH DATABASES

ADEC/art price annual and Falk's art price index. (1998-). St. Romain au Mont d'Or, France: Art Price Annual S. A.

ADEC Art Price Annual [Online]. St. Romain au Mont d'Or, France: Art Price Annual. Retrieved July 22, 1999. URL: <http://www.artprice. com>.

Auction catalogs and their indexes are beneficial to librarians as reference tools in assisting users with art research topics. Not only do they assist in verifying the value of a work of art, but also provide detailed information about a particular work of art that often is not found in traditional print sources. "Auction catalogs may be the scholar's only opportunity to identify objects passing from one set of private hands to another" (Robinson, 1999, p. 24).

In 1998 *ADEC: Annuaire des Cotes International* (published since 1988) and *Art Price Index International* (published in 1994) merged to become *ADEC/Art Price Annual & Falk's Art Price Index* (St. Romain au Mont d'Or, France: Art Price Annual S. A., 1999-) and *ADEC Art Price Annual* on the Internet. This resource is one of the best for identifying the sale price of works of art sold at auctions worldwide.

The current print annual of *ADEC* sells for $119, with other annuals dating back to 1987 costing $70 each or $620 for 11 volumes. Each volume has approximately 2,800 pages and includes all of the information that is available on the Internet, plus brief provenance auction house information. *ADEC* is expected to become more Internet-based in the near future because the company went public in the fall of 1999. The company still plans to produce print and CD-ROM versions of its work, however, recognizing that not everyone is Internet-ready.

According to the Web site, the database currently holds approximately 1,500,000 auction results from over 1,630 auction houses in 40 countries, with information on the sale of works by over 149,000 listed artists. It focuses on most forms of visual media: painting, drawing, sculpture, prints, and photography. The site is updated daily as auction houses post new sales. One accesses the database with a search engine. Currently, a search by artist's name is the only option, but other fields will be added. Searching the database on the Internet is free. A search on an artist will generate an index list of items that have been sold at auction since 1987. Information here includes the date of the sale, the title of the work, and the medium. However, in order to access the full record on the sale, you must sign up for "units." It is not a subscription price, but a usage price. Since each record constitutes one unit, blocks of units may be purchased online by credit card or by faxing information. Currently, the rates are approximately $1.00 per unit/record with volume discounts. The full record includes the same information as in the index, but also the auction house, whether reproduced in a catalog, lot number, expected selling price, and hammer price in pounds, francs, and dollars.

The Web site for this free part of the auction index is useful for doing basic research, and the cost involved for accessing the specific information is certainly within range for most libraries or individual patrons themselves who are intent on finding information about an artist. The print editions of *ADEC* would only seem useful to those libraries that prefer to have complete collections, but patrons need to recognize that print indexes require searching each year for accurate results. The online and print versions complement one another, allowing an individual to search on the free database and identify the years in which items were sold, and then consult the print volumes for specific information on the sale itself. In either case, the information assembled here will always prove useful.

There are numerous other online resources for auction information. For example, the most famous auction houses, Christie's and Sotheby's, now provide auction information on their Web sites. The Christie's site is useful, but detailed information requires a subscription. URL: <http://www.christies.com>. Auction information is available through the database entitled "LotFinder" at a cost of approximately $25 for 10 records. Here, a keyword search identifies Christie sales on items in all media (painting, sculpture, decorative arts, etc.) from all of its agencies worldwide. In turn, the Sotheby's Web site offers information on past and upcoming sales based on information gathered from their auction catalogs and sales results dating back to April 1998. URL: <http://www.sothebys.com>. The lot number is required in order to search, but this is available from the catalogs themselves. Abridged information from these catalogs and auction guides is provided. With past sales, some entries include extensive background information and hammer price, although no graphics are included.

Art index. (1929-). New York: H. W. Wilson.

Art Index/Abstracts/Full Text/Art Retrospective [Online]. Bronx, NY: H. W. Wilson. Retrieved July 8, 1999. URL: <http://www.hwwilson. com/Databases/artindex.html>.

For 70 years now, the monthly Wilson *Art Index* has been one of the most popular sources for the indexing of articles, reviews, visual reproductions of works of art, and publication types found in art journals, museum bulletins, and other art-related resources published primarily in English, but other European languages as well. Currently, the index covers 370 titles. Topics include traditional art history, architecture, and museology, as well as video and television. Since 1994, Wilson has published *Art Abstracts,* which includes the same information as *Art Index* but adds a brief abstract of 50 to 150 words. Subscription rates for both vary depending on the number of art journals to which a library subscribes.

On the Internet, *Art Index* provides citation information dating from September 1984 to the present. *Art Abstracts* provides citations and an abstract from January 1994 to the present. URL: <http://www.hwwilson.com/Databases/artindex.html>. Starting in the fall of 1999, there will be a major enhancement to the Internet version of *Art Abstracts*: the inclusion of 90 titles with full-text articles dating back to 1997. Prices are similar to those for CD-ROM versions, ranging from approximately $1,500 to $3,800 per year depending on the subscription database (*Art Index* or *Art Abstracts*) and the number of simultaneous users.

The other exciting development in the history of the *Art Index/Art Abstracts* has been *Art Index Retrospective,* which also is available over the Internet. *Art Index Retrospective* ultimately will include all of the data found in the volumes spanning 1929 through September 1984, all searchable in conjunction with the later dates currently available. Information dating back to 1971 is currently available, with the rest of the database scheduled for release in November 1999. Currently this information is only available through WilsonWeb, but contract negotiations are being conducted to make this database available through OCLC and SilverPlatter, vendors which also provide access to *Art Index* and *Art Abstracts.* The one-time fee for this product ranges from approximately $6,000 to $9,000 depending on the number of simultaneous users.

The move towards Internet access for the *Art Index* reflects the transition throughout arts-related research. It seems appropriate here, as it does for all indexes. Print indexes force individuals to search volume after volume to ensure that they gather all available information. Electronic access expedites searching, and the availability of some titles in full-text makes this research even less time-consuming and more comprehensive in the long run. The largest gap has been in searching older material, but projects like *Art Index Retrospective* are gradually providing this once obscure material online as well. This too is an area which will only improve research in the future.

Turner, J. (Ed.). (1996). *Dictionary of art* (Vols. 1-34). London: Macmillan.

Dictionary of Art Online [Online]. New York: Grove Dictionaries. Retrieved July 8, 1999. URL: <http://www.groveart.com>.

The publication in 1996 of the Grove *Dictionary of Art* was a monumental project welcomed by the art world. One reviewer called it "an astounding feat" (Doumato, 1997, p. 23). The last quality, comprehensive multi-volume art encyclopedia had been the *Encyclopedia of World Art* published in 1959. The 34 volumes of the print edition of the *Dictionary of Art* include 41,000 articles on worldwide topics ranging from prehistory through art of the 1990s in just about every visual medium: architecture, painting, sculpture, photography, and others. There are 6,802 contributors from 120 countries with 15,000 visual reproductions and 300,000 bibliographic citations. The index alone holds over 720,000 terms. The print version currently sells for $8,800.

As in the case with all encyclopedic sources, however, in ten years (if not sooner) the *Dictionary of Art* will be outdated with respect to information on contemporary artists and new research on past artists. This has led to the creation of the *Dictionary of Art Online,* the Internet version of the print encyclopedia. URL: <http://www.groveart.com>. Launched in November 1998, the online version includes the full-text of the articles, index, and bibliographic citations found in the original version. The main page also has links to special features, one of which is ingenious. Grove advertises for special exhibitions being held in museums worldwide by offering background information from the *Dictionary of Art Online* as introductory reading material before visiting the exhibit.

The *Dictionary of Art Online* is a frames-based site that is very easy to use by either browsing the entries alphabetically A-Z or consulting the online subject index. In both cases, every entry is hyperlinked to the article itself. One may also use the search engine, which seems powerful, offering concept, pattern, and Boolean options. It can search article titles or the full-text of articles. Some of the articles have hyperlinks within them to other articles, although this is not consistent for all articles. Entries appear in the main frame of the site with additional information in a side link. The appendices include a list of the contributors and a name and location list of all of the museums and galleries that are cited in the text.

The visual images that were reproduced in the print version are not included here because Grove does not have copyright permission to reproduce them online. To make digital images of works of art available through their database, Grove recently signed an agreement with The Bridgeman Art Library Online. Clicking on the link to the Bridgeman images launches their Web site, where one can use another search engine to find numerous works by a particular artist or images depicting a specific subject. A search on Sir Edward Burne-Jones, for instance, produced not only paintings but also photographs of him, which is a wonderful feature. Currently there are 30,000 images available; by the end of 1999 another 70,000 are scheduled for release.

Grove also provides links from the articles to digital art collections on the Internet. For instance, the entry on Burne-Jones provides links to images of his works on servers owned by the Tate Gallery and other museums worldwide. This means of providing visual images has actually caused concerns among some libraries and museums, because the *Dictionary of Art Online* is subscription-based, hence profit-earning, and it is providing free access to digitized information located within museum Web sites without seeking permission from the museum (Costello, 1999: W9).

The power of this database is in its future. In much the same way that the print edition was welcomed when it first premiered, so too will the online version be praised when articles are updated regularly and more images are included. The subscription rate is relatively reasonable at the academic level: $1,500 per year for one to five simultaneous users. Grove offers institutions that own the print version an incentive for the first year subscription price at a reduced rate of $1,000. Subsequent rates have not yet been established, but Grove offers multiple-year subscriptions at the current introductory rate. Together, the print and Internet versions of this product work well to provide comprehensive and up-to-date information in all areas of visual arts research.

Eureka on the Web [Online]. Mountain View, CA: Research Libraries Group. Retrieved June 17, 1999. URL: <http://www.rlg.org/eurekaweb.html>.

Eureka is an Internet database available by subscription and/or with membership in the Research Libraries Group (RLG). URL: <http://www.rlg.org/eurekaweb.html>. It is perhaps the database of choice for many art and architecture libraries, specifically because many of the databases are geared towards humanities research. Some of the more prestigious art institutions which are members of RLG include the Avery Architecture and Fine Arts Library at Columbia University, the Getty Information Institute, the National Art Library at the Victoria and Albert Museum, and the art libraries of the Smithsonian Institution. Membership in RLG includes discounts on Eureka databases.

Eureka was first made available on the Internet in 1993 in a telnet version. In November 1996, RLG released a limited access version on the World Wide Web. Mass distribution to RLG members and Eureka subscribers began on the Web in 1997. The interface is user-friendly, allowing both simple and advanced search options. JavaScript is used to launch new windows for descriptions of the databases and for the exporting of data for printing, downloading, or emailing. Subscriptions to the Web version of Eureka are priced individually within each database and are based on a single site and the number of users.

Some of the databases in *Eureka* are also available in print. However, some of these print publications, such as the *Avery Index to Architectural Periodicals,* may be discontinued by the publishers because of the cost involved in their publication and production. If the print version of any product is discontinued, then the electronic version will be pivotal to research in all areas. Were this to happen in the fields of art and architecture, then the following *Eureka* databases would be of vital importance for art and architecture researchers.

- *RLIN Bibliographic File* is a union catalog of the holdings of the 159 major research libraries and institutions worldwide, that belong to RLG. It includes books, serials, archives, manuscripts, music scores, photograph collections, and so on. It is updated daily. Its subscription rate starts at approximately $12,000.
- *Anthropological Literature* indexes and abstracts information related to anthropology and archaeology in both English and non-English sources dating back to the nineteenth-century. The data is provided by Tozzer Library, Harvard University. It is updated quarterly with subscription rates starting at $2,800. *Anthropological Literature* is also available in print as a quarterly index. It is

also published by Harvard University Tozzer Library at an annual subscription rate of $225.

- *Avery Index to Architectural Periodicals* indexes articles from over 1,000 serials on architecture, interior design, archaeology, and related disciplines from 1977 to the present. Updated daily, this resource is provided by the Avery Architecture and Fine Arts Library at Columbia University. Subscriptions start at $2,400 per year. *Avery Index to Architectural Periodicals* is available as an annual print publication for G. K. Hall and Co. at a rate of $595 a year.
- *Bibliography of the History of Art (BHA)* is one of the leading indexing services covering European and American art topics from late antiquity to the present. BHA provides abstracts on articles from over 2,500 journals, chapters in books, dissertations, exhibition catalogs, and conference proceedings. Updated quarterly, it spans the years 1973 to the present, providing extended coverage of its famous predecessors, RAA (Repertoire d'Art et d'Archeologie) from 1973 to 1989 and RILA (International Repertory of the Literature of Art) from 1975 to 1989. Data is provided by the Getty Information Institute and the Institut de l'Information Scientifique et Technique du Centre National de la Récherche Scientifique. Subscription rates start at $2,600 per year. *Bibliography of the History of Art* is also available in print from the J. Paul Getty Trust. Current annual subscription rates for this quarterly are approximately $425.
- *FRANCIS* indexes English and non-English sources, mostly European, which focus on the humanities, particularly in the areas of art history and religion. The database is updated monthly, with coverage from 1984 to the present. The data is provided by the Institut de l'Information Scientifique et Technique du Centre National de la Récherche Scientifique and the Getty Information Institute. Subscription rates start at $3,000.
- *Index to 19th-Century American Art Periodicals* is one of the best databases for those studying art history. It indexes the entire contents of 42 American art journals that were published over the span of the nineteenth century. One of its highlights is the indexing not only of articles but also of all pictures and advertisements found in the journals as well, providing a comprehensive data-

base of nineteenth-century life. This is a closed database, with subscription rates starting at $850.

- *SCIPIO: Art and Rare Book Sales Catalogs* is updated daily. It describes art auction and rare book catalogs for sales dating from the late sixteenth century to scheduled auctions not yet held. The project began in 1980 as a collaborative effort by the Art Institute of Chicago, the Cleveland Museum of Art, and the Metropolitan Museum of Art, and has since expanded to include contributions from 17 other museums. Records include the dates and places of sales, the auction houses, sellers, institutional holdings, and titles of works. Art historians and museum researchers will find the information most useful when tracing provenance and cultural history. Subscription rates start at $1,400.

CONCLUSION

If there were any doubts as to the availability of art and architecture resources on the Internet, such concerns should be put aside. The World Wide Web has made art and architecture resource material readily available in ways no one would have ever expected five years ago, particularly because of enhancements in visual image technology. However, it is important to remember that the key to conducting good research in art and architecture is to use the Internet as a complement to the print resources that humanities scholars historically have found most useful. Art and architecture resources on the Internet will only enhance their research.

NOTES

1. Information on the use of the World Wide Web by faculty is a necessity. Tim Devine (Head of Circulation/Current Periodicals and Microforms, FAU), Amy Shepper (Systems Librarian, FAU), and I are conducting research on this topic. Our quantitative survey will track usage of the World Wide Web by faculty in the humanities and social sciences at a randomly selected group of research universities across the United States. The survey will ask questions related to instruction, research, and library-faculty interaction. We hope to publish the results of this survey in the year 2000.

2. Jones, L. S. (1978). *Art research methods and resources: a guide to finding art information.* Dubuque, IA: Kendall/Hunt.

3. See Neth, M. (1998, Spring). Citation analysis and the Web. *Art Documentation, 17*: 29-33. Citation analysis of Web sites is a new and fascinating means of studying the popularity of Web links. However, it is interesting to note that in Neth's article, from the list of 900 individual sites, only four were linked more than twenty-five times, with *ArtSource* linked 32 times from the library Web pages analyzed. In turn, of the Web sites discussed in this article, only five appear in the top twenty obtained by Neth. These two points would seem to suggest that while citation analysis of Web links is an intriguing means of determining their popularity, they may not necessarily reflect the most current information. For example, *Artcyclopedia* did not exist at the time Neth's article was published. Also, opinions on the most useful Web resources for art and architecture, or any discipline, may differ from one individual to another.

WEBLIOGRAPHY

ADEC Art Price Annual [Online]. St. Romain au Mont d'Or, France: Art Price Annual. Retrieved July 22, 1999. URL: <http://www.artprice.com>.

Art Index/Abstracts/Full Text/Art Retrospective [Online]. Bronx, NY: H. W. Wilson. Retrieved July 8, 1999. URL: <http://www.hwwilson.com/Databases/artindex. html>.

Center for Cultural Technology. *Arthur Image Search System* [Online]. Los Angeles: Information Sciences Institute. Retrieved July 21, 1999. URL: <http://www.isi.edu/cct/arthur/>.

Brown, J. *Architecture and Building* [Online]. Las Vegas: University of Nevada. Retrieved April 28, 1999. URL: <http://library.nevada.edu/arch/rsrce/webrsrce/contents.html>.

Christie's [Online]. Retrieved June 22, 1999. URL: <http://www.christies.com>.

Dictionary of Art Online [Online]. New York: Grove Dictionaries. Retrieved July 8, 1999. URL: <http://www.groveart.com>.

Eureka on the Web [Online]. Mountain View, CA: Research Libraries Group. Retrieved June 17, 1999. URL: <http://www.rlg.org/eurekaweb.html>.

Getty Research Institute. *The Art & Architecture Thesaurus Browser* [Online]. Los Angeles: Getty Research Institute. Retrieved July 8, 1999. URL: <http://shiva. pub.getty.edu/aat_browser/>.

Harden, M. *Mark Harden's Artchive* [Online]. Retrieved July 6, 1999. URL: <http://www.artchive.com/>.

Jones, L. S. *Art Information and the Internet Updates* [Online]. Phoenix: Oryx. Retrieved June 17, 1999. URL: <http://www.oryxpress.com/artupdate/>.

Kohl, A. T. *AICT: Art Images for College Teaching* [Online]. Minneapolis: Minneapolis College of Art and Design. Retrieved July 6, 1999. URL: <http://www.mcad.edu/AICT/>.

Liu, A. *Voice of the Shuttle* [Online]. Santa Barbara: University of California. Retrieved June 21, 1999. URL: <http://humanitas.ucsb.edu>.

Malyon, J. *Artcyclopedia: The Guide to Museum-Quality Art on the Internet* [Online]. Calgary, Canada: Artcyclopedia. Retrieved July 6, 1999. URL: <http://www.artcyclopedia.com>.

Midkiff, A. *Mother of All Art History Links Pages* [Online]. Ann Arbor: University of Michigan. Retrieved June 21, 1999. URL: <http://www.umich.edu/~hartspc/histart/mother/>.

Molinaro, M. *ArtSource* [Online]. Lexington: University of Kentucky. Retrieved September 21, 1999. URL: <http://www.ilpi.com/artsource/>.

Scour.Net [Online]. Beverly Hills, CA: Scour, Inc. Retrieved September 21, 1999. URL: <http://www.scour.net>.

Tolub, B. T. *Sotheby's* [Online]. New York: @radical.media. Retrieved July 6, 1999. URL: <http://www.sothebys.com>.

Witcombe, C. L. C. E. *Art History Resources on the Web* [Online]. Sweet Briar, VA: Sweet Briar College. Retrieved April 28, 1999. URL: <http://witcombe.sbc.edu/ARTHLinks.html>.

World Wide Arts Resources [Online]. Retrieved June 22, 1999. URL: <http://wwwar.com>.

Yahoo! *Image Surfer* [Online]. Retrieved September 21, 1999. URL: <http://ipix.yahoo.com/>.

REFERENCES

ADEC/art price annual and Falk's art price index. (1998-). St. Romain au Mont d'Or, France: Art Price Annual S. A.

Anthropological literature. (1979-). Cambridge: Harvard UP.

Art & architecture thesaurus. (1990). (Vol. 1-3). New York: Oxford UP.

Art index. (1929-). New York: H. W. Wilson.

Bates, M. J. (1996). The Getty end-user online searching project in the humanities: report no. 6: overview and conclusions. *College and Research Libraries, 57(6)*: 514-23.

Berinstein, P. (1996). *Finding images online.* Wilton, CT.

Bibliography of the history of art. (1990-). Santa Monica, CA: J. Paul Getty Trust.

Blazek, R. & Aversa, E. (1994). *The humanities: a selective guide to information sources.* Englewood, CO: Libraries Unlimited.

Columbia University Avery Architectural Library. (1963-). *Avery index to architectural periodicals.* Thorndike, ME: G. K. Hall.

Costello, D. (1999, February 12). "Art & money." *Wall Street Journal*, p. W9.

Doumato, L. (1997, Spring). Overview. [Review of the *Dictionary of art*]. *Art Documentation, 16*: 23-24.

Jones, L. S. (1999). *Art information and the Internet.* Phoenix: Oryx.

Jones, L. S. (1978). *Art research methods and resources: a guide to finding art information.* Dubuque, IA: Kendall/Hunt.

Montaigne, M. de. (1963). *Essays and selected writings.* 1588. Ed. D. Frame. New York: St. Martin's.

Neth, M. (1998, Spring). "Citation analysis and the web." *Art Documentation, 17*: 29-33.

Research Libraries Group. (1998). *Rates for user services.* (Available from the Research Libraries Group, 1200 Villa Street, Mountain View, CA 94041-1100).

Robinson, L. (1999, Spring). "Auction catalogs and indexes as reference tools." *Art Documentation, 18*: 24-28.

Turner, J. (Ed.). (1996). *Dictionary of art.* (Vols. 1-34). London: Macmillan.

Wilde, O. (1912). The critic as artist. *Impressions.* 1891. New York: Brentano's.

Biology Sites on the World Wide Web:
A Brief Survey

John E. Sisson

SUMMARY. Access to biological information on the World Wide Web continues to grow at a rapid pace. Many resources that previously required a trip to the library are now accessible from the desktop PC. Three major categories of biology Web sites are explored: those with citation information, those functioning as clearinghouses or directories to other Web sites, and those that present biological information in innovative ways. The suggested Web sites are some of the best and may serve as models for future Web development. Many useful citation Web sites are fee-based and are likely to continue as such for the near future; MEDLINE and AGRICOLA are important exceptions. Many significant clearinghouse and information Web sites are not fee-based and allow innovative ways of finding and sharing information. The state of research information on the WWW is not developed enough for the researcher to forego using paper sources. *[Article copies available for a fee from The Haworth Document Delivery Service: 1-800-342-9678. E-mail address: <getinfo@haworthpressinc.com> Website: <http://www.HaworthPress.com>]*

KEYWORDS. Biology, Internet research in, Internet resources in, online research in, online resources in

John E. Sisson is Biological Sciences Librarian at the Science Library, University of California at Irvine, Irvine, CA 92623-9556 (E-mail: jsisson@uci.edu). He received his MLIS from the University of Hawaii, Honolulu, his MS in Zoology from University of Maine, Orono, and his BA in Biology from University of California, San Diego. He is the current President of the Board of the Orange County Library Association.

[Haworth co-indexing entry note]: "Biology Sites on the World Wide Web: A Brief Survey." Sisson, John E. Co-published simultaneously in *Journal of Library Administration* (The Haworth Information Press, an imprint of The Haworth Press, Inc.) Vol. 30, No. 1/2, 2000, pp. 63-73; and: *Academic Research on the Internet: Options for Scholars & Libraries* (ed: Helen Laurence, and William Miller) The Haworth Information Press, an imprint of The Haworth Press, Inc., 2000, pp. 63-73. Single or multiple copies of this article are available for a fee from The Haworth Document Delivery Service [1-800-342-9678, 9:00 a.m. - 5:00 p.m. (EST). E-mail address: getinfo@haworthpressinc.com].

INTRODUCTION

Biology on the Web is a "growing" subject area. Besides the many sites covering aspects of general biology, there are numerous subject-specific sites for every area of biology. This highly selective list presents some of the "must see" sites that conceivably could be models for similar sites in other areas of biology. These sites are not only well-built, they are also helpful in meeting information needs. Finally, the selected sites are those that seem likely to continue and grow increasingly useful over time.

CITATION WEB SITES

The most important research need in most areas of biology is access to journal article citations. Citation Web sites address this need. A major source of citations in biology, as well as in many other areas of science, is *Science Citation Index*, now available though the Web as **Web of Science: Institute for Scientific Information (ISI)**. URL: <http://www.isinet.com/products/citation/wos.html>. Currently, according to the Web site, "The *Science Citation Index Expanded* ™ fully covers over 5,600 journals (2,000 more titles than the print or CD-ROM versions) and is updated with 16,000 new records every week." Although very expensive, the search interface is accessible to all levels of users. As in the paper and CD-ROM products, the lack of subject access is a difficulty but title word searches are highly effective. The use of *Web of Science* for citation checking is relatively simple provided the user checks all variations (i.e., title abbreviations, minor volume number or date errors) under which an article may have been cited.

A second set of important resources that are only available for a fee, and unfortunately are presently not Web-based, are **BIOSIS Previews and Zoological Record**. These are currently available only in paper or as CD-ROMs or data tapes for onsite installation. Thus these are not accessible from the Web unless the user has purchased a license and developed a Web-based interface for them. Alternatively, participating licensed search systems such as **DIALOG** do have Web-based search interfaces. URL: <http://www.dialogweb.com>. The DIALOG Web interface allows access to **BIOSIS Previews** (1969-present) and **Zoo-**

logical Record (1978-present) with many useful extra features for the frequent searcher. **DIALOG** allows both guided and command searching and has options such as saving search strategies, alerts, and setting up default display and delivery preferences.

Other citation indexes are both Web-based and free. **AGRICOLA** is produced by the National Agricultural Library and organized into two bibliographic data sets, *Books, etc.* (1970-present) and *Articles, etc.* (1979-present). URL: <http://www.nal.usda.gov/ag98/>. There are three ways to search both databases: browse, keyword, and advanced keyword. The databases must be searched separately. The databases are indexed by author word, subject word (Commonwealth Agricultural Bureau [CAB] Thesaurus term), or title word.

Although it is discussed more thoroughly in the article on medical information elsewhere in this volume, no article on biology can be complete without mentioning **MEDLINE**, available through the National Library of Medicine's **PubMed** Web site. URL: <http://www.ncbi.nlm.nih.gov/PubMed/>. A great deal has been written about the free access to *MEDLINE*, and it is indeed a wonderful tool. The search interface allows either a simple keyword search of authors, titles, and subject or a more advanced search that opens the many search options available in the *MEDLINE* database. By using the advanced search option, a user can construct complex searches taking advantage of the MeSH subject headings. Advanced searching allows access to substance name searches, author contact information (through an affiliation search), and provides the ability to search by CAS (Chemical Abstracts Service) number. While PubMed is relatively weak in its coverage of journals traditionally used by biologists, it is quite strong in its coverage of many important molecular and cell biology journals.

CLEARINGHOUSE WEB SITES

Clearinghouse Web sites are directories of the best Web sources on a topic. Scholarly societies and other professional groups are beginning to make an impact in this area by using their reputations and the expertise of their members to create definitive subject clearinghouses. There are many rich biology clearinghouse Web sites. They all adopt slightly different selection strategies based on their perceived audiences. The following Web sites are examples of some of the most unusual.

The first site is **CELS: Coalition for Education in the Life Sciences**. URL: <http://www.wisc.edu/cbe/cels/edulinks.html>. *CELS* is a national coalition of professional societies in the biological sciences that have joined together in an effort to improve undergraduate education in the life sciences. Especially interesting is the section labeled *Educational Activities Links*, which includes links to 64 professional societies' homepages (as of April 1999). Annotations accompany each of these links, highlighting which resources of the site would be useful for undergraduate education.

It is often said that the Web needs librarians to catalog it. Although this may never be fully achieved considering the rate of growth of Web resources, selective cataloging is quite possible. An excellent example of how librarians can help identify the important resources of the Web is **BioSites: A Virtual Catalog of Selected Internet Resources in the Biomedical Sciences**. URL: <http://www.library.ucsf.edu/biosites/>. It was produced as part of a collaborative project by staffs in the 12 Resource Libraries within the Pacific Southwest Region of the National Network of Libraries of Medicine. Officially released in January 1997, it provides identification and description of high-quality biomedical resources in 76 subject areas, each with 5-20 sites. Sites are submitted by the health science librarians within the project based on their utility to their populations. Each site has a data entry with title, creator, URL, description, and MeSH subject heading. Information can be found by browsing one of the subject areas or by a search of site titles or full text via search engine.

An excellent example of a single scholar creating an authoritative clearinghouse is **Neurosciences on the Internet**. URL: <http://www.neuroguide.com/>. A searchable and browsable index of neuroscience resources available on the Internet, maintained and edited by Dr. Neil A. Busis (Chief, Division of Neurology at the University of Pennsylvania Medical Center), it is a commercial site with banner advertisements on each page. The **NOTI** Web site includes resources in neurobiology, neurology, neurosurgery, psychiatry, psychology, cognitive science, and information on human neurological diseases. It is updated regularly, so links often have been added since the last time you checked. The starting page offers browsing by topic, with links to the 20-odd sections of this Web site. On this site, searching by keyword, title or URL is the easiest way to find what you need. Quality control is loose in that the author/compiler is inclusive rather than exclusive, but it is an excellent starting point for any neuroscience topic.

An example of a scholarly society helping create and support a clearinghouse is **Virtual Library-Developmental Biology**. URL: <http:// sdb.bio.purdue.edu/Other/VL_DB.html>. The **VL-DB** is maintained by the Society for Developmental Biology and functions as a true clearinghouse, allowing the user to identify where research is being done on a particular organism or developmental biology topic. It has a simple front page with a Subject index, an Organisms index, and major subdivisions under these headings. The Subject index and the Organisms index show which labs are doing which kinds of research, as well as some of the important databases on that topic. There are also indexes for Departments and Institutes, Societies and Organizations, Educational Resources, Research Resources, and Journals and Publishers. The Web site includes a search engine for locating sites by titles or by the brief annotations. Use of the search engine is necessary to take full advantage of this resource. However, users will need to sort carefully through search results because of the multiple occurrence of certain terms within the **VL-DB**.

The **Virtual Library: Bio Sciences** site indexes many other biology subject clearinghouse Web sites (27 as of April 1999). URL: http://www.vlib.org/Biosciences.html>. The "libraries" do vary a great deal in usefulness and content, depending upon the diligence of the individuals or professional organizations which maintain and update the Web site. One example of excellent design among these "libraries" is the **Virtual Library of Ecology and Biodiversity**, maintained by Alan D. Thornhill (Clinical Assistant Professor, Ecology and Evolutionary Biology Department, Rice University). URL: <http://conbio.rice.edu/vl/>. Its simple design allows a researcher quickly to find if there is a Web site on a species or subject without having to wade through multiple pages.

An important biology Web site available from the U.S. Government is the **National Biological Information Infrastructure**. URL: <http:// www.nbii.gov/>. Quoting from the site, "The goal of the NBII (created by the Biological Resources Division of the USGS), is to provide swift user access to biological databases, information products, directories, and guides maintained by Federal, State, and local government agencies, non-government institutions, and private sector organizations in the United States and around the world."

Information is accessible in three ways: by using the site's search engine, the *NBII Metadata Clearinghouse* (NBII MC), or by browsing the select subject lists. These select lists include information for students and teachers, invasive species in U.S. ecosystems, amphibian declines and abnormalities, biodiversity, systematics, biology collections, and U.S. and international biological information sites.

The *NBII MC* gateway allows the user to locate, evaluate, and access biological data and information from a distributed network of cooperating data and information sources, including government sponsored data sets and reports. It also allows access to software tools to use in analyzing, integrating, and applying biological data. The *NBII Metadata Clearinghouse* contains standardized metadata-based descriptions of biological data sets and information products. Searching is enabled by keyword, geographic location of study area, date of publication, and all taxonomic levels.

INFORMATION WEB SITES

The most exciting sort of Web sites in biology may be those that arise out of the ability to organize information in new ways. The information Web sites take advantage of the ability of the Web to allow all sorts of information to be shared within a "common computer." In biology there are especially strong needs to keep as current as possible, as well as to be able to answer "instant" information needs.

An extraordinary Web site that will continue to gain utility as the years pass is **The Tree of Life: A multi-authored, distributed Internet project containing information about phylogeny and biodiversity**. URL: <http://phylogeny.arizona.edu/tree/phylogeny.html>. Coordinated and edited by David R. Maddison (Associate Professor, Ecology and Evolutionary Biology, University of Arizona), **The Tree of Life** Web site was formally begun in January 1996. The Tree of Life is "a collection of over 1380 World Wide Web pages containing information about the diversity of life . . . housed on 20 computers in four countries, and . . . authored by biologists from around the world." It is structured like an evolutionary tree with a page about a group, then links from that one Web page to subgroups and links from that subgroup to individual species.

Because it does have a complex structure, the beginning page gives several options for movement through **The Tree**. Possibilities include beginning at the root (the hypothetical common ancestor/s of all life), searching for a particular organism via its search engine, examining popular groups on **The Tree** (FAQ species and groups), or examining the recently added pages. Some sections of **The Tree** are not fully realized, but it is growing into an important resource for understanding phylogenetic relationships.

Each section contains its own phylogenetic tree, a short discussion of the relationships and characteristics represented by that particular tree, and a list of references for that interpretation. Some branches of **The Tree** have links, which allow movement to "higher" levels. Also of great utility are the navigation buttons on the top and bottom of each section, allowing movement up and down **The Tree** by either a single level or down to a major branch. There are many blank spaces in **The Tree**, but listings for the species it does contain include characteristics, natural history, discussion of phylogenetic relationships, and a list of references.

Another resource that showcases new ways to connect information is **The Interactive Fly: A Cyberspace Guide to Drosophila development** (19th edition, posted March 25, 1999). URL: <http://sdb.bio.purdue.edu/fly/aimain/1aahome.htm>. This is an excellent example of the kind of information that an individual can gather together as a resource and develop into a definitive source. **The Interactive Fly** was written by and is being updated quarterly by Thomas B. Brody (Neurogenetics Unit, Laboratory of Neurochemistry, National Institute of Neurological Disorders and Stroke, National Institutes of Health). Since its beginning in July 1996, it has attempted to synthesize the flow of new information about *Drosophila* into a continuously evolving hypertext encyclopedia of fly genes and developmental processes. Currently residing on the Society for Developmental Biology home page, this very specialized site, about one of the most important biological organisms, has become a standard source.

It features a large number of possible starting points, all accessible from a single starting page. Organized into two major categories, the Gene Index and Tissue and Organ Development, there are also links to *Drosophila* images and other online resources. There are also two separate introductions, one for the developmental biologist and one for the new biologist.

Like the National Library of Medicine and the National Agricultural Library, many other units of the U. S. government have been placing important data sets on the Web for free use. One of the best is the **PLANTS National Database,** located at the National Plant Data Center and produced by the Natural Resources Conservation Service (NRCS), a branch of the U.S. Department of Agriculture. URL: <http://plants.usda.gov/plantproj/plants/plantspage.html>. This database functions as a botanical dictionary as well as an encyclopedia. Its primary utility is in finding the name of or information about a plant using a variety of different starting points. According to the Web site, the PLANTS database is a list of "native or naturalized vascular and nonvascular plants known to occur in the United States."

The site allows searches by scientific name, common name, PLANTS symbol, family, or genus. It does support the use of wildcard symbols for single or multiple characters. In addition, searches can be limited by state or region. The data in PLANTS can also be searched by phylum, by wetland region, and by threatened or endangered status. There are also links to government lists of noxious plants and economically important plants.

The elements in the data record include the common and scientific name, the PLANTS symbol, the family, economic importance (yes or no), growth habits, duration, and origin (native or introduced). The record also includes, if available, plant synonyms, geographic distribution, and plant reference information (a bibliographic list of references to the plant and the contributor/s of the record).

BioTech's Life Science Dictionary is a searchable dictionary containing 8,300+ terms dealing with biochemistry, biotechnology, botany, cell biology, and genetics. URL: <http://biotech.icmb.utexas. edu/search/dict-search.html>. It is part of the Indiana University and University of Texas Institute for Cellular and Molecular Biology Web site called **BioTech: Life Sciences Resources and Reference Tools**. URL: <http://biotech.icmb.utexas.edu/>.

Classical Genetics: Foundations is part of the **ESP: Electronic Scholarly Publishing** Web site. Respective URLs: <http://www.esp. org/foundations/genetics/classical/> and <http://www.esp.org/>. **Classical Genetics** gives the full text of important books and papers relating to the foundations of classical genetics. The classic writings of Mendel, Darwin, Malthus, and Bateson are available to download or examine. The other feature that is still under construction is the outstanding, *Genetics in Context–A Comparative Timeline*. It provides links to what was going on in history at the same time these landmarks of genetics were written.

WHAT NEXT?

What does this brief tour of biology Web sites show us about the future of biological research on the Web? Clearly, we are in the midst of a massive migration of information, but serious research cannot yet be conducted completely or exclusively from the desktop computer.

As indexing tools and full text journals continue moving to the Web in the near future, we can anticipate that most recently published research papers will be available to researchers over the Web. The access to these indexes and journals will probably continue to be fee-based so only researchers with a sponsor organization (or deep pockets) will be able to take full advantage of this "instant research."

Libraries will play an important role, on behalf of their users, as the gateways and subscribers to this information. It is not unreasonable to expect that there will be online access to the most recent 5-10 years of most major journals, with libraries supplying or holding the older issues. Librarians will need to continue to advocate that publishers create uniform interfaces for their users.

The future of clearinghouse and information Web sites is less clear. Researchers will need new and better guides to Web resources. In the future, more important reference monographs, data sets, and databases will be made available over the Web. This information will probably continue to be a mixture of fee-based and free material. The continued growth of scholarly individual and professional society "free" subject pages will be important new sources of information for the researcher.

In the foreseeable future, as in the present, a mixture of paper journals, monographs, and Web-based resources will be needed to do the best quality research. The most important research resources will continue to be fee-based for the latest material. Older material may become more available inexpensively (or free) through some sort of central Web archive, but there are still many problems to be solved.

Researchers need to focus on the Web as a tool and not allow it to drive the direction of their research. Different subject areas in biology have different research needs, and some types of information may appropriately never be Web based. There are vast stores of research information that will never be converted to an electronic format because of cost. And even as the cutting edge of biology accelerates, the "mining" of paths not taken may continue to be a rich source of research ideas.

All we can do is to continue creatively to explore this rapidly expanding information environment. We must do our best to be "jungle guides" so that those who follow can find the treasures and avoid the quicksand.

WEBLIOGRAPHY

Citation Web Sites

The Dialog Corporation. *Dialog* [Online]. Retrieved April 15, 1999. URL: <http://www.dialogweb.com>.
Institute for Scientific Information. *Web of Science* [Online]. Retrieved April 15, 1999. URL: <http://www.isinet.com/products/citation/wos.html>.
National Agricultural Library. *AGRICOLA* [Online]. Retrieved April 15, 1999. URL: <http://www.nal.usda.gov/ag98/>.
National Library of Medicine. *PubMed* [Online]. Retrieved April 15, 1999. URL: <http://www.ncbi.nlm.nih.gov/PubMed/>.

Clearinghouse Web Sites

BioSites: A Virtual Catalog of Selected Internet Resources in the Biomedical Sciences [Online]. Retrieved April 15, 1999. URL: <http://www.library.ucsf.edu/biosites/>.
Busis, Neil A. *Neurosciences on the Internet* [Online]. Retrieved April 19, 1999. URL: <http://www.neuroguide.com/>.
CELS: Coalition for Education in the Life Sciences [Online]. Retrieved April 15, 1999. URL: <http://www.wisc.edu/cbe/cels/edulinks.html>.
Thornhill, Alan D. *WWW Virtual Library–Virtual Library of Ecology and Biodiversity* [Online]. Houston, TX: Center for Conservation Biology, Department of Ecology and Evolutionary Biology, Rice University. Retrieved April 15, 1999. URL: <http://conbio.rice.edu/vl/>.
USGS, Biological Resources Division. *National Biological Information Infrastructure* [Online]. Retrieved April 15, 1999. URL: <http://www.nbii.gov/>.
WWW Virtual Library: Bio Sciences [Online]. Retrieved April 15, 1999. URL: <http://www.vlib.org/Biosciences.html>.
WWW Virtual Library–Developmental Biology [Online]. Retrieved April 15, 1999. URL: <http://sdb.bio.purdue.edu/Other/VL_DB.html>.

Information Web Sites

Brody, Thomas B. *The Interactive Fly: A Cyberspace Guide to Drosophila development* (19th edition, March 25, 1999) [Online]. Bethesda, MD: Society for Developmental Biology. Retrieved April 15, 1999. URL: <http://sdb.bio.purdue.edu/fly/aimain/1aahome.htm>.

The Electronic Scholarly Publishing Project. *Classical Genetics: Foundations* [Online]. Retrieved April 15, 1999. URL: <http://www.esp.org/foundations/genetics/classical/>.

Maddison, David R. *The Tree of Life: A multi-authored, distributed Internet project containing information about phylogeny and biodiversity* [Online]. Tucson, AZ: University of Arizona. Retrieved April 15, 1999. URL: <http://phylogeny.arizona.edu/tree/phylogeny.html>.

USDA, Natural Resources Conservation Service, National Plant Data Center. *PLANTS National Database* [Online]. Baton Rouge, LA: NRCS. Retrieved April 15, 1999. URL: <http://plants.usda.gov/plantproj/plants>.

University of Texas Institute for Cellular and Molecular Biology and the Indiana Institute for Molecular and Cellular Biology. *BioTech's Life Science Dictionary* [Online]. Retrieved April 15, 1999. URL: <http://biotech.icmb.utexas.edu/search/dict-search.html>.

University of Texas Institute for Cellular and Molecular Biology and the Indiana Institute for Molecular and Cellular Biology. *BioTech: Life Sciences Resources and Reference Tools* [Online]. Accessed April 15, 1999. URL: <http://biotech.icmb.utexas.edu/>.

Choosing Wisely
from an Expanding Spectrum of Options:
Business Information and the Internet

Steven J. Bell

SUMMARY. Owing to the exponential growth of business information Web sites, it is increasingly challenging to identify those sites that are of value and worthy of recognition. Compounding this situation is the phenomenon of "Web-centricity" in which business professionals and students limit their information searching behavior to Internet resources, ignoring the vast riches of traditional print and online resources. This article will serve as a guide to some of the Internet's contemporary, outstanding business Web sites and examine how they mesh with traditional print and electronic resources. Business information is likened to a spectrum that runs the gamut from traditional print to CD-ROM to commercial online database to Internet Web site. Business researchers must choose wisely from this expanding spectrum. Doing so requires a strong knowledge of the resources or enlisting an experienced business information specialist to serve as a guide. *[Article copies available for a fee from The Haworth Document Delivery Service: 1-800-342-9678. E-mail address: <getinfo@haworthpressinc.com> Website: <http://www.HaworthPress.com>]*

KEYWORDS. Business, Internet research in, Internet resources in, online research in, online resources

---

Steven J. Bell is Director of the Gutman Library at Philadelphia University. He writes and speaks frequently about online searching, technology topics, and academic librarianship. He received his MSLS from Drexel University and his EdD from the University of Pennsylvania.

[Haworth co-indexing entry note]: "Choosing Wisely from an Expanding Spectrum of Options: Business Information and the Internet." Bell, Steven J. Co-published simultaneously in *Journal of Library Administration* (The Haworth Information Press, an imprint of The Haworth Press, Inc.) Vol. 30, No. 1/2, 2000, pp. 75-104; and: *Academic Research on the Internet: Options for Scholars & Libraries* (ed: Helen Laurence, and William Miller) The Haworth Information Press, an imprint of The Haworth Press, Inc., 2000, pp. 75-104. Single or multiple copies of this article are available for a fee from The Haworth Document Delivery Service [1-800-342-9678, 9:00 a.m. - 5:00 p.m. (EST). E-mail address: getinfo@haworthpressinc.com].

For business information specialists the blessings are indeed mixed. Owing to demand for up-to-date, comprehensive corporate, industry, and product intelligence, there is no dearth of information packagers lining up to supply business information of almost any type–financial, management, market, or simple stock quotes and analysis–and in almost any format. This is not an Internet phenomenon. From the earliest days of online information retrieval, business databases were a significant component of available databanks. Despite the Internet juggernaut, however, there is no noticeable decline in the market for print business reference material. This abundance carries a burden. Business librarians must work diligently to keep up with an expanding universe of resources. The sad truth is that many business resources, especially on the Internet, duplicate existing offerings, offer little of value, require expensive subscriptions, or are simply poor in design and execution. Today's challenge is to identify and familiarize oneself with the true gems among the rocks.

Because new gems are always becoming available, and today's gems may be tomorrow's rocks, this article will serve as a guide to some of the Internet's contemporary, outstanding business Web sites and examine how they mesh with traditional print and electronic resources. The glut of Internet business information is creating access to business news and data in volumes and dimensions previously unparalleled in the history of business librarianship. How, as library administrators, are we to react to this phenomenon and successfully build our business collections as both our students and superiors grow ever more Web-centric in their thinking about how business information is retrieved? What becomes of the print collection and traditional online databases? Where do they fit into the picture as we approach the new millennium?

BUSINESS INFORMATION IN THE INTERNET GENERATION

From my perspective as a business information specialist and an instructor of business research skills for executive MBA students at a local university, the revolution in Internet business information, as reflected in the business research habits of American businessmen and businesswomen, is both undeniable and chilling. Two personal observations are notable. First, the average EMBA student (characteristically someone who has been a business manager or executive for 6-10 years and who has also been away from the business library for quite some time) will almost always initially consult the Internet for information before seeking out other sources. Second, unless otherwise educated, these students will also be completely unconvinced that most library resources are of any value. The good news is that course-related bibliographic instruction can help create the awareness needed to get students to remove their Internet blinders.

In any case, business librarians cannot ignore the Internet. Efforts to persuade business students that only traditional print and electronic library resources will provide the kind of authoritative and quality information needed for business decision-making will ring hollow. It is common knowledge that the Internet contains some exceedingly good sources of business information. In the company information realm alone, there are dozens of Web sites that can lead to profiles, financial data, and market information. For example, **Hoover's Company Information** will provide some basic company financials at no charge. URL: <http://www.hoovers.com>. If the researcher needs pre-calculated financials, however, he or she will find that this is available only to subscribers. Most business libraries are already likely to subscribe to Disclosure (on CD-ROM, online or on the Web) which contains similar or superior data.

That is why students and academic administrators must understand that the Internet is but one choice on the spectrum of business information resources. None of the resources, not paper, CD-ROM, traditional online, nor Internet, can be used to the exclusion of others. The key is making wise choices, and doing so requires a thorough knowledge of the available options–or knowing a business information specialist who can explain the options and recommend the best choices. As the types and intricacies of Web-based business resources grow in size and complexity, the line between traditional print and electronic resources and Web resources blurs. The differences were distinct in the past. On one side was the Web: free information for the masses found with an easy-to-use interface, but much-too-broad results and needle-in-the-haystack-like searches for things of quality or uniqueness. On the other side was the traditional commercial online databank system: costly, arcane, command language databases driven by keyword searching offering quality information and a set of powerful retrieval tools, but accomplished only with steep learning curves or by seeking out an information professional. In this environment, print has been relegated to delivering specialized reference books, monographs and journals (though all are increasingly evolving into Web formats).

Now, traditional commercial online systems such as Dialog and Lexis/Nexis offer Web interfaces and search engine-like relevancy and natural language capabilities that should open up these once "professionals only" databanks to a broader range of users. Sophisticated business data, at a cost, can be retrieved on the Web from sites such as **XLS**, a provider that specializes in information that can be directly downloaded into spreadsheet programs. URL: <http://www.xls.com>. And hybrid resources, such as **Northern Light**, part-search engine, part-commercial database, and now part-provider of Wharton Econometrics reports and Investext reports, are shaking up our conventional thinking about how business information can be delivered via the Internet. URL: <http://www.northernlight.com>. This trend is likely to continue. Business information is moving to the Web, and as the number of providers and options grows, choosing the appropriate resource is becoming increasingly difficult. Business information in the Internet generation and beyond will require the researcher's toolbox to include resources from every point along the expanding information spectrum.

A CASE STUDY

Business educators are primary users of the case study method, using actual events and decisions occurring in companies and industries to teach business principles and practices. Some schools, such as Harvard Business School and Virginia's Darden School of Business, are well known for the case studies they publish. Business librarians spend fair amounts of time both assisting and reassuring students as they gather information needed for a case study analysis. The value of the case method is its ability to identify best practices by studying how individuals and organizations met challenges and resolved difficult situations. A case study is constructed below to illustrate the complexity of information gathering for a business research project. It is based on an actual interaction between the author and an undergraduate business major. This case study will make two points. First, the path to answers for a non-routine research project is rarely direct and is likely to require resources from the traditional print/electronic sectors, supplemented by Internet resources. Second, typical business students are more likely to begin their research on the Internet, but after seeking guidance from a skilled business researcher, students will expand the material they use to include the traditional print/electronic resources.

A fairly common business school assignment requires students to develop an idea for a product or business service and to then design a business plan to explain how to obtain financing, how to market the product, and how the business will be managed for growth. Completing the business plan requires a student to collect different types of information, of which several are described below. The student in this case study developed a new model of athletic shoe for sale in specialty athletic footwear stores in the Northeast United States region. When first encountered by the author, the student explained the nature of the research. At the point of this encounter, the student had already spent a few hours conducting research on the Internet. Using a common search engine, searches on terms such as "athletic shoe" and "athletic footwear" yielded thousands of Web pages, few of which had any substantive information, and most of which were commercial in nature. After these few hours of frustrated searching with little to show, the student sought librarian assistance.

We decided to concentrate on using library and Internet resources to focus on collecting the marketing and demographic information needed for the business plan. For example, the plan needed to demonstrate that there is an identifiable target market for the product and that there is room for a new competitor in the marketplace. This means finding out who will buy the product, what their numbers are, who already sells the product, determining if competitors are moving into the target market, and developing a plan for promoting and selling the product. The Internet will work best for targeted information retrieval using known Web sites. For example, to identify the industry code for athletic footwear, which would help in gathering market information, we went to the Standard Industrial Classification Search page maintained by the U.S. Occupational Safety & Health Administration (OSHA) at URL: <http://www.osha.gov/oshstats/sicser.html>. The search engine makes finding SIC codes easier than the printed manual (yes, the North American Industry Classification System [NAICS] is the latest version of the classification codes, but many business information resources are still using the SIC code scheme). From there, we went to the library's reference section to find the *U.S. Industry & Trade Out-*

look for an overview of the industry. There the student discovered a few other books, such as the *Encyclopedia of American Industry*. The serendipity of discovering information resources through shelf browsing, thanks to subject classification, is still a unique strength of the print domain.

The printed industry sources didn't list the major companies in the market, so we turned to one of the library's commercially licensed databases. This one, the Gale Group's *General Business File*, included a company profile module that could be searched by SIC code. We quickly generated a list of the largest companies in the athletic shoe industry, ranked by sales. Without a librarian, the student would never have known how to get this information out of the database. With a list of major companies in hand, the student went back to the Internet, this time identifying and locating each company's Web site. These sites contained the bulk of the product information the student needed, but some of it was not up-to-date. The student wanted to find recent news stories on the industry and market. It was back to the library's subscription business database, where a search on the phrase "athletic footwear and market" turned up dozens of potentially useful articles. The student later found a Web site that contained an industry overview of the athletic shoe industry. However, it did not contain needed sales data for the Northeast region.

Where, the student asked, could regional business information be found? This library subscribes to the Dialog Classroom Instruction Program (CIP), a version of the powerful Dialog system available to academic institutions at reduced search rates. Of the numerous business databases available through Dialog, the student used one called *Marketfull*. It provides access to full-text market research reports from companies such as FIND/SVP and DataMonitor. The Dialog system, traditionally used by professional librarians, is considered difficult for students to search, but this library provided access to DialogWeb, a Web-based, graphical user interface version of Dialog. With DialogWeb, there is no need to know database names or numbers, and the search interface (there is a simple or advanced mode) is not much more difficult than an Internet search engine. The student found more than a dozen reports, within the last year, on the topic, and one did contain regional sales information for a leading footwear retailer. The student also needed some demographic data for a few major East Coast cities. On the librarian's recommendation, the student used File

581 on Dialog, the *Population Database*, to locate the needed information effortlessly.

This abbreviated case study reinforces the point that while there is a lot of business information on the Web, there is still a great deal more that is not. There are two important things library administrators will want to learn from this and communicate to students and administrators. First, as stated above, business information should be viewed as a spectrum encompassing many different types of information in a variety of formats. The function of the library is to gather, organize, and make accessible to its constituents (within the constraints of its budget) that spectrum of information. Second, accessibility is of little help without the added value of information professionals who can guide information seekers through the maze of resources. Library administrators must continually remind Web-centric colleagues and students that traditional print and electronic library resources are still critical to research. Collaborative programs with faculty that involve course-related bibliographic instruction and assignments that are designed to facilitate students' education about information skills will reinforce these two points.

WHERE TO BEGIN

Looking for quality business information on the Internet can be a daunting task owing to the sheer volume of sites. The recommended entry point for the less experienced business researcher is the business "megasite," a Web page that attempts to provide a comprehensive portal to sites on a wide range of business subjects. These are excellent starting points and have almost eliminated the necessity for generalist academic libraries to create and maintain their own set of business information links. Business schools' libraries, however, will certainly want to continue to maintain their own comprehensive listings. Most of today's best business megasites are three or more years old, ancient by Internet standards. One rarely sees the emergence of a new megasite because the existing ones do the job so well. Their success would be difficult to replicate. That aside, starting a new megasite from scratch is a formidable task.

Two senior and popular business megasites are **Yahoo's Business and Economy Page**, URL: <http://www.yahoo.com/Business>, and **Galaxy: Business and Commerce**, URL: <http://www.einet.net/galaxy/Business-

and-Commerce.html>. Of the two, Yahoo is more comprehensive and, like all Yahoo pages, has the advantage of offering sites selected by researchers. Galaxy leans more towards the needs of the business professional or consumer seeking business information. Either of these sites is a good, general purpose jumping-off point for research on the major sub-disciplines of business. Both have the weakness of concentrating on more general rather than specialized sites. Neither is likely to identify and link to sites of interest to scholars and academic researchers. For example, neither Yahoo nor Galaxy provides quality links to resources in fields such as Operations Research or Decisions Science. For these one would need to explore other megasites.

While this article recommends a Yahoo site as a starting point for business research, library administrators and their instructional specialists will be challenged to convince their constituencies to expand their horizons beyond these popular Internet directories. One drawback to directories such as Yahoo, SNAP, or Looksmart is that they quickly breed a familiarity with their users that leads to a reluctance to use additional sources. Given the challenges of finding business information on the Web, these users tend to fall into a pattern of always using the same resource, neglecting the reality that no single source is all inclusive or that other resources may offer better features. Overcoming the "familiarity breeds comfort" syndrome is no simple task. Strategies can include a well-designed, library-supported Internet resources page that introduces users to resources beyond Yahoo, an on-going program of instruction on finding business information on the Internet, collaborative efforts with faculty to design assignments that require exploration and evaluation of comparative Web pages, and more proactive reference techniques.

There may be a dozen or so business megasites that could qualify for inclusion here. Three sites in particular are notable for their consistent quality and breadth and depth of links. **Business and Economics Resources** is a site produced by Larry Schankman, a librarian at Mansfield University. URL: <http://www.mnsfld.edu/depts/lib/business.html>. It is simple in design and execution. It begins with a list of the top all-purpose sites, and then proceeds logically through general resources, reference resources, and then more specialized resources. A more comprehensive megasite is **A Business Researcher's Interests**, also referred to as the BizTech Research Library. URL: <http://www.brint.com/interest.html>. It is sponsored by @BRINT. Geared to the needs of business professionals, this site is a searchable knowledge map for information and tools for which executives are most likely to be searching. Its categories include topics such as "knowledge management," "e-commerce," and "reengineering." **Business Information Sources on the Internet** is a site maintained by Sheila Webber at the University of Strathclyde in Glasgow. URL: <http://www.dis.strath.ac.uk/business>. In existence since 1994, this site continues to be a selective guide to business information whose focus is on basic business needs. Like **A Business Researcher's Interests**, this one has a feature that makes the site fully keyword-searchable. Company, country, statistical, and economic information are the mainstays of this site. One specialty of this site is the emphasis on United Kingdom Internet resources. Despite the presence of some UK resources, however, international information is not this site's strength. That forte belongs to several other international business megasites.

Of these, **Virtual International Business & Economic Sources (VIBES)** is perhaps the best known. URL: <http://libweb.uncc.edu/ref-bus/vibehome.htm>. Maintained by Jeanie Welch, the Business Librarian at the University of North Carolina–Charlotte, VIBES provides links to over 1,500 sites for international business and economic information. There are no links to fee-based services or business directories. The resources are organized for access by comprehensive topic, region, or specific country. A government's agency sites are clearly marked. Owing to its longevity, VIBES now is a rich source for international information. The resource would create more added value by adding distinctive summaries or ratings to linked sites. An alternative to VIBES is **International Business Resources on the WWW (IBR)**, maintained by the Center for International Business Education and Research at Michigan State University. URL: <http://www.ciber.msu.edu/busres.htm>. The two are actually organized in a rather similar fashion, providing access by region or country, and both contain government resources, statistical data, and trade information. IBR does include business directories, and has more direct links to news and article sources. IBR also is developing into something of a hybrid. It now provides its own full-text articles on international business topics (written primarily by the school's faculty), links to relevant conferences, and executive summaries from related journals.

Beyond VIBES and IBR, there are a number of sites that offer links to international information. **Worldclass Supersite**, maintained by

Mike Kuiack & Associates, has been on the Web since 1995. URL: <http://web.idirect.com/~tiger/supersit.htm>. There are links to over 1,000 sites from 95 countries. The site's organization could use improvement, but if one is willing to browse through the major categories, there are some real finds. One area in particular is the "market guide" section, which contains some excellent, free Latin American information sources. A newer, not yet very comprehensive site is **BIRD–the Business Information Resources Directory**. URL: <http://www.bird-online.co.uk/entry.html>. Maintained by Business Administrative Services (Wales), it includes international information links, but does focus on the UK and Ireland. This site is of interest because it uses the "virtual reference library" approach instead of the more familiar organization by categories of information. All links are accessed by searching the database by subject term(s). Searches on broad subjects, particularly technology topics, gave good results. For example, a search on the term "E-commerce" quickly located links to several E-commerce associations, a report on Internet commerce from a major consulting firm, and the home page of an E-commerce research center. However, searches on narrower or non-technology topics, such as the fashion industry, yielded no links. BIRD is an interesting site, and if it grows in scope, it may rival some of the more established international megasites.

The home pages of the major international business school libraries are not typically thought of as megasites, but given the sheer number of links one finds there, they can certainly qualify as potential starting points for business research on the Internet. Rather than specify one particular site, since all are quite good, this author's preference is to refer the reader to the **Academic Business Libraries Web Pages** maintained by the Foster Business Library at the University of Washington. URL: <http://www.lib.washington.edu/business/abl.html>. This page has links to the Web sites of the libraries at the Wharton School, Harvard Business School, Stanford's Graduate School of Business, and a dozen others. One caveat must be observed by the users of these sites. Most of the business school libraries feature links to commercially licensed databases (e.g., Lexis/Nexis, Dow Jones, etc.) that are only available to that school's constituency. Most of the B-school Web pages will clearly identify those sites that are restricted.

A LOOK AT BUSINESS SUB-DISCIPLINES

Moving beyond megasites, the typical researcher is likely next to explore a specific discipline within business, not all of which can be covered within the scope of this article. Some sub-disciplines, such as finance, have their own sub-disciplines or focus areas (e.g., stocks, bonds, futures, options, commodities, etc.), each of which, in turn, has an entire sub-culture of Web sites. Eight representative major sub-disciplines listed below have been selected for coverage. Those areas are:

- Accounting/Taxation
- Advertising and Demography
- Company Information
- Economics
- Entrepreneurship
- Finance
- International Business
- Marketing and Market Research

Examining the impact of the Internet on these sub-disciplines reveals several trends that extend into other sub-disciplines (industry information, government resources, management, business statistics, real estate, health care management, etc.). First, business information is moving to the Web. Business libraries will no doubt continue to acquire large amounts of print information; the majority of books and journals are still in print, as are the many specialized reference resources needed to satisfy the range of questions received at a busy reference desk. But many of those questions can now be answered with Web resources, and the range continues to expand. Second, the Internet is still incapable of competing with the dozens of specialized online business databases found in commercial online systems such as Dialog and Dow Jones News/Retrieval. But the traditional bibliographic searching performed with these services is slowly migrating its way to the Web, albeit with far less to choose from, but at significantly lower pricing. Third, the thirst for pure financial data among private investors and firms that previously could not afford to subscribe to many different business information providers is driving a vast increase in the number of companies offering business data on the Web.

ACCOUNTING AND TAXATION

With some 45,000 accounting firms and 400,000 CPAs eager to find up-to-date accounting and tax information, the Web is a robust environment for delivering information that appeals to accounting professionals. There is a need for access to reference information, such as directories of accountants and their firms, IRS regulations, tax forms, and recent tax news. Given the demand for and interest in this practitioner information, it is no surprise that the bulk of accounting and taxation Web sites are geared to the needs of practitioners. Some of these are the official sites of primary accounting organizations such as **AICPA** (URL: http://www.aicpa.org), **FASB** (URL: http://www. fasb.org), and other state and professional associations. Aside from these organizations, where else can one find information of interest to accountants and tax professionals on the Internet?

AccountingNet is among the more comprehensive sites for the accounting professional. URL: <http://www.accountingnet.com>. It was begun by a former manager of a Big Six accounting firm. The site's mission is "to create the most comprehensive and valuable asset on the Internet for accountants, their firms and anyone interested in reaching the accounting community." The site features a forum for exchanging information, headlines and summaries of stories from over 700 publications, and a research library (that only searches the text of state regulations and course guides, not the accounting literature). There are two similar, but equally worthwhile sites. **Electronic Accountant**, "the accountant's Web magazine and resource guide," is maintained by Faulkner and Gray, a publisher of accounting journals. URL: <http://www.electronicaccountant.com>. **Rutgers Accounting Web** (RAW), maintained by the Rutgers Accounting Research Center, is a site that any user of accounting information will want to bookmark. URL: <http://www.rutgers.edu/Accounting>. Of the various accounting sites, this one will better meet the needs of the academic accounting researcher as it provides more links to the types of finance, economic, and quantitative information that appeal to researchers, with far fewer practitioner-oriented links.

The domination of practitioner information in the accounting domain is paralleled in taxation information on the Web. The majority of taxation sites provide tax advice and information for completing tax forms, access to the tax forms themselves, other Internal Revenue Service materials, tax planning information, and, of course, sites selling tax books, software, and "tax-saving" tips. There are probably about a dozen core taxation sites. They include advice sites such as **J.K. Lasser's Your Income Tax Site** (URL: http://w3.mgr.com/mgr/lasser) and **Intuit's TurboTax** (URL: http://www.intuit.com/turbotax) site. Several other sites, such as **1040.COM**, offer access to both tax forms and tax publications (1040.COM is notably faster than the IRS's own site). URL: <http://www.1040.com>. These sites are a godsend at tax time–and have all but eliminated the need for libraries to keep those pesky tax forms on hand. Those with more involved research needs may find the **U.S. Tax Code On-Line** a worthwhile site. URL: <http://www.fourmilab.ch/ustax/ustax.html>. This site provides access to the complete text of the United States Internal Revenue Code, Title 26 of the U.S. Code. To facilitate research, the site has a WAIS-based search engine to the text of the Code, and it is embedded with hypertext links for fast cross-references between code sections. However, anyone other than a tax accountant or lawyer using the raw Code for tax research may find the going a bit rough.

If your institution supports an accounting or taxation program, you will likely want a resource page with links to all of these sources. Those with infrequent requests in this area will probably want some links to tax-advice sites, but may be better off with a single link to what may be the best all-around site in this area. **Tax and Accounting Sites Directory**, maintained by Schmidt Enterprises, is essentially a comprehensive compilation of all types of tax and accounting sites. URL: <http://www.taxsites.com>. There is virtually no text here, just links, and it contains all of the sites mentioned above. In addition, there are sections for academic sites, and these links will be of more interest to accounting and taxation researchers. There is also a fairly comprehensive set of links to accounting and taxation sites for other countries, an important feature because international information can be difficult to obtain.

All of these free accounting and taxation sites will provide access to a range of good informational resources, but they don't quite satisfy if some serious research is necessary. For example, trying to locate journal articles, IRS code sections with commentary and case examples, or relevant court cases on a topic such as the amortization of goodwill will require a higher level database, most likely a commercial source. Two good examples are the **CCH Tax Research Network** and UMI's *Accounting and Tax Database*. The former is on the Web (URL: http://

tax.cch.com/NetWork), available through subscription from Commerce Clearing House, and the latter is available to any Dialog subscriber (File 485) and is available in Web format on DialogWeb Version 2. Tax Research Network is a necessity for any serious tax research. Not only does it contain a fully-searchable version of the *Standard Federal Tax Reporter*, as well as on-line versions of other CCH loose-leaf reporters, but its holdings of tax court cases rival what will be found on Lexis/Nexis or Westlaw. Since the demise of the AICPA-published *Accountant's Index* many years ago, *Accounting and Tax Database*, which still has a print counterpart, has served as the primary research tool for the literature of accounting and taxation. It indexes and abstracts articles from virtually all accounting and tax journals, both professional and scholarly, as well as books, dissertations, AICPA and FASB publications, and other miscellaneous accounting and tax material. More recently, full-text articles have been added to the database.

ADVERTISING AND DEMOGRAPHY

The most common reference questions in advertising are requests for agency information. The most frequently used book to answer these questions is the "Red Book," the *Standard Directory of Advertisers*, an indispensable tool for advertising information. Many agencies now have their own Web sites. This won't make the Red Book dispensable any time soon, but, along with the agency profiles, much advertising information is moving to the Web. To locate ad agency information and other Web-based resources on advertising, it is a good idea to start at a specialized sub-megasite for this area. One of the best is **Advertising World,** found at the University of Texas at Austin. URL: <http://advertising.utexas.edu/world>. The site appropriately advertises itself as the most extensive collection of advertising-related links on the Web. There are many links to other advertising and tangential Web sites.

The Web is a great creativity tool thanks to advertising aficionados who have mounted extensive tribute pages to ads of all media and format. From Speedy Alka-Seltzer to Calvin Klein ads, the Web is becoming a repository of ad campaign information. There is no single site for locating ads. Links can be found at Advertising World or found through search engines. This concept is taken a step further by **TelevisionCom-**

mercials.com, a commercial site that sells access to television ads from a growing archive. URL: <http://www.televisioncommercials.com>. Using a searchable database of over 30,000 commercials dating back to the 1950s, this site offers an array of production services. Advertising researchers can find many samples for viewing. The Web is also a resource for links to national advertising organizations, such as the Ad Council or Advertising Education Foundation, or for research on advertising events, such as winners of the CLIO awards. URL: <http://www.clioawards.com>. What the Web has not yet provided is a source comparable to any of several commercial online databases. General business databases, such as *ABI/Inform, Management Contents, Business & Industry* and *PROMT* (all available on DialogWeb), cover selected advertising literature. A more comprehensive online resource is *Marketing and Advertising Reference Services* (MARS). This is File 570 on Dialog. Its strength is the advertising-specific indexing that makes it possible to retrieve articles by fields such as spokesperson, slogan, or advertising agency. Do not expect to find anything comparable to MARS for free on the Web.

If you recall the concept of segmentation from your Marketing 101 class, you know that demographic information is certainly of interest to advertisers and the agencies. Demographics, not unlike advertising, is something of a crossover subject, so links to relevant sites may be found through marketing Web sites. There are hundreds of potential sites for demographic data, domestic, international, state and regional. An excellent starting point is the **WWW Virtual Library Page for Demographics and Population Studies** maintained at the Australian National University. URL: <http://coombs.anu.edu.au/ResFacilities/ DemographyPage.html>. It contains 190+ links for demographic information, but does not contain as exhaustive a listing of U.S. Census Bureau sites as may be found elsewhere. **American Factfinder** is a new data access and dissemination system that provides useful facts and information about your community, your economy, and your society. URL: <http://factfinder.census.gov/java_prod/dads.ui.homePage. HomePage>. The system will find and retrieve the information needed from some of the Census Bureau's largest data sets. True, most of the data can also be found at the main Census Bureau site (URL: http://www.census.gov), but American Factfinder lets users select, extract, and post-process the data, as well as produce custom tabulations from the data sets. For more sophisticated demographic research needs, there are commercial vendors of demographic data that can supply virtually any demographic data needed at a price. For example, **USADATA.com** sells a variety of populations and market segment demographic reports for any geographic location for approximately $100. URL: <http://www.usadata.com>. An alternate site offering both free and fee-based demographic reports is **The Right Site**. URL: <http://www.easidemographics.com>.

COMPANY INFORMATION

One of the earliest reasons to go to the Internet was to locate company information. As companies created Web sites, business researchers and the public-at-large had a new source for company news and financial information, albeit a somewhat subjective source. Company information abounds on the Internet. The difficulty is in finding a site that has the necessary information. For publicly-held companies, free sites will provide some news, general background information, and financial data, but without subscribing to a more comprehensive source don't expect to find much comprehensive information. For private companies, most free sites will yield little more than the most basic directory information. While the quality and depth of company information on the Internet still lags significantly behind what can be obtained by a professional searcher using databanks, such as Dialog or Lexis/Nexis, the Web has had a democratizing impact on access to company information. The end-user is now able to choose from a vast array of free company information resources, and if desired, can pay a reasonable amount of money for more valued information.

Because of the sheer mass of company information sites, it is virtually impossible to select a few to present here. Individuals should identify their own favorites, and megasites are a good starting point for hunting them down. Experienced business researchers will already likely have a slew of bookmarks for their trusted company information sites. For the rest, here are some suggestions and profiles of newer entrants to the crowded field. Everyone should know how to use an EDGAR site for obtaining Securities and Exchange Commission documents on U.S. public companies. A relatively new variant is **Edgar-Scan**. URL: <http://bamboo.tc.pw.com>. Maintained by PriceWaterhouseCoopers, EdgarScan pulls filings from the SEC's holdings and automatically brings up the key financial tables. It also creates hyperlinks for faster access to specific sections of a filing. This site is a good example of a third party creating a site that makes a good source of information even better.

EDGAR covers only public companies. There are also dozens of personal investment sites available to gather additional information on public firms. Almost all are there to sell something. Despite the commercial nature of these sites, however, valuable information is there for the taking. The previously mentioned **Hoover's Online** is a good example, though Hoover's, of late, is positioning itself as a fee-based vendor of company information to the academic market. Perhaps a better example of a site offering valuable, but still free, company information is the **Wright Research Center**. URL: <http://profiles. wisi.com/profiles/comsrch.htm>. Here, one can find detailed analysis on over 18,000 companies worldwide (over 20 countries are represented). What sets Wright apart is not that it provides a company analysis, stock price data, and earnings information, but rather that it provides ten years of annual data in each of these areas. Access to historical data greatly enhances the site's value as a worthy research resource. In addition, Wright allows the user to convert the data to any currency for easier international comparisons.

Getting public company information on the Internet is easy. Getting private company information however–details beyond the address and phone number–is much more difficult. Expect to pay for something of value. Again, there are quite a few vendors of this information, and it may require some trial and error to find a source that is reliable. A relatively new service is **aRMadillo**, from the Raymond Morris Group. URL: <http://www.rmonline.com/armusa.htm>. Currently available for 44 states, the service can identify how long a private firm has been in business; provide its credit worthiness; provide officer information; and tap into state filings. Fees are typically based on the amount of information extracted about the company. They range from $15 to $45 depending on the size of the report produced. Experienced online searchers can find similar types of information on traditional databases from Dun & Bradstreet or American Business Information, also at a cost, but perhaps with more company coverage and a greater sense of faith in the validity of the information.

Experienced business researchers know that hard-to-find company information, such as corporate strategies, product development news, and market share, is not free for the taking on the Internet, and certainly is not easy to locate with standard search engines. Traditional electronic sources include those databases that cover the trade and industry literature, such as *ABI/Inform, Trade and Industry Database*, and a few others. For public companies, investment reports written by company analysts at major brokerage firms, available through the *Investext* database on Dialog and other systems, are excellent ways to gather serious competitive analysis information. In one of the more promising Internet developments, this information is moving to the Web as well. **Northern Light**, a progressive search engine system, is making a hybrid product of itself. URL: <http://www.northernlight.com>. It retrieves all the standard Web sites that other search engines will locate, but its "special collection" of articles from traditional online databases is simultaneously searched, providing full-text articles at prices from $1.00 to $4.00. More recently, Northern Light has added access to selected *Investext* reports at reasonable prices. Granted, the selection and years of archival reports is no match for *Investext* (file 545) on Dialog, but it clearly points to a trend in which company information, previously available only to a few, is now available for mass consumption.

Those with little experience in performing company research will find little help from this brief discussion, but can find considerable help on the Internet. A basic site frequently consulted is **Researching Companies Online** by Deb Flanagan. URL: <http://home.sprintmail.com/~debflanagan/index.html>. It is clearly written and well-organized, and includes some self-paced tutorials and lots of hypertext links to sources of Internet company information. Other sites worth examining are **Company Research**, at URL: <http://iws.ohiolink.edu/companies/maincontentwindow.htm> and **Searching for Company Information**, at URL: <www.babson.edu/library/company>. As more individuals and business libraries create on-line, Web-based tutorials for performing business research, the skills required for finding much of this elusive information will gradually be passed on to the layperson.

ECONOMICS

A good understanding of economics is fundamental to understanding many underlying principles and practices of business. Many academic researchers require economic data. Economics Web sites generally fall into one of three categories: data, instructional, and informational. For data, government sites, both domestic and foreign, are key sources of information. Instruction in economics can be found on the Web pages of professors who have created tutorials to help their students. The worldwide banking community offers sources for timely news on economic developments. There is so much economic data on the Web that, for the majority of individuals, the Web will suffice. Serious business researchers, those needing large volumes of historical data, daily time series of data (at best, most free Web sites offer only several years of monthly data), or obscure types of data, will need to seek out fee-based sources such as *Econbase* (file 565 on Dialog) or *Datastream*, a UK-based provider of international economic data. Despite the expansion of electronic economic data, larger academic research libraries will want to continue their subscriptions to the major print sources of economic data, such as the IMF's *International Financial Statistics*. These sources remain indispensable for quick reference lookups and satisfying the needs of undergraduates or the less demanding researcher.

Users of economic information can immediately help themselves by bookmarking two or three sites that provide numerous economics links. Recommended sites include **RFE: Resources for Economists on the Internet**, URL: <http://econwpa.wustl.edu/EconFAQ/EconFAQ.html>, **EconLINKS**, URL: <http://www.ncat.edu/~simkinss/econlinks.html>, and **Econ Data & Links**, URL: <http://www.csufresno.edu/Economics/econ_EDL.htm>. The latter contains a good list of other sites that carry links to economic information. One site that is nearly universally linked to most business or economic sites is **FRED**, the Federal Reserve Economic Data, maintained by the Federal Reserve Bank at St. Louis. URL: <http://www.stls.frb.org/fred/>. This is a good starting point for obtaining many U.S. government reported economic time series. For a site with more features, try **EconoMagic.Com**. URL: <http://www.economagic.com>. Boasting over 100,000 data series, this site allows more added value by letting users create charts for the data, by including a convenient "most requested time series" page, and by making it easy to download data in Excel spreadsheet format. This site also has a subscriber option for those who want to create forecasts for their data. These sites do focus on domestic economic data, but also have links to sources of international data.

Just using some of the economic data or dealing with the jargon can be intimidating. Thanks to the Internet anyone can delve into a range of Economics 101-type sites. Two frequently linked pages are **Cyber-Economics**, maintained by Robert Schenk at St. Joseph's College, URL: <http://ingrimayne.saintjoe.edu/econ/TitlePage.html>, and **Essential Principles of Economics: A Hypermedia Text**, maintained by Roger McCain at Drexel University, URL: <http://william-king.www.drexel.edu/top/prin/txt/EcoToC.html>. Either of these pages will provide an overview of economics. McCain's page has a good quiz module, which is a great way to get feedback after reading new material. Once you've mastered some of the basic principles of economics, it will be time to put that knowledge to practice by exploring how economics impacts on the world of business and finance. A site worth mentioning is **Dr. Ed Yardeni's Economics Network**. URL: <http://www.yardeni.com>. Dr. Yardeni is the Chief Economist at Deutsche Bank Securities, and his page also has many good links for sources of economic information, but particularly notable are his series of weekly audio programs and analytical papers on current economic issues. Most banks and the United States Government also provide news that is more data oriented, such as current economic indicator releases.

ENTREPRENEURSHIP

Compared to sub-disciplines such as economics or marketing, entrepreneurship is much more specialized. However, the needs and interests of small business fall into this category, so the interest level is high, especially among the general public. In public libraries, after company and industry questions, questions about starting a business are the most frequent. There isn't any one single best page that contains all the top links, so business librarians will likely want to put together their own resource listings. As with economic data, the United States Government is an important source of information for small businesses. The **Small Business Administration's Web Site** is a good starting point for information on programs and finance. URL: <http://www.sbaonline.sba.gov>. Better and more comprehensive links are found at the Web site of the Small Business Development Center's **SBDC Research Network**. URL: <http://www.smallbiz.suny.edu>. From this site, one can find a fair number of resources all geared to help budding entrepreneurs get started.

Other sites in this area provide advice and are usually maintained by an accounting firm or business advisor trying to sell a service; entrepreneurship research centers, usually based at business schools and opportunity sites; or others offering ideas and support for new businesses and start-up trends. In the latter category, a unique site is the **Idea Café**. URL: <http://www.IdeaCafe.com>. It includes threaded bulletin board discussions, one of the more lively ones dealing with ideas for home businesses. Idea Café also provides information from business experts, special pricing deals, and financing advice. A fair amount of this plays to the average person's dream of owning his or her own business. An alternate site is the **Smart Business Supersite**. URL: <http://www.smartbiz.com>. This site claims "thousands of how-to resources" geared specifically to the needs of entrepreneurs.

FINANCE

An important part of the Internet's democratization of access to information is the virtual revolution it has created in the world of personal investment. By providing market information that was previously only available to the investment community, personal investors, from their desktops, can now exert greater control over their own investing. When financial information first became available on the Web, it seemed terribly exciting to be able to find a stock quote. Now there are a multitude of such sources, with some giving fairly detailed data. Through a combination of investment information and advice and electronic trading capability, private investors can now be their own investment advisors. Owing to the proliferation of commercial sites, finance is an area in which Internet searchers are challenged to find reliable, credible purveyors of investment information. Virtually anyone or any organization can mount a Web site with investment advice. For every good site, there may be a dozen poor ones. The other challenge is to find good sites for academic financial research.

Three sites are good starting points. They will give novices many other links to review and choose. Of the three **Yahoo Finance** is most directed to the needs of the personal investor. URL: <http://quote.yahoo. com>. It provides quotes on a wide variety of investment instruments, from stocks and bonds to mutual funds. There are even some tools for stock analysis, but the stock screening tool is not as sophisticated as that found with many commercial financial databases. The **WWW**

Virtual Finance Library, maintained by the Fisher College of Business at Ohio State University, is probably the best choice for sheer number of links to finance information sources on the Web. URL: <http://www.cob.ohio-state.edu/dept/fin/overview.htm>. This site recognizes that the needs of personal investors and researchers are quite different, so it provides different groupings of links for each one. Though its focus is the banking industry, **FINDEX** is another good source of general purpose finance information. URL: <http://www.findex.com>. The good list of links is found under "FINMedia."

Most of the financial data being sought by researchers and investors was never conveniently found in print resources, unless one considers *The Daily Stock Price Record,* published by Standard & Poor's, a good way to obtain a long time series of stock prices. The radical shift to electronic financial information was not an outcome of the Internet. Rather, spreadsheets changed everything. Once analysts and researchers saw the value of spreadsheets, suddenly, if the data was not in electronic, machine-readable format, there was no interest. Prior to the Web, online data files from Dialog, via *Tradeline,* and Dow Jones News Retrieval, were frequently used sources of financial data. Even more sophisticated, and significantly more expensive services, such as Bloomberg, Securities Data Corporation, and First Call, came along and raised the bar for comprehensive financial analysis data.

Within the last year or two, the Web has created an entirely new market for more affordable, more highly targeted types of financial data. One of the more impressive vendors of fee-based data is **XLS**. URL: <http://www.xls.com>. The service takes its name from the Excel file extension for good reason. All of the data, which come from over 60 different commercial databases, are easily downloaded into Excel spreadsheets. Telescan is another example of the trend towards fee-based access to financial data on the Internet. URL: <http://www.telescan.com>. Providing more detailed information than free sites, **Telescan**, for a number of low cost monthly subscription plans, allows the investor or researcher to access a fair amount of current and historical financial data. Will these services eliminate resources such as Bloomberg and Dow Jones? Of course not, but they do signal that the Internet, not print, will be the wave of the future for delivering financial data.

INTERNATIONAL BUSINESS

The Internet hasn't replaced printed material for information on international business, but it has made it easier to access information that was difficult to obtain in print sources and has provided access to information that wasn't previously available in any format. Consider currency exchange rates. Before the Internet, a quick exchange rate check required a run to the newspaper rack. Now there are several sites on the Web that make exchange rate data retrieval simple and fast. **The Currency Site**, maintained by Olsen and Associates, provides daily historical data back to 1990 for 164 currencies. URL: <http://www.oanda.com>. This is but one example of how the Internet is changing things and will continue to change them into the new millennium. We will see more information that was conventionally delivered in paper format migrating to the Web, particularly reference and data-oriented information.

For the uninitiated, there are some good starting points for international business research on the Internet. In addition to the two international business megasites mentioned above, **VIBES** and **International Business on the WWW**, **Everything International** is a well-rounded compendium of sources for international information. URL: <http://ib.philacol.edu/ib/russow.html>. Maintained by Lloyd Russow, a professor at Philadelphia University, this site is particularly strong in pointing to sources of economic data and trade information.

As with many other types of information, the Internet has greatly enhanced the ability of United States (and other countries') government agencies to produce and disseminate current international and trade information. One area in particular is country information. It used to be quite difficult to get up-to-date data and analysis on the political, social, and economic state of foreign countries. **The Spire Project** is a single site with many links to country information. URL: <http://cn.net.au/country.htm>. The **Country Studies** (URL: http://lcweb2.loc.gov/frd/cs/cshome.html) Web site with area reports produced by the Library of Congress, and the State Department's **Country Commercial Guides** (URL: http://www.state.gov/www/about_state/business/com_guides/) are two particularly good sites for basic country information. Then there are more outstanding sites for country data, such as **Infonation**, maintained by and with information on the United Nations member countries. URL: <http://www.un.org/Pubs/

CyberSchoolBus/infonation/e_infonation.htm>. It lets the user select the data required and up to four countries, and then generates a report. And there are regional Web sites, such as CAMENA, which just covers the Middle East, North Africa, and Central Asia, URL: <http://www.ifc.org/camena/country.htm>, and **LatInvestor**, for Latin American information, which is a mix of country and financial information. URL: <http://www.latinvestor.com>.

MARKETING AND MARKET RESEARCH

With certain sub-disciplines in business, the distinction between what can be found on the Internet for free and for a fee is more noticeable. Marketing is such an area. There are some good, free Web sites marketing professionals will want to bookmark. These sites can lead to services, reports on new developments, and summaries of market research findings. For example, the Gartner Group, a leading computer technology consulting firm, maintains a Web site for their Dataquest division. **Dataquest** performs market research in the computer industry. URL: <http://gartner5.gartnerweb.com/dq/static/dq.html>. This site provides news about development in the computer industry and summaries of Dataquest market research, but a fee is required to access the full-text research. The type of information found in these elusive market research reports, whether from Dataquest or other providers such as FIND/SVP, such as the identifying of markets, the gathering of exhaustive product information, and the analysis of target markets can be collected by searching traditional electronic database systems. Some, such as Dialog, offer access to all these types of business information as well as the full-text market research reports. Collecting market research data on Dialog can be expensive, but, if done selectively, it can be more cost effective than purchasing entire research reports from an Internet Web site.

As with other categories, there are several megasites for this sub-discipline. Any search for marketing or market information can begin with these sites. Many business school libraries link to the **Marketing Virtual Library**. URL: <http://www.knowthis.com>. This is a comprehensive listing of marketing resources on the Web. Many sites related to marketing are commercial. There are some sites, but they are far fewer, that attempt to steer the user to research-oriented information. One example is the **AACSB Marketing Departments Online**, which leads to the Web sites of marketing departments at AACSB accredited schools; the AACSB is the premier accrediting agency for bachelor's, master's, and doctoral degree programs in business administration and accounting. URL: <http://mkt.cba.cmich.edu/aacsbmkt>. Marketing Virtual Library contains links to this type of academic research-oriented site. There is also crossover into related areas, such as advertising. For those who want to explore other megasites for marketing, try **Marketing Today** (URL: http://www.marketware-tech. com/marketing.htm) or the **Marketing Webliography** at Louisiana State University. URL: <http://www.lib.lsu.edu/bus/marketin.html>. Market researchers will also discover some traditional print reference materials that are now being made available on the Web. *The Worldwide Directory of Marketing Research Companies and Services,* referred to as the "Green Book," identifies companies offering many different types of marketing services. A version of the **Green Book** can be searched on the Web, though the extent to which this electronic counterpart reproduces or improves upon the print version is not yet known for this relatively new resource. URL: <http://www.greenbook. org>. Presumably, it is less comprehensive, however, because if an equivalent electronic resource were provided for free, who would buy the book?

Beyond these free sites, much of the marketing or market research-related information on the Web is fee-based. Many sites are selling marketing services and are of little use to a researcher looking for information about a product, industry, or service. Here, online databank systems provide a competitive edge. Yes, they are fee-based, but only databases such as *Trade & Industry, PROMT* and *Business & Industry,* all files on the Dialog system, are going to provide access to the full-text of articles from the marketing literature. In addition to their superior search engines, these commercial databases provide several interface options; users can choose from an old-style command-driven, character-based interface (still the fastest way for some) or a Web interface. In academic libraries, this type of information can be made accessible through subscriptions to commercial products, such as Gale Group's *General Business File*, Ebsco's *Business Elite*, or UMI's *ABI/Inform*. Any of these options allows an academic library director to give business students access to marketing information at predictable, fixed-fee costs. Libraries that want to provide access to full-text market research reports can do so through Dialog. Subscribers to Dialog's Classroom Instruction Program can search market research reports from several general and specialized firms, such as FIND/SVP, Frost and Sullivan, Jupiter Market Research, and Euromonitor Market Research.

IDENTIFYING AND TRACKING THE NEW GEMS

It is always hazardous to write about electronic information sources. There is a good chance that by the time one's article gets to the reader, some of the sources will be located elsewhere or have been made obsolete by newer, better resources or will simply have disappeared from the landscape. To combat that syndrome this article has attempted to focus on Web sites that have already withstood the test of Internet time and which are recognized in the business librarian community for their value and reliability. They will be around for a while longer. Even so, new sites will undoubtedly appear on the Internet that may be even better. It is critical for anyone with a need for Internet business information to monitor these new sites. Here are some strategies for maintaining current awareness.

First, bookmark sites that routinely identify new and valuable business Web sites. One of the better ones is the **Scout Report for Business & Economic**s. URL: <http://scout.cs.wisc.edu/scout/report/busecon/index.html>. Every other week a new list of annotated Web sites is published. An informal poll of business librarians indicates that the Scout Report is the number one site for current awareness. Another site worth bookmarking is **Bookmark Central**. URL: <http://www.onlineinc.com/bookmark/index.html>. Sponsored by Online Inc., this site offers links in more specialized subject areas, such as cost-of-living or environmentalism (not strictly business), and all the sites are reviewed by the contributors. Second, listen to what the experts are talking about. The best resources for this are the **BUSLIB-L** (URL: http://www.willamette.edu/~gklein/buslib.htm) and SLABF-L listservs (URL: http://www.sla.org/division/dbf/resource/slabf-l.htm). The former is a general listserv for business librarians and researchers, and the latter is the listserv for members of the Special Library Association's Business and Finance Division. The URLs listed provide information on how to subscribe to each list. Listserv participation presents an opportunity to ask others for Web site recommendations or simply to wait and see if new and exciting Web sites are mentioned. Don't let all connections with the business librarian community be electronic. Get to know some business librarians in your vicinity and just visit or call them occasionally. Ask them if they have spotted any good Web finds lately.

Though they don't always report solely on business Web sites, a number of library publications have become good sources for monitoring new Web sites. Many of the publications by Online Inc. and Learned Information are reporting new Web sites in business or feature business information columns that report new subject-specific sites. For example, Marydee Ojala, writing about business resources in both *Online* and *EContent*, frequently covers Internet resources. URL: <http://www.onlineinc.com/index.html>. Her counterpart for Learned Information, Amelia Kassel, writes frequently on business topics for *Searcher* magazine. URL: <http://www.infotoday.com>. A related strategy is to attend the respective conferences of these publishers. Many of the conference tracks now discuss Web sites in fields like business, and it presents an opportunity to hear what the experts are using. The Internet update columns in both *Library Journal* (Web-Watch) and *College & Research Libraries News* (Internet Resources On . . .) occasionally cover business topics also. These are but a few examples. It has become more common for library and information science journals to report new and interesting Web sites, much as they still do for professional books and journals. To save some time on all of this monitoring, it may be preferable simply to review *CHOICE*. This venerable collection development resource now contains Web site reviews along with its current book reviews; there is also an annual issue that collects all of the Web site reviews contained in the year's issues. No matter what monitoring strategy you use, you won't catch everything, but it is highly unlikely a new Web site of major significance will be missed.

CONCLUSION

"Doesn't all the business information on the Internet make your library pretty much obsolete," is a remark that business information experts are finding themselves responding to more frequently as the new millennium approaches. Who can blame laypersons, and even some administrators, for harboring such thoughts? Wave after wave of media assault, bolstered by television and radio advertising, has created the myth that all the information in the universe is free on the Internet and can be located instantly with search engines. The reality of the situation, as serious researchers know, is that for many types of queries the Internet is not yet as effective a tool as traditional electronic databank systems, and for some questions, is not even as effective as some standard print resources. For some types of information, on the other hand, the Internet can be more effective than those traditional resources. It all goes back to the idea of the information spectrum, the need to be knowledgeable about the spectrum, and having the skill to identify where along the spectrum information is to be obtained most efficiently and at the best price.

If the trends in business information continue, the landscape for information retrieval will grow increasingly convoluted. The boundaries between the traditional and the new are less well defined. In a mix of free, cheap, moderately priced, and unaffordable information, the need for guidance will become much more critical. So while the Internet is changing the way we think about, retrieve, and use business information, one thing that remains the same is the need for specialists who can navigate the maze and lead information seekers to their destination. The problem is that everyone thinks he or she is a specialist. In the new millennium, business information professionals will have a dual challenge. Not only must they keep up with and maintain their expertise with an expanding universe of resources, but they must also fight a constant battle to justify their existence and prove that individuals who organize the information and serve as guides for others are a necessity. Otherwise, finding business information in the new millennium will have people wishing for the good old days.

WEBLIOGRAPHY

Baker School Library at Harvard University. (1999) *BizInfo*. Cambridge, MA: Harvard University. [Online] Retrieved September 1, 1999. URL: http://www.hbs.edu/applegate/bizinfo3–Calling itself "a guide to conducting business research on the Internet," this page links to many of the most basic resources for business research, including both company and industry research. Users will find links to proprietary databases accessible only to those affiliated with Harvard, but there are still many links to public Internet sites.

Dow Jones & Company. (1999) *Dow Jones Business Directory*. New York, NY: Dow Jones & Company. [Online] Retrieved September 5, 1999. URL: http://busdir.dowjones.com–Business researchers will certainly want to link to a site with current business news that provides added value by providing high quality links to business information. Dow Jones Business Directory is a selective source that only adds links that meet its criteria for content, speed, navigation, and design.

Flanagan, D. (1998) *Researching Companies Online*. Houston, TX: Debra Flanagan. [Online] Retrieved August 30, 1999. URL: http://home.sprintmail.com/~debflanagan/index.html–Flanagan's tutorials remain among my favorites and I continually point students to them. With so many business researchers looking for company information and not knowing how to go about it, this is the site to go to before the research begins.

Hoover's Company Information. (1999) *Hoover's Online: The Business Network*. [Online] Retrieved August 24, 1999. URL: http://www.hoovers.com–A top list of business Web sites should contain a link to a source for company information, news, directory listings, annual reports and more. Though the more in-depth information on the Hoover's site requires a subscription, there is much here to be mined that is free and of value.

Lippincott Library Home Page. (1995), Philadelphia, PA: Wharton School of the University of Pennsylvania. [Online] Retrieved September 3, 1999. URL: http://www.library.upenn.edu/lippincott–Many business schools have good listings of business Web sites, but I really like this site's business reference page. If I'm looking for a calculator, a business glossary, an NAICS code look-up, places to find case studies, or quick S&P data, I know I can find it here–frequently updated and maintained.

Lott, Z. (1999) *The Investment FAQ*. [Online] Retrieved September 5, 1999. URL: http://www.invest-faq.com–No business Webliography should be without a link to a site for personal finance. Investment advice is one of the highly sought out pieces of information on the Web, and many of the investment sites will lead to other kinds of important research information. But there are many personal investment sites, so it is difficult to choose one. The Investment FAQ is designed to answer questions and provide sources of information for investor education. Whatever is needed for investment, it can be found here or there will be a link to it.

Price, G. (1997) *Price's List of Lists*, Washington, D.C.: George Washington University. [Online] Retrieved August 30, 1999. URL: http://gwis2.circ.gwu.edu/~gprice/listof.htm–One of the most common business questions is for lists of rankings, from the Fortune 500 to the top advertising spenders. Price's list remains the best collection of links to "rankings" lists found on the Internet.

PriceWaterhouseCoopers. (1999) *EdgarScan*, Menlo Park, CA: PriceWaterhouseCoopers. [Online] Retrieved August 31, 1999. URL: http://bamboo.tc.pw.com–No business resources page should be without a link to SEC documents. This one has enhanced search and data reporting features that make it superior to the SEC's own Edgar site.

TheStreet.com. (1999) *Basics of Business History*, New York, NY: TheStreet.com. [Online] Retrieved September 3, 1999. URL: http://www.thestreet.com/basics/countdown–Billing itself as the one hundred events that shaped business history, this is a great site for those who want to get a perspective on how business has changed our society in this century. You won't use this as a quick reference, but it's a fascinating site that anyone with an interest in business should visit.

United Feature Syndicate, Inc. (1999) *Dilbert Zone*. [Online] Retrieved September 3,

1999. URL: http://www.unitedmedia.com/comics/dilbert/career–You obviously won't find any serious business information here, but the Dilbert Zone deserves to be on any list of top business sites because business researchers will need to go there to take a humor break, and the mission statement generator alone is worth the visit.

University of Washington Foster Business Library. (1997) *Academic Business Libraries Web Pages*, Seattle, WA: University of Washington. [Online] Retrieved September 1, 1999. URL: http://www.lib.washington.edu/business/abl.html–Almost any of the business resource pages of the major business school libraries will make a good starting point, and all deserve further exploration for those specialty areas in which each will excel.

Welch, Jeannie. (1996) *Virtual International Business & Economics Sources*, Charlotte, North Carolina: North Carolina State University. [Online] Retrieved September 3, 1999. URL: libweb.uncc.edu/ref-bus/vibehome.htm–Welch's site has received awards and other recognition that distinguish it as the site to start any international business research project. **The International Business Resources on the WWW**, http://www.ciber.msu.edu/busres.htm, at Michigan State University is also worth bookmarking for international business research.

Yahoo! Inc., *Yahoo! Business and Commerce*. Santa Clara, CA: Yahoo! Inc. [Online] Retrieved August 25, 1999. URL: http://www.yahoo.com/Business–Too many students are already Yahoo-centric and need to be pointed elsewhere, but for those needing to start broad or for anyone looking for a resource page, Yahoo's business section is worth the occasional visit, especially when other sites are leading to dead ends.

Yardeni, E. (1999) *Dr. Ed Yardeni's Economics Network*, New York, NY: Deutch-Bank. [Online] Retrieved May 12, 1999. URL: http://www.yardeni.com–Eventually all business researchers' paths will lead them on the road to economics, and for news, projections, resources, and data, Yardeni's site is highly regarded as a well-rounded source. When in need of data only, just remember FRED at the Federal Reserve Bank of St. Louis. *FRED–Federal Reserve Economic Data*. [Online] Retrieved May 12, 1999. URL: http://www.stls.frb.org/fred.

Internet Resources for Educational Research

Linda Marie Golian

SUMMARY. This article focuses on the current status of the Internet for scholarly research in the field of education on the eve of the millennium, highlighting several categories of resources: commercial databases, government and educational association Web sources, and specialty Web pages. After a brief speculation concerning the possible future of Internet and World Wide Web information in future educational research and scholarly activities, the chapter concludes with a Webliography of the Internet sites highlighted in the article. *[Article copies available for a fee from The Haworth Document Delivery Service: 1-800-342-9678. E-mail address: <getinfo@haworthpressinc.com> Website: <http://www.HaworthPress.com>]*

KEYWORDS. Education, Internet research in, Internet resources in, online research, online resources in

Linda Marie Golian is a founding library faculty member at Florida Gulf Coast University Library in Ft. Myers, Florida. She is the Reference Team Leader and is also a member of the Library Leadership, Library Training, Collection Development, Library Instruction, and Technical Service Teams. She began her library career in the Periodicals Department of the University of Miami Otto G. Richter Library in Coral Gables. She has worked as the Serials Librarian for the University of Miami Law Library and the Serials Department Head for Florida Atlantic University. She received a BA in Sociology from the University of Miami, MLIS from Florida State University, EdS in Adult and Community Education from Florida Atlantic University, and an EdD in Higher Education Administration from Florida Atlantic University. In addition to these activities, Dr. Golian is also Adjunct Professor for the University of South Florida's School of Library and Information Science and for the Florida Gulf Coast University's College of Arts and Sciences.

[Haworth co-indexing entry note]: "Internet Resources for Educational Research." Golian, Linda Marie. Co-published simultaneously in *Journal of Library Administration* (The Haworth Information Press, an imprint of The Haworth Press, Inc.) Vol. 30, No. 1/2, 2000, pp. 105-119; and: *Academic Research on the Internet: Options for Scholars & Libraries* (ed: Helen Laurence, and William Miller) The Haworth Information Press, an imprint of The Haworth Press, Inc., 2000, pp. 105-119. Single or multiple copies of this article are available for a fee from The Haworth Document Delivery Service [1-800-342-9678, 9:00 a.m. - 5:00 p.m. (EST). E-mail address: getinfo@haworthpressinc.com].

THE CURRENT STATE OF EDUCATIONAL RESEARCH USING THE INTERNET AND THE WORLD WIDE WEB

Although Internet search engines and databases are remarkable tools, it is important to realize as we begin the new millennium that these tools do not obviate the scholarly process. In fact, many researchers comment that the Internet has greatly compounded the common research problem of "too much information." It is not uncommon for scholars to spend countless hours searching the Internet for relevant Web sites and then spend additional hours sifting through enormous amounts of information in order to locate high quality scholarly information that is reliable and relevant to their research project.

Effective researchers are familiar with what can be expected from the Internet, how to phrase their information requests, where to look for specific information, how to structure their questions, and how to evaluate the results.[1] To assist beginning scholars with these tasks, librarians and educators are developing cyber guides to help researchers through the Internet maze and critically review World Wide Web information. Two examples of cyber guides are: Esther Grassian's *Thinking Critically about World Wide Web Resources* and *The WWW CyberGuide*. Respective URLs: <http://www.library.ucla.edu/libraries/college/instruct/web/critical.htm> and <http://cyberbee.com/guides.html>.

Many student researchers comment that full-text proprietary databases (databases which require payment arrangements before access privileges are granted) provide some of the most attractive packaging of information over the Internet. Unlike business, law, or medicine, the field of educational research is relatively new to the arena of full-text proprietary databases.

At one time, all electronic database searches were conducted with the assistance of a skilled library professional. If the student researcher were unfamiliar with the subject content, the librarian would assist the researcher through a reference interview process to help the researcher narrow, expand, or redefine his/her search strategy.

Today's full text proprietary databases are noteworthy because they allow for independent and self-directed research. However, it is important to realize that they move the responsibility of content knowledge and searching responsibility down the information stream from the educator to the user. Today, and in the next millennium, users must have a fundamental knowledge of the subject and a basic understanding of how to combine words and phrases that will retrieve the information they seek. Infrequent Internet information users can find this especially challenging.

Information competency is not simply a matter of computer literacy; it is a combination of subject knowledge, information-seeking behaviors, and technology training. Unless students are educated to seek the best and most appropriate information (not just what is easily found), they will simply use these new technologies to find the most convenient information. Full-text sources will win out over abstracting resources simply because they eliminate one step. Electronic resources will win out over print, simply because they appear to be easier and faster to use and thus present the illusion of comprehensiveness. For those doing Internet research, it is easy to forget that what appears on the screen is frequently but a small drop in the sea of information.[2]

Some of the more important resources for the education community are noted below, including several core databases and World Wide Web sites necessary for conducting scholarly research in the field of education. The recommended resources are broken into the following three categories: commercial databases, governmental and educational association-sponsored Web sites, and specialty Web sites. Many variables, such as number of users, remote access, consortium pricing, and database packages affect the final institutional price of the following products. Institutions interested in subscription information should contact the publisher directly.

COMMERCIAL DATABASES

Bell & Howell's ProQuest Education Complete. *ProQuest Education Complete* is a full-text proprietary database produced by the company formerly known as University Microforms International. URL: <http://proquest.umi.com/>. This database provides instant access to an extensive collection of published educational materials, including journals, periodicals, and newspapers. *ProQuest Education Complete* provides a mix of article searching, information access, and information delivery. The database uses an easy searching interface that is effective for both the novice and professional researcher. *ProQuest Education Complete* provides a solid basic collection of core titles in education that assists researchers on the undergraduate level.

Numerous help screens are available, with a high percentage of readily available full-text materials. It should quickly become a product purchased by most academic institutions with an undergraduate education program. Publication coverage is broken down into the following categories: current, backfile, and deep backfile. Current coverage includes articles published in the current year and the two previous years. Current coverage is a strength of this product with materials added daily upon receipt from the originating source. Backfile coverage includes materials published after 1986, not including the current or previous two years. Backfile coverage from the early 1990s is excellent, but coverage from 1986 to the early 1990s needs to be strengthened. Deep backfile coverage includes materials published prior to 1986. Like all other full text databases, deep backfile coverage is weak, but continued efforts are being made with publishers to acquire this essential information.

H. W. Wilson's Education Abstracts Full-Text. *Education Abstracts Full-Text* is marketed as a full text proprietary database produced by H. W. Wilson. The database is based upon the popular paper index, *Education Abstracts*, which provides author, title, and subject coverage of more than 500 core international periodicals, monographs, and yearbooks. Topics include a wide range of contemporary education issues, including government funding, instructional media, multicultural education, religious education, student counseling, competency-based education, and information technology. *Education Abstracts Full-Text* includes indexing coverage of most titles covered in *Education Abstracts* from June 1983, of which approximately 70 titles are not currently available in other commercial proprietary databases. The remaining database is comprised of abstracting coverage from June 1984 and full text coverage from January 1996. *Education Abstracts Full Text* provides both a core undergraduate collection of educational materials and advanced educational materials that can be used by students and professors on a graduate level. International coverage of educational publications is an additional strength of this publication. Many researchers complain that the title of this database, *Education Abstracts Full Text*, is misleading, since a large portion of the database provides only bibliographic citations or citations with abstracts. The publisher is aware of this problem and is making great progress in adding more full text materials to the database quickly. Researchers using this product comment that the searching interface is not as sophisticated as other products. For example, although *Education Abstracts Full Text* provides a link to "PDF Full-Text" materials, students comment that the addition of icons for abstracts, full text, and scanned information (a method used by *ProQuest Education Complete*) would make this product easier to use.

OCLC's FirstSearch. *FirstSearch* is available on the World Wide Web as a product of the Online Computer Library Center, Inc. URL: <http://firstsearch.altip.oclc.org/htm/>. *FirstSearch* is an interactive online system that provides information about books, journal articles, films, computer software, and other materials in a wide variety of subject areas. This interactive database access system is one of the few sponsored by a nonprofit organization serving libraries and educational institutions worldwide. Libraries can purchase customized, proprietary access to over 85 databases, some full text, and many which are relevant to a researcher in the field of education. Several of the databases are specifically suggested for researchers in either academic, public, or school settings. Researchers unsure about which database(s) cover their subject can quickly find recommendations through help screens and broad subject guides. For research in the field of education, the following general databases are helpful: **WorldCat** (provides information concerning books and other materials held in libraries worldwide), **ArticleFirst** (provides access to full-text articles from nearly 12,500 journals intended for the beginning researcher), **Electronic Collections Online (ECO)** (provides access to full-text scholarly journals), and **NetFirst** (provides hyperlinks, which are updated daily, to recommended World Wide Web sites on a wide variety of informational and scholarly information).

PsycINFO. Produced by the American Psychological Association and available via OCLC FirstSearch or by individual subscription, **PsycINFO** covers scholarly literature in these subject areas and more: experimental psychology (human, animal, and comparative), psychosexual behavior, educational psychology, applied psychology, and sports psychology. It includes original research and journal articles, literature reviews, reports of surveys, case studies, theoretical discussions, bibliographies, and descriptions of tests and apparatus. Indexed materials are selected from more than 1,300 journals published in 50 countries and 28 languages. Most records have abstracts. This index is very helpful for scholars conducting research in counselor education.

Dissertation Abstracts. Produced by Bell & Howell and accessible via OCLC *FirstSearch* or by individual subscription. It covers every doctoral dissertation completed in the U.S. at accredited institutions for the last 150 years and includes some master's theses and foreign language materials. The database allows for author, title, subject, and key word searching. Most citations include abstracts, which are also searchable using author, title, subject, and key words.

ERIC. Access available via OCLC *FirstSearch* or by individual subscription. ERIC (Educational Resources Information Center) is a national indexing and abstracting database sponsored by the U.S. Department of Education and the National Library of Education. ERIC is considered the father of all educational databases and the database of choice by most educational researchers, with the most complete bibliography of educational materials available since 1966. The ERIC database is an index to thousands of educational topics, which include citations to journal articles from *Current Index to Journals in Education (CIJE)* along with citations to unpublished materials, books, government documents, conference proceedings, and theses/dissertations from *Resources in Education (RIE)*. One strength of this database is the inclusion of well written, highly factual abstracts for most citations. Another strength is the numerous links of both major and minor descriptions listed for each citation. The database is divided into journal citations (EJ) and documents (ED). Educational documents can run from one page to several hundred pages in length. ED documents are typically available in microfiche format at most higher education institutions specializing in educational and teacher certification programs. In some rare circumstances, ED documents are not available in microfiche. The information is then typically available in a print format from the institutional library or inter-library loan. ED documents are considered so important that most major style guides, such as the American Psychological Association, include special instructions on how to cite these publications. The lack of full text journal articles is a current weakness of the ERIC database. Currently, ERIC provides limited access to a small number of full text journal articles. In the near future ERIC plans on aggressively expanding the availability of full text journal materials and also plans on providing newer ED documents in an electronic full text format. URL: <http://www.accesseric. org/>.

GOVERNMENT WEB SITES

United States Department of Education. The mission of the U.S. Department of Education is to ensure equal access to education and to promote educational excellence throughout the nation. Its World Wide Web page provides information on U.S. national priorities for improving education, including renewed emphasis on reading and math, reduction in class size, and promotion of school and community partnerships. The site provides links to research funding opportunities, financial assistance, educational statistics, highlights of current research studies, brief summaries of news and current events, a listing of federal programs and services, a listing of free and fee based federal publications and products, and contact information for workers and departments of the U.S. Department of Education. One special feature is a listing of links associated with the "Most Requested Items" received by the DOE from educators, policy makers, parents, students, researchers, and other citizens with an interest in education. URL: <http://www.ed.gov/>.

Office of Bilingual Education and Minority Languages Affairs (OBEMLA). The U.S. Department of Education also sponsors OBEMLA. The site is designed to support the special needs of bilingual education by serving as a clearinghouse of information concerning funding opportunities, technical assistance, current research, and the latest bilingual education news. Of special interest is the research funding information provided on this Web site. In addition to providing a link to the *Federal Register*, an essential resource for research funding, this site provides additional funding opportunities from a wide variety of educational associations, social agencies assisting non-English speaking minorities, and some state funding opportunities. The site provides tips for beginning researchers applying for new funding opportunities in the area of bilingual and multi-cultural education. URL: <http://www.ed.gov/offices/OBEMLA>.

National Library of Education. The National Library of Education is the U.S. federal government's main resource center for education information. The NLE is charged with being the nation's collector and creator of education research information. The NLE sponsors the National Clearinghouse for Educational Facilities which acquires, manages, and disseminates information relating to educational facilities, including the design, construction, equipment, furnishing, maintenance, renovation, rehabilitation, mechanical operation, and demolition of educational facilities. NLE produces the Advances in Education Research series, which promotes recent research findings and disseminates the latest education information. This site includes a link to NLE publications, resources, explanations of free and fee services, and a link to other sites, including ERIC. URL: <http://www.ed.gov/NLE>.

National Library of Education–Educational Resources Information Center (ERIC). This site provides full access to the many specialized ERIC sites, including a link to all ERIC Clearinghouses, adjunct ERIC clearinghouses, affiliate clearinghouses, ERIC support components, searchable ERIC databases, information concerning special projects, and a FAQ site. All 18 of the ERIC clearinghouses include hypertext links. Each of these 18 clearinghouses is filled with research and scholarly information concerning a specific educational area, such as the ERIC Clearinghouse on Educational Management. URL: <http://www.accesseric.org/>.

ERIC Clearinghouse on Languages and Linguistics. Operated by the Center for Applied Linguistics, a private nonprofit organization, ERIC/CLL provides a wide range of services, materials, and specialized research links for language educators, most of them free of charge. These include two-page information digests and short bibliographies, a semiannual newsletter, and a questions-answering service via e-mail at eric@cal.org. All of these are available at no cost. Computer searches of the ERIC database are available for a nominal fee. URL: <http://www.cal.org/ericcll/about.html>.

National Center for Education Statistics. The NCES is part of the U.S. Department of Education. It is considered the primary federal entity for collecting and analyzing data that are related to education in the United States and other nations. The NCES fulfills a congressional mandate to collect, collate, analyze, and report complete statistics on the condition of American education; conduct and publish reports; and review and report on education activities internationally. It is intended that Congress, federal agencies, state and local officials, educational organizations, the news media, business organizations, and the general public will use this helpful site for finding statistical information concerning all aspects of education from K-12 to continuing education. This site provides direct links to the latest NCES survey results and information about data access tools. The site also acts as an electronic catalog with information about publications and data products. URL: <http://nces.ed.gov/index.html>.

National Distance Learning Center. The NDLC is a centralized electronic information source for distance learning programs and resources. The NDLC contains listings of K-12, higher education, and continuing education courses as well as teleconference offerings. This site is recommended for individuals designing and researching distance learning Web sites or for learners seeking distance learning courses. The NDLC is designed to distribute available courseware. URL: <http://www.ucm.es/INET/hytelnet_html/ful/fu1070.html>.

National Institute on Early Childhood Development and Education. The Department of Education sponsors NIECDE, to support research and share information about the three Rs of early childhood education: relationships, resilience, and readiness. The NIECDE Research and Development Center provides a stable foundation for long-term research and development regarding the development and education of young children. The Institute awards competitive grants to support research projects that focus on child development and learning. There is a special interest in funding and supporting research that involves communities, families, and educational professionals. As a special service to researchers, the NIECDE has created the Early Childhood Research Working Group from approximately 30 Federal agencies in an attempt to support research, data collection, and services for young children and their families. URL: <http://www.ed.gov/offices/OERI/ECI/about.html>.

Developing Educational Standards. Each state is responsible for developing, implementing, researching, and evaluating educational standards. The passage of the *Goals 2000* in the early 1990s created a renewed emphasis upon educational standards. Today, good teachers have both the national standards of *Goals 2000* and their specific state standards in mind when they create lesson plans and research curriculum development. The Internet has provided the opportunity to index the sources of educational standards in one place. Charles Hill and other educators from the Putnam Valley Central School System in New York have established, and constantly update, a resource page that serves as a repository for information about educational standards and curriculum frameworks from all sources (national, state, local, and other sources). This Web site also acts as a clearinghouse for numerous research links in the area of curriculum development. URL: <http://putwest.boces.org/Standards.html>

Florida Sunshine State Standards. As an example of a state educational standard, the Sunshine State Standards are a set of statewide academic standards that represent the core knowledge and skills Florida students are expected to achieve in order to succeed in the world of work or college. They provide clear, identifiable goals for learning so parents, teachers, and the community can understand what students are expected to know in each subject and at each grade level. They provide standards for teachers for their lesson plan development. The site provides specific information on core academic subjects, the arts, and miscellaneous subjects. URL: <http://SunshineStateStandards.net>.

National Association for the Education of Young Children. NAEYC is a professional organization in support of early childhood education. The Web site provides information for parents and professionals in the field. There are short one- or two- page articles about various topics concerning young children, such as selecting a child care facility, accreditation standards, attributes of a quality child program, advocacy information, play and learning, guidance, and diversity issues. This site also provides professional development opportunities, such as conference information and job openings for early childhood education professionals. It also provides a searchable index for the journal *Young Children*, which is published by the parent organization. URL: <http://www.naeyc.org>.

SPECIALTY WORLD WIDE WEB SITES

Kathy Schrock's Guide for Educators. Kathy Schrock is a Technology Coordinator for the Dennis-Yarmouth Regional School District in Yarmouth, Massachusetts. Her Web site is a categorized list of sites on the Internet found to be useful for enhancing curriculum and teacher professional growth. It is updated daily to keep up with the tremendous number of new World Wide Web sites. The site is broken down into logical subject access points that support academic research. She also includes information concerning search engines and how to evaluate Internet sites. The site includes audio components. URL: <http://discoveryschool.com/schrockguide/>.

Web66: A K-12 World Wide Web Project. Web66 is designed to act as a catalyst to help integrate the Internet into K-12 school curricula. It is a project of the University of Minnesota College of Education & Human Development, Office of Information Technology and Center for Applied Research and Educational Improvement. The Web66 project is designed to facilitate the introduction of Internet technology into schools with the following three goals:

1. help K-12 educators learn how to set-up their own Internet servers,
2. provide a link for interested K-12 Web servers, educators, and students to those schools, and
3. help K-12 educators find and use appropriate K-12 resources on the Web. URL: <http://web66.umn.edu>.

American Memory. Educators are noticing an increased emphasis on multicultural perspectives and discovery learning. To help increase classroom dialogue and an awareness of other cultural perspectives in the classroom, teachers are including more audio-visual materials into their lessons. Supporting the concept that "a picture is worth a thousand words," this site incorporates the use of dramatic images for educational discussions. Each collection of dramatic images and sounds is accompanied by a "learning page" of additional scholarly information. This learning page typically includes links to related research articles on the collection, lesson plan ideas, feature articles written by education professionals, and detailed information concerning the specific collection. Researchers and students can click through a dramatic gallery of digitized photographs from the American Memory Collection (supported in part by funding from the National Science Foundation Digital Libraries Initiative), including explanations of each image's significance, origin, and story. The site is designed to share comments about the collections and supporting research. URL: <http://memory.loc.gov>.

Center for Educational Leadership & Technology. The Center for Educational Leadership and Technology is a nonprofit educational service agency whose primary mission is to integrate current education reforms and research with effective uses of technology by using a unique blend of educational and technological expertise. The staff understands the culture of schools, colleges, and universities and combines this with their specialized understanding of how the appropriate application of technology in these settings can greatly enhance the teaching, learning, and management process. Their Web page provides links concerning jobs, helpful educational and developmental links, upcoming seminars, and recommended products. URL: <http://www. celt.org>.

21st Century Teachers Network. This Web site highlights a national grassroots network of teacher leaders helping themselves and their colleagues through hands-on research and the use of education technology. Under the support and direction of the McGuffey Project, volunteer teachers throughout the nation are encouraged to become members in this three year pilot study with the goal of building 21st century schools by committing to four actions: (1) building their own expertise using new learning technologies, (2) sharing their expertise and experience with other educational professionals, (3) using their expertise with students as part of the daily learning process, and (4) working to make classroom technology available. Each volunteer is asked to share the information, knowledge, and research materials they learn with five colleagues. URL: <http://www.21ct.org/>.

Test Locator. Test Locator is a joint project of the ERIC Clearinghouse on Assessment and Evaluation, the Library and Reference Services Division of the Educational Testing Service, the Burros Institute of Mental Measurements at the University of Nebraska in Lincoln, the Region III Comprehensive Center at George Washington University, and Pro-Ed Test Publishers. This Web site describes more than 11,000 assessment instruments and provides information concerning research studies using the instruments, along with reliability and validity information. The site also provides information concerning instrument availability via phone, fax, and Web links. URL: <http://ericae.net/testcol. htm>.

Virtual Reference Desk (VRD). The National Library of Education and the ERIC Clearinghouse on Information and Technology (ERIC/IR) sponsor the Virtual Reference Desk project with support from the Office of Science and Technology Policy. This Web site is the result of a national cooperative digital reference service for the field of education. The Web site provides digital reference services, also called "Ask-An-Expert," that connect users with experts in specific subjects or skills. For example, practitioners conducting math curriculum research can forward their questions to "Ask Dr. Math." The Web site also provides guidance to students in the K-12 community. URL: <http:// www.vrd.org>.

Encyclopedia Britannica's E-Blast: A Guide to the Web's Top

Sites. This free Internet guide by the editors of the *Encyclopedia Britannica* is a World Wide Web navigation service that classifies, rates, and reviews thousands of Web sites. Britannica editors search the Web to identify the highest-quality Web resources, which are then clearly and concisely described, rated according to consistent standards, and indexed for superior retrieval. E-Blast brings context, structure, and a distinctive editorial voice to the Web. Advanced search and retrieval technology enables users to locate relevant and appropriate sites. Clear, unbiased site descriptions and ratings allow the user to make an informed site selection. Extensive and detailed organizational hierarchy efficiently organizes thousands of topics. URL: <http://eblast.com>.

CONCLUSION

The popularity of the Internet and the World Wide Web is having a major impact on contemporary learning institutions. The Internet has something to offer to almost everyone. However, to the novice user and the information illiterate, the abundance of available information can cause frustration.

The development of Internet technology adaptable to research is both a blessing and a curse. As we enter a new millennium, Internet technology is viewed as a blessing because of the continuous development of sophisticated, user-friendly, and reliable features at relatively low costs. Databases are continually adding backfiles and additional scholarly materials. These attributes, and new options not yet imagined today, provide the researcher with new and effective tools that help make information and instruction interesting, varied, and meaningful.[3]

Finding scholarly information on the Internet and the World Wide Web will continue to be a principal challenge to researchers in the Information Age. Effective utilization of the World Wide Web for scholarly purposes requires a focus upon both the strengths and weaknesses of the tool. While the printed word no longer provides exclusive access to information, it is important to realize that Internet technology does provide limited access to high quality information, but unlimited access to disreputable materials. We have much to learn, and ultimately to share about the art and practice of using these resources effectively. It is critical to remember that information and data are not knowledge, knowledge is not wisdom, and wisdom is not foresight. Each grows out of the other and we need them all.[4]

NOTES

1. Judith M. Pask & Carl E. Snow, "Undergraduate Instruction and the Internet," *Library Trends* 44 (Fall 1995), 306-317.
2. Michael Perkins, "Bibliographic instruction? More than ever!" *Journal of Academic Librarianship* 22 (May 1996), 212-213.
3. D. Randy Garrison, and Doug Shale, *Education at a Distance: From Issues to Practice* (Malabar, Florida: Krieger, 1990), 67.
4. Judi Harris, "Educational telesearch: A means, not an end," *Learning and Leading with Technology* 126:3 (November 1998), 45.

WEBLIOGRAPHY

American Memory [Online]. Retrieved September 20, 1999. URL: <http://memory. loc.gov>.

Center for Educational Leadership & Technology [Online]. Retrieved September 20, 1999. URL: <http://www.celt.org>.

Cyber Bee [Online]. Retrieved September 20, 1999. URL: <http://cyberbee.com/guides. html>.

Developing Educational Standards [Online]. Retrieved September 27, 1999. URL: <http://www.ucm.es/INET/hytelnet_html/ful/fu1070.html>.

Encyclopedia Britannica's E-Blast: A Guide to the Web's Top Sites [Online]. Retrieved September 20, 1999. URL: <http://eblast.com>.

ERIC Clearinghouse on Languages and Linguistics [Online]. Retrieved September 20, 1999. URL: <http://www.cal.org/ericcll/about.html>.

Florida Sunshine State Standards [Online]. Retrieved September 20, 1999. URL: <http://SunshineStateStandards.net>.

Kathy Schrock's Guide for Educators [Online]. Retrieved September 20, 1999. URL: <http://discoveryschool.com/schrockguide/>.

National Association for the Education of Young Children [Online]. Retrieved September 20, 1999. URL: <http://www.naeyc.org>.

National Center for Education Statistics [Online]. Retrieved September 20, 1999. URL: <http://nces.ed.gov/index.html>.

National Distance Learning Center [Online]. Retrieved September 20, 1999. URL: <http://www.ucm.es/INET/hytelnet_html/ful/fu1070.html>.

National Institute on Early Childhood Development and Education [Online]. Retrieved September 20, 1999. URL: <http://www.ed.gov/offices/OERI/ECI/about. html>.

National Library of Education [Online]. Retrieved September 20, 1999. URL: <http://www.ed.gov/NLE>.

National Library of Education–Educational Resources Information Center (ERIC) [Online]. Retrieved September 20, 1999. URL: <http://www.accesseric.org/>.

Office of Bilingual Education and Minority Languages Affairs [Online]. Retrieved September 20, 1999. URL: <http://www.ed.gov/offices/OBEMLA>.

Test Locator [Online]. Retrieved September 20, 1999. URL: <http://ericae.net/testcol. htm>.

Thinking Critically about World Wide Web Resources [Online]. Retrieved September 20, 1999. URL: <http://library.ucla.edu/libraries/college/instruct/web/critical.htm>.

21st Century Teachers Network [Online]. Retrieved September 20, 1999. URL: <http://www.21ct.org/>.

United States Department of Education [Online]. Retrieved September 20, 1999. URL: <http://www.ed.gov/>.

Virtual Reference Desk (VRD) [Online]. Retrieved September 20, 1999. URL: <http://www.vrd.org.>.

Web66: A K-12 World Wide Web Project [Online]. Retrieved September 20, 1999. URL: <http://web66.umn.edu>.

Engineering Information Resources on the Web

Thomas W. Conkling

SUMMARY. Engineering information is steadily moving onto the Internet in a mixture of fee-based and free sites. Printed resources are still very important to the field, but Web-based electronic journals, databases, and document image files are now bringing information directly to the desktop. Commercial organizations, professional societies, and government agencies are all actively developing online products. This paper examines the current state of engineering information on the Web. The available formats and access options for the major types of resources used by engineers and engineering students are reviewed. *[Article copies available for a fee from The Haworth Document Delivery Service: 1-800-342-9678. E-mail address: <getinfo@haworthpressinc.com> Website: <http://www.HaworthPress.com>]*

KEYWORDS. Engineering, Internet research in, Internet resources in, online research in, online resources in

The Internet is providing engineers and engineering students with new options to access the information needed for their work, studies, and research. Engineers traditionally consult a wide variety of resources to gather information, including journals, trade publications,

Thomas W. Conkling has a BS in physics and mathematics from SUNY at Stony Brook and an MLS from Queens College. He has been Head of the Engineering Library at Pennsylvania State University since 1981. He previously served as Assistant Plasma Physics Librarian at Princeton University. Address correspondence to: Pennsylvania State University, 325 Hammond Building, University Park, PA 16802

[Haworth co-indexing entry note]: "Engineering Information Resources on the Web." Conkling, Thomas W. Co-published simultaneously in *Journal of Library Administration* (The Haworth Information Press, an imprint of The Haworth Press, Inc.) Vol. 30, No. 1/2, 2000, pp. 121-138; and: *Academic Research on the Internet: Options for Scholars & Libraries* (ed: Helen Laurence, and William Miller) The Haworth Information Press, an imprint of The Haworth Press, Inc., 2000, pp. 121-138. Single or multiple copies of this article are available for a fee from The Haworth Document Delivery Service [1-800-342-9678, 9:00 a.m. - 5:00 p.m. (EST). E-mail address: getinfo@haworthpressinc.com].

books, conference proceedings, technical reports, standards, patents, and company catalogs. The printed page is still the preeminent format for these materials, but they are beginning to appear in electronic format on the Web with increasing frequency. The tools used to access the primary engineering literature are now routinely found on the Web. Databases, publisher's directories, and online library catalogs permit desktop access for users to review what publications are being produced in their areas of interest. Some of these resources can be used for free, while others have associated fees.

This paper looks at the current state of engineering information on the Internet. A different category of resources is discussed in each section, and the options for accessing that type of information are reviewed. No attempt has been made to be exhaustive and include all engineering-related sites on the Internet. Rather, the emphasis is on examining core resources and suppliers and providing a sampling of other sites to give a sense of what types of useful information can be found on the Internet. The Web is a dynamic environment, and sites are modified and created on an ongoing basis.

COMMERCIAL DATABASES

Bibliographic databases are one of the pioneering online information tools. Engineering related databases came online in the early 1970s on systems such as DIALOG, BRS, and SDC. The end user typically accessed these systems through an intermediary, such as a librarian or search specialist. Before the advent of online databases, engineers had to use printed indexes, such as *Engineering Index* and *Science Abstracts,* to review the literature. The online databases permitted powerful keyword searching and the use of Boolean operators to refine the search strategy. One drawback to searching in the 1970s was the lack of back files–most of the engineering database coverage began in the mid-1960s to 1970.

Now, almost thirty years later, engineers have an increased selection of databases that provide more retrospective coverage. The odds are also very good that they are doing their own searching from an office PC. Printed indexes are still available for engineering, but the speed and power offered by their online counterparts are strong disincentives to their use.

The best databases on the Internet for searching the engineering journal and conference literature are proprietary, and payment arrangements must be made before access is permitted. A variety of subscription, leasing, and pay-as-you-go arrangements are open to individuals and institutions.

CompendexWeb is the most comprehensive database for bibliographic searching in engineering. URL: <http://www.ei.org/>. It covers all fields of engineering from 1970 and is produced by Engineering Information, Inc. It is the online version of the printed *Engineering Index*. **INSPEC** is another strong database covering electrical engineering, computer engineering, and physics back to 1969. URL: <http://www.iee.org.uk/publish/inspec/>. It is produced by the Institution of Electrical Engineers. **Applied Science and Technology Abstracts** covers almost 400 core engineering journals back to 1983. URL: <http://www.hwwilson.com>. It is produced by Wilson and provides excellent coverage of short news items as well as regular length articles.

There are a number of other important commercial databases for accessing engineering literature. The most significant of these include *Metadex, Aerospace Database, Ceramics Abstracts, Pollution Abstracts, Mechanical Engineering Abstracts, SAE Global Mobility Database, Energy Science and Technology Database, Transport, Science Citation Index*, and *Dissertations Abstracts*. Web versions of all of these databases are available from one or more of the commercial vendors listed in the "Webliography."

In addition to the subject specific databases, there are several broad interdisciplinary databases that are popular with engineers because of their coverage. **SWETSCAN** (covering 14,000 journals), **ArticleFirst** (12,600 journals), and **Uncover** (17,000 journals) provide excellent coverage of the journal literature in most fields of interest to engineering. Each database permits subject searching as well as browsing tables of contents. Respective URLs: <http://www.nrc.ca/cisti/source/toc_e.html>, <http://jake.prod.oclc.org:3055/html/fs_homepage.htm>, <http://uncweb.carl.org/>.

GOVERNMENT DATABASES

Government agencies maintain bibliographic databases to provide access to technical reports, which are the main vehicle for announcing research results done on government contracts. Technical reports have been available since the early part of the twentieth century. Their numbers increased drastically after the Second World War when government funding for engineering and science projects was strong. There have always been two bodies of this literature–a publicly available segment and another segment with restrictions on distribution, usually for reasons of national security. The concentration here will be on the public collection. Printed indexes served as the main access points until the early 1970s when online databases began to appear. By the mid-1990s, all of the major technical report indexes had ceased publication. The newest technical reports from these agencies are now announced in Web-based databases.

The broadest coverage of the technical report literature can be found at the **National Technical Information Service** (NTIS) Web site. URL: <http://www.ntis.gov>. They have a searchable database containing records of technical reports issued during the last ten years. Several commercial vendors offer the full NTIS database back to 1964. NASA, the National Aeronautics and Space Administration, provides coverage of its technical reports on the **NASA CASI Technical Report Server**. URL: <http://www.sti.nasa.gov/RECONselect.html>. There are over 2 million records here, covering technical reports and much of the open journal and conference literature for aerospace engineering. NASA maintains a related database, RECONPlus, for the use of its facilities and contractors. This database contains publicly available reports as well as those with distribution limitations.

The U.S. Department of Energy (DOE) offers the **DOE Reports Bibliographic Database** on the Web. URL: <http://www.doe.gov/dra/dra.html>. It covers reports issued since 1994. Access to the early nuclear and energy literature can be found through the "Energy Science and Technology Database" and "Nuclear Science Abstracts," available from commercial vendors. The U.S. Department of Defense (DOD) provides access to its publicly available reports on the **DOD STINET** site. URL: <http://www.dtic.mil/stinet>. It covers reports issued since 1985. Limited distribution documents are covered by a secure version of STINET, available only to DOD facilities and contractors.

An example of a smaller government-sponsored database is **Earthquake Engineering Abstracts**. URL: <http://www.eerc.berkeley.edu/eea.html>. The National Science Foundation sponsors this database which covers technical reports, journal articles, conference papers, and other types of publications.

SPECIALTY DATABASES

There are numerous non-bibliographic databases on the Internet of potential interest to engineers. Some are produced by government agencies or with government support, others come from individuals and universities. Only a sampling is presented here–many more can be found by diligent searching on the Web.

NASA has a searchable database of images at its **NIX–NASA Image Exchange** site. URL: <http://nix.nasa.gov/nix.cgi>. The site contains 300,000 photos and images collected by the agency. The **National Institute of Standards and Technology** (NIST) has developed a selection of numeric databases containing useful data for engineers and scientists. URL: <http://www.nist.gov>. There are databases covering physical constants, atomic spectra, radionuclides, thermochemical and physical properties, structural characteristics, and vibration spectra for a range of compounds. The site is worth bookmarking for most engineers and scientists.

Thermodex: An Index of Selected Thermodynamics Handbooks was developed by the libraries at the University of Texas. URL: <http://thermodex.lib.utexas.edu>. This index can be searched by property and compound, and it returns the title of the handbooks containing the requested data. There are many directory-type sites offering valuable data. For example, **EE Circuit Archive** is produced at the University of Washington and provides an archive of electronic circuit designs and related information. URL: <http://www.ee.washington.edu/pg_circuits.html>. The **Data Bookshelf** contains links to the data sheets for electronic components for dozens of manufacturers. URL: <http://www.crhc.uiuc.edu/~dburke/databookshelf.html>. A group at the University of Illinois maintains this site.

ELECTRONIC JOURNALS

Journals have served as the primary announcement and archiving media for advances in engineering for decades, and, until recently, printed copies were the only format available. Now, we are in the midst of a huge change in the production and distribution of journals. Electronic engineering journals were a rarity in the mid-1990s, but they are becoming more widespread as publishers continue to move to the new format. It is hard to predict the future in publishing, but we may be entering a period where virtually all printed journals have an electronic counterpart on the Internet. The next stage could be a complete move away from print for most journals, once satisfactory arrangements can be made for preserving the electronic archival copies. For the next several years, library managers should be prepared to support multiple formats of these publications.

COMMERCIAL E-JOURNALS

Commercial publishers are moving aggressively into electronic journal publishing. **Elsevier**, the largest publisher of scientific journals, now has over 1000 of its titles on the Web. URL: <http://www.sciencedirect.com>. The company has been marketing the journals a number of ways, from access to the entire collection down to subsets such as engineering. Elsevier recently purchased Engineering Information, Inc., and is now offering various packages of access to online journals linked to the references retrieved during searches on CompendexWeb.

Springer-Verlag has a collection of 400 electronic journals, primarily in engineering and science. URL: <http://link.springer-ny.com>. **Springer** allows free searching of tables of contents of its titles, but the full text can only be retrieved by subscribers. **Kluwer Academic** has 400 online journals, including titles from Chapman and Hall and Plenum. URL: <http://www.wkap.nl/>. The **IDEAL** system (Academic Press) contains 174 online journals. URL: http://www.apnet.com>. **Wiley, Taylor & Francis**, and **Thomas Telford** are other engineering publishers of note who are offering access to electronic journal collections. Respective URLs: <http://www.interscience.wiley.com>, <http://www.tandf.co.uk/>, <http://www.t-telford.co.uk/>. The most active university press in the area of electronic engineering journals has been **Cambridge University Press**. URL: <http://www.cup.cam.ac.uk>. Cambridge offers online access to about 70 titles in all subject areas to subscribers of the printed versions.

A number of trade journals have free online subscriptions. There are several journal gateways that are good starting points for investigating electronic journals: **e-Zine-list, Ejournal Siteguide, Electronic Journal Access: The Alliance,** and the **Engineering E-journal Search Engine**. Respective URLs: <http://www.meer.net/~johnl/e-zine-list>, <http://www.Library.ubc.ca/ejour>, <http://www.coalliance.org>, <http://www.eevl.ac.uk/eese>.

SOCIETY E-JOURNALS

Engineering societies have always held a vital publishing role in the field, specifically in the areas of journals, conference papers, and books. On the whole, however, the professional societies have been very deliberate in their approach to electronic journals. The one exception to this has been the Institute of Electrical and Electronics Engineers (IEEE), the largest engineering society in the U.S. The IEEE has been digitally scanning its journals, conference papers, and standards for years, and they market a CD-ROM collection of these materials. In late 1998, the society began offering access to a Web site with electronic versions of its publications issued since 1988. The **IEEE Electronic Library** (IEL) is a massive collection with over 500,000 articles and papers in full text. URL: <http://www.ieee.org/products/electronicproducts.html>. Included are over 100 journals published by IEEE and IEE, the Institution of Electrical Engineers. IEL is available to institutions on a subscription basis.

The **American Society of Mechanical Engineers** (ASME) currently has one of its 17 journals in electronic format with more to follow. Journal tables of contents are available for browsing at their Web site. URL: <http://www.asme.org/index.html>. The **American Society of Civil Engineers** (ASCE) offers journals on CD-ROM, but not on the Web. URL: <http://www.asce.org>. It does offer a useful bibliographic database of all of its publications since 1974, which is free. The **Society of Automotive Engineers** (SAE) has started offering Web access to its newer technical papers. URL: <http://www.sae.org>. These are an important resource in mechanical and automotive engineering. There is a charge for each paper downloaded, but the SAE does maintain a free searchable database of its technical papers issued in the last 12 months. The **American Institute of Aeronautics and Astronautics** (AIAA) does not have its journals available electronically at this time, but it does offer browsable tables of contents and a searchable database of AIAA papers issued since 1992. URL: <http://www.aiaa.org>. The **Society of Photo-optical Instrumentation Engineers** (SPIE) has three electronic journals available by subscription, and free access to tables of contents and abstracts. URL: <http://www.spie.org>. The **Institute of Industrial Engineers** (IIE) is putting its journals online for member and subscriber access. URL: <http://www.iienet.org>. To stay abreast of online publishing news for these and other engineering societies, check the society Web sites.

Several other professional societies in related fields have extensive online publishing programs that support certain areas of engineering. The Association for Computing Machinery (ACM), Society for Industrial and Applied Mathematics (SIAM), American Chemical Society (ACS), American Physical Society (APS), and the American Institute of Physics (AIP) all have extensive collections of electronic journals (and conference proceedings in some cases) on the Web.

TECHNICAL REPORTS

As mentioned in a previous section, technical reports constitute a valuable sector of the engineering literature. The bulk of the reports published in the last 50 years have been produced as the result of government sponsored research. The largest sponsoring agencies in the U.S. have been NASA, the Department of Defense, and the Department of Energy. Each of these agencies has made hard copy reports available to contractors and universities through a variety of distribution programs over the years. NTIS has also filled the role as the national warehouse and distributor of these items to the engineering community and the public. These agencies are moving toward digital distribution of technical reports, some more quickly than others.

The DOE has the most advanced Web-based technical report archive–the **DOE Information Bridge**. URL: <http://gpo.osti.gov:901>. This Web site contains the full text and bibliographic records of all DOE sponsored reports published since January 1996. The site contains over 30,000 electronic reports. Most of the reports have been scanned with OCR (optical character recognition) software, and once a report has been located in the bibliographic database, its individual pages can be searched for specific terms or pieces of data. This is a powerful tool for engineers and scientists.

NASA's digital technical report program is decentralized. The **NASA Technical Report Server** acts as a gateway to servers at NASA centers and facilities. URL: <http://techreports.larc.nasa.gov/cgi-bin/NTRS>. Users search the main interface and their queries go out to the distributed servers. Users can limit searches to particular NASA labs. The number of reports available online varies significantly between the NASA facilities–several have thousands of reports available, others relatively few. The historic NACA (National Advisory Committee for Aeronautics) technical report series is being digitized as well, and this will be a valuable resource to aeronautical engineers. As mentioned previously, the DOD operates both a public and a secure version of STINET. Full text technical reports are being added to these systems, but only in limited numbers at this point.

These agencies all maintain information centers for fulfilling orders for technical reports not available online, primarily for the use of their own research facilities and contractors. The main public distributor for technical reports in this country is NTIS–they have several million in their inventory. The NTIS Web site has two searchable bibliographic databases containing the most recent 90 days and the last 10 years of their acquisitions. NTIS sells most technical reports in paper or microfiche format, but has started offering image files that can be downloaded for a fee. NTIS also maintains the Fedworld Web site that acts as a gateway to other federal agency servers. URL: <http://www.fedworld.gov>. Searches of this site can lead users to online full text copies of assorted publications and regulations.

Other federal agencies have technical reports on the Internet. One of the more substantial collections can be found at the **Environmental Protection Agency** Web site. URL: <http://www.epa.gov>. Searchable databases there provide access to thousands of online publications, regulations, and technical reports. Exploring the Web sites of non-U.S. scientific agencies can also turn up electronic publications. The **European Space Agency** (ESA) has a selection of its publications on the Internet for browsing and downloading. URL: <http://www.esa.int/Info>.

The number of online technical reports decreases once you leave the government domain. At this time, corporations aren't posting their proprietary reports online for the most part. One segment of academia has been active in sharing technical reports online–Computer Science departments. The **Networked Computer Science Technical Refer-**

ence Library (NCSTRL) is a cooperative system, tying together over 150 computer science departments. URL: <http://www.ncstrl.org>. A central index can be searched, and reports that are located can be downloaded from the supplying institution's server. Another directory site is **On-line CS Techreports**. URL: <http://www.cs.cmu.edu/~jblythe/cs-reports.html>. This page provides links to almost 400 sites with online technical reports in computer science.

STANDARDS

Standards are documents that specify performance requirements for materials and equipment, testing methods, and related activities. Committees and groups of experts from professional societies, industry, government agencies, and the military develop these publications. A number of societies and vendors have made bibliographic databases of standards available on the Web, so it is now relatively easy for engineers to locate applicable documents. The standards themselves are not generally available on the Web for free, but Web access to online collections of standards is available in some cases.

The **American National Standards Institute** (ANSI) is the largest standards producer (aside from the military) in the U.S. URL: <http://web.ansi.org/>. Their Web site offers site licenses to organizations for access to the full text of selected standards collections. ANSI participates in the **National Standards System Network** (NSSN) with several hundred other organizations. The NSSN Web site contains a searchable standards database with 250,000 records. URL: <http://www.nsn.org/>. Searches on this database return standards information along with ordering information. The site also permits access to certain full text standards for a fee. As mentioned earlier, the IEEE has full text standards online for subscribers to its electronic library.

The **International Organization for Standardization** (ISO) maintains a Web site with a searchable database that provides ordering information. URL: <http://www.iso.ch>. The **World Standards Service Network** (WSSN) provides links to the servers of international standards producing bodies. URL: <http://www.wssn.net/WSSN>. Access to standards bibliographic information is often available for free at the Web sites of professional societies in the U.S.

Information Handling Services (IHS) has supplied large collections of standards on microfilm and CD-ROM for years. IHS is now providing Web access to full text standards from selected producers by subscription. URL: <http://www.ihs.com>. Organizations can arrange for institution-wide access for their engineers in this manner. Several vendors offer searchable databases with ordering information at their sites. They include **Global Engineering, Document Center**, and **CCS–Custom Standards Service**. Respective URLs: <http://global.ihs.com>, <http://www.document-center.com>, <http://www.cssinfo.com>.

The military produces an enormous number of standards and specifications. The **DODISS** Web site has a free searchable database with military and federal specifications and standards, handbooks, and DOD-adopted industry standards. URL: <http://www.dtic.mil/stinet/htgi/dodiss>. The site contains a link to DODSSP (DOD Single Stock Point) which can be used to order these documents. Government related standards can also be ordered from vendors and from NTIS.

PATENTS

Access to U.S. patents has improved markedly with the development of the Web. Users no longer have to view microfilm or wait for orders in the mail, at least for recent patents–desktop access is now the order of the day. The U.S. Patent and Trademark Office (PTO) Web site offers bibliographic searching of patents back to 1976 and free image files of those patents. URL: <http://www.uspto.gov>. The images are stored in TIFF format (Tagged Image File Format). The IBM Intellectual Property Network site holds a large database with over 4 million records and includes U.S. patents and patent applications from the European Patent Office and the World Intellectual Property Organization. URL: <http://www.patents.ibm.com/>. Images are available at no charge for U.S. patents issued since 1974.

Information on non-U.S. patents can be found in a number of databases. **The European Patent Register Online** site has bibliographic data and the legal status of European patent applications. URL: <http://www.european-patent-office.org/>. The **Canadian Patent Database** has 75 years of patent data online. URL: <http://patents1.ic.gc.ca/>. Over 1.3 million patent image files can be found there. Additional international patent databases and copies of full text patents can be found online from DIALOG and other vendors.

COMPANY CATALOGS

Printed catalogs are still the mainstay for engineers searching for materials or equipment to use in their job assignments. However, the print format is now being complemented by Web-based information. Thousands of companies have a Web presence to some degree. Many have just a page or two that describe their products and services in general terms. Other companies have entire product catalogs online with pricing. This section presents a sampling of the types of company information that can be found on the Web.

All engineers are familiar with the printed *Thomas Register*, the venerable tool for locating products and their producers. **Thomas Register** is also on the Web and lists 150,000 companies in its database. URL: <http://www.thomasregister.com>. A search by product or service returns a list of companies and has links to their Web sites, if they exist. It is interesting to note that fewer than 10% of the companies in **Thomas** have associated Web sites.

A number of Web sites provide searching of large collections of vendor catalogs in related product areas. For example, **Design-Info** offers a searchable database of testing equipment, sensors, gauges, motors, and other components. URL: <http://www.designinfo.com/>. Users search by the component needed, and the results give a choice of suppliers and their catalogs. **AMM Online Metals Marketplace** has a database of 675 metal suppliers. URL: <http://www.amm.com/marketplace>. Searches by metal and category of supplier return lists of companies with links to Web catalogs, when available. **Metals Supplier Online** has an online properties database for over 17,000 types of materials with suppliers. URL: <http://www.suppliersonline.com/>. **Electric Net** describes itself as a resource locator for the electric power industry. URL: <http://www.electricnet.com>. It offers directories of products, organizations, and companies. **Electronics Manufacturers on the Net** contains data from hundreds of electronics manufacturers. URL: <http://www.electricnet.com>. It is searchable by company name or product.

Some sites maintained by suppliers offer complete catalogs. **MSC Industrial Supply Company** lists 372,000 items from 1900 manufacturers. URL: <http://www.mscdirect.com>. The **Grainger Industrial Supply** Web site has an online catalog of 200,000 items. URL: <http://www.grainger.com>. **McMaster-Carr** offers a wide selection of mechanical and electrical components in its online catalog, including pricing data. URL: <http://www.mcmaster.com/>. Individual companies may have extensive online listings. The electrical component manufacturer **AMP** details 70,000 products on its site. URL: <http:// connect.amp.com>.

Organizations wanting to purchase single point access to catalog information can do so through **Information Handling Services**. IHS offers subscribers access to its "Product Selection Service," which contains over 1 million pages of catalog information from 10,000 manufacturers. The information is updated regularly, and a variety of access paths are provided.

SOFTWARE

Software is an indispensable tool in engineering, and there are many software-related resources on the Internet. The Web sites range from shareware and vendor sites to producer sites. This is a mere sampling of sites–many more can be located through engineering gateways or by browsing.

Shareware.com and **ZDNET** are sites that offer downloadable software. Respective URLs: <http://www.shareware.com/>, <http://www. zdnet.com/>. Both have a large collection, and each has a searchable index. For directories of commercial software, the **All Internet Shopping Directory** and **SciTech International Online** can be explored. Respective URLs: <http://www.all-internet.com/>, <http://www.scitechint. com/>. They provide access to information on hundreds of software packages, with the latter specializing in engineering and scientific packages.

The popular Linux operating system has several supporting Web sites. **The Linux User's WWW Page** offers links to documentation, kernels, patches, and related information. URL: <http://linuxwww. db.erau.edu>. For information on commercial software packages, consult the producer's site, which usually provides support data. These producers of important engineering software all have useful Web sites: **Autodesk**, **Mathworks**, and **Wolfram Research**. Respective URLs: <http://www.autodesk.com>, <http://www.mathworks.com>, and <http:// www.mindswap.com>.

BOOKS AND REFERENCE TOOLS

Engineering books haven't moved to the Internet yet. The same is true for most of the sciences–the printed versions will be required for some years to come. Testing is being done on e-books that can be downloaded to specialized portable readers, but the technology is still in the developmental stage. Books offer a more convenient and easy to use format. Users may not mind reading a short paper on their monitors, but using a screen to view several hundred pages is a more difficult proposition.

Information about books is easy to find on the Internet. **Publishers' Catalogues Home Page** provides an exhaustive listing of publisher information for the U.S. and other countries. URL: <http://www.lights.com/publisher/index.html>. **Books in Print** is available by subscription on the Web. URL: <http://www.silverplatter.com>. Its database contains information on 1.5 million titles that are currently in stock. The **Amazon.com** Web site has a huge searchable database of titles. URL: <http://www.amazon.com>. Out of print titles can be located on sites such as **Bibliofind**. URL: <http://www.bibliofind.com>.

There are many general reference tools on the Web. As with other resources, some are subscription-based while others are free. Engineering encyclopedias are appearing online–the 22 volume *Wiley Encyclopedia of Electrical and Electronics Engineering* will be published in both print and Web versions in 1999. The *Kirk-Othmer Encyclopedia of Chemical Technology* is also scheduled to appear on the Web. Dictionaries, almanacs, thesauri, and acronym glossaries are often available for free on the Web.

VIRTUAL LIBRARIES AND GATEWAYS

Links to most (if not all) of the resources mentioned in this paper can be located on engineering virtual library and gateway sites. These sites have been put together by individuals or groups who saw the need to consolidate Web site listings by subject. A good place to start exploring engineering Internet resources is the **WWW Virtual Library–Engineering**. URL: <http://arioch.gsfc.nasa.gov/wwwvl/engineering.html>. This site has links to the discipline-based virtual libraries such as acoustics and mechanical, electrical, and civil engineering. The site contains an extensive list of broadly applicable engineering resources.

ICE–Internet Connections for Engineering was one of the first resource gateways and was developed by the Engineering Library at Cornell. URL: <http://www.englib.cornell.edu/ice/>. It is a searchable alphabetical subject list that provides links to more specific listings. **EEVL–Edinburgh Engineering Virtual Library** is a gateway to engineering sites, targeted to the university and research community in the U.K. URL: <http://www.eevl.ac.uk>. It does, however, cover the entire Web, and it provides links to over 4000 annotated Web sites. **EELS–Engineering Electronic Library** provides a classified subject arrangement of Web sites. URL: <http://www.UB2.lu.se/eel/eelhome. html/>. The sites have been reviewed for usefulness and the listing is searchable.

Ei Village is a subscription-based service that was developed by Engineering Information, Inc. URL: <http://www.ei.org/>. It is an attractive and innovative site that is divided into 11 subject areas, such as "Research & Industrial Park," "Industry Mart," "Datasphere," and "Careers and Education Campus." Thousands of Web sites are listed and all are annotated. **Ei Village** is a very useful tool for engineers.

The **Scout Report for Science and Engineering** is a free Internet service that notifies subscribers by email when new sites become available. URL: <http://wwwscout.cs.wisc.edu/scout/report>. The report is issued twice per month, and all of the Web sites listed are annotated. The report is produced by the University of Wisconsin Computer Science Department and is sponsored by the National Science Foundation.

CONCLUSION

The move of resources onto the desktop will facilitate the information-seeking efforts of engineering students and engineers. They will be able to locate data faster, and there will be an opportunity for quicker delivery. The value of gateway-style sites will be increasingly important. If done properly, these one stop Web sites can pull together widely scattered resources and save people Web searching time. The acquisition of electronic materials needs to be supported with appropriate instruction and guides, either print or online. Their usefulness can't be overstated as more users access information remotely. The range of resources available in a field such as engineering must seem overwhelming to users at times, and any type of assistance that can be given them to simplify their online tasks should be considered.

This paper provides a snapshot of engineering resources on the Internet in mid-1999. There is a definite trend among information producers to make their products available online. However, it will be a long time until everything is on the Web. We are in a transition period now in which many resources are being produced in both print and online versions, and it could take years before the bulk of current engineering information is on the Web. In addition, many producers are only putting current materials up–the enormous quantity of engineering research done in the last seven or eight decades may never be available online. In the near term, total costs for collections will increase as librarians and administrators are forced to maintain multiple formats for these resources. The long term will see a broader range of online materials, with most resources requiring purchase or lease. However, any future savings realized from the cancellations of duplicate print resources could be consumed by the ongoing need to update network and computer equipment.

WEBLIOGRAPHY

Database Vendors

Cambridge Scientific Abstracts [Online]. Retrieved April 10, 1999. URL: http://www.csa.com.

The Dialog Corporation. *Dialog* [Online]. Retrieved April 10, 1999. URL: http://www.dialog.com.

Engineering Information, Inc. *Ei* [Online]. Retrieved April 10, 1999. URL: http://www.ei.org/

Institution of Electrical Engineers. *INSPEC* [Online]. Retrieved April 10, 1999. URL: http://www.iee.org.uk/publish/inspec/

SilverPlatter Information [Online]. Retrieved April 10, 1999. URL: http://www.silverplatter. com.

STN International. *Databases in Science and Technology* [Online]. Retrieved April 10, 1999. URL: http://www.fiz-karlsruhe.de/stn.html.

Government Sites

NASA Center for AeroSpace Information. *CASI Technical Report Server* [Online]. Retrieved April 2, 1999. URL: http://www.sti.nasa.gov/RECONselect.html.

U.S. Department of Commerce. *National Technical Information Service (NTIS)* [Online]. Retrieved April 2, 1999. URL: http://www.ntis.gov/.

U.S. Department of Defense. *Scientific and Technical Information Network (STINET)* [Online]. Retrieved April 2, 1999. URL: http://www.dtic.mil/stinet/.

U.S. Department of Energy. *DOE Information Bridge* [Online]. Retrieved April 2, 1999. URL: http://gpo.osti.gov:901/.

Selected Professional Societies

American Chemical Society. *ACS Publications* [Online]. Retrieved March 31, 1999. URL: http://pubs.acs.org/about.html.

American Institute of Physics. OJPS: Online Journal Publishing Service [Online]. Retrieved March 31, 1999. URL: http://ojps.aip.org/.

American Society of Civil Engineers. *ASCE–American Society of Civil Engineers Homepage* [Online]. Retrieved March 31, 1999. URL: http://www.asce.org/.

American Society of Mechanical Engineers. *ASMENET–Website of ASME International* [Online]. Retrieved March 31, 1999. URL: http://www.asme.org/.

Association for Computing Machinery. ACM Digital Library [Online]. Retrieved March 31, 1999. URL: http://www.acm.org/dl/.

The Institute of Electrical and Electronics Engineers, Inc. *IEEE* [Online]. Retrieved March 31, 1999. URL: http://www.ieee.org/index.html.

Society of Automotive Engineers. SAE International [Online]. Retrieved March 31, 1999. URL: http://www.sae.org/.

Society for Industrial and Applied Mathematics. *SIAM Journals Online* [Online]. Retrieved March 31, 1999. URL: http://epubs.siam.org/.

Virtual Libraries and Gateways

Engineering Information, Inc. *Ei Village* [Online]. Retrieved April 7, 1999. URL: http://www.ei.org/.

Engineering Library. *The ICE Index: Internet Connections for Engineering.* Ithaca: Cornell University. Retrieved April 7, 1999. URL: http://www.englib.cornell.edu/ice/.

Heriot-Watt University Library. *EEVL: Edinburgh Engineering Virtual Library* [Online]. Retrieved April 7, 1999. URL: http://www.eevl.ac.uk/.

Waterbury, S. *WWW Virtual Library: Engineering* [Online]. Greenbelt, MD: Goddard Space Flight Center. Retrieved April 7, 1999. URL: http://arioch.gsfc.nasa.gov/wwwvl/engineering.html.

REFERENCES

Berinstein, Paula. "Technically Speaking: Nuts and Bolt Images from HIS." *Online* 21, no.6 (1997): 43-48.

He, Jimin. "Databases on the Internet for Engineers." *Experimental Techniques* 22, no.4 (1998): 38-41.

He, Jimin. *Internet Resources for Engineers: A Practical Handbook for Engineers and Students*. Port Melbourne, Australia: Butterworth-Heinemann, 1998.

Lawrence, Steve, and C.L. Giles. "Searching the Web: General and Scientific Information Access." *IEEE Communications Magazine* 37, no.1 (1999): 116-122.

MacLeod, Roddy. "Discover: Engineering Information." *Managing Information* 5, no.3 (1998): 27-30.

Schwarzwalder, Robert. "Engineering Information Village: A New Spin on the Web." *Online* 20, no.2 (1996): 33-37.

Thomas, Brian J. *The World Wide Web for Scientists & Engineers*. Bellingham, WA: Society for Photo-Optical and Instrumentation Engineers, 1998.

Sound, Image, Action:
Remaking History on the Internet

Michael Seadle

SUMMARY. This article begins with discontinuity. Its review of Web-based historical information discards traditional taxonomies and builds instead on the new capabilities that separate digital publishing from its paper-based predecessor. The article emphasizes dynamic, transformative, and multimedia sources that specialize in images, sound, searchability, and the conversion of data into visually digestible tabular and spatial forms. The goal is not to make a one-to-one comparison with print resources, or in any way to denigrate them, but to highlight the kind of sources which a generation of historians brought up on Alistair Cooke's *America* and Ken Burns's *Civil War* are learning to exploit. *[Article copies available for a fee from The Haworth Document Delivery Service: 1-800-342-9678. E-mail address: <getinfo@haworthpressinc.com> Website: <http://www.HaworthPress.com>]*

KEYWORDS. History, Internet research in, Internet resources in, online research in, online resources in

INTRODUCTION

Discontinuity–the fact that within the space of a few years a culture sometimes ceases to think as it had been thinking up till

---

Michael Seadle has a PhD in modern European history from the University of Chicago and a library degree from the University of Michigan. He is Digital Services and Copyright Librarian at Michigan State University, where he also serves as the German bibliographer. He has written over 25 articles, chapters, and books, and is Editor of the peer-reviewed journal *Library Hi Tech*.

[Haworth co-indexing entry note]: "Sound, Image, Action: Remaking History on the Internet." Seadle, Michael. Co-published simultaneously in *Journal of Library Administration* (The Haworth Information Press, an imprint of The Haworth Press, Inc.) Vol. 30, No. 1/2, 2000, pp. 139-155; and: *Academic Research on the Internet: Options for Scholars & Libraries* (ed: Helen Laurence, and William Miller) The Haworth Information Press, an imprint of The Haworth Press, Inc., 2000, pp. 139-155. Single or multiple copies of this article are available for a fee from The Haworth Document Delivery Service [1-800-342-9678, 9:00 a.m. - 5:00 p.m. (EST). E-mail address: getinfo@haworthpressinc.com].

> *then and begins to think other things in a new way–probably begins with an erosion from outside, from that space which is, for thought, on the other side, but in which it has never ceased to think from the very beginning.*
>
> –Foucault, 1970, p. 50

Did it begin with Shakespeare? Or perhaps as far back as Euripides? The urge to depict history in something more visual and sensual than the written word is probably older than the written word itself. In recent centuries professional historians have concentrated on the written word for a variety of excellent reasons having to do with the power of the printing press to disseminate their works and their ability to use print to establish standards and reliability. But the desire for seeing history live in non-sequential, non-textual forms has persisted. Historical movies like *Gone with the Wind* and *Ben Hur* were enormously popular. In recent decades the almost scholarly sets of series by Alistair Cooke (*America*) and by Ken Burns (*Civil War*) have cut tracks in the imaginations of contemporary historians. To create such a series remained, however, beyond the means of the ordinary academic–until the advent of the Web.

It is essentially a commonplace that the Internet represents a discontinuity in our means of communication. Web publishing also represents a discontinuity in the way history and historical sources are presented, because it has radically lowered the barrier to creating multimedia history. This seems so sudden and jarring to a field of study which many love as a refuge from the present that the categories of discourse, the taxonomies of subjects and methodologies, still tend to carry over from the old pre-Web world. The easy and obvious way to approach a resource-review article like this remains through an organization that classifies sites by country, period, or methodology. But that would obscure the elements of real, underlying importance.

Probably we stand too close to the beginning of this discontinuity to analyze accurately the forms and elements which will seem important to historians a decade hence, but six groupings appear to be significant now:

1. *Discussion groups.*
   Although the discussions are text based, they bear more resemblance to hallway conversations than to print-based notes or articles. This is partly because of the number of contributors and

the wandering themes. What they do is to liberate the isolated specialist. The most vigorous and important groups often correspond to the smallest, most focused, least well supported fields. They open collegial interaction and idea sharing to the whole of the intellectual community, not just those who travel to conferences. This means they are source of information about trends, as well as a place to put questions.

2. *Multimedia collections.*
   Sound and video still require somewhat expensive and uncommon digitization tools, so public sources of these are particularly important. One of the problems is that standards for format, segmentation, and metadata do not exist for all practical purposes, though that is changing.

3. *Photographic image collections.*
   The number of images of historical subjects on the Web is huge, but the number of well-organized collections with reliable quality standards and good metadata is noticeably smaller. Images represent the cornerstone of most multimedia history sites. The equipment to create new images from paper originals is readily available, but old problems of physical access make Internet-based collections a necessity.

4. *Searchable text collections.*
   The written word remains a fundamental tool on the Web as in paper, but its manner of use has changed as sites increasingly use Optical Character Readers (OCR) or inexpensive typists to create searchable ASCII versions of works once available online only in image form. Online historians today generally expect to be able to search for key words and want a level of precision in the result set that makes the fullest possible use of their own knowledge of the item sought.

5. *Indexes and reviews.*
   These are categories of print as well as digital publishing, but in the digital world they work differently and cover different subjects. Indexes are interactive, with hyperlinks to relevant Web-based material. There are many well-marketed commercial databases that fit this category, but equally interesting are the small, highly focused, and often free indexes supported by individual scholars or departments. Likewise, reviews on the Web will link to the items they are discussing (if they are also Web-based), and they are more likely to cover multimedia resources.

6. *Maps, data, and transformative systems.*
   Maps deserve a separate category from images, although many
   appear in image format. Maps are common in print sources too,
   but on the Internet maps can also be built dynamically from
   otherwise unwieldy sets of data. This kind of spatial and multi-
   dimensional representation is growing more common and becoming more integrated into the historian's toolkit.

These resources are not necessarily substitutes for traditional paper
materials. It will be a long time, for example, before some of the
archival materials I used decades ago in my dissertation appear on the
Web because they include confidential letters. The same will be true
for a lot of historically interesting records.

Web-resources offer something different–not just passive information sources in different forms, but access to publishing tools which
are changing the relationship between the historian and the source on
the one hand, and the historian and the audience on the other. Some of
these tools allow historians to use sound, color, and movement in
making their arguments. Others are transformative, like the Geographic Information System (GIS) software that turns one form of data, such
as census numbers, into visually comprehensible maps. Some of the
sites listed below represent attempts by professional historians to explore the possibilities. One key limiting factor for all materials on the
Internet is copyright. Anything put on the Web in an unprotected
folder counts as being published. This means that every book, every
photograph, every compilation that is not in the public domain ought
to have an accompanying permission from the rights holder. Most of
the sites listed below are copyright-aware and attempt to be scrupu-
lously careful. But the copyright law is complex. Before copying
anything for public use, a good understanding of the copyright law is
essential, and, increasingly, libraries and universities provide some
measure of help. As a very rough rule of thumb, for works published
in the U.S., it is best to assume that they are protected unless they were
published before 1923 or were created by a Federal (not state or
foreign) government employee in the course of his or her duties.

The attentive reader may notice a strong bias toward university and
government sites in the selection below. This is because of the problem of reliability. Many interesting Web sites vanish abruptly after a
few months or years. Those with institutional backing are usually

more persistent and may even survive the format changes of the next wave of technological improvements. Many interesting sites have inevitably been left out for no good reason except space, time, and the author's ignorance.

DISCUSSION GROUPS

H-Net: Humanities and Social Sciences Online [online]. Retrieved May 26, 1999. URL: <http://www.h-net.msu.edu/>

H-Net is an international complex of moderated discussion lists, reviews, and, increasingly, multimedia projects. It is arguably the most organized and wide-ranging of all the history-related lists. In many respects each list functions like a journal. There are on-line editors, editorial boards, regular "scholarly" book reviews, a description of current discussion threads, and archived copies of the discussion. H-Net can be thought of as a new kind of digital press that is pushing the boundaries of online publication to cover that half-explored but still uncivilized territory between the formal, peer-reviewed article or book, and informal hallway-style mailing list chatter.

The sheer number of history-oriented discussions on H-Net is too large to detail here. Some are fairly traditional area/country oriented lists, such as: H-Africa (African History and Culture), H-Albion (British and Irish History), H-Canada (Canadian History and Studies), or H-France (French History and Culture). Others focus on teachers and teaching: H-AfrTeach (Teaching African History and Studies), H-Survey (Teaching United States History Survey Courses), and H-Teach (Teaching College History). Others deal with regional topics: H-Appalachia (Appalachian History and Studies) and H-California (History and Culture of California). History of religion is represented: H-Bahai (Culture and History of the Baha'i Faith) or H-Mideast-Medieval (The Islamic Lands of the Medieval Period). Not all lists are in English: H-Francais (H-Net liste des Clionautes, sur l'histoire et la geographie en France) and H-Soz-u-Kult (Methoden, Theorie und Ergebnisse neuerer Sozial-und Kulturgeschichte). Many cover special topics: H-Childhood (History of Childhood and Youth), H-CivWar (U.S. Civil War History), H-CLC (Computers and Literary Studies), H-Demog (Demographic History), H-Ethnic (Ethnic and Immigration History),

H-Film (Cinema History; Uses of the Media), and H-Frauen-L (Women and Gender in Early Modern Europe).

Association of College and Research Libraries, Western European Specialists Section. **WESS-SSH Electronic Discussion Group** [online]. Retrieved May 26, 1999. URL: <http://www.lib.virginia.edu/wess/discussion.html>

This discussion list is an outgrowth of the WESS Social Sciences and History discussion group that began in 1997. Its focus is on librarians and collection development, and it is useful as a way for library colleagues to ask each other those difficult subject specialist questions that no one else in their institution can deal with. Unfortunately, no archive is currently available.

Computer Professionals for Social Responsibility. **Community Memory–Discussion List on the History of Cyberspace** [online]. Retrieved May 26, 1999. URL: <http://memex.org/community-memory.html>

This discussion list is important because it is a primary source of information about computing history. As the original announcement said: "Many of the people involved in the creation of important technologies and organizations are on-line . . ." and, in fact, have joined the list. Often there is no other record, or, at least, no easily available record for the memories that are recorded here.

The topics on the list include a broad range of computing and network issues, including ethics, privacy concerns, hacking, and intellectual property rights. Topics can be as abstract as the origin of the term "vaporware." They can be as concrete as a debate over the earliest transistorized computer (see archive 4 in the URL above) or how to pronounce ENIAC (see archive 7). The June 4 to August 15 1996 posts are at the address above. Additional archives (up to the present) are available at the server site. URL: <http://maelstrom.stjohns.edu/archives/cyhist.html>

MULTIMEDIA COLLECTIONS

Goldman, J. (1996-8). **The Oyez Project** [online]. Northwestern University. Retrieved May 27, 1999. URL: <http://oyez.nwu.edu/>

This site contains full audio versions of major recent U.S. Supreme Court decisions, as well as the transcripts. It also has transcripts of earlier decisions back as far as 1935. Unfortunately, earlier court decisions often were not captured on a sound recording medium, so the full multi-media value is limited to very recent history: the oldest presently on the site is the 1975 *Eastland vs. U.S. Serviceman's Fund*, which dealt with the constitutional separation of powers.

Among the unusual features of this site is a virtual tour of the Supreme Court, which allows the visitor to click on an image of the court, to go into different rooms, and to get up-close views of objects like the Advocate's lectern. Other major sections include "cases" (which leads to the transcripts and oral decisions) and "justices" (which gives biographical, educational, and family information about each of the current justices).

Michigan State University. **Vincent Voice Library** [online]. Retrieved May 27, 1999. URL: <http://www.lib.msu.edu/digital/vincent/index.htm>

The Vincent Voice Library (VVL) is arguably the largest academic voice library in the country, with materials from the earliest days of recorded sound. Its digital offerings at present include short clips from presidential speeches, beginning with Grover Cleveland in 1892 and running through Woodrow Wilson. There are also clips of Big Ben ringing in the new century, Edwin Booth reading "Othello" in 1890 onto Edison cylinder, and an 1890 rendition of the sound of the bugle used in the charge of the Light Brigade.

The number of selections will grow substantially. The voices of all the presidents since Cleveland will soon be up, and the VVL is part of a major multimedia digitization project called the National Gallery of the Spoken Word, which hopes to digitize thousands of hours of sound, make it searchable, and accompany it with text and photographic materials. The sound files are currently available in both Real Audio and MP3 formats. Photographs accompany most of the current items.

Bailey, D. and Halsted, D. **Pluralism and Unity** [online]. Michigan State University. Retrieved: May 27, 1999. URL: Expo98 site: <http://www.expo98.msu.edu/>

This began as the official site for the U.S. Pavilion at Expo98. That might conjure up a misimpression of fluff. In fact the site is a scholarly exploration of key intellectual history issues from the period of heavy immigration to the U.S. at the start of the twentieth century.

Bailey and Halsted also used the opportunity to explore how to integrate multimedia sources into an academic discourse. All of the photographs, for example, are clickable and lead to pages that explain who or what is in the image. They provide background material and give related links. The site includes a dozen sound files (from the Vincent Voice Library). Each sound file comes with a photograph of the speaker, biographical information, and a transcript.

The major subdivisions of the site are: the Idea of Pluralism, the Idea of Internationalism, Race and Pluralism, Labor and Pluralism, Culture and Pluralism, Gender and Pluralism, and Pluralism and Unity.

Webcorp multimedia. *Richard Nixon Video Archive/Senator Joe McCarthy–A Multimedia Celebration/***The Webcorp Multimedia Archive/Historic Audio Archive** [online]. Retrieved May 27, 1999. URL: <http://www.webcorp.com/mccarthy/>

The Internet has relatively few historical video collections, since the digitization is expensive and film is fraught with copyright issues. This collection may have some copyright problems, too, but happily no one has closed it yet. Webcorp is a multimedia company that specializes in content-creation using Internet audio and video applications.

The Nixon archive has ten short videos that run from his "Republican cloth coat" and Checkers talks to the Watergate era "I am not a crook" and resignation speeches. The Joe McCarthy section has another 10 video and audio files, including one of his witch-hunting speeches and the speech by Joseph Welch, the Counsel for the army, that brought McCarthyism to an end.

The Multimedia Archive section is larger (over 25 items) and more eclectic. It mixes historical video and sound files of Neville Chamberlain and Hitler with contemporary recordings of Clinton and Gingrich. The captions explaining the clips in this section are particularly flip and leave out critical name and date provenance information. Some still photographs also accompany the items.

The Historic Audio Archive has some additional material, though there is duplication with items in the sound portion of the Multimedia Archive.

Galafilm. **War of 1812** [online]. Retrieved: May 27, 1999. URL: <http://galafilm.com/1812/e/index.html>

This Quebec-based site was created as a companion to Brian McKenna's four part documentary film on the war. Access can be rather slow, and it requires plug-ins like Shockwave and Quicktime. Text accompanies each of the six major sections: Introduction, People and Stories, Events and Locations, Background and Ideas, Exploration and Quiz, and Image Gallery and Catalogues. The site is particularly interesting as a self-conscious Web-based recreation of the kind of aural and visual history that has long been possible on television. Galafilm is a Canadian television production company specializing in documentaries, children's programming, and feature films.

The Image Gallery and Catalogs section offers a good selection of images. These include portraits of active participants, such as: John Quincy Adams (American), Henry Clay (American), Robert Barclay (British), Tecumseh (First Nations), and Laura Secord (Canadian). The site also has a large and excellent collection of historical maps relating to the war. Those interested in images of forts can also get an extensive set of images with some textual explanation about each.

PHOTOGRAPHIC IMAGE COLLECTIONS

Library of Congress. **American Memory** [online]. Retrieved May 25, 1999. URL: <http://memory.loc.gov/>

This collection is a prime resource for those interested in American history and could well fit several categories, including multimedia, since it has sound files as well as photographs, images, and searchable text. It represents an effort to publish digitally rare and generally otherwise unavailable source material on nineteenth century American history. The result appears eclectic because the intention is so far-reaching and comprehensive that the current offerings fill in only a few random squares of the whole canvas. In time this will change.

The site is organized by collection rather than topic. This comes in part from the way it has been built, both through internal departmental contributions and from the well-known Library of Congress/Ameritech awards, whose winners either contribute or make their materials available to the site. An important feature is the teaching guide, since school teachers rank as one of the prime target audiences.

National Library of Scotland. **Photographs of John Thompson at National Library of Scotland** [online]. Retrieved May 25, 1999. URL: <http://www.nls.ac.uk/digframe.htm>

The National Library of Scotland has begun a digitization program to make more of its rare materials available. The items currently on their Web site include an exhibit of the first Scottish books, photographs which John Thompson made in China a century ago, and a wide-ranging collection of notable acquisitions (letters by Sir Henry Raeburn, a catalog of sanitary appliances from 1893, the miniature Ellen Terry Shakespeare, and a collection of songs by Free Masons). The latter section generally has only a single image of the newly acquired item, though there are exceptions: some of the Raeburn letters are available in digital form.

The section on the first Scottish books has full color page by page images (as well as transcriptions) of the first nine books that Chepman & Myllar published in 1508. It also includes discussions of the provenance and binding and a short article on where they fit in the history of printing.

The John Thompson collection includes a fairly limited number of images, but they come with information about the title, date, and size, as well as a text explaining something of the context.

National Library of Canada (1998). **Cultivating Canadian Gardens: the History of Gardening in Canada** [online]. Retrieved May 25, 1999. URL: <http://www.nlc-bnc.ca/events/garden/>

This small exhibit is included less for its own importance as an information source, than as a representative of an increasing trend to put recent historical exhibitions online. Topics like the history of gardening in Canada are not ones which most libraries, even research libraries, necessarily buy. Yet gardening and many other similar topics of small exhibits at major libraries represent a valuable slice of social or political or intellectual history.

Gardening is a highly visual art. Since histories of gardening often have at least some plates illustrating past sites or techniques, the printed volumes tend to be expensive. This exhibit from the National Library of Canada has the virtue of being free. The exhibit has four major sections: Planting the Seeds, Cultivating the Garden, The Cultivators, and Reaping the Harvest. It also has a bibliography whose organization follows the section structure. Most of the illustrations come from cover art on the books cited, since this is really as much an exhibit about the printed works as it is about the history of gardening itself. Some of the covers consist of nothing more exciting than words and logos, but others have photographs or full color images.

SEARCHABLE TEXT COLLECTIONS

JSTOR (1999), **Journal Storage: Redefining Access to Scholarly Literature** [online]. Retrieved: May 27, 1999. URL: <http://www.jstor.org/>

JSTOR is not free, but it is a definite must-have for any library that supports serious historical research. JSTOR began in 1995 as a Mellon Foundation funded pilot project to convert full runs of the back issues of paper journals to digital format. It is now up to 117 titles in 15 subject areas ranging from African American Studies to Statistics. The largest collection is history journals (14 titles, 19 counting title changes).

JSTOR may seem as if it just reproduces works already in the stacks of every major research library. In fact, JSTOR's own difficulties in finding complete copies suggests that no library has a reliable run of any backfile. JSTOR adds value in other ways too. It has a search engine that runs against "dirty" (uncorrected) text from an OCR process. The search can use AND, OR, or two versions of NEAR (within 10 words and within 25), can be limited to, for example, all history journals, and can be further limited to searching either full text, author, title, or abstract. Printing is done either via PDF or JSTOR's own JPRINT software.

University of Bielefeld (1998). **Berlinischen Monatsschrift/Ältere Drucke aus dem Besitz der Bibliothek als digitale Rekonstruktionen** [online]. Retrieved May 27, 1999. URLs: (1) <http://www.ub.uni-bielefeld.de/diglib/Berlinische_Monatsschrift/> and (2) <http://www.ub.uni-bielefeld.de/diglib/rara.htm>

These items from the University of Bielefeld will interest German historians, especially the Berlinischen Monatsschrift, which dates from 1783 and offers excellent source material about early Berlin. Although only page images are presented, JSTOR style, Bielefeld has made the text searchable by title, author, and year.

The "old printing" offerings include a range of topics, such as incunabula, the history of political ideas, legal history, economic, social, and cultural history, and travel narratives. None of the categories has a large number of entries, but whole works are available and can be examined page by page. These works are not searchable. The books came from the 15th through 18th centuries.

Making of America [online]. Retrieved: May 28, 1999. URLs: (1) <http://www.umdl.umich.edu/moa/> and (2) <http://moa.cit.cornell.edu/MOA/MOA-JOURNALS2.html>

Making of America is a Mellon-funded collaborative project of the University of Michigan and Cornell. The Michigan site has 634,068 pages and 4038 volumes online. Cornell has nearly 900,000 pages from 114 books and 24 journals. The combined totals make Making of America one of the largest free full-text resources on the Internet.

The navigation is slightly different on each site, though both offer page images with a variety of size options (100%, 75%, 50%, thumbnail). Michigan also provides a PDF format, and Cornell will scale either one or two pages to the width of the browser window. For most contemporary monitors, every option below 75% is just another variation on illegibility, but as monitor resolution improves, this should change. Michigan provides full text search capabilities, with the ability to limit a search to books, journals, or both, and to set a year range.

Copyright law has constrained the contents of this project largely to nineteenth-century materials. Otherwise the subject range is so broad that neither site makes any attempt to organize the items by subject.

LINK-BASED BIBLIOGRAPHIES AND REVIEWS

H-Net:Reviews [online]. Retrieved May 26, 1999. URL: <http://www.h-net.msu.edu/reviews/>

Although the H-Net discussion lists have already been mentioned, the H-Net reviews deserve separate notice. These are scholarly reviews done by subject specialists, generally people with PhDs in a relevant field or advanced graduate students. All reviews are signed, and the reviewer's affiliation is listed. Most importantly, the H-Net reviews are often the first scholarly review of a work to appear, because there is no waiting for printers, mailers, or other parts of a journal issue. And the reviews are substantial. A typical one might run 3000 words.

The reviews can be sorted in a number of different ways: by author, by title, by date, by reviewer, by list name, by publisher, by ISBN, or by LC number. Each discussion list has its own review editor, so the topics for reviews are as broad as the lists themselves and tend to follow the interests of list members. Reviews are available from back as far as 1993.

The site has an online registry for qualified persons who would like to apply to become reviewers.

Haverford College (1999). **Medieval Feminist Index**. Retrieved May 28, 1999. URL: <http://www.haverford.edu/library/reference/mschaus/mfi/mfi.html>

The Medieval Feminist Index is an example of a very focused and effective Web-based index. It covers only "journal articles, book reviews, and essays in books about women, sexuality, and gender during the Middle Ages," and fills an important gap in access because the interdisciplinary nature of the topic means that no traditional index covers it all. This sort of index used to appear in typed, facsimile-style copies that were expensive to buy and invariably out of date. The Internet makes this kind of niche-market, low volume, high quality publishing relatively cheap and easy.

The index itself allows searches by author, title, or subject, and it returns basic bibliographic information: author, title, source, year of publication. An advanced search page increases the search fields substantially, with items like source, publication type, language, century, author's affiliation, and geographic area. Unfortunately, there are no pull-down menus for fields like century, but a clickable list of "correct vocabulary and proper forms" is nearby on the page.

University at Albany–State University of New York (1998). **Journal of Multimedia History**. Retrieved: May 28, 1999. <URL: http://www.albany.edu/jmmh/>

The intentions of this journal, as much as the contents themselves, represent the new way of thinking about and presenting historical information. Its territorial claim is substantial: "The *JMMH* is the first peer-reviewed electronic journal that presents, evaluates, and disseminates multimedia historical scholarship." The site is not comprehensive and not as up-to-date as it should be, since the last issue appeared in the fall of 1998. Since that was also the first issue, it could be a bad sign. Nonetheless, it is worth watching, not for what it is, but for what it may become.

One of the feature articles contains ordinary historical fare that might appear in any print journal. Another is actually a talk, which is available in full audio format (without any transcript). A third has the full audio version of a broadcast by Elijah Muhammad, which is a key source "document" for the historical analysis that follows. There are also three sections of reviews: (1) CD-ROM and DVD works, (2) Web sites, and (3) film and video reviews. The issue ends with short links to "noteworthy" Web sites.

MAPS, DATA, AND TRANSFORMATIVE SYSTEMS

University of Virginia, Fisher Library, Geospatial and Statistical Data Center. *United States Election Data: 1788-1900* [online]. Retrieved: May 28, 1999. URL: <http://fisher.lib.Virginia.EDU/elections/us.elections/>

This site represents a true transformative system which takes numerical data, in this case from ICPSR (Inter-university Consortium for Political and Social Research) datasets, and dynamically builds tables and maps. The results may seem somewhat plain compared to printed versions, but the number of software-enabled combinations and permutations transforms this site into the equivalent of a substantial historical atlas.

For the table data, the user can select either presidential, senatorial, congressional, or gubernatorial elections, and then further select a state and a year. Unfortunately, it is possible to select a year which is impossible for a particular state, such as the Alaska gubernatorial election of 1790–the software responds with a user-unfriendly blank screen. The site developers have offered some help, however: the date of statehood is listed beside each state.

Maps are available only for presidential elections since 1860. They give color-coded representations of who won in each state, and the percentage of the popular vote.

University of Virginia, Fisher Library, Geographic Information Center. **Interactive Resources** [online]. Retrieved: May 28, 1999. URL: <http://www.lib.virginia.edu/gic/interactive.html>

This is not, strictly speaking, an historical resource, but it is a tool many modern historians will want to use because it provides relatively quick, accurate maps where the user can choose any of a wide variety and combination of features, including railroads, rivers, religious institutions, hospitals, schools, parks, power lines, and more.

The site has four sections. One maps Virginia counties. Another does USGS maps for all 50 states (and the District of Columbia). A third helps to locate geographic names in Virginia, either through mapping from a name on a list or from clicking on a map. The fourth section is a search tool that shows where to find information about, for example, major cities in a state like Connecticut.

University of Texas at Austin, Perry-Castañeda Library Map Collection. **Historical Map Web Sites** [online]. Retrieved May 28, 1999. URL: <http://www.lib.utexas.edu/Libs/PCL/Map_collection/historical/history_main.html>

Good maps are hard to find, especially maps that are in the public domain and are easy to copy for a class or to include in an article. This site has a wealth of full-color historical maps from nineteenth- and early twentieth-century sources. The age of the originals means that they present mainly political boundaries and geographic features and ignore social and economic dimensions. These maps are just images rather than data-driven products of an interactive system. They are beautiful, but static and a bit slow to load.

The site divides the maps into nine sets by region: Africa, the Americas, Asia, Australia and the Pacific, Europe, the Middle East, polar regions and oceans, Russia and the former Soviet Republics, and the United States. The latter is an especially large category, with more than 100 historical city maps in addition to maps on topics like Indian lands, exploration, territorial growth, and even national parks.

A linked page leads to a long list of historical maps at other sites.

CONCLUSION

The obvious question about any discontinuity is "from what, to what?" The first part seems deceptively clear. History as written by academically trained professionals has been fundamentally document-based and book-dominated. Will that vanish? This seems unlikely. Documents in image form on the Web may soon cease to seem any different than the paper originals in archives. Even fully searchable documents may be so taken for granted in a few years that people think about them in the same way that they think about computer-based word processing packages as fancy typewriters. The real discontinuity may lie less in how people think about the sources themselves than in how historians integrate them into their own new works.

To readers increasingly accustomed to sound files, moving images, and non-linear structures, a printed 500-page tome may seem oddly specialized, purely academic, and as inaccessible as a highly mathematical economics article seems today to readers of the standard business press. This is not to suggest that Web-based history will be or should be less serious–only that its appeal may well be broader. The mass market lies with the new medium. Historians are learning to exploit it in order to keep up with the reading public.

WEBLIOGRAPHY

Association of College and Research Libraries, Western European Specialists Section. *WESS-SSH Electronic Discussion Group* [online]. URL: http://www.lib.virginia.edu/wess/discussion.html.

Bailey, D. and Halsted, D. *Pluralism and Unity* [online]. Michigan State University. Retrieved: May 27, 1999. URL: Expo98 site: http://www.expo98.msu.edu/.

Computer Professionals for Social Responsibility. *Community Memory–Discussion List on the History of Cyberspace* [online]. Retrieved May 26, 1999. URL: http://memex.org/community-memory.html.

Galafilm. *War of 1812* [online]. Retrieved: May 27, 1999. URL: http://galafilm.com/1812/e/index.html.

Haverford College (1999). *Medieval Feminist Index*. Retrieved May 28, 1999. URL: http://www.haverford.edu/library/reference/mschaus/mfi/mfi.html.

H-Net: Humanities and Social Sciences Online [online]. Retrieved May 26, 1999. URL: http://www.h-net.msu.edu/.

H-Net:Reviews [online]. Retrieved May 26, 1999. URL: http://www.h-net.msu.edu/reviews/.

Goldman, J. (1996-8). The Oyez Project [online]. Northwestern University. Retrieved May 27, 1999. URL: http://oyez.nwu.edu/.

Journal of Multimedia History (1998). University at Albany–State University of New York. Retrieved: May 28, 1999. URL: http://www.albany.edu/jmmh/.

JSTOR (1999), *Journal Storage: Redefining Access to Scholarly Literature* [online]. Retrieved: May 27, 1999. URL: http://www.jstor.org/.

Library of Congress. *American Memory* [online]. Retrieved May 25, 1999. URL: http://memory.loc.gov/.

Making of America [online]. Retrieved: May 28, 1999. URLs: (1) http://www.umdl.umich.edu/moa/ and (2) http://moa.cit.cornell.edu/MOA/MOA-JOURNALS2.html.

Michigan State University. *Vincent Voice Library* [online]. Retrieved May 27, 1999. URL: http://www.lib.msu.edu/digital/vincent/index.htm.

National Library of Canada (1998). *Cultivating Canadian Gardens: the History of Gardening in Canada* [online]. Retrieved May 25, 1999. URL: http://www.nlc-bnc.ca/events/garden/.

National Library of Scotland. *Photographs of John Thompson at National Library of Scotland* [online]. Retrieved May 25, 1999. URL: http://www.nls.ac.uk/digframe.htm.

University of Bielefeld (1998). *Berlinischen Monatsschrift/Ältere Drucke aus dem Besitz der Bibliothek als digitale Rekonstruktionen* [online]. Retrieved May 27, 1999. URLs: (1) http://www.ub.uni-bielefeld.de/diglib/Berlinische_Monatsschrift/ and (2) http://www.ub.uni-bielefeld.de/diglib/rara.htm.

University of Texas at Austin, Perry-Castañeda Library Map Collection. *Historical Map Web Sites* [online]. Retrieved May 28, 1999. URL: http://www.lib.utexas.edu/Libs/PCL/Map_collection/historical/history_main.html.

University of Virginia, Fisher Library, Geographic Information Center. *Interactive Resources* [online]. Retrieved: May 28, 1999. URL: http://www.lib.virginia.edu/gic/interactive.html.

University of Virginia, Fisher Library, Geospatial and Statistical Data Center. *United States Election Data: 1788-1900* [online]. Retrieved: May 28, 1999. URL: http://fisher.lib.Virginia.EDU/elections/us.elections/.

Webcorp multimedia. Richard Nixon Video Archive/Senator Joe McCarthy–A Multimedia Celebration/The Webcorp Multimedia Archive/Historic Audio Archive [online]. Retrieved May 27, 1999. URL: http://webcorp.com/mccarthy/.

REFERENCE

Foucault, Michel, *The Order of Things: an Archaeology of the Human Sciences*. NY: Vintage, 1973 (©1970).

Legal Information on the Internet

Yvonne J. Chandler

SUMMARY. This article reviews legal and government information resources that are available on the Internet. Information technology of the 21st century has revolutionized the way much of this information is disseminated by the judiciary, legislature, and governmental agencies and the way that it may be accessed by all citizens and information users. Primary and secondary resources of Anglo-American law are identified and evaluated. The primary sources of law that are made available through this technology are: judicial and administrative decisions or case reports; federal, state, and municipal government laws or ordinances; rules and regulations; presidential documents; agency serials and reports; and other governmental information at both the federal and state government levels. Secondary sources, including guides and directories, search engines, dictionaries, encyclopedias, directories, law reviews, and sources of topical law information, are also discussed. These resources are developed and maintained by government departments and agencies, law schools and

Yvonne J. Chandler is the author of the *Neal Schuman Guide to Legal and Regulatory Information on the Internet*. She has a PhD in Information Studies from the University of Michigan School of Information and an MSLS from Atlanta University. She is Associate Professor at the University of North Texas School of Library and Information Sciences. Dr. Chandler teaches in the areas of information access and retrieval, legal information access and retrieval, government information access and services, social sciences information access and retrieval, and law library management. She has written and spoken on a range of topics including library and information science education, competencies for law librarianship, Internet resources for educators, children and public librarians, Internet resources for business executives, multi-cultural diversity in librarianship, and using technology to teach legal research.

[Haworth co-indexing entry note]: "Legal Information on the Internet." Chandler, Yvonne J. Co-published simultaneously in *Journal of Library Administration* (The Haworth Information Press, an imprint of The Haworth Press, Inc.) Vol. 30, No. 1/2, 2000, pp. 157-207; and: *Academic Research on the Internet: Options for Scholars & Libraries* (ed: Helen Laurence, and William Miller) The Haworth Information Press, an imprint of The Haworth Press, Inc., 2000, pp. 157-207. Single or multiple copies of this article are available for a fee from The Haworth Document Delivery Service [1-800-342-9678, 9:00 a.m. - 5:00 p.m. (EST). E-mail address: getinfo@haworthpressinc.com].

other educational institutions, professional associations, and commercial organizations. *[Article copies available for a fee from The Haworth Document Delivery Service: 1-800-342-9678. E-mail address: <getinfo@haworthpressinc. com> Website: <http://www.HaworthPress.com>]*

KEYWORDS. Law, legal resources, Internet research in, Internet resources in, online research in, online resources in

INTRODUCTION TO LEGAL INFORMATION IN THE 21ST CENTURY

The primary sources of Anglo-American law are created and produced by governmental institutions at the federal, state, and municipal levels. At all governmental levels, legal information is produced by the branches of government that are empowered to produce and disseminate this information to citizens. Legal information includes judicial rulings or administrative decisions, legislation that is signed into laws or municipal ordinances, rules and regulations, presidential documents, and agency serials or reports that must be followed by all citizens and government agencies.

The specialized nature, organizational system, and language of legal and government information cause some hesitation and difficulty for those people not trained in legal research. In addition to these factors, the use of legal and government resources is problematic for a number of other reasons:

1. Legal and government information is constantly growing as cases are continuously being decided and pieces of legislation, rules, or regulations are being passed or revised.
2. Users must consider sets of resources rather than individual volumes as is characteristic of traditional information tools.
3. Traditional catalogs, indexes, databases, and other finding aids used in libraries for other subject disciplines are not used to identify legal and government information resources.
4. Bibliographic citations used to find information resources are different for legal and government publications than for other subject disciplines and are unique for each type of resource.[1]

Resources to identify, access, retrieve, and publish legal and government information are available in print, micromedia, and computer-assisted electronic database formats. Information technology of the 21st century has revolutionized the way much of this information is disseminated by the judiciary, legislature, and administrative agencies and the way that it may be accessed by all citizens and information users. Users no longer need specialized resources or have to wait for weeks or even months to access many legal and government information resources. The number of legal and government information resources that are published or made available on the Internet is continuing to grow at a phenomenal rate.

Federal, state, and local government departments and agencies are committing to electronic dissemination of the primary sources of law, which include case decisions, legislation, laws, reports, rules, and regulations via the Internet to disseminate this information to the public. Secondary sources of the law are also digitally published on the Internet. These resources include directories of legal professionals and experts, encyclopedias, dictionaries, legal forms, treatises, citation manuals, legal newspapers, and law reviews or journals. Law schools, courts, government agencies, and law firms also produce, in-house, a variety of legal information resources, special reports, opinion letters, articles, guidebooks, or legal memoranda available through the Internet. Electronically published reports or studies by law school students, faculty, libraries, attorneys, or other participants in the legal process provide valuable information on the Internet.

GUIDES AND DIRECTORIES TO LEGAL AND GOVERNMENT INTERNET RESOURCES

Guides, specialized indexes, or directories for government and regulatory information on the Internet include Web sites or pages created by law schools and universities, law firms, and government courts, departments, or agencies. Because of the specialized language, arrangement, and diversity of sites on which legal and government information are published, these compendia provide an important link in using these resources on the Internet. One of the first sites to provide evaluation of Web sites for users was the **Argus Clearinghouse**, which provides a central access point for value-added topical guides that identify, describe, and evaluate Internet-based information resources. URL: <http://www.clearinghouse.net/>. The **Government and Law Page** includes guides on topics pertaining to government, law, and intellectual property, military, politics, elections, and the rulings of nations, states, and provinces, municipalities, and other political regions. URL: <http://www.clearinghouse.net/cgibin/chadmin/viewcat/Government___Law?kywd++>. Subject guides cover legal and government topics, including patents, copyright, legal resources, congressional sources, and international law.

Part of the World Wide Web Consortium and selected as one of the top fifty legal research Web sites by *Law Office Computing*, the **World Wide Web Virtual Law Library** is maintained by the Indiana University School of Law. URL: <http://www.law.indiana.edu/law/vlib/lawindex.html>. The site is a collection of subject-related Web sites maintained by institutions throughout the world. There is a searchable index to the site, and a directory listing allows users to browse the list of linked sites. There is also a list of sites organized by legal information topic, such as administrative law, constitutional law, family law, and foreign or international law.

The **Legal Information Institute at Cornell University School of Law (LII)** was the first law site developed on the Internet and thus is the grand-daddy of legal and government information sites. URLs: <http://lii.law.cornell.edu/> or <http://www.law.cornell.edu:80/>. The development of this site was one of the pioneering experiments in the delivery of legal information via the Internet when it began operating in 1992. In addition to core collections of federal law, New York state legal resources are accessible or downloadable in several formats. There are two searchable indexes to the Web site: **Materials Organized by Topic** and **Materials Organized by Source of Law**. URL: <http://www.law.cornell.edu:80/topical.html> and URL: <http://www.law.cornell.edu:80/source.html>.

The **Washlaw WWW Washburn University School of Law** is recognized as one of the best sites on the Internet for legal and government information. There is a hypertext matrix to all resources and a searchable index to the entire site. URL: <http://www.washlaw.edu/>. **REFLAW Virtual Law Library Reference Desk WWW** provides a directory of links to Web sites for federal and state government offices, legislation, law journals and publishers, legal directories, and other reference material on the Internet. URL: <http://www.washlaw.edu/reflaw/>. **Hieros Gamos (HG) The Comprehensive Legal and**

Government Portal, maintained and operated by Lex Mundi, a consortium of law firms, provides access to virtually all online and many offline published legal information resources. URL: <http://www.hg.org/>. The recently redesigned site includes directories containing information on foreign governments, U. S. federal and state governments, over 6,000 legal organizations, law schools and students, law firms, continuing legal education programs, employment and job listings, practice areas, discussion groups, doing business guides, and electronic law journals and newsletters.

The **Guide to Law Online**, prepared by the Law Library of Congress for the Global Legal Information Network (GLIN), is an annotated hypertext guide to free, online sources of information on government and law worldwide. URL: <http://lcweb2.loc.gov/glin/worldlaw.html>. It includes links to legal information sites available for every country. Each site is evaluated by GLIN for completeness, accuracy, and authenticity of the legal information. There are three geographical guides to United States and international resources. **GUIDE: United States**–URL: <http://lcweb2.loc.gov/glin/us.html>, **GUIDE: Nations of the World**–URL: <http://lcweb2.loc.gov/glin/xnation.html>, and **GUIDE: Multinational & International Legal Sources**–URL: <http://lcweb2.loc.gov/glin/xmulti.html>. The **Library of Congress** has also developed a collection of guides to Internet resources called the **Browse Topical Guides–Government Resources by Category**. URL: <http://lcweb.loc.gov/global/subject.html>. Five guides are available to identify federal and state legal or government information resources.[2]

The **U.S. Government Printing Office** (GPO) prints, binds, and distributes publications of Congress, executive branch departments and agencies, and the judicial branch. URLs: <http://www.access.gpo.gov> or <http://www.gpo.gov>. **GPO Access** from the GPO provides online access to a number of important executive, legislative, judicial, and regulatory information sources. URL: <http://www.access.gpo.gov/su_docs/index.html>. It was created after passage of the Government Printing Office Electronic Information Access Enhancement Act of 1993.[3] This act called for the GPO to develop an electronic directory of federal information, to operate an electronic storage facility for online access to federal information, to disseminate government information products online, to provide a system of online access to major government publications, and to provide online access to depository libraries. Titles accessible on **GPO Access** include the *Congressional Record, U.S. Government Manual, U.S. Reports, Code of Federal Regulations*, and *U.S. Code*. Users can search these databases one at a time or search across multiple databases from the **Connect to Databases Online via GPO Access** page. URL: <http://www.access. gpo.gov/su_docs/db2.html>. The GPO also provides directories called "**Finding Aids**" to resources from the **Legislative, Executive**, and **Judicial** branches of government and the **regulatory agencies**. Legislative–URL: <http://www.access.gpo.gov/su_docs/legislative.html>, Executive–URL: <http://www.access.gpo.gov/su_docs/executive.html>, Judicial–URL: <http://www.access.gpo.gov/su_docs/judicial.html>, and Regulatory Agencies–URL: <http://www.access.gpo.gov/su_docs/regulatory. html>. **GPO Access** is available from 22 Federal Depository Library Gateway and SWAIS sites that are authorized by the GPO to encourage greater use and accessibility.

Part of **GPO Access**, the **Core Documents of U.S. Democracy** electronic collection provides direct online access to a core group of current and historical federal government documents and information sources through the **GPO Access** Web site. URL: <http://www.access. gpo.gov/su_docs/dpos/coredocs.html>. This collection was created to provide American citizens with direct, free, permanent, and public online access via the **GPO Access** service to basic government documents that define democratic society. Current government documents linked to this page include the *Weekly Compilation of Presidential Documents,* Census *Catalog and Guide, Statistical Abstract*, and the *U.S. Government Manual*. Historical documents on this page include the *Bill of Rights* and *U.S. Constitution, Declaration of Independence, Gettysburg Address,* and the *Federalist Papers.*

FindLaw WebGuide of Legal Information and Web Sites is a comprehensive directory of legal resources with links to primary legal sources, government resources, Web sites, publications, software, law reviews, mailing lists, Usenet discussion groups, and related FindLaw pages. URL: <http://www.findlaw.com/>. The **Internet Legal Research Guide** is a comprehensive categorized index to more than 4000 Web sites from 238 nations and territories concerning law and the legal profession. URL: <http://www.ilrg.com/>. Sites are selected and evaluated by the editors on two principles: the extent to which the resource is unique and the relative value of the information it provides. While international material is included, the site emphasizes U.S. legal and government information. The **United States Federal Government Sites** page provides a directory to government agencies. URL: <http://www.ilrg.com/gov/us.html>. The **American Government Index** analyzes information for each state. URL: <http://www. ilrg.com/gov.html>.

Two major and well known legal and government information resources are making changes in their structure and accessibility. The **Center for Information Law and Policy (CILP)** was a joint effort between the Villanova University School of Law and the Illinois Institute of Technology/Chicago-Kent College of Law. URL: <http://www. cilp.org/>. This site began as a research institute and developed sources of legal information from governmental sources, including courts and agencies. Some members of the developing team of the Center have moved to other institutions, and the joint initiative ended in September, 1999. The responsibility for continuing portions of the Center's work and housing its archives will be administered directly by the library staff of both law schools. The Center produced some well known publications, such as the Federal Web Locator, which will continue to be maintained by Chicago-Kent. URL: <http://www. infoctr.edu/fwl/>. The **Federal Court Locator** and **Tax Master–the Tax Law Locator** will be housed at Villanova. URL: <http://vls. law.vill.edu/Locator/fedcourt.html> and URL: <http://vls.law.vill.edu/prof/maule/taxmaster/taxhome.htm>. Both institutions are developing new directories to these resources, such as the **Internet Legal Research Compass** from Villanova. URL: <http://vls.law.vill.edu/compass/>. Chicago-Kent is providing access to many of the Center's publications from its **Legal Resources** page. URL: <http://www.kentlaw.edu/legal_resources/>. As of this publication, the Center's **U.S. Government** page was still providing links to six sites providing identification and access to federal case law, regulations, and legislation. URL: <http://www.cilp.org/newhome/mainpages/usgovtam.html>. The **Law Library** page includes a directory of information from CILP publications, collections, and links to Internet sites covering areas of information law, including intellectual property, access rights, dissemination policy, and the use of information technology. URL: <http://www. cilp.org/vcilp/vcilplibam.html>.

Another guide to legal and government information that is currently undergoing major changes is the **U.S. House of Representatives Internet Law Library**, which was developed and maintained by the

House Information Resources and the Office of the Law Revision Counsel. URL: <http://law.house.gov/>. The directory contains over 1,600 links to law resources on the Internet, including federal and state laws, treaties and international law in fulltext. Maintenance of the existing Internet Law Library was discontinued on May 28, 1999. The **U.S. Code Database** will continue to be available at this site after the official closing. URL: <http://uscode.house.gov/>. Law schools, professional associations, government agencies and commercial companies have agreed to host and administer the site. Thirteen institutions and firms have made the Internet Law Library available to the public through the Internet. These institutions and firms include **Etext Archives**–URL: <http://law.etext.org/>, **LawGuru.com**–URL: <http://www.lawguru.com/ilawlib/index.html>, '**Lectric Law Library**–URL: <http://www.lectlaw.com/inll/1.htm>, and the **Illinois Institute of Technology Information Center**–URL: <http://www.infoctr.edu/ill>. As of this publication, 20 other firms, professional associations, and institutions have received copies of the Internet Law Library, but have not yet made the site available on the Internet.

LEGAL SEARCH ENGINES

Legal information search engines provide legal researchers or ordinary citizens with better precision when searching for legal resources or documents than is available using general information indexes or search engines such as Yahoo or AltaVista. There are currently over 100 legal indexes or search engines that provide databases of resources in exclusively legal information domains rather than the entire Internet. **LawCrawler** uses intelligent agents combined with the AltaVista search engine and database and other legal code and case law databases to retrieve information related to the information needs of legal professionals. URL: <http://www.lawcrawler.com/>. **LawCrawler** provides legal researchers with precision by enabling them to focus their searches on sites with legal information and within specific domains. **LawCrawler** is accessible from the **FindLaw Web Guide of Legal Information and Web Sites on the WWW**. URL: <http://www.findlaw.com/>. **LawCrawler** provides for searching of the entire FindLaw Web site, or queries can be limited to specific FindLaw databases. The **LawCrawler** search engine also includes special search options for particular legal resources at the international and national levels. **LawCrawler International** searches for legal information within individual country domains. URL: <http://web.lawcrawler.com/>. **LawCrawler USA** provides a searchable index for federal government departments, statutes, regulations and court decisions. URL: <http://lawcrawler.findlaw.com/federal.html>. There are also search options for researching state government resources.

Some Web sites provide multiple search engines or indexes to legal resources from one site. These sites help speed research by arranging all of the indexes into a uniform meta-index. One of the multiple indexes or catalog Web sites that provides one gateway to all legal and government indexes is **CataLaw**, which was designed to be a "catalog of catalogs" of law on the Internet. URL: <http://www.catalaw.com/>. The index is divided into three sections that provide hyperlinks to sub pages within all other indexes on a legal subject. The **CataLaw–Usual Suspects** page provides a list of major catalogs of law and government organized geographically. URL: <http://www.catalaw.com/info/suspects.shtml>. **Regional Law** includes links to catalogs about regional or international government, courts, and legislation. URLs: <http://www.catalaw.com/region/Region.shtml> or <http://www.catalaw.com/info/map.shtml#Region>. **Legal Topics** includes all catalogs that are classified by a legal topic. URL: <http://www.catalaw.com/topics/Topics.shtml>. **Extra Information** provides catalogs of law-related resources, such as legal directories, professional organizations, employment resources, education resources, and support services. URL: <http://www.catalaw.com/extra/Extra.shtml>.

Law Guru–Legal Research Page searches can be conducted on more than 435 legal search engines, resources, and tools for many of the legal and government research resources across the Web. URL: <http://www.lawguru.com/search/lawsearch.html>. The "Multiple Resource Research Tool" allows searches to be conducted on different legal resources from one interface and search box and offers "parallel searching" capability. The drop-down menu search form lists the resources, search engines, and tools in alphabetical order and includes federal and state cases, statutes, legislative bills, and administrative regulations. The **Law.Com** search engine offers a meta-index of 400 legal search engines, databases, and tools. URL: <http://www.legal.com> or URL: <http://legal.com>. The **Georgia State University Meta-Index for U.S. Legal Research** incorporates multiple legal search tools on the internet. URL: <http://gsulaw.gsu.edu/metaindex/>. The

Georgia State Meta-Index provides access to search engines for judicial opinions from FindLaw, congressional legislation, statutes, federal regulations, law reviews, and professional directories.

LawRunner is a feature of the **Internet Legal Resource Guide**. URL: <http://www.lawrunner.com/>. The search engine offers predefined intelligent agents to facilitate usage of the most complex query parameters built into the AltaVista search engine as well as select legal databases. With Law Runner, users can limit searches from the Alta-Vista database to a particular jurisdiction or to Web sites with a specific domain suffix. The **LawRunner American State Index** allows users to limit searches to the jurisdictions of any of the fifty United States. URL: <http://www.ilrg.com/gov.html>. The LawRunner **Global Index** provides a search mechanism for legal and government information from 238 jurisdictions worldwide. URL: <http://www.ilrg.com/nations/>. The **Law Engine** offers access to online law sources in an easy, single-page format organized into a directory listing of federal and state cases, courts, legal newspapers and law reviews, reference sources, government agencies, legal associations, law school and firm directories, forms, and other sites or resources concerning special areas or topics of the law. URL: <http://www.fastsearch.com/law/index.html>.

A comprehensive search engine to retrieve government federal and state sites around the country is the Center for Intelligent Information Retrieval/U.S. Business Advisor **GOVBOT Database of Government Web Sites (GOVBOT)**. URL: <http://ciir2.cs.umass.edu/Govbot/>. This software and database was developed by The Center for Intelligent Information Retrieval (CIIR) at the University of Massachusetts at Amherst. The CIIR **GOVBOT** has gathered 1,204,943 Web pages from U.S. Government and Military sites around the country.

JUDICIAL BRANCH INFORMATION SOURCES: FEDERAL AND STATE CASE LAW

The major focus of American law is case law, the statement of decisions of a court made in settlement of a litigated civil or criminal case. The courts interpret the laws and regulations made by the legislative and executive branches. The judicial system in this country is divided into federal and state levels. The **Federal Judiciary Home Page** published by the Administrative Office of the Courts provides a clearinghouse for information from and about the judicial branch. URL: <http://www.uscourts.gov/>. Historical and explanatory information about the federal court systems, the judicial branch and its judges, and press releases are provided. The site includes the **Directory of Electronic Public Access Services to Automated Information in the United States Federal Courts**. URL: <http://pacer.psc.uscourts. gov/pubaccess.html>. The publication, **Third Branch–The Newsletter of the Federal Courts**, is updated monthly and includes back issues since February 1995. URL: <http://www.uscourts.gov/ttb/index. html>. For detailed explanatory information about the federal judicial system, **Understanding the Federal Courts** gives a description and overview of court operations and a directory of the organization and administration of the courts. URL: <http://www.uscourts.gov/ understanding_ courts/899_toc.htm>. The West Group also provides an overview of the U.S. court system in **LawOffice.Com** with excerpts of an article from West's publication, *Encyclopedia of American Law.* URL: <http://lawoffice.com/>. The resource *Overview of US Courts* provides information about the **Federal Courts** and **State Courts**. URL: <http://www.lawoffice.com/tools/usfed.htm> and URL: <http://www.lawoffice.com/tools/usstate.htm>.

Federal and State Opinions

The written opinions of the federal and state courts are accessible via the Internet from a number of government, academic, and commercial sites. One important impact of the Internet is an increase in the number of court decisions made accessible as courts and other sites can electronically publish the decisions from these courts directly to the Internet. Prior to the publication of legal cases on the Internet, the most current case law was only available via the commercial computerized databases of LEXIS and WESTLAW. The cost of these databases and access to the systems are cost prohibitive as well as inaccessible to many users of legal information.

The availability of current case law over the Internet is increasing daily, but these databases do not offer comprehensive or archival coverage of all decisions from the courts. On average, most databases only offer access to decisions from the past five years. The exception to the problem of limited availability and comprehensiveness of case law databases is the U.S. Supreme Court, which now has decisions online dating back to 1937 and collections of selected historical opinions. Federal appellate court decisions are available for all circuits because a consortium of law schools provides free access to slip opinions through each school's Web site. Court information and case law is now available for most states and many local court jurisdictions.

Federal Case Law Information Resources

The United States judicial system is composed of three types of courts at the federal and state government levels: trial courts, appellate courts, and supreme courts. In the federal court system, the trial courts are the District Courts, the appellate courts are termed the Courts of Appeals; and the highest court is the U.S. Supreme Court. A number of Internet sites offer access to all of the federal cases. While there are numerous sites on the Internet that provide access to these court decisions, a few sites have the most accessible and explanatory organizational scheme and structure for use. **American Law Sources On-Line (ALSO)–United States Government–Law Page** includes searchable indexes for Supreme Court and Court of Appeals decisions. URL: <http://www.lawsource.com/also/usa.cgi?us1>. Cases can be retrieved by party name, citation, and keyword. Users can also browse the cases by year and volume. The site also provides a hypertext listing of other sites for federal case law, court rules, and newsgroups.

Three sites provide links to federal opinions with a graphical map of the country divided by the thirteen circuit courts and the Supreme Court which allows users to retrieve the desired court's home page or opinion site. The **Federal Court Locator** at the **Villanova University School of Law** serves as a gateway to Supreme Court, circuit court, and district court decisions. URL: <http://vls.law.vill.edu/Locator/fedcourt.html>. The **Federal Court Opinions–Georgetown University Legal Explorer,** created by the Georgetown University Law Library, was designed as a home page for the federal court system on the Internet. URL: <http://www.ll.georgetown.edu:80/Fed-Ct/>. The page provides links to information concerning the federal judiciary, including slip opinions from both the Supreme Court and the appellate courts. The **U.S. Federal Courts Finder from the Emory University Law School** includes opinions from the U.S. Court of Appeals for the Armed Forces and U.S. Court of Federal Claims opinions. URL: <http://www.law.emory.edu/FEDCTS>.

The **Findlaw Case Law Index** provides a well organized and comprehensive listing of links to federal and state opinion law sites. URL:

<http://www.findlaw.com/casecode/>. The search engine allows users to select databases to search courts individually or at the same time. **The Courthouse** produced by Law Journal Extra provides searchable databases and links to decisions for federal and state courts. URL: <http://www.ljx.com/courthouse/>. The **U.S. Federal Courts** page offers two searchable databases for retrieving case law. URL: <http://www.ljextra.com/courthouse/feddec.html>. **Search The Federal Courts** is a natural language search engine. URL: <http://search.ljx.com/>. **Search All Circuit Courts** is a keyword searchable database that allows users to retrieve cases from the circuit courts. URL: <http://www.ljextra.com/cgibin/cir>. **Washlaw Web–Federal Case Law** is one of the most comprehensive database indexes. URL: <http://www.washlaw.edu/searchlaw.html#FederalCaselaw>. The **Washlaw Query Interface to the Federal Court Opinions Broker** offers full text searching for all federal case law that exists on the Internet. URL: <http://cat.wuacc.edu/Harvest/brokers/fed/query.html>. The site also provides links to the federal court rules, court bulletin boards, and biographies of justices.

Subscription Databases

Subscription databases to case law are also accessible via the Internet. These databases provide more sophisticated and authoritative search mechanisms and more comprehensive databases. *LEXIS* and *WESTLAW* are now accessible for subscribers via the Internet. **Law Office Information Systems (LOIS)** (subscription required) publishes a subscription database of federal electronic primary law materials. URL: <http://www.pita.com>. The databases, called libraries, cover federal and state courts. There is a searchable database for users to search one or multiple libraries by citation, docket number, date of decisions, party names, or keywords. **VersusLaw** is a subscription database produced by Timeline Publishing that offers access to databases of federal and state case law. URL: <http://www.versuslaw.com>. Retrieval of cases is provided by the VersusLaw search engine, Agent V, which can search multiple databases using keywords or concepts.

Supreme Court Decisions

United States Supreme Court decisions are published in print and electronic format from the earliest rulings made in 1790. The published print reporters are the *U.S. Reports,* officially published by the GPO, *Supreme Court Reporter,* published by West Group, and *U.S. Supreme Court Reports Lawyers Edition,* published by Lexis Law Publishing. The cases are also published in looseleaf reporters and on both major legal research database systems, *LEXIS* and *WESTLAW.*

One of the potential impacts of the Internet was to increase the number of decisions accessible to users who do not have access to the fee-based legal databases. This potential has been achieved with the digital publication of federal and state case law and, most successfully, with the decisions from the Supreme Court. Opinions of the Court are available on the Internet in a number of Web sites. The problem of inequity of access to case law was addressed by the Court in 1990 with Project Hermes. Through a collaboration of private publishers, academic institutions, and the federal government, this project was designed to experiment with disseminating opinions electronically and to provide public access via Internet technology. The Hermes archive is maintained at Case Western Reserve University, and at the LII, through streamed conversion, all of the decisions are now available in HTML.[4]

In 1996, Supreme Court decisions from 1937 to 1975 were made available on the Internet by the Office of Information and Regulatory Affairs of the Office of Management and Budget. These opinions were created by the U.S. Air Force's Federal Legal Information Through Electronics (FLITE) project, conducted during the seventies to computerize the historic file of decisions.[5] The FLITE database offers a search engine and access to a database of over 7400 Supreme Court opinions. The addition of the FLITE database of opinions expanded the comprehensiveness and depth of the Supreme Court case law provided via the Internet, but with the exception of some historic decisions, the majority of earlier opinions of the Court are not accessible via this technology.

The first major site to provide Internet access to Supreme Court decisions was the **Legal Information Institute (LII)–Supreme Court Collection**, sponsored by Cornell University School of Law. URL: <http://supct.law.cornell.edu/supct/>. The **Supreme Court Collection** includes a searchable database of nearly all opinions of the court issued from May 1990 to the present. Two pages on this site–the **Historic Supreme Court Decisions by Party Name** and **Selected Historic Decisions of the US Supreme Court**–contain a searchable collection of more than 580 important decisions decided before 1990. URLs: <http://www.law.cornell.edu/supct/cases/name.htm>, <http://supct.law.cornell.edu/supct/cases/name.htm>, or <http://supct.law.cornell.edu/supct/cases/historic.htm>.

Databases providing Supreme Court decisions are available from the GPO on the **GPO Access Judicial Branch Resources** page. URL: <http://www.access.gpo.gov/su_docs/judicial.html>. This page from GPO Access provides links to two databases of Supreme Court opinions. The **Search Supreme Court Decisions 1937-1975** is a database of the FLITE opinions that is searchable by case name, by case or docket number, and full text. URL: <http://www.access.gpo.gov/su_docs/supcrt/index.html>. Current case decisions since 1992 are retrievable from the **Federal Bulletin Board Online via GPO Access–Supreme Court Opinions** Web page which includes decisions released and transmitted by the Court from the Hermes Project. URL: <http://fedbbs.access.gpo.gov/court01.htm>.

There are a number of other sites that maintain collections of current and historic decisions of the Supreme Court. **FindLaw** provides a database of Supreme Court decisions since 1893 or Volume 150 of the *US Reports* to the present that can be searched by citation, case name, and volume as well as browsed by volume number and year. URLs: <http://www.findlaw.com/casecode/supreme.html> or <http://www.unilegal.com/ussc.htm>. **USSC+ Online** from Infosynthesis, Inc. provides full coverage of Supreme Court decisions from 1945 to the present and more than 450 older cases dating back to 1793. URL: <http://www.usscplus.com/>. The site provides a searchable research database option "**Conduct Research**" that allows viewers to search the full database by words and phrases using boolean logic, by subject, by citation, by parties or by case name, and by docket number. The full text of the retrieved cases and a list of all cases citing that case is provided. The opinions can be viewed and downloaded for a subscription fee. The **View Current Term Cases Decisions** page provides a listing of recent cases handed down by the Court that can be viewed in **reverse-chronological order**–URL: <http://www.usscplus.com/current/> or **alphabetical order**–URL <http://www.usscplus.com/current/cases_alpha.htm>.

The Oyez Project (formerly called **Oyez, Oyez, Oyez**) offers an innovative use of technology to provide access to Supreme Court information with its U.S. Supreme Court Multimedia Database from

Northwestern University. URL: <http://oyez.nwu.edu/>. This project provides abstracts, audio of oral arguments, and other materials for leading cases in constitutional law decided by the Court. **Oyez** also includes panoramic images of the Supreme Court Building and offers a virtual tour of the courthouse. URL: <http://court.itservices.nwu. edu/oyez/tour/>. Two other sites provide searchable access to the FLITE database of opinions. **FedWorld** sponsored by the National Technical Information Service provides access to this Supreme Court decisions database. URL: <http://www.fedworld.gov/supcourt/index. htm>. FLITE decisions are also accessible from the **U.S. Supreme Court Page in the Federal Court Locator at Villanova University**. URL: <http://vls.law.vill.edu/Locator/fedcourt.html>.

Supreme Court and Justice Information

Information about the history, procedures, and practices of the Supreme Court and biographies of the justices can be found in a World Wide Web version of the information booklet written by the Court, The **United States Supreme Court** at the USSCPlus site developed by InfoSynthesis, Inc. URL: <http://www.usscplus.com/info/>. The **Oyez Project** includes a comprehensive database of information about current and past judges on the **Justices Page**. URL: <http://oyez. nwu.edu/justices/justices.cgi>. This page provides extensive background, educational, judicial career, and biographical information for each justice in alphabetical order or in chronological order of appointment. Biographical information about the justices of the current court is also published on the **Supreme Court Justices Web Page** on the **LII** site and from **USSC Plus–About The Court**. URL: <http://www. law.cornell.edu/supct/justices/fullcourt.html> and URL: <http://www. usscplus.com/info/index.htm>.

Lower Federal Courts–Federal Court of Appeals, District Court, and Other Courts

There are thirteen federal circuit courts of appeal, including eleven circuit courts geographically dispersed across the country, the District of Columbia Circuit, and the Federal Circuit. These circuit court decisions are published in the sole case reporter for these courts, the *Federal Reporter,* published by the West Group. The **Courts Publish-**

ing Project from the **Emory University School of Law** publishes the decisions for a number of circuit courts. URL: <http://www.law. emory.edu>. This project began with the distribution of cases from the Eleventh Circuit Court of Appeals in 1994. Today each court has at least one Web site where the decisions of the court are published on the Internet. Appendix I provides a listing of the federal courts, dates of coverage, and the URL for each court. Web sites for each court can be accessed from one of the federal court multi-site directories, such as the **Federal Court Locator**. URL: <http://vls.law.vill.edu/Locator/ fedcourt.html>. The **Federal Circuit Court Opinions** page includes a searchable page for each circuit on the FindLaw database as well as directory listings to links for the specific Web site for each court. URL: <http://WWW.FINDLAW.COM/casecode/courts/index.html>.

Federal District Court Case Law

The opinions of the district courts that hear and adjudicate cases in 94 district courts in the fifty states, District of Columbia, and all U.S. territories are published in the print resource, *Federal Supplement* by the West Group. While digital publication of circuit court opinions has been implemented, the majority of federal district courts do not publish their decisions on the Internet. These courts do provide Web sites where other court information is available. A small number of district courts are providing their decisions as well. The **U.S. District Court for the Northern District of Illinois** publishes recent opinions and orders that have been designated for posting on the Web page. URL: <http://www.ilnd.uscourts.gov/Opinions/opinlist.htm>. Decisions from the **U.S. District Court for the Northern District of Mississippi** are digitally published and maintained by the University of Mississippi School of Law Library. URL: <http://home.olemiss.edu/~llibcoll/ ndms/>. The site provides case law since October 1994. Opinions from the **U.S. District Court of South Carolina** are published by the University of South Carolina Law Center Coleman Karesh Law Library from January 1997 to the present. URL: <http://www.law.sc. edu/dsc/DSC.HTM>.

Administrative and Agency Decisions

Agencies engage in "order making" as well as "rule making." A number of federal agencies exercise quasijudicial power in determining cases and questions arising under their statutory and regulatory powers. More than two dozen federal agencies, such as the regulatory commissions, publish official reports of their administrative decisions, reports, letter rulings, orders, and advisory opinions. These rulings and decisions are also subject to review and appeal by the courts and are published in official GPO documents. Some decisions are printed in both the official government editions as well as through looseleaf services and topical law reporters, such as *Environment Law Reporter, Standard Federal Tax Reporter*, or *Labor Relations Reporter*. A large number of agency decisions are available online on *WESTLAW* and *LEXIS*. Many agencies have also made their administrative opinions or rulings available on the Internet at their sites. The **GPO Access** site offers a directory of these decisions in the **Administrative Decisions Guide**. URL: <http://www.access.gpo.gov/su_docs/admin.html>. Links are provided to the decisions of a number of administrative agencies, such as Decisions of the Comptroller General from the U.S. General Accounting Office.

State Case Law State MultiCourt Sites

Publication of state case law is primarily done by the West Group's "National Reporter System." This system publishes case reports for all fifty states in a uniform format for all jurisdictions. State case law is published in chronologically numbered volumes called "regional reporters." The units of regional reporters are grouped together geographically based on the country's population during the early twentieth century. New York and California have separate reporters.[6] The geographic grouping allows for the case reports from neighboring states to be published within the same set of books. The "National Reporter System" is linked by West's editorial treatment and enhancements, which provide for uniform subject access to all cases from each jurisdiction.

State case law is available online for many states for the past five years, but there is no consistency among the states concerning how many years of case reports are made available via this technology. Those states that do have case law databases may only publish summaries of decisions, but without the editorial treatments or finding aids that are available from the commercially published print or electronic formats. Some sites do provide full text search engines, tables of cases or docket numbers, or other indexes. The full text databases, *LEXIS* and *WESTLAW*, provide full text searching and coverage for all 50 states from at least 1945 and for many states back to the nineteenth century.

A number of sites provide access to all fifty states or multiple states from one location and utilize various uses of Web-based technology to present and organize these case law databases. The **State Court Locator** from Villanova University was designed with the intention of being the home page for state court systems on the Internet. URL: <http://vls.law.vill.edu/Locator/statecourt/>. This site presents the states in an alphabetically organized directory linking to the judicial opinion sites for state courts. **FindLaw State Resources**–URL: <http://www.findlaw.com/11stategov/>, **StateLaw–WashLawWEB State Case Law**–URL: <http://www.washlaw.edu/uslaw/statelaw.html>, and **ALSO American Law Sources Online–United States**–URL: <http://www.lawsource.com/also/usa.htm> all provide a hypertext table of the states linking to individual pages for each state and list court information as well as opinion sites. The **Internet Legal Resource Guide–American Government Index** also provides individual pages for each state with hypertext links to court sites. URL: <http://www.ilrg.com/gov.html>. A search engine allows users to limit searches to the jurisdictions of any of the states. The **Georgetown University Law Center–Legal Explorer–State, Local, Territorial** page provides a hypertext graphical map of the fifty states which links to pages for each state, identifying judicial information and case law. URL: <http://www.ll.georgetown.edu:80/lr/lg/state.html>.

LEGISLATIVE AND STATUTORY INFORMATION SOURCES

The legislative branch makes or writes statutes or laws that are passed by Congress or the jurisdictional law-making branch. Legislation includes constitutions, statutes, treaties, municipal charters, ordinances, interstate compacts, and reorganization plans. Federal, state, and local legislative and statutory information is available in print and electronic formats, including on *LEXIS* and *WESTLAW*.

Constitutional Law

The text of the *U.S. Constitution* is published in legal resources in the *U.S. Code* and in all state codes. It is available in digital format at numerous sites on the Internet. The Library of Congress Global Legal Information Network publishes the **Guide to the U.S. Constitution and Legal System,** which provides an annotated list of information sources available on the Internet about the Constitution. URL: <http://lcweb2.loc.gov/glin/usconst.html>. This document includes hypertext links to historical documents that influenced the content and history of the Constitution, such as the *Articles of Confederation* and the *Iroquois Constitution.* The **Annotated Constitution** Web page is a joint project that was developed by the GPO with the Congressional Research Service. URL: <http://www.access.gpo.gov/congress/senate/constitution/toc.html>. This **GPO Access** database contains the text of Senate Document No. 103-6, "The Constitution of the United States of America," which provides an analysis and interpretation of the Constitution.

An important use of Internet and Web technology is the digital scanning of historical documents that were previously not accessible, but can now be viewed and studied. The **National Archives and Records Administration Constitution of the United States** Web page includes a transcript of the complete text and a high-resolution image of each page. URL: <http://www.nara.gov/exhall/charters/constitution/conmain.html>. There are also hypertext links to information about the history of the Constitutional Convention and the 55 attendees and biographical information about the 39 signers. The **Constitution Society** on its **Founding Documents** page also includes scanned copies of the original pages and the Bill of Rights. URL: <http://www.constitution.org/constit.htm>. The scanned copy on the Emory University School of Law Web site includes a searchable database to the Constitution and all amendments. URLs: <http://www.law.emory.edu/FEDERAL/conpict.html#const> or <http://www.law.emory.edu/FEDERAL/usconst.html>. The **LII** publishes the **Constitutional Law Materials** Web page which provides an overview of constitutional law and a hypertext menu of source materials. URL: <http://www.law.cornell.edu/topics/constitutional.html>. The site includes links to other materials on constitutional law including historic and recent constitutional law decisions from the Supreme Court and U.S. Court of Appeals.

State constitutions of most states are published in the codes of the states, usually with annotations as well as the text of previous constitutions. Both *WESTLAW* and *LEXIS* provide comprehensive coverage of the codes for all the states. A number of sites offer access to state constitutions on the Internet, such as **American Law Sources On-line–United States**. URL: <http://www.lawsource.com/also/#[United States]>. The **FindLaw State Resources State Constitutions** Web site provides a directory of the states with links to the location of digital publications of their state constitutions. URL: <http://www.findlaw.com/11stategov/indexconst.html>. The **Know Your Constitutional Rights! Constitutions of the States** Web page provides direct links to the digital publication of the *Bill of Rights* from the constitutions of each state. URL: <http://www.harbornet.com/rights/states.html>.

Congressional Servers

The United States House of Representatives and United States Senate maintain sites to provide information from and access to members. The **United States Senate World Wide Web Server** provides information from and about the members, the Committees, and leadership and support offices. URL: <http://www.senate.gov>. The page also presents information about legislation and background information about Senate legislative procedures, facilities, and the history of the Senate. Databases on the server include a search mechanism for legislation, "Bill Search," and lists identifying Senate leadership, committee structure, and assignments. **Contacting the Senate** is a directory of the members by name and state with hypertext links to member Web pages and e-mail addresses. URL: <http://www.senate.gov/contacting/index.cfm>.

The **United States House of Representatives' World Wide Web Service U.S. House of Representatives' Home Page** provides public access to legislative information and to other U.S. government information resources, as well as information about members, committees, and organizations of the House. URL: <http://www.house.gov/>. The **U.S. House Of Representatives Member Office Web Services** includes a directory of all members Web sites. URL: <http://www.house.gov/house/MemberWWW.html>. The search engine can identify representatives' sites by state or member name. Constituents can identify and contact individual members on the **Write Your Representative Web Page** by state and zip code. URL: <http://www.house.gov/writerep/>. The *U.S. Code* is also accessible from this site by the Office of the Law Revision Counsel of the House of Representatives. URL: <http://uscode.house.gov/>.

Legislative Information Sites

Thomas: Legislative Information on the Internet (THOMAS) was introduced on January 5, 1995, at the inception of the 104th Congress, as the legislative information site on the Internet to provide access to current information on Congress and Congressional documents. URL: <http://thomas.loc.gov>. Named for Thomas Jefferson, it provides access to the full text of all of the documents created during preliminary consideration of legislation and the legislative process, including bills, the *Senate Calendar*, the *House Calendar, Congressional Record*, session laws, and public laws. **THOMAS** is updated as soon as new files are received from the GPO. New documents are indexed and made available for searching immediately and the text files of bills are updated several times during the day.

The **Legislative–Congressional Publications** Web page on **GPO Access** provides a directory of links to all congressional information resources that are available from this database. URL: <http://www.access. gpo.gov/su_docs/legislative.html>. Legislative resources on GPO Access include: *Congressional Record, History of Bills and Resolutions, Congressional Directory, Congressional Pictorial Directory*, congressional hearings, congressional reports, congressional calendars, public laws, and other legislative resources. These databases are accessible at all depository libraries and through a federal depository library gateway.

Guides to the Legislative Process

Many reference books covering American politics include a description of the legislative process, and a number of sites on the Internet provide these guides. Two guides are published on the **THOMAS** database. One that contains a very thorough and in-depth discussion and presentation of the overall process is *How Our Laws Are Made*, revised and updated by Charles Johnson, Parliamentarian of the U.S. House of Representatives. URL: http://thomas.loc.gov/home/lawsmade. toc.html. This guide is also available on the House of Representatives Web page. URL: <http://www.house.gov/house/HOLAM.TXT>. *Enact-*

ment of a Law by Robert B. Dove, Parliamentarian of the Senate, is also available on this site. URL: <http://thomas.loc.gov/home/enactment/enactlawtoc.html>. Two other guides are published by the House of Representatives and are accessible from the **U.S. House of Representatives Educational Resources** page. URL: <http://www.house.gov/house/Educat.html>. *The Legislative Process, A House of Representatives Guide* provides access to a wealth of information about bills and resolutions being considered in the Congress. URL: <http://www.house.gov/Legproc.html>. The guide also includes current information about activities on the House floor. The second guide, *The Legislative Process Tying It All Together,* includes explanations of each form of congressional action and each step in the process. URL: <http://www.house.gov/Tying_it_all.html>.

Subscription Databases

Congressional Universe, published by Congressional Information Service, a subsidiary of Lexis-Nexis, is a comprehensive index to U.S. legislative information, including the full text of proposed legislation, legislative history information, and current member and committee information. URL: <http://www.cispubs.com>. This fee-based database and the print index, *CIS Index*, provide reliable indexing and abstracting of the U.S. Congress from 1970 forward. The Web-based **Congressional Universe** provides a seamless link to the full range of legislative and public policy resources.

Legislative History

Legislative histories provide insight into the legislature's "original intent" in passing a specific law or in interpreting the meaning of particular provisions of a law. To identify this intent, all of the information and documents used or created during the legislative process must be examined. Both the **LOCIS** and **THOMAS** databases provide access to these resources. The Documents Center at the University of Michigan has prepared a guide to assist students with their legislative history assignments. The **Legislative History** page gives guidance for identifying legislative documents since the 103rd Congress in 1993. URL: <http://www.lib.umich.edu/libhome/Documents.center/legishis.html>. This guide provides step by step directions for preparing histories, recommendations to help students identify bills or new laws, and the names of multiple sources or databases that include the needed documents or information to compile histories. Links are made to the print, electronic, and Web-based resources.

The **Legislative Histories–Bill Summary and Status** on the **THOMAS** database provides searchable summaries of the bill's progress through the congressional process and legislative histories for bills and amendments. URL: <http://thomas.loc.gov>. The database can be searched by type of legislation, stage of the legislative process, sponsor, committee, keyword or phrase, bill or amendment number, date, or any combination of the fields. Another database maintains a list of public laws and vetoed bills during either congressional session that can be browsed.

Congressional and Government Directories

There are a number of directories that allow citizens to contact their congressional representatives. These directories offer information about the Washington, D.C. offices as well as district, city, and state offices of officials. The Web sites for congressional directory information include personal and biographical information, as well as contact numbers and email addresses. One of the most used government documents is the *Congressional Directory*, which is published for each Congress every two years by the GPO. Linked from the U.S. Congress page at **GPO Access**, there are two congressional directories at this site. The **Congressional Directory** is a searchable online version that is published by the GPO. URL: <http://www.access.gpo.gov/congress/cong001.html>. The *Directory* presents short biographies of each member of the Senate and House, committee memberships, terms of service, administrative assistants and/or secretaries, and room and telephone numbers. It also lists officials of the courts, military establishments, and departments and agencies, D.C. government officials, governors of states and territories, foreign diplomats, and media information. GPO Access provides two different methods of accessing the *Congressional Directory*: a traditional simple-search interface and a table of direct links to each section of the directory. Editions of the *Congressional Directory* are available on the Internet from the **GPO Access** Web site through the 106th Congressional session. **GPO Access** also publishes the **Congressional Pictorial Directory**, which has pictures of the members for the current Congress. URL: <http://

www.access.gpo.gov/picdir/title.html>. The **Congressional Pictorial Directory** identifies Congressional leadership. Member information is accessed by browsing the members' pictures, which are listed in alphabetical order.

The **Congress.Org** Web site provides a complete directory of information about the members of the U.S. House of Representatives and Senate. URL: <http://congress.org/main.html>. Users can search for any congressional member's name or use the browseable list by state and jurisdictional district. Through the Congressional Directory page member information can be retrieved by name from the alphabetic listings, by state, or by committee assignments. The Congressional Email page provides electronic mail addresses for congressional members. The Find Your Member page identifies members of Congress and congressional district by the five-digit zip code. **Mr. Smith E-mails Washington**, published by InfoSearch, also identifies the e-mail addresses of members of the U.S. Congress. URL: <http://www.mrsmith.com/>. **Congress Web** also provides a "zip code lookup" feature, with the **CongressWeb ZipLookUp** as well as a complete directory of information about members. URL: <http://www.congressweb.com/html/ziplookup.cfm>.

CapWeb is an unauthorized and unofficial guide to the members of the U.S. Congress. URL: <http://www.capweb.net/classic/index.morph>. It serves as a link to all Senate and House of Representatives members who have Web pages. The **CapWeb** page is organized into a directory of the two houses and provides e-mail addresses, bills, votes, public laws, information about congressional support agencies, caucuses, Capitol Hill and Washington, D.C., and links to the other two government branches. The Senate and House of Representatives **CapWeb** pages offer specific information unique to each house. Users can search for any congressional member's name or browse the list by state and jurisdictional district.

Contacting the Congress is a very up-to-date database of congressional contact information. URL: <http://www.visi.com/juan/congress/>. This directory is maintained by Juan Cabanela and provides Washington, D.C., district offices and fax numbers for members. Congressional members from a particular state, commonwealth, or territory can be identified from a hypertext map. Member information can also be retrieved by searching the **Zip To It** search database for zip codes that is accessible at this site. URL: <http://www.visi.com/juan/congress/ziptoit.html>.

The **Biographical Directory of the United States Congress 1774 to Present** is a searchable directory of biographical information about each member, including education, family, professional experience, and government service. URL: <http://bioguide.congress.gov/>. Other resources on the site include information for planning visits to the Senate and a virtual tour of the Capitol building. The search mechanism allows users to search for Congressional members by name, position, or state.

Statutory Information Resources Codification of Federal Statutes

The *U.S. Code* is published by the GPO and two commercial publishers. The official printed bound edition of the *U.S. Code* and the CDROM edition are available in all depository libraries and for purchase through the GPO by phone, fax, or mail. The West Group publishes the *U.S. Code Annotated*, which includes all of the editorial treatments included in the West Key Number System. Lexis Law Publishing publishes the *U.S. Code Service*. Both publications provide the codified statutes as well as references to court decisions, regulations, and encyclopedia and law review articles. These two sets are available in all formats including print, CD-ROM, and online via *WESTLAW* and *LEXIS-NEXIS*. Electronic copies on the Internet are accessible on a number of Web sites. Like the official GPO edition of the *U.S. Code*, the Internet-published versions do not include any of the references to judicial decisions, explanatory materials, or other finding aids that are included in the commercial annotated codes. The versions of the *U.S. Code* on the Internet are not as current as the official government published or commercial editions. Use of these copies must be supported by examination of one of the commercially published printed or online codes to insure the currency of the law.

The most up to date online version of the *U.S. Code* is published by the Office of the Law Revision Counsel on the **U.S. House of Representatives** page. URL: <http://uscode.house.gov/usc.htm>. The latest edition includes Titles 1 to 15, which is current as of Supplement IV (January 5, 1999), to the 1994 edition of the *U.S. Code* and Titles 16 to 50, the Organic Laws, the Table of Popular Names, and Tables IIX of the database which is based on Supplement III (January 26, 1998). Each section of the *U.S. Code* database contains a date in the top right corner, indicating that laws enacted as of that date and affecting that section are included in the text of that section. The *Code* can be searched by keyword or title.

The *U.S. Code,* available on the **GPO Access** Web site, is part of the Legislative Collection of government resources. URL: <http://www.access.gpo.gov/congress/cong013.html>. This version of the *U.S. Code* is generated from the most recent version of the Government Printing Office CDROM. The database includes the 1994 edition of the *U.S. Code* and three supplements that include all general and permanent laws in effect as of January 26, 1998. This full-text database can be accessed through the Federal Depository Library Gateways or on site at any depository library. It can also be searched from the **Connect to Databases Online via GPO** access that provides for searching across multiple databases. URL: <http://www.access.gpo.gov/su_docs/aces/aaces002.html>. The **GPO Access Gateway at the University of California, GPO Gate** provides a more detailed search screen for its copy of the *U.S. Code.* URL: <http://www.gpo.ucop.edu:80/search/uscode.html>. The full text of the code can be searched by keyword or phrase, or the search can be limited to words in the title of laws. This site also provides for retrieval of code sections by a browseable hypertext list organized by code section and by the **Acts by Popular Name Table**. URL: <http://www.gpo.ucop.edu:80/catalog/uscode.html#popname>.

The *U.S. Code* from the **LII** is generated from the most recent version made available by the U.S. House of Representatives. URLs: <http://www.law.cornell.edu/uscode/> and <http://www4.law.cornell.edu/uscode/>. The database includes all official *U.S. Code* notes and appendices, as well as the **Table of Popular Names**. URL: <http://www4.law.cornell.edu/uscode/topn>. The site has an update service that integrates the services of the House servers and of the Library of Congress's THOMAS service to supply accurate updates to any section that has been amended or has had additions passed in the Congress. The site provides hypertext links to the **THOMAS** site to update the *U.S. Code* by title number, by subject, or by keyword. The **LII** site has a hypertext directory listing of each *Code* title and provides search forms to identify laws by title and section number, subject, or keyword.

The **ALSO! American Law Sources Online Federal Government–U. S. Code** search form links to the LII and the House of

Representatives editions of the *Code*. URL: <http://www.lawsource.
com/also/usa.cgi?us1#Z3Q>. The **Popular Names of Public Acts–
Complete List (1 of 6)** includes the names of public acts passed
through January 1994 that is published by the GPO. URL: <http://
www.lawsource.com/also/usa.cgi?usp1>. The **Popular Names of Significant New Laws** lists the names of public laws enacted since the
104th Congress which are compiled by the Library of Congress. URL:
<http://www.lawsource.com/also/usa.cgi?usp0>. The **Popular Names
of Selected Public Acts** is an alphabetical list of the popular names of
selected federal acts and codified statutes that are available on the
Internet. URL: <http://www.lawsource.com/also/usa.cgi?usp>.

Statutory Multistate Finders

All states have published legislative information and statutory
codes on the Internet, and there are a number of sites that provide
access. The Washburn University School of Law sponsors **StateLaw
State Government and Legislative Information** which provides a directory of the states and links to the codes. URL: <http://www.washlaw.
edu/uslaw/statelaw.html>. There is a full text search engine of the Web
site. Hypertext matrixes of the states provide state legislature sites,
legislative bill searches, chaptered bill information, and legislative
history on the **Legislative Information Sites Listing** page. URL:
<http://www.washlaw.edu/uslaw/search.html#legislative>. A matrix to
state statutes, state codes, and uniform crime reports is accessible on
the **State Statutes Sites** Web page. URL: <http://www.washlaw.edu/
uslaw/search.html#statutes>. The **FindLaw–State Resources Index**
site includes a search engine for each state's government Web sites.
Links are also made to municipal codes. URL: <http://www.findlaw.
com/11stategov/index.html>.

Municipal Codes

Two Web sites are making municipal and local codes more accessible by publishing them on the Internet. The **Municipal List of Codes**
page from the Municipal Code Corporation includes links to many city
codes. URL: <http://www.municode.com/database.html>. The database
consists of local government Codes of Ordinances from around the
United States, organized in alphabetical order by state. The Seattle

Public Library maintains the **Municipal Codes Online** Web site. This project was begun by the library in an effort to make municipal codes throughout the nation more accessible to the public. URL: <http://www.spl.org/govpubs/municode.html>. The site includes an alphabetically ordered list of links to city and county codes by state. This site was named as one of the top fifty legal research Web sites by *Law Office Computing*.

ADMINISTRATIVE AND EXECUTIVE BRANCH INFORMATION SOURCES

Guides to the Federal Government Departments and Agencies

The administrative or executive branch is comprised of the regulatory and independent agencies and departments. These administrative agencies make a great impact on governmental operations as they write and develop rules and regulations that implement the laws that have been enacted by the legislative branch, set procedures, detail technical distinctions, issue opinions, and interpret and apply the governing statute.

One of the best-selling publications issued each year by the GPO is the *U.S. Government Manual*. The *U.S. Government Manual* is an indispensable resource to identify titles, addresses and phone numbers for government officials, agencies, or departments. Published by the GPO in print and digitally on the **GPO Access** Web site, the **U.S. Government Manual** is the official directory for information on the agencies and officials of the legislative, judicial, and executive branches. URLs: <http://www.access.gpo.gov/nara/nara001.html> and <http://www.access.gpo.gov/nara/browsegm.html>. For each agency the *Manual* provides a list of principal officials, the statement of the agency's purpose and role, brief history and legislative/executive authority of the agency, a description of its programs and activities, and a "Sources of Information" section. The "Sources of Information" section provides information on consumer activities, contracts and grants, employment, and publications. The *Manual* is available at a number of sites on the Internet, including through the GPO gateway sites project.

A number of Web sites providing directories of government departments and agencies have based their organizational structure on the *U.S. Government Manual.* The **Great American Web Site–A Citizen's Guide to the Treasures of the U.S. Government on the World Wide Web The Internet Guide to the U.S. Government** is organized according to the *Manual* and provides access to the three Branches of Government and the Independent Agencies and Commissions. URLs: <http://www.unclesam.com/guide.html>. A major Internet resource used to identify government departments and agencies is the **Federal Web Locator from the Center for Information Law and Policy**. URL: <http://www.infoctr.edu/fwl/l>.[7] This site is one of the most comprehensive Internet indexes to United States government Web sites. The site motto is the "one stop shopping point for federal government information on the World Wide Web." The Villanova University School of Law Library has produced a new directory to government sites, the **Federal Web Navigator–Villanova University School of Law**. URL: <http://yolanda.law.vill.edu/fedweb/index.html>. Government sites can be searched by agency name or subject on two indexes.

Some Web sites provide exhaustive directories of the government departments and agencies. The **U.S. Federal Government Agencies Directory**, which is part of the **Louisiana State University Libraries WWW Virtual Library,** provides a list of federal agencies on the Internet organized according to the branches of government and divided according to executive; independent; boards, commissions, and committees; and quasiofficial agencies. URL: <http://www.lib.lsu.edu/gov/fedgov.html>. The **Federal Information by Agency Duke University Public Documents and Maps Department of Perkins Library Federal Information Official Government Agencies** is an alphabetically organized list according to the structure outlined in the *U.S. Government Manual.* URL: <http://www.lib.duke.edu/pdmt/federal/official/index.htm>. It serves as a directory to Web sites created and maintained by a Department, Agency, Subagency, Office or Bureau of the Federal Government, and government-supported Web sites. The directory also provides links to publications, news, and data sites from each agency, department, or institutional link. The **Government Information Exchange Federal Directory–Executive Branch** and the **Library of Congress Official Federal Government Web Sites** provide a hypertext alphabetical list of the executive branch departments, agencies, and commissions. URL: <http://www.info.gov/Info/html/executive.htm> and URL: <http://lcweb.loc.gov/global/executive/fed. html>.

The **Interactive Citizen's Handbook** on the White House Web server provides links to the administrative departments and independent agencies. URL: <http://www.whitehouse.gov/WH/html/handbook. html>. Federal government departments, independent agencies, or commissions can be identified by graphical icons of the seal of each office, department, agency, or commission linked to their official government Web site for the **President's Cabinet**-URL: <http://www. whitehouse.gov/WH/Cabinet/html/cabinet_links.htm> and the **Federal Agencies and Commissions**-URL: <http://www.whitehouse.gov/WH/ Independent_Agencies/html/independent_links.html>. The names of current cabinet members are identified with links to the departments that they head on the **Cabinet Secretaries** Web page. URL: <http:// www.whitehouse.gov/WH/Cabinet/html/secretary.html>. The **White House Offices and Agencies** page provides the names and links to offices and commissions that are administered under the office of the President. URL: <http://www.whitehouse.gov/WH/EOP/html/EOP_org. html>.

DocLaw WWW from the Washburn University School of Law provides a gateway to federal government Internet resources and documents by subject, by organizational chart, and with a search engine. URL: <http://www.washlaw.edu/doclaw/doclawnew.html>. The site includes the hypertext linked **U.S. Government Organizational Charts** Web page, which provides direct links to departments and agencies. URL: <http://www.washlaw.edu/doclaw/orgchart/orgchart2. html>. The site is organized by subject and includes an **Agency Index** to department or agency home pages, publications, electronic forms, and opinions. URLs: <http://www.washlaw.edu/doclaw/subject5m.html> and <http://www.washlaw.edu/doclaw/executive5m.html>.

GUIDES TO ADMINISTRATIVE LAW AND FEDERAL REGULATIONS

The regulatory process includes the proposal and final approval of rules and regulations that are completed by the executive branch departments and independent agencies. These rules and regulations carry out the laws that have been passed by the Congress. A number of digital publications provide guides and explanatory material about this process and identify Web sites where the federal and state regulations may be accessed on the Internet. These guides have been written and published by government offices, commercial organizations, individuals, and libraries.

Regulatory information and documents are made accessible from **GPO Access**. Two **GPO Access** Web pages, **Executive Branch Resources on GPO Access** and **Regulatory Resources on GPO Access** serve as guides to administrative branch resources and documents that are retrievable from this site. URL: <http://www.access.gpo.gov/su_docs/executive.html> and URL: <http://www.access.gpo.gov/su_docs/regulatory.html>. Executive branch resources accessible from **GPO Access** include the *Federal Register, Code of Federal Regulations* (CFR), and the *Semiannual Regulatory Agenda (Unified Agenda)*. Larry Schankman, Cyber-Librarian at Mansfield University, developed the excellent guide–**Federal Regulations Library Guide Series**. URLs: <http://www.mnsfld.edu/depts/lib/fedregs.html> or <http://www.clark.net/pub/lschank/web/fedregs.html> (mirror site). This guide provides background and explanatory information about government regulations and regulatory information. Hypertext links accessing the *Federal Register, CFR*, regulatory agencies or departments, government regulations for specific topics, and state regulatory information sites are imbedded within the text. **Federal Regulations**, supported by the LII, provides background information on the regulatory system with links to sites on the Internet. URL: <http://www.law.cornell.edu/library/fedregs1.html#toc>.

FEDERAL REGISTER

The rules and regulations that are proposed and finalized by the administrative branch departments and independent agencies are published in the *Federal Register* as they are being written, codified, and enacted. Created in 1936, the *Federal Register* is published by the Office of the Federal Register, U.S. National Archives and Records Administration and is legislatively mandated to publish: Presidential proclamations and executive orders, final and proposed rules and regulations, regulatory agendas, notices of hearings, administrative documents, rulings, notices, announcements of application deadlines, license revocations, congressional documents, lists of acts approved by the President, and public laws. The *Federal Register* is published by the U.S. Government every business day.

The **Federal Register** has been hosted by the National Archives and Records Administration Web site on the **GPO Access** Web page since Volume 60, January 1, 1995. URL: <http://www.access.gpo.gov/ nara/index.html>. It can be searched from the Federal Register **GPO Access Database** and from the **Connect to Databases Online via GPO Access**, which lets users search across multiple databases. URLs: <http:// www.access.gpo.gov/su_docs/aces/aces140.html> and URL: <http:// www. access.gpo.gov/su_docs/aces/aaces002.html>. The database includes proposed and final rules and regulations, presidential documents, and government notices. The *Federal Register* is also available through the **EPA Electronic Federal Register Project Environmental Documents and the Unified Agenda**. URL: <http://www.epa.gov/fedrgstr/ search.htm>.

Code of Federal Regulations

The final repository for all general and permanent federal rules and regulations published in the *Federal Register* by the executive departments and agencies is the *Code of Federal Regulations* (CFR). The *CFR* is divided or codified into an arrangement of fifty titles, representing broad areas subject to Federal regulation. Each title is divided into chapters which usually bear the name of the issuing agency. The chapters are further subdivided into parts covering specific regulatory areas. Each title of the *CFR* is revised once each calendar year and issued on a quarterly basis. The GPO publishes print editions of the *CFR* and *Federal Register* and makes them available through its Superintendent of Documents sales service. Both publications are also published by a number of commercial publishers, including *WESTLAW* and *LEXIS*.

The purpose of the *CFR* online is to provide the public with enhanced access to government information. The *CFR* is officially published online on the **GPO Access–Code of Federal Regulations** Web site by the Office of the Federal Register (OFR) and the National Archives and Records Administration, in partnership with the GPO. URL: <http://www.access.gpo.gov/nara/cfr/index.html>. The *CFR* volumes are added to the online service concurrent with the release of the paper editions. When revised *CFR* volumes are added, the prior editions remain on **GPO Access** as the historical set. Both the current or historical volume are accessible on the **GPO Access–Search or browse your choice of CFR titles and/or volumes page,** which provides an up-to-date listing of available titles. URL: <http://www. access.gpo.gov/nara/cfr/cfrtablesearch.html#page1>. The current set of the *CFR* can be searched by keyword on this page and on the Connect to Databases Online via GPO Access, which lets users search across multiple databases. URL: <http://www.access.gpo.gov/su_docs/ aces/aaces002.html>. The *Code* can also be accessed through the **GPO Access Depository Library Gateways**. The *CFR* is also available from the **LII Code of Federal Regulations** and **FindLaw: Laws: Cases and Codes: US Constitution, Code and CFR** pages which serve as front ends to the most recent version of the *CFR* placed on the Internet by the GPO. URL: <http://www4.law.cornell.edu/cfr/> and URL: <http://www.findlaw.com/casecode/code.html>.

The *Federal Register* is connected to the *CFR* by finding aids that are published daily and cumulated in the *List of CFR Sections Affected (LSA)*. The *LSA* is used to update the rules and regulations in the CFR as they are proposed and finalized in the *Federal Register.* The **List of CFR Sections Affected** is also made available online by the National Archives and Records Administration in three parts so that *CFR* sections and parts can be monitored on a daily basis. URL: <http:// www.access.gpo.gov/nara/lsa/aboutlsa.html>.

State Administrative Law

Like the legislative law, the state system of administrative law parallels that of the federal government. Because of online publication, these resources have been made more accessible to legal professionals, government administrators and officials, business persons, and citizens. While these regulations were accessible on commercial databases such as *WESTLAW* and *LEXIS*, there are now a number of online Web sites that have made agency information and state rules and regulations retrievable for all fifty states. The **American Bar Association (ABA) Administrative Procedure Database** is being developed and maintained through a joint initiative by the ABA's Section of Administrative Law and Regulatory Practice and the Florida State University College of Law. URL: <http://www.law.fsu.edu/ library/admin/>. The **State Resources** page provides hypertext tables to state agencies, administrative procedure acts, and other information for all fifty states. URL: <http://www.law.fsu.edu/library/admin/state.

html>. A search engine for the **Administrative Procedure Database** accesses the contents of all materials on the database, including links to and descriptions of offsite materials. URL: <http://www.law.fsu. edu/library/admin/new_search.html>.

A number of other Web sites provide access to the administrative resources for each state. The **State Web Locator** from the Center for Information Law and Policy provides hypertext tables linked to state directory pages listing the Internet sites. URL: <http://www.infoctr. edu/swl/>. The URLs link to sites for administrative law, agency, and state government information. The **ALSO American Law Sources Online United States** directory pages for each state also provide administrative law sources with links. URL: <http://www.lawsource. com/also/#[UnitedStates]>. Other sites with excellent state administrative resources include **FindLaw State Resources Index** and **State-Law,** which publish individual pages for each state with links to administrative law and agency sites on the Internet. URL: <http:// www.findlaw.com/11stategov/> and URL: <http://www.washlaw.edu/ uslaw/statelaw.html>. Two Web sites provide hypertext linked graphic maps of the U.S. which link to each state's administrative resources. Both the General Services Administration's **Government Information Xchange U.S. State and Local Government** and the **Georgetown University Legal Explorer–States and Territorial Pages** publish pages with links for each state to executive branch and other state government information, including state home pages; governor's offices; agency, board, and commission listings; and administrative codes. URL: <http://www.info.gov/Info/html/state_government.shtml> and URL: <http://www.ll.georgetown.edu:80/lr/lg/state.html>.

PRESIDENTIAL INFORMATION

The White House Web page is the central access point on the Internet for information about the activities, public presentations, and papers of the President. URL: <http://www.whitehouse.gov>. Information about and history of the Presidency, the White House, and the government are included on this site on such pages as the "**Interactive Citizen's Handbook**" and the "**White House for Kids Page**." URL: <http://www.whitehouse.gov/WH/html/handbook.html> and URL: <http://www.whitehouse.gov/WH/kids/html/kidshome.html>. The **White House: Search All White House Publications** provides for searching by keywords and document type within date ranges. URL: <http://www.pub.whitehouse.gov/search/everything.html>. The **White House Virtual Library** provides access to speeches, press briefings, radio addresses, executive orders, photographs, and other publicly released White House publications since 1993–the beginning of the Clinton administration. URL: <http://www.whitehouse.gov/WH/html/library.html>. The **White House Briefing Room** includes summaries of current press releases and press briefings, the President's radio addresses (in English and Spanish), government statistics, and information on other current issues and events. URL: <http://www.whitehouse.gov/WH/html/briefroom.html>. The **Search the White House Website** provides full text and title searching by key word. URL: <http://library.whitehouse.gov/Search/QueryWebsite.html>.

The *Weekly Compilation of Presidential Documents* is published every Monday by the Office of the Federal Register (OFR) of the National Archives and Records Administration. This publication contains statements, messages, and other Presidential materials released by the White House during the preceding week, and began publication with the Presidential papers of Harry S. Truman. The online edition of the **Weekly Compilation of Presidential Documents** is currently under development as a pilot project jointly authorized by the OFR and the GPO to provide the public with enhanced access to Presidential documents. URL: <http://www.access.gpo.gov/nara/nara003.html>. The *Weekly Compilation* is compiled annually into the *Public Papers of the Presidents of the United States* that is published by the OFR of the National Archives and Records Administration.

SECONDARY RESOURCES

Sources that provide evaluation and analysis of the primary law are secondary sources. They provide textual treatment and discussion of the official text of cases, laws, and rules or regulations. Secondary tools include legal citation and style manuals, encyclopedias, dictionaries or wordbooks, treatises and textbooks, directories, legal periodicals and newspapers, and law reviews.

Citation Manuals

The **Introduction to Basic Legal Citation** is based on the Sixteenth Edition of *A Uniform System of Citation*, known as the *"Har-*

vard Blue Book" or the *"Bluebook."* URL: <http://www.law.cornell.edu/citation/citation.table.html>. The citation manual was written by Peter W. Martin of the Cornell University Law School. This digital citation manual links to the compact disk version of the *Bluebook* on the Folio Webserver at the LII. The **Uncle Sam Brief Guide to Citing Government Publications** was developed by the staff of the Regional Depository Library and Government Publications Department of the University of Memphis. URL: <http://www.lib.memphis.edu/gpo/citeweb.htm>. The guide provides examples of bibliographic citations to the most common government documents that are used by researchers, students, and scholars in articles or research papers based on the *Chicago–Turabian Manual of Style* standard bibliographic form. The forms of the citations were patterned after Diane Garner and Diane H. Smith's *Complete Guide to Citing Government Documents: A Manual for Writers & Librarians.*

Legal Dictionaries

There is no comprehensive and authoritative legal dictionary published on the Web. A number of sites provide dictionaries that have been developed online and include excerpts from standardized dictionary resources. The **FindLaw Legal Dictionary** is the digital version of the *Merriam-Webster's Dictionary of Law* that is licensed to **Find-Law** by Merriam-Webster. URL: <http://dictionary.findlaw.com/>. **Oran's Dictionary of the Law** is published by the West Group and is a dictionary guidebook to the law. URL: <http://www.lawoffice.com/pathfind/orans/orans.asp>. The site provides definitions of many legal terms and phrases of Latin, French, and Old English etymology. Obsolete words and terms with technical definitions are also included.

Other sources providing definitions include Nolo Press, the publisher of legal self-help guides which is developing a digital legal dictionary to support the users of their guides. **Shark Talk: Everybody's Law Dictionary** provides plain-English definitions to legal terms and concepts. URL: <http://www.nolo.com/dictionary/wordindex.cfm>. The page includes a legal word game, "Shark Talk." **Duhaime's Law Dictionary from the World Wide Legal Information Association** is written by a Canadian barrister and solicitor, Lloyd Duhaime. URL: <http://www.duhaime.org/dictc.htm> or URL: <http://www.wwlia.org/diction.htm>. Each definition includes hypertext links to terms that are used in the definitions of the legal concepts. The **Lawcopedia**

Lectric Legal Lexicon includes explanations for more than 1000 law related Web sites, terms, and phrases. URL: <http://www.lectlaw.com/def.htm>. **Understanding the Federal Courts–The Glossary of Terms** is a glossary providing explanatory definitions to the specialized terms, language of law, and processes that are used in the federal court system from the **U.S. Courts** Web site. URL: <http://www.uscourts.gov/understanding_courts/gloss.htm>.

Legal Directories

Legal directories are one of the most popular legal and government information resources on the Internet. They are used by attorneys, law students and professors, government administrators, judges, business persons, and ordinary citizens. There are a variety of resources that provide directory and biographical information about individual attorneys or law firms, legal experts, professors, government officers, corporate attorneys, legal aid or assistance organizations, and elected officials.

Attorney and Law Firm Directories

The *Martindale-Hubbell Law Directory* is the primary directory of authoritative information on lawyers in the United States and in foreign countries. It is made available via the Internet as the **Martindale-Hubbell Lawyer Locator**. URL: <http://www.martindale.com>. It contains biographical and law firm information for more than 900,000 lawyers and law firms in 150 countries. Now owned by LEXIS-NEXIS, it is accessible via the Web and is available in print, on CD-ROM, and on the *LEXIS* database of legal information. The new Web site **lawyers.com** is a service that is made available at no cost from the Martindale-Hubbell Company. URL: <http://www.lawyers.com/>. The database includes profiles of 420,000 attorneys and law firms with links to the home pages of law firms that provide information, including practice focus, professional credentials, fees, office hours, and directions. The site also provides consumer-oriented legal information to help users better understand the law, consumer friendly explanations of 24 major areas of law, articles on current legal topics, links to legal resources on the Web, and a glossary of legal terms. The interactive page **Ask a Lawyer** provides a forum for submitting questions. URL: <http://learnlaw.lawyers.com/site/ask/default.cfm>.

The **West Legal Directory–Find A Lawyer** on the **Lawoffice.com** site provides profiles of more than 1,000,000 lawyers and law firms, international counsel, corporate counsel, and U.S. government attorneys. URL: <http://www.lawoffice.com/direct/direct.asp>. This directory is part of **Lawoffice.com**, a free service provided by the West Group for consumers and small businesses. URL: <http://www.lawoffice.com/>.

Expert Directories

Expert directories are used by attorneys, journalists and others in the media, and researchers to identify expert witnesses, subject matter experts, consultants, spokespersons, and authors. There are a number of directories of experts that are available on the Internet. The directory **EXPERTS.COM**, published by The Noble Group, provides a database to search for experts by keyword, topic, or location. URL: <http://www.experts.com>.

Law School and Faculty Directories

The **American Bar Association (ABA) Section of Legal Education and Admissions to the Bar–ABA Approved Law Schools** has six directories which provide direct links to the Web site of each school. URL: <http://www.abanet.org/legaled/approved.html>. The site includes four ways to identify approved law schools, including an alphabetical list, a list by state, lists of public and private schools, and lists of schools by year of ABA approval. The sixth directory, **Geographic Location**, provides hypertext linked regional maps that identify the names of schools and their location. URL: <http://www.abanet.org/legaled/map.html>. The **Association of American Law Schools (AALS) Member Schools** also provides a directory of hypertext links to the Web sites of the 162 member schools and 17 fee-paid schools of the AALS. URL: <http://www.aals.org/members.html>. This non-profit association is the learned society for law professors and the principal representative of legal education to the federal government and to other national higher education organizations. The digital publication is similar to the *AALS Directory of Law Teachers*, which is published annually by the Association and lists full-time faculty and professional staff of all member and fee-paid law schools by law school.

The **Hieros Gamos Every Law School on the Planet** directory includes the address, telephone number, fax number, and administrative information for over 1,300 law schools linked to their home pages. URL: <http://www.hg.org/schools.html>. Hieros Gamos also makes available Internet directories for the following geographic regions: North America, Latin America and the Caribbean, Asian Pacific, and African and Middle Eastern. The directory listing for each region is organized in alphabetical order by country and school.

Topical Law Information

There is no authoritative legal encyclopedia on the Internet, but there are a number of sites which identify published and unpublished resources on legal topics. The West Group's **Lawoffice.com** produces **Law Pathfinders** which are designed to assist users to find information on various topics. URL: <http://www.lawoffice.com/pathfind/pathfind.htm>. The **Law Pathfinders** page includes **Pathfinder Maps**, which organize pathfinders by topic, and allows for searching of lawyers, firm Web sites by city, topic-related Law Knowledgebase articles, Internet links, publications, and dictionary terms. URL: <http://www.lawoffice.com/pathfind/maps/mapsst.htm>. The **Legal Guides** are topic-driven resources written to give consumers a better understanding of different areas of the law. URL: <http://www.lawoffice.com/pathfind/guides/guides.htm>. The **Law Knowledgebase** consists of articles and newsletters written by law firms throughout the United States that are organized by topic. URL: <http://www.lawoffice.com/pathfind/knowbase/knowbase.asp>.

Two topical law Web pages are available from FindLaw. The **FindLaw Library** provides the full text of topical law publications that have been submitted to the site and made available on the Internet. URL: <http://library.findlaw.com/>. The **FindLaw Subject Index of Legal Resources** includes over 8,000 digital collections of information resources and articles developed by specialists in the field, government offices, law schools or educators, and law firms that are hypertext linked to the FindLaw site. URL: <http://www.findlaw.com/01topics/index.html>.

Other Web sites providing legal topical information have been developed by law schools and firms. Developed by the University of Southern California Law Library, the **Legal Topics Reference Desk: Topical Sites on the Web** provides a hyperlinked menu to a variety of legal resources available on the Internet, including publications arranged by subject. URL: <http://www.usc.edu/dept/lawlib/legal/topiclst.html>. **The LII–Law About** page provides summaries of law topics and sub-topics with links to primary source material, including documents on the Internet. URL: <http://www.law.cornell.edu/topical.html>. The **Law About–Alphabetical Listing of Topics** can be searched by key word through an index or by browsing the alphabetical list of topics. URL: <http://www.law.cornell.edu/topics/topic1.html>. The **World Wide Web Virtual Law Library** sponsored by the Indiana University School of Law Library and the World Wide Web Virtual Library includes a list of topical law that can be browsed by topical listing. URL: <http://www.law.indiana.edu/vlib/>.

CONCLUSION

Digital publication of legal and government information on the Internet is making this information more accessible and affordable for all information users. The development of this new information and communication technology supports the spirit of democracy that our government is based upon. The increased accessibility of official legal and government documents provides vital information resources for legal professionals, as well as support for ordinary citizens' awareness of the activities and actions of government offices. However, users of these Internet based tools are advised to verify and examine the authority and currency of the digital resource. Unlike other disciplines, examination of both current as well as historical legal and government resources is necessary for the proper use and understanding of the impact of these materials. While a great deal of Supreme Court and approximately ten years of federal circuit court case law has been published on the Internet, there is no complete database for federal and state case law. Case law databases and print publications, such as LEXIS-NEXIS, WEST-LAW, and the official and unofficial reporters, must be used to research judicial opinions. The information disseminated by the legislative and executive branch, at both the federal and state level, is also not as comprehensive as those resources produced by commercial database publishers. A number of the secondary legal and government information tools, such as encyclopedias and dictionaries, are not authoritatively reproduced or are not accessible via this technology.

NOTES

1. Yvonne Chandler, "The Nature of Legal Information on the Internet." *Neal-Schuman Guide to Finding Legal and Regulatory Information on the Internet*, 3.

2. Library of Congress Internet guides to legal and government resources: Sources of Government Information: URL: <http://lcweb.loc.gov/rr/news/extgovd.html>, Official Federal Government Web Sites–URL: <http://lcweb.loc.gov/global/executive/fed.html>, United States Legislative Branch: URL: <http://lcweb.loc.gov/global/legislative/congress.html>, U.S. Judicial Branch Resources–URL: <http://lcweb.loc.gov/global/judiciary.html>, and State and Local Governments–URL: <http://lcweb.loc.gov/global/state/stategov.html>.

3. "Government Printing Office Electronic Information Access Enhancement Act of 1993 (GPO Access Act), A Public Law 103-40." June 8, 1993, 107 Stat. 112 (Title 44, Sec. 4101 et seq.).

4. Supreme Court Collection. URL: <http://supct.law.cornell.edu/supct/cases/historic.htm>. The Legal Information Institute at Cornell has converted the entire Case Western Reserve archive backlist to HTML from Word Perfect 5.1 and ASCII formats and filled gaps in the collection of decisions. Since the October 1997 term, decisions of the Court have been distributed in Adobe Acrobat (PDF) and SGML tagged ASCII format.

5. FedWorld–Supreme Court Decisions, 1937–1975. URL: <http://www.fedworld.gov/supcourt/index.htm>. The file of Supreme Court decisions from the FLITE ("Federal Legal Information Through Electronics") system contains over 7,000 opinions dating from 1937 through 1975, from volumes 300 through 422 of U.S. Reports, the official reporter of Supreme Court decisions. The file was exempt from release under the Freedom of Information Act by court decision, but was released by the U.S. Air Force in September, 1996.

6. The regional reporters are *Pacific Reporter, Northwestern Reporter, Southwestern Reporter, Northeastern Reporter, Atlantic Reporter, Southeastern Reporter, Southern Reporter, California Reporter*, and the *New York Supplement*.

7. As discussed earlier, the Chicago-Kent College of Law and Villanova University School of Law have discontinued joint operation of the Center for Information Law and Policy. The two institutions divided the CILP databases and Web sites. Each institution is developing new Web products to make legal and government information more accessible.

WEBLIOGRAPHY

Guides and Directories to Legal and Government Internet Resources

Argus Clearinghouse–URL: http://www. clearinghouse.net/
Argus–Government and Law Page–URL: http://www.clearinghouse.net/cgibin/chadmin/viewcat/Government___Law?kywd++

Center for Information Law and Policy (CILP)–Chicago-Kent College of Law–
URL: http://www.cilp.org/
FindLaw Web Guide of Legal Information and Web Sites–URL: http://www.findlaw.
com/
GPO Access–U.S. Government Printing Office–URL: http://www.access.gpo.gov
Core Documents of U.S. Democracy–http://www.access.gpo.gov/su_docs/dpos/co-
redocs.html
U.S. House of Representatives Internet Law Library–URL: http://law.house.gov/
(List of institutions and firms that have made the Internet Law Library available to
the public through the Internet)
Internet Legal Research Compass–Villanova University School of Law–URL:
http://vls.law.vill.edu/compass/
Library of Congress–Guide to Law Online–URL: http://lcweb2.loc.gov/glin/worldlaw.
html
**Library of Congress–Browse Topical Guides–Government Resources by Cate-
gory–**URL: http://lcweb.loc.gov/global/subject.htm
Hieros Gamos–The Comprehensive Legal and Government Portal–URL: http://
www.hg.org/
Legal Information Institute at Cornell University School of Law–URL: http://
lii.law.cornell.edu/
Washlaw WWW Washburn University School of Law–URL: http://www.
washlaw.edu
World Wide Web Virtual Law Library–Indiana University School of Law Library–
URL: http://www.law.indiana.edu/law/vlib/lawindex.html

Legal Search Engines

CataLaw–URL: http://www.catalaw.com/
Georgia State University Meta-Index for U.S. Legal Research–URL: http://gsulaw.
gsu.edu/metaindex/.
GOVBOT–URL: http://ciir2.cs.umass.edu/Govbot/
Law.Com–URL: http://www.lawcrawler.com/
LawCrawler–URL: http://www.lawcrawler.com/
Law Engine–URL: http://www.fastsearch.com/law/index.html
Law Guru–Legal Research Page–URL: http://www.lawguru.com/search/lawsearch.
html
LawRunner–URL: http://www.lawrunner.com/

Judicial Branch Information Sources: Federal and State Case Law

Federal Courts Finder–Emory University Law School–URL: http://www.law.emory.
edu/FEDCTS
Federal Court Locator–Villanova University School of Law–URL: http://vls.
law.vill.edu/Locator/fedcourt.html
Federal Court Opinions–Georgetown University Legal Explorer–URL: http://
www.ll.georgetown.edu:80/Fed-Ct/

Findlaw Case Law Index–URL: http://www.findlaw.com/casecode/

Supreme Court Decisions

FindLaw Supreme Court Cases–URL: http://www.findlaw.com/casecode/supreme.
html or URL: http://www.unilegal.com/ussc.htm
Judicial Branch Resources–GPO Access–URL: http://www.access.gpo.gov/su_docs/
judicial.html
> **Supreme Court Decisions, 1937 to 1975–FLITE Database (Federal Legal
> Information Through Electronics)**–URL: http://www.access.gpo.gov/su_docs/
> supcrt/index.html
> **Supreme Court Decisions, 1992 Term Forward**–http://fedbbs.access.gpo.
> gov/court01.htm
Legal Information Institute (LII)–Supreme Court Collection–URL: http://
supct.law.cornell.edu/supct/

Supreme Court and Justice Information

Oyez Project–Justices Page–URL: http://oyez.nwu.edu/justices/justices.cgi

Administrative and Agency Decisions

Administrative Decisions Guide–GPO Access–URL: http://www.access.gpo.gov/su_
docs/admin.html

State Case Law State Multicourt Sites

State Court Locator–Villanova University School of Law–URL: http://vls.law.
vill.edu/Locator/statecourt/
FindLaw State Resources–URL: http://www.findlaw.com/11stategov/
StateLaw–WashLawWEB–URL: http://www.washlaw.edu/uslaw/statelaw.html
ALSO American Law Sources Online–United States–URL: http://www.lawsource.
com/also/usa.htm

LEGISLATIVE AND STATUTORY INFORMATION SOURCES

Constitutional Law

**Global Legal Information Network–Guide to the U. S. Constitution and Legal
System**–URL: http://lcweb2.loc.gov/glin/usconst.html
FindLaw State Resources State Constitutions–URL: http://www.findlaw.com/
11stategov/indexconst.html

National Archives and Records Administration Constitution of the of the United States–URL: http://www.nara.gov/exhall/charters/constitution/conmain.html

Congressional Servers

U.S. Senate World Wide Web Server–URL: http://www.senate.gov
U.S. House of Representatives' World Wide Web Service–URL: http://www.house.gov/

Legislative Information Sites

Legislative–Congressional Publications–GPO Access–URL: http://www.access.gpo.gov/su_docs/legislative.html
THOMAS: Legislative Information on the Internet–URL: http://thomas.loc.gov
Congressional Universe–Congressional Information Service (Subscription Based)–URL: http://www.cispubs.com/

Guides to the Legislative Process

The U.S. House of Representatives Educational Resources–URL: http://www.house.gov/house/Educat.html
> **The Legislative Process**–URL: http://www.house.gov/Legproc.html
> **The Legislative Process Tying it All Together**–http://www.house.gov/house/Tying_it_all.html
How Our Laws Are Made–THOMAS–URLs: http://thomas.loc.gov/home/lawsmade.toc.html or http://www.house.gov/house/HOLAM.TXT
Enactment of a Law–THOMAS–URL: http://thomas.loc.gov/home/enactment/enactlawtoc.html

Congressional and Government Directories

Biographical Directory of the U.S. Congress 1774 to Present–URL: http://bioguide.congress.gov/
CapWeb–URL: http://www.capweb.net/classic/index.morph
Congressional Directory–URL: http://www.access.gpo.gov/congress/cong001.html
Congress.Org–URL: http://congress.org/main.html

Statutory Information Resources Codification of Federal Statutes

U.S. Code–House of Representatives–URL: http://uscode.house.gov/usc.htm
U.S. Code–Legal Information Institute–URL: http://www.law.cornell.edu/uscode/ and URL: http://www4.law.cornell.edu/uscode/
U.S. Code–GPO Access–URL: http://www.access.gpo.gov/congress/cong013.html

U.S. Code–ALSO! American Law Sources Online–URL: http://www.lawsource. com/also/usa.cgi?us1#Z3Q.
> **ALSO! Popular Names of Public Acts–Complete List**–URL: http://www. lawsource.com/also/usa.cgi?usp1
> **ALSO! Popular Names of Significant New Laws**–URL: http://www.lawsource. com/also/usa.cgi?usp0.
> **ALSO! Popular Names of Selected Public Acts**–URL: http://www.lawsource. com/also/usa.cgi?usp.

Statutory Multistate Finders

StateLaw State Government and Legislative Information–Washburn University School of Law–URL: http://www.washlaw.edu/uslaw/statelaw.html
State Web Locator–Center for Information Law and Policy–Chicago-Kent College of Law–URL: http://www.infoctr.edu/swl/

Municipal Codes

Municipal Code Corporation List of Codes–URL: http://www.municode.com/ database.html
Municipal Codes Online–Seattle Public Library–URL: http://www.spl.org/govpubs/ municode.html

ADMINISTRATIVE AND EXECUTIVE BRANCH INFORMATION SOURCES

Guides to the Federal Government Departments and Agencies

DocLaw WWW–Washburn University School of Law–URL: http://www.washlaw. edu/doclaw/doclawnew.html
Federal Web Locator from the Center for Information Law and Policy–Chicago-Kent College of Law–URL: http://www.infoctr.edu/fwl/
Federal Web Navigator–Villanova University School of Law–http://yolanda.law. vill.edu/fedweb/index.html
The Great American Web Site–URL: http://www.unclesam.com/home.html# siteguide and URL: http://www.unclesam.com/guide_index.html
> **Internet Guide to the U. S. Government**–URL: http://www.unclesam.com/ guide.html

U.S. Government Manual–GPO Access–URL: http://www.access.gpo.gov/nara/nara001. html and URL: http://www.access.gpo.gov/nara/browse gm.html
The White House–URL: http://www.whitehouse.gov
Interactive Citizen's Handbook–URL: http://www.whitehouse.gov/WH/html/handbook. html
> **The President's Cabinet**–URL: http://www.whitehouse.gov/WH/Cabinet/html/ cabinet_links.html

Cabinet Secretaries–URL: http://www.whitehouse.gov/WH/Cabinet/html/secretary. html

Independent Federal Agencies and Commissions–URL: http://www. whitehouse.gov/WH/Independent_Agencies/html/independent_li nks.html

White House Offices and Agencies–URL: http://www.whitehouse.gov/WH/EOP/ html/EOP_org.html

White House Virtual Library–URL: http://www.whitehouse.gov/library/

Guides to Administrative Law and Federal Regulations

Executive Branch Resources–GPO Access–URL: http://www.access.gpo.gov/su_docs/ executive.html

Regulatory Resources–GPO Access–URL: http://www.access.gpo.gov/su_docs/ regulatory. html

Federal Register

Federal Register–GPO Access–URL: http://www.access.gpo.gov/nara /index.html

Code of Federal Regulations

Code of Federal Regulations–GPO Access–URL: http://www.access.gpo.gov/nara/ cfr/index.html

List of CFR Sections Affected–GPO Access–URL: http://www.access.gpo.gov/nara/lsa/ aboutlsa.html.

State Administrative Law

American Bar Association (ABA) Administrative Procedure Database–URL: http:// www.law.fsu.edu/library/admin/

State Web Locator–Center for Information Law and Policy–Chicago-Kent College of Law–URL: http://www.infoctr.edu/swl/

PRESIDENTIAL INFORMATION

White House–URL: http://www.whitehouse.gov

White House Interactive Citizen's Handbook–URL: http://www.whitehouse.gov/ WH/html/handbook.html

White House Virtual Library–URL: http://www.whitehouse.gov/WH/html/library. html

Weekly Compilation of Presidential Documents–URL: http://www.access.gpo. gov/nara/nara003.html

SECONDARY RESOURCES

Citation Manuals

Introduction to Basic Legal Citation–URL: http://www.law.cornell.edu/citation/citation.table.html

Legal Dictionaries and Glossaries

Findlaw Legal Dictionary–URL: http://dictionary.findlaw.com/.
Oran's Dictionary of the Law–URL: http://www.lawoffice.com/pathfind/orans/orans.asp

Legal Directories

American Bar Association–Approved Law Schools–URL: http://www.abanet.org/legaled/approved.html
Hieros Gamos Every Law School on the Planet–URL: http://www.hg.org/schools.html
MartindaleHubbell Lawyer Locator–URL: http://www.martindale.com
Martindale-Hubbell lawyers.com–URL: http://www.lawyers.com/
West Legal Directory–Find A Lawyer–URL: http://www.lawoffice.com/direct/direct.asp

Topical Law Information

FindLaw Subject Indexes of Legal Resources–URL: http://www.findlaw.com/01topics/index.html
FindLaw Library–URL: http://library.findlaw.com/
law.com–Law Pathfinders–URL: http://www.lawoffice.com/pathfind/pathfind.htm

APPENDIX I

Federal Courts/Dates of Coverage	Sponsoring Institution	Uniform Resource Locator
District of Columbia Circuit Court of Appeals 1995-present[1]	Edward Bennett Williams Law Library at the Georgetown University Law Center Law Library	http://www.ll.georgetown.edu/Fed-Ct /cadc.html
1997-present	U.S. Court of Appeals District of Columbia Circuit Homepage	http://www.cadc.uscourts.gov/opinions/ opinions.asp
First Circuit November 1995-present[2]	Emory University School of Law Library-Court Publishing Project	http://www.law.emory.edu/1circuit/
Second Circuit 1995-present[3]	Touro College-Fuchsberg Law Center	http://www.tourolaw.edu/2ndcircuit/ indexf.html
1995-present	Pace University School of Law	http://www.law.pace.edu/lawlib/legal /us-legal/judiciary/secondcircuit.html
Third Circuit 1994-present[4]	Villanova University Law School and Center for Information Law and Policy	http://vls.law.vill.edu/Locator/3/index. htm
Fourth United States Circuit Court of Appeals 1995-present[5]	Emory University School of Law Library-Court Publishing Project in cooperation with the Fourth Circuit	http://www.law.emory.edu/4circuit/
Fifth Circuit 1991-present[6]	University of Texas at Austin School of Law-Tarlton Law Library	http://www.law.utexas.edu/us5th/us5th. html
1990-present	U.S. Court of Appeals for the Fifth Circuit	http://www.ca5.uscourts.gov/opinions. HTM
Sixth Circuit 1994-present[7]	U.S. Court of Appeals for the Sixth Circuit	http://pacer.ca6.uscourts.gov/opinions/ main.php
1995-June, 1999	Emory University School of Law Library-Court Publishing Project	http://www.law.emory.edu/6circuit/
Seventh Circuit 1993-present (Browse) 1995-present (Searchable database)[8]	Chicago Kent College of Law-Center for Law & Computers	http://www.kentlaw.edu/7circuit/
August 1995 to the present	U.S. Circuit Court for the Seventh Circuit	http://www.ca7.uscourts.gov/

APPENDIX I (continued)

Federal Courts/Dates of Coverage	Sponsoring Institution	Uniform Resource Locator
Eighth Circuit August 1995 to the present[9]	Washington University School of Law	http.//www.wulaw.wustl.edu/8th.cir/
Ninth Circuit June 1995[10]	Villanova University Center for Information Law and Policy	http://www.cilp.org/Fed-Ct/ca09.html
Current decisions	United States Court of Appeals for the Ninth Circuit	http://www.ca9.uscourts.gov/
Tenth Circuit 1995-October 1997	Emory University School of Law-Court Publishing Project	http://www.law.emory.edu/10circuit/index.html
1995 to the present[11]	Washburn University School of Law	http://www.washlaw.edu/searchlaw.html#10th Circuit
Eleventh Circuit November 1994[12]	Emory University School of Law Library-Court Publishing Project	http://www.law.emory.edu/11circuit
July 1998-present	Administrative Office of U.S. Courts	http://www.ca11.uscourts.gov/opinions.htm
United States Court of Federal Claims 1997-present	United States Department of Commerce-Office of General Counsel	http://www.ogc.doc.gov/fedcl/cofc.html
U. S. Court of Appeals for the Armed Forces 1997-present[13]	U.S. Court of Appeals for the Armed Forces	http://www.armfor.uscourts.gov/Opinions.htm

1. The cases on appeal from Washington, D.C. are heard in the District of Columbia Circuit Court. This court hears most of the appeals from the Federal administrative agency decisions

2. The First Circuit hears cases from Maine, New Hampshire, Massachusetts, Rhode Island, and Puerto Rico.

3. The Second Circuit Court hears cases from Connecticut, New York, and Vermont.

4. The Third Circuit hears cases from the states of Pennsylvania, New Jersey, and Delaware.

5. The Fourth Circuit hears cases on appeal from West Virginia, Virginia, Maryland, and North Carolina.

6. The Fifth Circuit Court of Appeals hears cases from Texas, Louisiana, and Mississippi.

7. The Sixth Circuit hears cases on appeal from Michigan, Ohio, Kentucky, and Tennessee.

8. The Seventh Circuit hears cases from Wisconsin, Illinois, and Indiana.

9. The Eighth Circuit Court hears cases from North Dakota, South Dakota, Nebraska, Minnesota, Iowa, Missouri, and Arkansas.

10. The Ninth Circuit Court hears cases on appeal from the states of Hawaii, Alaska, Washington, Oregon, California, Idaho, Montana, Nevada, and Arizona.

11. The Tenth Circuit hears cases from Wyoming, Utah, Colorado, Kansas, Oklahoma, and New Mexico.

12. The Eleventh Circuit Court hears cases on appeal from Georgia, Alabama, and Florida.

13. The official reports are published by the West Group and are known as the Military Justice Reporter (MJ). These reports contain Daily Journals of the Court's filings, summary disposition orders and other day-to-day actions of the Court, as well as selected opinions of each of the Courts of Criminal Appeals.

English and American Literature Internet Resources: A Selective List

Scott Stebelman

SUMMARY. Humanities scholars have generally been reluctant to incorporate the Web into their research and teaching. Because humanists have placed such a high value on printed texts, have worked independently, and have been less dependent on current research data, their reliance on the Web is less urgent than for colleagues in other disciplines. Most primary and secondary literature is still published exclusively in print, and those literary texts that are available on the Web are often in popular rather than scholarly editions. Although the predominance of printed texts will continue to exist, probably for several decades, a shift is underway to enhance the authority and uniqueness of information available on the Web. Particularly instrumental in the shift is the emergence of hypermedia and hyperliterature, which are producing new modes for creating, experiencing, and analyzing texts. This essay discusses the effect these changes are having for scholars and librarians and identifies some of the most important Web resources in the area of English and American literature. *[Article copies available for a fee from The Haworth Document Delivery Service: 1-800-342-9678. E-mail address: <getinfo@haworthpressinc.com> Website: <http://www.HaworthPress.com>]*

KEYWORDS. Language and literature, Internet research in, Internet resources in, online resources in

---

Scott Stebelman is the selector for English and American literature at the Gelman Library, George Washington University, Washington, DC. He has a PhD in English from the University of Wisconsin–Madison and a MLS from the University of California–Berkeley (E-mail: scottlib@gwu.edu).

[Haworth co-indexing entry note]: "English and American Literature Internet Resources: A Selective List." Stebelman, Scott. Co-published simultaneously in *Journal of Library Administration* (The Haworth Information Press, an imprint of The Haworth Press, Inc.) Vol. 30, No. 1/2, 2000, pp. 209-229; and: *Academic Research on the Internet: Options for Scholars & Libraries* (ed: Helen Laurence, and William Miller) The Haworth Information Press, an imprint of The Haworth Press, Inc., 2000, pp. 209-229. Single or multiple copies of this article are available for a fee from The Haworth Document Delivery Service [1-800-342-9678, 9:00 a.m. - 5:00 p.m. (EST). E-mail address: getinfo@haworthpressinc.com].

Internet resources in English and American literature, as with other disciplines, have proliferated over the last five years. From reproductions of primary works, such as novels, plays, and poetry, to publication of original scholarly essays, resources on the Web are competing with traditional print formats to draw the scholar's attention. In some cases, such as the use of e-mail, the resource has become indispensable for communicating new research activities and strengthening collegial relationships; in other cases, the resource is viewed with skepticism, its claim to advancing knowledge seriously questioned. Although numerous examples might be cited of the latter, those frequently discussed among literary scholars are electronic editions or self-published secondary criticism. To many scholars, reading a brief essay might be instructive, especially if it contains new factual information or an original interpretation, but the computer is the last place to peruse a Victorian novel or a scholarly monograph. Given the skepticism of many humanists, a key task for librarians is to demonstrate what is valuable and what is marginal or questionable, and to assist users in acquiring both the technical and critical skills to find resources germane to a project.[1]

Equally key is to acknowledge that while the Internet is becoming increasingly important for scholarly research, the majority of humanities research is still being published in print. Most scholarly monographs and journals, although probably composed electronically, are not accessible electronically. Important reference tools, such as author bibliographies, dictionaries of literary terms, literary gazetteers, and many other works are still being published exclusively in print. Some, such as Gale's *Dictionary of Literary Biography, Contemporary Authors,* and *Biography and Genealogy Master Index,* are available both electronically and in print; however, in some cases, the electronic version is an abridgement of the print. Given many students' exclusive reliance on electronic resources and the dwindling purchasing power of most libraries, librarians must ask themselves whether it is prudent to continue to buy print materials which may contain unique information but information which may go unread. Examples that readily come to mind are the author bibliography series published by Greenwood, Scarecrow, and Garland presses; in addition to secondary criticism, they often contain "critical reception" (i.e., reviews published at the time of a work's initial publication) citations and citations to minor regional publications. These references will not be indexed by the

MLA International Bibliography, but except for the most specialized and conscientious of scholars, they probably won't be consulted by most students, who can use the *MLAIB* to generate a quick 20-30 citation bibliography that will satisfy most instructors.

In selecting both print and electronic tools, librarians must have a sound understanding of how humanists conduct research and what issues affect their selection and evaluation of materials. Unlike students, who may want only the cheapest and most legible edition of a text, scholars need texts that have undergone editorial scrutiny. Variant editions need to be identified and examined, inconsistencies noted, and decisions made about which textual emendations to accept. Variorum or critical editions, such as those authorized by the Modern Language Association's Center for Scholarly Editions, or editions published by distinguished university presses (e.g., Oxford University Press's Illustrated Authors editions) are valued above popular editions. One of the problems with editions found on the Internet is that–to avoid problems of copyright–only those in the public domain are usually included, and these editions may be the most spurious; an example are some of the editions made available through Project Gutenberg. However, as Harris has demonstrated, some reputable editions are rife with errors: over 100 Web sites link to *The Collected Poems of Yeats* (1956), an edition with incorrectly titled poems, several poems inadvertently joined, and stanzas split to form separate poems.[2] Another problem is the preference for HTML rather than SGML many transcribers use for encoding a text. Weibel and Price-Wilkin have argued that HTML cannot capture the myriad textual characteristics scholars often need for describing a work physically.[3]

Scholarly credentials are often important to faculty. Hence a literary critic, to be considered a peer, should have a Ph.D. and be affiliated with an academic or research institution. Most scholarship is also vetted by an editorial board or by a group of experts contacted by the publisher. Peer review can occur with Web documents, but it need not, as anybody can publish any opinion or any data, regardless of how dubious the source or the research design used to gather it. Even if a study published on the Web exhibits high standards of scholarship, other scholars may be reluctant to cite it, because to do so would reflect poorly on them–i.e., scholars who cite un-refereed research themselves become suspect.

Some of the problems attending Web publications are not peculiar to the humanities but are endemic to the Web itself. An acute example is the impermanency of many Web sites. A scholar may compile a bibliography on Charles Lloyd, a minor British poet, and mount it on a Web site; within a few years, however, the bibliography becomes somewhat dated and the scholar decides to expunge it from the site. Unlike a book or an article, which will continue to exist in some library, the Lloyd bibliography is lost forever. The problem may not be so radical as expungement but may instead be transfer of the document to another URL; in this case, the document remains but the record of access (i.e., a footnote) is now erroneous. The frequency of this occurrence came home to the author during the teaching of a graduate English workshop; an article, which discussed the development of course Web pages, was distributed to students and the request made that students visit the cited URLs. Unfortunately, approximately a third of all the URLs were broken, even though the article was only two years old. The point here is that faculty are either hearing or experiencing these problems on their own, and every time URL error messages are received, they undermine the Web's authority as a reliable transmitter and archiver of scholarly research.

If the unregulated dissemination of information vexed librarians and faculty, the acquisition of full-text journal databases was perceived as a partial solution. By acquiring digitized collections published by Elsevier, the Johns Hopkins University Press, JSTOR, and other prestigious publishers/vendors, librarians believed that some form of quality control would be exercised (if perhaps unconsciously) in student papers. The result was, indeed, the citing of reputable scholarship, but at a cost: students, instead of trying to identify the best literature on a topic, increasingly defer to the path of least resistance, which is to incorporate *only* those articles that can be downloaded from a full-text database. Some of these articles are scholarly, but often they are popular and hence inappropriate for many research papers (not, of course, for papers dealing with popular culture). The library, which may still expend hundreds of thousands of dollars on its print subscriptions, may find that money wasted as print titles languish on the shelf. As for the students, they acquire negative research skills, believing that a self-contained database of articles can substitute for the diversity of opinion that is more likely to come from a multitude of publishers and information formats. Again, it will not be long before faculty discern a sameness to their students' bibliographies and the authorities that are cited.

Although there are many reasons to be skeptical about the Web's value, there is one fundamental feature of the Web that will force literary scholars to become more receptive: hypermedia. In a seminal essay about the importance of hypermedia to textual production, Jerome McGann argues that critical editions should no longer be printed now that the option of hypermedia has become available.[4] Among the writers he uses to illustrate his points are Robert Burns and William Blake. In the case of Burns, much of his poetry was meant to be sung, and any modern edition should include the score as well as auditory recitations. Blake, an artist as well as a poet, included engravings with his poetry; it is difficult to understand Blake's conception of Urizen, Job, and other key figures without viewing these almost psychedelic images.[5] What hypermedia permits is the linking of almost an infinite number of texts with the central text under discussion; for example, collocating all the editions of *Leaves of Grass* within a variorum edition would be a monumental task, but a contemporary editor could link to them as independent texts, or to altered passages. Within that same edition could be links to pictures of Whitman, of Washington and New York during the late 19th century, and to essays about surgical practices during the Civil War (Whitman attended many of the soldiers). Incorporating these resources into a printed text would elevate the price; however, linking to texts and photographs located on other sites would be free.

Libraries have been one of the main purchasers of bibliographies. The advantage of a print medium, as previously noted, is stability: a printed text cannot be "deleted" in the way a computer file can, and changes in location are usually documented. Yet a printed text also has several handicaps which disappear in a hypermedia environment. Bibliographies (more aptly named Webliographies) can be continuously updated, and they permit categories of information that could not be rendered in print. For example, the author has produced a bibliography on hypertext and hypermedia that nullifies traditional format boundaries.[6] Included in this document are not only conventional citations, but also links to the full-text of many of the publications, as well as links to a writer's Web site (which often supplies biographical and contact information). In addition, there are links for conference announcements, courses teaching hypermedia, usenet groups and e-lists, hypermedia journal Web sites, a hypermedia timeline, a hypermedia glossary, and links to other Webliographies devoted to the subject. The advantage to having this published on the Web is that other resources do not have to be reproduced, or embedded, within the original document; the disadvantage, one that is also significant, is that the links must be continuously checked to verify their currency.

Finally, a new literary genre has mutated from a pre-existing one, a genre that is revolutionizing the way critics conceptualize creative writing: hyperliterature.[7] Poems, novels, and short stories now exist that have no linear plot; instead, the reader chooses a narrative pathway among many, in the process negating the authority of the "original" author and recreating the work anew. The response to hyperliterature has not been uniformly positive (many readers do not find the anarchy stimulating), but hyperliterature–like hypermedia in general–has decentered the text in ways anticipated by many postmodern theorists.[8]

The resources that follow are meant to be representative, rather than comprehensive, listings for their categories. For those readers who desire more extensive directories, they should consult the designated meta-sites. The categories were chosen because they reflect the information needs of literary scholars (which, in several instances, are identical to the needs of scholars in other disciplines). Because no two people would probably agree on what constitutes the best resources within an area, the listings are necessarily subjective. The pleasure in compiling such a list is sharing the information with faculty and librarians who will incorporate it into their research and teaching; the unavoidable regret is knowing that (as stated earlier) many of these sites will not exist, or their URLs will change, within the next few years.

ELECTRONIC LISTS

There are several excellent directories of e-lists, such as The Directory of Scholarly and Professional EConferences (http://www.n2h2. com/KOVACS/), Liszt, the mailing list directory (http://www.liszt. com/), and TILE.NET/LISTS (http://tile.net/lists/), and The List of Lists (http://catalog.com/vivian/interestgroupsearch.html). These directories are global in subject, attempting to identify all e-lists regardless of discipline or topic. Usually classified by topic, or arranged alphabetically, the e-lists can also be searched by key word. For scholars wanting to confine their searches to English and American literature, they may want to begin with the List of Electronic Discussion Groups, maintained by the Department of English Language and Literature, Southern Illinois University at Edwardsville. URL: <http://www.siue.edu/ENGLISH/listserv.html>. In addition to classifying lists by literary period (no distinction is made between English and American literatures), the site also includes other subjects of interest to literary scholars, such as African-American Studies, Education and Pedagogy, and Theory and Cultural Studies. The major drawbacks to using this directory are its lack of timeliness (the last update, at the time of this writing, was March of 1997) and–in spite of its assertion that it covers all nationalities–the omission of postcolonial literatures.

For professional development, English and American literature librarians should subscribe to EALSL (listserv@hermes.circ.gwu.edu), the official list of ACRL's English and American literature section and to the MLAIB (listserv@hermes.circ.gwu.edu), the official list of ACRL's MLA International Bibliography in Academic Libraries Discussion Group. Both of these lists provide valuable information about their committee's conference programs as well as guidance for literary collection development, reference work, Web development, and other professional issues.

META-SITES

Voice of the Shuttle
URL: <http://humanitas.ucsb.edu>

Created and maintained by Alan Liu and his staff, the Voice's scope is humanities, although a few social science subjects, such as "Anthropology," are included. Given Liu's background as an English professor at the University of California at Santa Barbara, the focus is particularly strong for English and American literature and for cultural studies. In the case of English and American Literature, sites are arranged by literary periods and by nationalities. Included among the resources are links to author Web sites, sites devoted to a particular movement or genre, museum or special exhibit sites, and sites containing the full-text of books, articles, and manuscripts. Of particular value are the links to sites specializing in conference announcements, course Web pages, journals and series, and e-lists, all arranged by literary period or by topic. The Voice even has a search engine which allows users to search key words throughout the entire site. The major weakness of the Voice is its failure to monitor site currency for URL changes or to ascertain whether a site still exists. Having said that, the Voice is clearly the pre-eminent Web site for literary scholars.[9]

Literary Resources on the Net
URL: <http://andromeda.rutgers.edu/~jlynch/Lit>

Created and maintained by Rutgers University English professor Jack Lynch, LRN's focus is English and American literature, with links to important ancillary topics, such as Theatre and Drama, Theory, and Bibliography and History of the Book. Resources are arranged by literary period and by nationality; particularly strong is The Eighteenth-Century, a separate archive established by Lynch and more cross-disciplinary than other periods within LRN. Like the Voice (to which LRN has links), LRN includes conference announcements, literary e-lists, and links to course Web pages among its resources. Single electronic texts are excluded, as well as those resources which are viewed as non-academic. A search engine permits cross-sectional searches.[10]

Mitsuharu Matsuoka's Home Page
URL: <http://www.lang.nagoyau.ac.jp/~matsuoka>

An English professor at the University of Nagoya in Japan, Matsuoka has constructed a site that is somewhat irregular in its organization: there is a broad link for English literature but not American, for 19th century British authors but not for other literary periods; entries are arranged chronologically rather than alphabetically, requiring users to know the birth and death dates of a particular writer; many entries are not hyperlinked, which provides an inflated impression of the site's value. Included among traditional resources, such as "Literary Magazines" and "Scottish Writers on the Internet," are Britannica's Great Books, Yahoo's Fonts, and the British Rail Timetables. The exceptional strength of this site is its concentration on English and American authors, ranging from canonical writers, such as Milton and Forster, to minor writers and those on the margins, such as Francis Ledwidge and Quentin Crisp. Sometimes the choice of hyperlinked materials is incomplete or superficial; for example, under Thomas Shadwell are links to a biographical essay and the Shadwell papers at the University of Michigan, but also a brief listing of Shadwell books at the Library of Congress and a Shadwell quotation.

The Literary Web
URL: <http://www.people.virginia.edu/~jbh/books.html>

Created by students attending the University of Tennessee, Knoxville, the site's major strength is fiction and poetry. Included are sections for books, children's literature, literary magazines, literary resources, poetry, and writing resources. The annotations are often thoughtful and discriminating. A site more for the book lover than for the conventional literary scholar.

Online Literary Criticism Collection
URL: <http://www.ipl.org/ref/litcrit>

Maintained by the Internet Public Library, this site links to the full-text of many scholarly publications, ranging from bibliographies to monographs. The links may contain original research available only through a Web site as well as reprints of articles and books originally appearing elsewhere (often the link is to the Northern Light, which requires a fee to download the document). Entries can be accessed by author's last name, by title of a work, and by literary period. Most of the resources are well annotated and include subject descriptors, the author's name, and the original source. A useful feature of this site, especially for undergraduate students unfamiliar with an author, is to identify a few major Web resources rather than attempt comprehensiveness. Like the Voice, it suffers from one drawback: many of the links are broken.

LSU Libraries Webliography: LITERATURE
URL: <http://www.lib.lsu.edu/hum/lit.html>

A model subject site maintained by Steven R. Harris at Louisiana State University. Categories include "General Guides," "Bibliographies," "Library Catalogs," "Dictionaries," "Discussions," "Organizations," "Periodicals," "Style Guides," "Electronic Texts," and "Individual Authors." Includes annotations. The "Author Webliography" links to many continental European as well as British and American writers; however, there appear to be few postcolonial writers.

LITERARY PERIOD SITES

The Labyrinth: Resources for Medieval Studies
URL: <http://www.georgetown.edu/labyrinth/labyrinthhome.html>

Created and maintained by Deborah Everhart and Martin Levine of Georgetown University, Labyrinth is the premier medieval studies Web site. Its resources are not restricted to literature but are multidisciplinary, including History and most humanities disciplines. In addition to Britain, its national scope includes France, Germany, Iberia, Italy, Byzantium, and Scandinavia. Like the meta-sites, Labyrinth lists pedagogical resources, discussion lists, conference announcements, and professional organization information. Finally, it includes links to Medieval Studies Text, Image, and Archival Databases, such as The Thesaurus Linguarum Hiberniae and the Online Medieval and Classical Library. No other site devoted to a literary period is as impressive and as comprehensive as Labyrinth.

Luminarium
URL: <http://www.luminarium.org/lumina.htm>

Luminarium is unusual in that it has no institutional affiliation and was created and is maintained by a Medieval and Renaissance aficionado rather than by a scholar. Divided into three sections (the Renaissance includes a separate 17th century division), Luminarium includes links to texts from major writers of the periods, as well as scholarly essays, chronologies, and biographical information. A troublesome problem with this site is textual reliability: many of the texts were developed at research institutions, but others come from sources whose editing is not consistent with current scholarly practices. The site is particularly useful for undergraduates, with numerous background notes, summaries, and plot outlines included; also attractive–to any user–are the numerous artistic reproductions and musical files (representative of the selected period) that complement reading.

Romantic Circles
URL: <http://www.rc.umd.edu>

General Editors are Neil Fraistat, Steven E. Jones, and Carl Stahmer, with an Advisory Board comprised of over 30 eminent Romanticists. Romantic Circles is a model site, publishing conventional scholarship as well as innovative projects. The following categories of information are included: publications, conference announcements, electronic editions, reviews, Romantic praxis (hypermedia articles devoted to specialized subjects), scholarly resources (includes links to editions, journals, exhibits, and chronologies of individual writers), and features (currently contains articles and conference reports). The site is also one of the few to contain an interactive MOO (a MOO is an object-oriented MUD [Multi User Domain], here serving as a virtual conference center). Still in its infancy, Romantic Circles has much room for development (e.g., its electronic editions are few), but it promises to be one of the most cutting-edge literary sites.

The Victorian Web
URL: <http://www.stg.brown.edu/projects/hypertext/landow/ victorian/victov.html>

Maintained by George Landow, Professor of English and Art History at Brown University, and based upon contributions from faculty and students from around the world, this site exemplifies what successful collaboration can produce. It was originally intended as an instructional aid for Brown's survey of English literature class, but the breadth of its interdisciplinary topics, and the cogency of its essays (which serve as basic introductions for undergraduate students), make it invaluable for anybody beginning a study of Victorianism or teaching Victorian studies. Categories of information include: "Gender Matters," "Social Context," "Political Context," "Economics," "Religion," "Philosophy," "Literature," "Visual Arts," "Science," and "Technology." Within each of these categories will be found articles with hyperlinks to other information sources or to paintings and illustrations when relevant. Continuing the spirit of collaboration, Landow welcomes contributions from visitors to the site.

THEORY, CULTURAL STUDIES, AND POSTCOLONIALISM

Theory, Culture & Society
URL: <http://tcs.ntu.ac.uk>

Produced by the Theory, Culture & Society Centre at the Notting-ham Trent University, this site includes information about confer-ences, journals, and research projects, and provides links to major sites devoted to theory and cultural studies. The strength of Theory, Cul-ture, and Society is its inclusion of sites from a variety of countries and that represent a variety of scholarly formats. For example, its site links include prominent theorists (Bakthin), journals (*CTheory* and *Octo-ber*), and institutes (Knowledge Media Institute and Institute for Cul-tural Research).

Sarah Zupko's Cultural Studies Center
URL: <http://www.popcultures.com>

Like the creator of Luminarium, Sarah Zupko is a non-academic who has produced an extensive set of resources for her subject. Categories of information include: journals/archives; articles/papers; theorists and crit-ics; calls for papers/conferences; book reviews; academic programs; bib-liographies/reading lists; publishers; newsgroups/listservs; general links; film; international; mass media/communication; cyberspace/sci fi; and television. What is particularly valuable about this site is the plethora of full-text hyperlinks to articles about sub-areas (e.g., "queer studies") and major theorists within cultural studies. Zupko has also simplified search-ing within some of the categories; for example, in the journals/archives section, users can conduct searches of specific journals without having to go to those Web sites. The "paper/conferences" section not only contains announcements for special issues, but in many cases links to the publish-er's requirements for manuscript submission. Zupko's site is an excellent example of how anticipation of an audience's research needs can inform site content and structure.

Contemporary Postcolonial and Postcolonial Literature in English
URL: <http://www.stg.brown.edu/projects/hypertext/landow/ post/misc/postov.html>

Created and maintained by George Landow of Brown University, the site–like his Victorian Studies site–is a collaborative project of students and faculty from around the world. Countries or continents covered include Africa, India, Australia, New Zealand, the United Kingdom (writers born in other countries who established residency in the UK), the Caribbean, and Singapore. Many of the contributions are from Brown students who post essays in the context of their course work. For most writers, separate categories have been established for specialized aspects of their life or work; among these are a work's setting, characterizations, political and religious themes, and the imagery used. Bibliographies are also included. The only weakness of this site is the numerous broken links.

Postcolonial Studies
URL: <http://www.emory.edu/ENGLISH/Bahri/>

Created by Deepika Petraglia-Bahrito, an English professor at Emory University, to assist students studying postcolonial writers and theorists, this site is not as neatly organized as Brown University's, nor is it as visually attractive, but it does include commentary about individual writers, covers many theorists, and provides bibliographies and some links to secondary materials. Of particular value are the definitions of key concepts and issues, such as "essentialism," "divorce in India," and "Yoruba Women and Gelede," the identification of key journals addressing postcolonial issues, and the linking to other important sites on the subject. How often the site is updated is unclear.

FULL-TEXTS OF BOOKS AND JOURNALS

So many important collections exist that it is impossible to catalogue them all here. Of paramount value are the *Humanities Text Initiative* at the University of Michigan (http://www.hti.umich.edu), the *Electronic Text Center* at the University of Virginia (http://etext.lib.virginia.edu), the *Making of America* (http://www.umdl.umich.edu/moa), and specialized collections, such as the *Victorian Women Writers Project* (http://www.indiana.edu/~letrs/vwwp/index.html) at Indiana University. Most of the major sites are linked in *Books and Journals (Full-Text) Accessible on the Web* (see next entry). Also useful is the *Sunsite Digital Collections* site (http://sunsite.berkeley.edu/Collections/) from the University of California at Berkeley, which not only provides access to California materials but also includes links to major digital collections around the world.

Books and Journals (Full-Text) Accessible on the Web
URL: *<http://www.gwu.edu/~gelman/train/books.htm>*

Compiled by Scott Stebelman, this site provides one-stop shopping for full-text books and journals. In addition to listing the metasites, which link to thousands of texts and provide author and title searching, this site includes gateways to foreign text collections, specialized sites (such as those dealing with mystery fiction or Renaissance literature), online booksellers, and sites covering journal collections. Annotations included.

Literature Online
URL: *<http://lion.chadwyck.com>*

Available by subscription from Chadwyck-Healey, LION provides access to important bibliographic databases, such as the *Annual Bibliography of English Language and Literature,* and to the full text of thousands of novels, poems, and plays published in America and the UK. Some of the collections are highly specialized, such as African-American Poetry and Editions and Adaptations of Shakespeare. A search engine permits users to search individual collections or to search for a word across collections. Many of the editions included in LION are first editions or editions published within the writer's lifetime. Although LION is an invaluable resource for students who need a quick copy of a specific text (especially if the text is not held by their library), some scholars have criticized the editions chosen for inclusion and the accuracy of the text reproduced.[11]

Project Muse
URL: *<http://muse.jhu.edu>*

A digitized collection of journals published by The Johns Hopkins University Press, Project Muse includes some of the most important scholarly publications in the humanities and social sciences. Titles range from traditional literary criticism, such as *ELH* and *Milton Quarterly,* to journals dealing with theory and cultural studies, such as

New Literary History and *Postmodern Culture*. The earliest issues were usually published in the early 1990s; no attempt is being made retrospectively to include a journal's entire run (such as is being done by JSTOR). A search engine permits users to search key words within a specific journal or across the entire database. Accessible by subscription.

ARCHIVAL AND MANUSCRIPT REPOSITORIES AND SEARCH AIDS

Literary scholarship is often based on the identification and analysis of primary documents, such as diaries, correspondence, autobiographies, and manuscripts. The tools below, some of which were only available in print or in microform, have simplified the process for scholars.

ArchivesUSA
URL: <http://archives.chadwyck.com>

Produced by Chadwyck-Healey, this subscription database provides holdings information for over 5,000 repositories and 110,000 special collections. Much of the information is based on the *National Union Catalogue of Manuscript Collections* (*NUCMC*) and the *National Inventory of Documentary Sources in the United States* (*NIDS*). Terms can be searched across several fields, such as "keyword," "collection name," "repository name," and "repository city" or "repository state." Hyperlinks to a repository Web site may allow visual and auditory materials to be examined.

Repositories of Primary Sources
URL: <http://www.uidaho.edu/specialcollections/Other. Repositories.html>

Maintained by Terry Abraham at the University of Idaho, this site is useful for scholars who already know what repository will have materials relevant to a research topic. Included are links to over 3300 repositories that contain manuscripts, archives, rare books, and historical photographs. Especially valuable are the links to foreign repositories, as well as to specialized resources, such as *The Directory of Corporate Archives in the United States and Canada* and *Guide to the Archives of Intergovernmental Organizations.*

DICTIONARIES OF LITERARY TERMS

A Glossary of Literary Terms and A Handbook of Rhetorical Devices
URL: *<http://www.uky.edu/ArtsSciences/Classics/Harris/rhetform.html>*

Created by Robert Harris, Professor of English at Southern California College in Costa Mesa, with search capability provided by Ross Scaife, Associate Professor of Classics, University of Kentucky, the *Glossary* includes the usual literary and rhetorical terms, such as "oxymoron," "zeugma," and "epistolary novel." Two features make this site more useful than its print counterparts: the examples used to illustrate (and hence help clarify) a concept are plentiful, and the search engine will look for a term within an entry's complete text as well as its title.

The Johns Hopkins Guide to Literary Theory & Criticism
URL: *<http://www.press.jhu.edu/books/hopkins_guide_to_literary_theory>*

Based on the print title of the same name, the electronic *Guide* claims added value by including additional terms not found in the print, by establishing hyperlinks for cross-referenced terms, and by enabling users to search by field or phrase across entries. Accessible on the Web by subscription, it is available to its users 24 hours a day. Because it is unclear how complicated, or simple, most search requests are (i.e., does the average user merely want a quick definition of a term?), this tool may be less essential than products offering unique information critical for research and teaching.

ENGLISH DEPARTMENT HYPERLINKS

English Departments Worldwide
URL: *<http://www.nyu.edu/gsas/dept/english/links/engdpts.html>*

Created and maintained by David Hoover of New York University's English Department, this site links to about 1300 departments, about

1000 of them in the United States. Attempts are made to be comprehensive; it does not include annotations.

English Departments Online
URL: <http://www.marist.edu/humanities/english/engdep.html>

Created and maintained by Tom Goldpaugh of Marist College's English Department, English Departments Online is not as extensive as English Departments Worldwide, but it does include useful annotations. These annotations not only indicate whether there is information on the program and the faculty, but also cite (and link) to unique scholarly resources developed by a department.

COURSE SYLLABI AND WEB PAGES

As indicated earlier, both the Voice of the Shuttle and Literary Resources on the Net include links to course Web pages. Two other useful sites are:

Library of Syllabi for Teaching the American Literatures
URL: <http://www.georgetown.edu/tamlit/teaching/syllabi_lib.html>

Maintained by the Electronic Archives for Teaching the American Literatures at Georgetown University, this site does not link to course Web pages but instead provides syllabi information from cooperating American literature courses. Categories include survey courses, courses on specific literatures (e.g., literature by women), period courses, and courses organized around issues and themes. A category exists for genre courses, but no hyperlinks exist. Although the syllabi included will be useful for instructors, this site would be even more valuable if it attempted to be a comprehensive directory of American literature course Web sites.

World Lecture Hall
URL: <http://www.utexas.edu/world/lecture/index.html>

Maintained by the University of Texas at Austin, the World Lecture Hall is a multidisciplinary directory of course Web sites. The "English" section includes literature courses, but many of the links are to writing courses. Annotations provide a brief summary of course content and what can be found on the pages. The World Lecture Hall is useful for faculty who want to see what categories of information, or pedagogical aids, are being used by colleagues.

PROFESSIONAL ASSOCIATION SITES

The Modern Language Association of America
URL: <http://www.mla.org>

Since the MLA is the primary professional association for English Department faculty, English and American literature librarians should become familiar with this site. It provides information about conferences, association publications (both scholarly and those related to association governance), professional jobs, MLA prizes and awards, and style guidelines for scholarly papers.

ACRL's English and American Literature Section
URL: <http://www.lib.uconn.edu/EALS>

This is the official ACRL site serving academic librarians responsible for English and American Literature collections. It provides access to the Section's newsletter, a directory of current and past officers and committee chairs, important Section documents, and information about conference programs and meetings.

ACRL's MLA International Bibliography in Academic Libraries Discussion Group
URL: <http://gwis2.circ.gwu.edu/~scottlib/mla.html>

The *MLA International Bibliography* is the premier bibliographic database for literary scholars. This site provides information about the Group's officers, a bibliography of studies about the *MLAIB*, some original research, and links to user aids to teach the *MLAIB*.

CONCLUSION

Although humanities scholars have been slower than colleagues in other disciplines to embrace computer technology, the proliferation of

Internet resources and their role in much cutting edge research can no longer be ignored. Aside from e-mail and e-lists, which facilitate scholarly networking, those Web sites devoted to literary periods, genres, archival and manuscript documents, and professional associations provide information that in many cases is unique; moreover, as more and more instructors develop course Web pages to enhance and supplement classroom teaching, faculty from other institutions will find them invaluable models for pedagogical experimentation. Because new knowledge formats, such as hyperliterature, are influencing the evolution of both primary and secondary texts, librarians who are often most cognizant of these developments need to share them with faculty. Print will probably continue to remain the most popular medium for scholarly communication, but its displacement by electronic networks and artifacts will accelerate.

As important as electronic research is becoming for humanities scholars, their acceptance of it will remain provisional. Particularly alarming to the humanist, whose research has traditionally been archived and referenced for decades (or, in the case of premodern literature, centuries), is the ephemeral nature of Web documents. Given the recent repudiation of the canon as a governing criterion for research, teaching, and collection building, any attempt to identify "significant" literature and house it in permanent electronic storage sites is problematic: if a writer or genre is perceived to be minor, documents associated with them will eventually be deleted and any future research abrogated. Until librarians and archivists can assure scholars that the most ephemeral of documents will be preserved, and that the digital representation is as accurate as the print, humanists will respond to electronic research with a healthy skepticism. Such skepticism can actually be beneficial for libraries: it can motivate selectors to establish more critical standards for the acquisition of electronic materials.

NOTES

1. In an effort to provide some guidance for librarians and scholars, several reviews of Internet resources in English and American literature have been published. They include Loss Pequeño Glazier, "Internet Resources for English and American Literature," *C & R L News* (July/August 1994): 417-422; James R. Bottino and William Baker, "World Wide Web Resources for English Studies," *Library Review* 46 no. 1 (1997): 45-51; Pam Day, "Internet Reference Resources in Language and Liter-

ature." *The Reference Librarian* 57 (1997): 153-59; and Byron Anderson, "The World Wide Web and the Humanities: Superhighway to What? Research, Quality and 'Literature.'" *Humanities Collections* 1 no. 1 (1998): 25-40.

2. Steven R. Harris, "Webliography: The Process of Building Internet Subject Access," *The Acquisitions Librarian* 17/18 (1997): 33.

3. Stuart L. Weibel, "The World Wide Web and Emerging Internet Resource Discovery Standards for Scholarly Literature." *Library Trends* 43 (1995): 627-44; and John Price-Wilkin, "Using the World Wide Web to Deliver Complex Electronic Documents: Implications for Libraries." *Public-Access Computer Systems Review* 5 no. 3 (1994): 5-21. Retrieved June 18, 1999. URL: <http://info.lib.uh.edu/pr/v5/n3/pricewil.5n3>

4. Jerome McGann, "The Rationale of HyperText." Last modified May 6, 1995. Retrieved June 18, 1999. URL: <http://jefferson.village.virginia.edu/public/jjm2f/rationale.html>

5. An excellent example of the integration of hypermedia with hypertext is John Tolva's essay on Blake, "The 'bounding line': Verbal and Visual Linearity in Blake's 'Laocoön' and Book of Urizen." Retrieved June 18, 1999. URL: <http://www.mindspring.com/~jntolva/blake/line.html>

6. Scott Stebelman, "Hypertext and Hypermedia: A Select Bibliography." Updated December, 1997. Retrieved June 18, 1999. URL: <http://www.gwu.edu/~gelman/train/hyperbib.htm>

7. The most comprehensive hyperliterature Web site, focusing on fiction, is Michael Shumate's "Hyperizons." Updated July 22, 1997. Retrieved June 18, 1999. URL: <http://www.duke.edu/~mshumate/hyperfic.html>

8. One of the first, and most important, works to note the correspondence between hypermedia and critical theory was George P. Landow's *Hypertext: The Convergence of Contemporary Critical Theory and Technology* (Baltimore and London: The Johns Hopkins University Press, 1992). A second edition was published in 1998.

9. For a discussion of the background and scope of the Voice, see Alan Liu, "Globalizing the Humanities: Voice of the Shuttle: Web Pages for Humanities Research." *Humanities Collections* 1 no. 1 (1998): 41-56.

10. For a review of LRN, see John Creech, "On-Line Literary Resources," *College & Research Libraries News* 57 (1996): 307.

11. The most important of these problems are addressed in Gail Paster Kern, "Literature Online (LION): A Scholar's Perspective." *Biblio-Notes: Issued by the English and American Literature Section of the Association of College & Research Libraries, a division of the American Library Association* 33 (Spring 1999). Retrieved June 18, 1999. URL: <http://www.lib.uconn.edu/EALS/biblio/spring1999.html>

WEBLIOGRAPHY

ArchivesUSA [Online]. Alexandria, VA: Chadwyck-Healey, Inc. Retrieved June 18, 1999. URL: http://archives.chadwyck.com.
Association of College and Research Libraries. The English and American Literatures Section (EALS) [Online]. Chicago: American Library Association. Retrieved June 18, 1999. URL: http://www.lib.uconn.edu/EALS.

Electronic Text Center [Online]. Charlottesville: University of Virginia Library. Retrieved June 18, 1999. URL: http://etext.lib.virginia.edu.

English Departments Worldwide [Online]. New York: New York University, Department of English. Retrieved June 18, 1999. URL: http://www.nyu.edu/gsas/dept/english/links/engdpts.html.

Humanities Text Initiative at the University of Michigan [Online]. Ann Arbor: University of Michigan Press, School of Information, University Library. Retrieved June 18, 1999. URL: http://www.hti.umich.edu.

Irvine, M. and Everhart, D. *The Labyrinth: Resources for Medieval Studies* [Online]. Washington, D.C.: Georgetown University. Retrieved June 18, 1999. URL: http://www.georgetown.edu/labyrinth/labyrinth-home.html.

Landow, G. *The Victorian Web* [Online]. Providence, RI: Brown University. Retrieved June 18, 1999. URL: http://www.stg.brown.edu/projects/hypertext/landow/victorian/victov.html.

Landow, G. *Contemporary Postcolonial and Postcolonial Literature in English* [Online]. Providence, RI: Brown University. Retrieved June 18, 1999. URL: http://www.stg.brown.edu/projects/hypertext/landow/post/misc/postov.html.

Liu, A. *Voice of the Shuttle: Web Page for Humanities Research* [Online]. Santa Barbara, CA: University of California, Santa Barbara. Retrieved June 18, 1999. URL: http://humanitas.ucsb.edu/.

Lynch, J. *Literary Resources on the Net* [Online]. Newark, NJ: Rutgers University. Retrieved June 18, 1999. URL: http://andromeda.rutgers.edu/~jlynch/Lit.

Matsuoka, M. *Mitsuharu Matsuoka's Home Page* [Online]. Nagoya, Japan: Nagoya University. Retrieved June 18, 1999. URL: http://www.lang.nagoya-u.ac.jp/~matsuoka.

Stebelman, S. *Books and Journals (Full-Text) Accessible on the Web* [Online]. Washington, D.C.: George Washington University. Retrieved June 18, 1999. URL: http:// www.gwu.edu/~gelman/train/books.htm.

Medical Reference Tools

Steve Foote

SUMMARY. The current state of medical reference tools is confusing. Traditional sources are available in print and electronic formats, but the electronic formats range from CD-ROMs to locally mounted or Internet-based databases accessed by Web browsers. The National Library of Medicine was an early producer of reference tools and an early adopter of electronic means of distribution, a pioneering role it continues at the turn of the century. NLM's premier product, MEDLINE, is available from a variety of vendors, as are the electronic versions of traditional print indexes. An industry has grown up around distribution of electronic databases in the health sciences, an industry that has extended onto the World Wide Web to include resources unique to that medium. *[Article copies available for a fee from The Haworth Document Delivery Service: 1-800-342-9678. E-mail address: <getinfo@haworthpressinc.com> Website: <http://www.HaworthPress.com>]*

Steve Foote has been a medical librarian for 25 years, 20 of those as a cataloger of medical serials at the Emory University Health Sciences Center Library, where he also was involved with various aspects of library automation and remote connectivity. An infatuation with the Internet that began in 1985 turned into teaching classes at Emory, the Centers for Disease Control and the American Medical Writers Association; handouts for those classes evolved into MedWeb. In 1994 he created Emory MedWeb, a WWW-based resource, which grew to be one of the largest health sciences indexes of WWW sites. In 1998 he left Emory to co-create MedWebPlus, a resource which has extended beyond the boundaries of the original Emory MedWeb project and continues to grow with over 900,000 pages viewed per month. URL: <http://www.medwebplus.com>. Steve has been cataloging medical journals, monographs, and audio-visual materials since 1978 and medical WWW resources since 1994.

[Haworth co-indexing entry note]: "Medical Reference Tools." Foote, Steve. Co-published simultaneously in *Journal of Library Administration* (The Haworth Information Press, an imprint of The Haworth Press, Inc.) Vol. 30, No. 3/4, 2000, pp. 231-270; and: *Academic Research on the Internet: Options for Scholars & Libraries* (ed: Helen Laurence, and William Miller) The Haworth Information Press, an imprint of The Haworth Press, Inc., 2000, pp. 231-270. Single or multiple copies of this article are available for a fee from The Haworth Document Delivery Service [1-800-342-9678, 9:00 a.m. - 5:00 p.m. (EST). E-mail address: getinfo@ haworthpressinc.com].

KEYWORDS. Health/medicine, Internet research in, Internet resources in, online research in, online resources in

INTRODUCTION

On the eve of the new millennium, medical reference tools are experiencing the acceleration of a transition from paper to electronic media that began over 30 years before; yet the basic unit, the fundamental particle of information in the medical sciences, remains as it has for over 100 years: the journal article. The principal means of finding journal articles, indexes of periodical literature, are as important as ever, although they "went electric" in the 1970s. Recent events have altered the means of access, from fee-based services with arcane search commands that often required trained mediators, to fill-in-the-blanks form-based interfaces that may be offered as free services of umbrella Web sites. The intent to provide electronic access has remained unchanged for 30 years, but the technology and business climate for doing so have changed considerably.

At present, and probably for the immediate future, the standard medical reference works are the indexes to peer-reviewed scientific journals: *Index Medicus* (print format) or *MEDLINE* (electronic version), *Excerpta Medica* (print) or *EMBASE* (electronic), *Cumulative Index to Nursing and Allied Health Literature* (print) or *CINAHL* (electronic), *Psychological Abstracts* (print) or *PsycINFO* (electronic).

Almost from the beginning, the National Library of Medicine sold its MEDLINE data to commercial concerns, thus encouraging the growth of an industry of database vendors. Such vendors as Bibliographic Retrieval Service (BRS) and Dialog, initially in the online arena, and CDPlus and SilverPlatter in the CD-ROM market, aggregated electronic databases and sold them in packages distinguished by means of access and search interface. The publishers of scientific journals have embraced the Web with un-uniform enthusiasm in the last 6 years, and electronic distribution of journal content is becoming a primary, though not the primary, means of distribution. Efforts by library consortia and the National Institutes of Health may hasten the transition.

In the 1970s and 80s, access to medical databases was through dial-up connections over different commercial telecommunications networks or on locally mounted CD-ROMs. Often, each publisher or distributor of a reference source had to create and maintain its own electronic means of presenting data. The increasing ubiquity of the Internet and the 1993 release of the graphical Web browser Mosaic gave information providers a public domain, non-proprietary, and free means of distribution over the Internet, a communications medium whose use was growing so rapidly that it became a fad by 1995.[1] Even in 1992 the Internet was "the world's largest computer network and the largest electronic network of any kind, except for the telephone network."[2] The popularity of the World Wide Web has supported the proliferation of information providers. A. J. Liebling said that "Freedom of the press is guaranteed only to those who own one," and the Web has given a printing press to practically everyone. Universities, government agencies, libraries, and pharmaceutical companies have all put health-related information on the Web, in the spirit of the free exchange of ideas, of establishing good will, of self-aggrandizement, and of salesmanship. Effective use of the vast amount of information requires both focused catalogs of health related Web sites and criteria for determining quality.

The eve of the millennium finds the world of biomedical information in a most interesting situation: there is an almost overwhelming embarrassment of riches available to those rich enough to get them. The electronic forms of indexes to printed sources are available in a variety of formats from a variety of sources at a variety of prices. New forms of information distribution have clouded the picture as the same data appear in a variety of guises in varying degrees of completeness. Database aggregators provide packages of a limited number of databases; those same databases appear intermixed with content from a variety of sources, commercial and noncommercial, making choice difficult at best.

NATIONAL LIBRARY OF MEDICINE

The U.S. **National Library of Medicine** (NLM) was one of the first government agencies to have a strong presence on the Internet with its HyperDoc site in mid-1994, but the NLM had been a major provider of biomedical information since it began publishing *Index Medicus* in 1879.[3] URL: <http://www.nlm.nih.gov/>. *Index Medicus* is an index to the biomedical literature printed on paper. As the numbers of biomedical journal articles grew, so grew the size of *Index Medicus* and the task of producing it in a timely fashion. In 1964, NLM began using a computerized system for index production; this evolved into a pilot study in 1967 and became a full-fledged searchable online database called MEDLINE in October 1971.[4]

The National Library of Medicine MEDLINE (MEDlars onLINE) is a database containing over 9 million bibliographic citations "from over 3,900 biomedical journals published in the United States and 70 foreign countries."[5] The original bibliographic database has grown into a family of over 30 bibliographic and factual databases.

Early on, the NLM licensed its databases to commercial vendors in hopes of making the information more widely available: Bibliographic Retrieval Service (BRS) began offering MEDLINE in January 1977, DIALOG in May 1981.[6] Today the number of MEDLINE providers is larger and more varied; some offer it for free, some as part of a free service requiring registration, some for a fee.[7]

On June 26, 1997, NLM announced that the MEDLINE database may be accessed free of charge on the Web through its end-user interface called Internet Grateful Med and through a new service called PubMed. Internet Grateful Med began in 1986 as a program designed for end-user, rather than for mediated searching.[8] PubMed was an entirely new service designed for all kinds of end-users, sophisticated or novice.[9] It is important to note that not all available versions of MEDLINE are identical; they differ mainly in dates of coverage and in search capabilities.[10]

MEDLINE

National Library of Medicine PubMed. Retrieved May 30, 1999 URL: <http://www.ncbi.nlm.nih.gov/PubMed/>

PubMed searches MEDLINE and Pre-MEDLINE (the basic citations for articles before subjects are assigned to them, entered daily) plus links to on-line journals–the "Pub" of PubMed. ("As of 27-Aug-99, there are 404 journals on this list.")[11] It offers both simple and sophisticated search options and a clinical query form that provides preconstructed search filters for diagnosis, etiology, therapy and prognosis. Taking advantage of the hypertext capabilities of the World Wide Web, PubMed also links to related articles from each citation, has links to molecular biology databases of DNA/protein sequences and 3-D structure data, and to NLM's Loansome Doc Document Delivery service.

The combination of free and WWW access to the MEDLINE data through PubMed has encouraged others to create new approaches to the data. The University of Iowa Hardin Library **PubMed MEDLINE Search: Dermatology & Skin Diseases** consists of pre-written searches for dermatological topics. URL: <http://www.lib.uiowa.edu/hardin/pm/derm.html>. The Oregon Health Sciences University **Clini-Web International** is a database of medical Internet resources pertaining to anatomy or diseases categorized with the Medical Subject Headings (MeSH) thesaurus developed for MEDLINE. URL: <http://www.ohsu.edu/cliniweb/>. Each disease entry also includes a "canned" PubMed search for review articles, therapy, diagnosis or all articles pertaining to the disease. **MedWebPlus**, another database of medical information on the Web, includes a database of the journals indexed for MEDLINE (the List of Serials Indexed for Online Users) with a "canned" search of PubMed that produces a table of contents of sorts for each journal. URL: <http://www.medwebplus.com/>.

National Library of Medicine Internet Grateful Med. Retrieved May 30, 1999
URL: <http://igm.nlm.nih.gov/>

The National Library of Medicine Internet Grateful Med began in April 1996 as a fill-in-the-blank end-user interface to the MEDLINE data that has slowly acquired most of the characteristics of PubMed. It differs mainly by assuming the user wishes advanced searching capabilities (fielded searching, ability to limit searches by language, age groups, publication type) and by including NLM databases other than MEDLINE: AIDSLINE, AIDSDRUGS, AIDSTRIALS, BIOETHICS-LINE, ChemID, DIRLINE, HealthSTAR, HISTLINE, HSRPROJ, OLDMEDLINE, POPLINE, SDILINE, SPACELINE, and TOXLINE.

BioMedNet Evaluated MEDLINE. Retrieved May 30, 1999
URL: <http://www.biomednet.com/db/medline>

BioMedNet Evaluated MEDLINE is another interesting leveraging of Web technology. BioMedNet calls itself "the Internet community for biological and medical researchers." It includes access to the full text of 208 journals for a fee, a database of biomedical Web sites, a job listings exchange, a weekly science magazine (**HMS Beagle** at http://www.biomednet.com/hmsbeagle/current/about/index), and several databases: Macromolecular Structures Database, Mouse Knockout and Mutation Database, Swiss-Prot, and Evaluated MEDLINE. Evaluated MEDLINE includes access to the tables of contents and full text (for a fee) of the BioMedNet collection of journals, plus 964 others (a total of 1172 on March 30, 1999) plus access to the user's search history. The "evaluated" part of the name comes from the fact that the MEDLINE citations are linked to their critical evaluation in articles in the series of "Current Opinion" review journals included in BioMedNet. There are links between MEDLINE citations and the full-text journals that have cited it. Free, but requires registration.

HealthGate. Retrieved June 8, 1999
URL: *<http://www.healthgate.com/medline/search-medline.shtml>*

HealthGate MEDLINE access includes both an advanced and a simple search, the latter offering the option to use "ReADER," which translates "layman's terms" into the MeSH vocabulary to insure search results. HealthGate also provides access to other databases: AgeLine, AIDSDRUGS, AIDSLINE, AIDSTRIALS, BIOETHICSLINE, CANCERLIT, CINAHL, EMBASE, HealthSTAR, PsycINFO. A registered user is allowed to search all these databases, but some of them require a small fee to view full citations. HealthGate also has a consumer health site called **beWELL.com** that offers MEDLINE searching. URL: <http://beWELL.com/>. Free, but requires registration.

Medscape. Retrieved May 30, 1999
URL: *<http://www.medscape.com/misc/FormMedline.html>*

Medscape offers a sophisticated interface to MEDLINE from 1996 to the present, AIDSLINE and TOXLINE. The MEDLINE search can be rerun against Medscape's collection of full-text journals and to its online bookstore. Free, but requires registration.

Ovid. Retrieved May 30, 1999
URL: *<http://www.ovid.com/>*

Ovid Technologies uses the motto "Platform-independent access to bibliographic and live full text databases for academic, biomedical and scientific research" and has a history almost as long and as venerable as MEDLINE itself. Ovid Technologies is the name taken by the CD-ROM based MEDLINE vendor CDPlus after it bought the online services portion of Bibliographic Retrieval Services (with its licenses for full text journals).[12] BRS was the first company to sell access to MEDLINE and the first to link MEDLINE citations to the full text of journals. Ovid sells access mainly to institutions, offering a variety of databases, from NLM products (MEDLINE, AIDSLINE, Bioethics-Line, and HealthSTAR) to other major biomedical databases (BIOSIS Previews, CancerLit, Cumulative Index to Nursing and Allied Health Literature, Current Contents, EMBASE the Excerpta Medica database, Health Reference Center, International Pharmaceutical Abstracts, MANTIS: Manual, Alternative, and Natural Therapy Index System, and PsycINFO). Ovid provides the full text of several hundred journals and includes links between the MEDLINE citations and the full text articles, and between the articles' bibliographic citations and their MEDLINE citations and full text, if available. Ovid allows one to restrict a search to "Evidence-Based Medicine Reviews" (the Cochrane Database of Systematic Reviews and Best Evidence) designed to support clinical decision making.[13]

PaperChase. Retrieved May 30, 1999
URL: <http://www.paperchase.com/>

PaperChase was an early distributor of MEDLINE that offers a combined search of MEDLINE, AIDSLINE, Healthstar, CancerLit (from the National Cancer Institute), and OLDMEDLINE (Index Medicus citations from 1960-1965). Offers document delivery.

These are only a few of the ways to access MEDLINE that are available on the Web. To find more, look at **Dr Felix's Free MEDLINE Page** (http://www.docnet.org.uk/drfelix/) from the Gloucestershire Royal Hospital Library or the **OMNI Medline** page (http://omni. ac.uk/medline/). **Medical Matrix** presents a chart comparing the features of many of the different ways to access MEDLINE. URL: <http://www.medmatrix.org/info/medlinetable.asp>.

OTHER TRADITIONAL BIBLIOGRAPHIC DATABASES

Besides MEDLINE, other printed indexes have made the transition to electronic format. They are available through institutional and, sometimes, individual subscription, and often appear as part of packages offered by database aggregators or Web portals.

CINAHLsources. Retrieved May 30, 1999
URL: <http://www.cinahl.com/>

CINAHL Information Systems produces the CINAHL database, an index to nursing and allied health literature since 1982, which is distributed through database vendors and health portals and is directly available on the World Wide Web to subscribers. Recently CINAHL has expanded services by adding access to the full text of 18 journals at $12 per article and has even added access to MEDLINE.

EMBASE. Retrieved June 8, 1999
URL: <http://www.elsevier.nl/locate/inca/523328>

EMBASE began in 1946 as an international effort to report medical research with 14 manually produced abstract bulletins that evolved into an online index that began distribution in 1969.[14] Today *EMBASE: the Excerpta Medica Database* from Elsevier Science is a medical database best known for drug information from 4,000 journals published in 70 countries. URL: <http://www.elsevier.com/>. Updated monthly, EMBASE is one of the most current biomedical databases available. Fully indexed citations and complete author abstracts appear on average twenty days after receipt of the journal–most appear earlier. The database contains over three million records from 1980 to the present, with 375,000 new records added annually. Each record contains the full bibliographic citation, indexing terms, and codes. More than 65% of the records contain abstracts. The database includes EMTREE, a hierarchically ordered controlled thesaurus, which contains 38,000 preferred terms and more than 150,000 synonyms. Eighteen field-specific subsets of EMBASE are also available.

PsycINFO. Retrieved June 8, 1999
URL: <http://www.apa.org/psycinfo/>

PsycINFO, developed by the American Psychological Association, began as *Psychological Abstracts* in 1927. It contains all of the citations that *Psychological Abstracts* has created in electronic form–more than 1.5 million references to psychological literature spanning 1887 to the present day. Although the references themselves are all written in English, the covered literature includes material published in over 45 countries and written in more than 30 languages. Updated monthly with approximately 5,500 new references, the Psyc-INFO database covers all types of publications that APA examines regularly to identify psychologically relevant material, including journal articles, dissertations, reports, English-language book chapters and books, and other scholarly documents. PsycINFO data is found in systems from DIALOG, DIMDI (a service of the German Institute for Medical Documentation and Information), HealthGate, a service of HealthGate Data Corporation, OCLC's EPIC service, and Ovid.

Science Citation Index

The Institute for Scientific Information publishes **Current Contents** (a current awareness database featuring the tables of contents of the current issues of journals in the humanities, sciences, social sciences, and technology), the **Science Citation Index** (which traces the citation history of scientific and technical journal articles), and other products based on the journal literature. URL: <http://www.isinet.com/>. Current Contents is available in print, CD-ROM, and over the Web through **Current Contents Connect** (http://www.isinet.com/products/cc/ccc.html), Ovid, SilverPlatter, and Information Access Company's InfoTrac SearchBank. The company's **Web of Science** product, available only to institutional subscribers, offers a Web interface to *Science Citation Index Expanded, Social Sciences Citation Index, Arts & Humanities Citation Index,* and *BioSciences Citation Index, Chem Sciences Citation Index,* and *Clinical Medicine Citation Index.* URL: <http://www.isinet.com/products/citation/wos.html>.

DATABASE AGGREGATORS

Dialog. Retrieved May 30, 1999
URL: <http://www.dialog.com/>

Dialog Corporation is a database aggregator whose **DialogWeb** offers a Web interface to over 4500 databases divided into 12 subject collections. URL: <http://www.dialogweb.com/>. The Medicine collection includes AIDS Database, AIDSLINE, AMED Allied & Alternative Medicine, BIOETHICSLINE, BIOSIS Previews, CANCERLIT, CINAHL, EMBASE, MEDLINE, SciSearch (variant of Science Citation Index), full text of the AMA journals, *General Practitioner, Lancet, New England Journal of Medicine.*

EBSCO Information Services. Retrieved May 30, 1999
URL: <http://www.ebsco.com/home/>

EBSCO Information Services is a company that began as a journal subscription agent and now offers access to databases and to full text journals. It offers a number of packages to institutions; the medical set includes MEDLINE back to 1966 coupled with the full text from 80 medical journals, a consumer health database called Health Source Plus that includes the full text of over 1000 pamphlets, the USP Pharmacopoeia DI: Volume II Advice for the Lay Patient, full text for over 260 medical journals and abstracts and indexing for 430 general health, nutrition and professional health care publications. URL: <http://www.epnet.com/medical.html>.

MICROMEDEX. Retrieved May 30, 1999
URL: <http://www.micromedex.com/>

MICROMEDEX specializes in pharmacological and toxicological resources (DRUGDEX System, Index Nominum, Physicians' Desk Reference, U.S. Pharmacopeial Convention Material Safety Data Sheets and others) but includes some clinical databases as well (CareNotes, Clinical Decision Support Tools). It is sold to institutions.

OCLC FirstSearch. Retrieved May 30, 1999
URL: <http://www.oclc.org/oclc/menu/fs.htm>

OCLC, a long-time library support organization, offers its FirstSearch only though libraries. URL: <http://www.oclc.org/>. FirstSearch offers such databases as ContentsFirst (a tables of contents service), CINAHL, Health Reference Center, MDX Health Digest, MEDLINE, PsycINFO.

Ovid. Retrieved May 30, 1999
URL: <http://www.ovid.com/>

Ovid Technologies has been discussed in the MEDLINE section.

SilverPlatter. Retrieved May 30, 1999
URL: <http://www.silverplatter.com/>

SilverPlatter is a database aggregator whose offerings include: AgeLine, AIDSLINE, AMED Allied and Complementary Medicine, BIOETHICSLINE Plus, British Nursing Index, CANCERLIT, CINAHL, Current Contents, EMBASE, HealthSTAR, International Pharmaceutical Abstracts, MDX Health Digest, MEDLINE, Mental Measurements Yearbook, Material Safety Data Sheets from the Canadian Centre for Occupational Health and Safety, POPLINE, PsycINFO, TOXLINE.

DICTIONARIES AND OTHER REFERENCE WORKS

Electronic versions of traditional printed reference works, originally sold for installation on stand-alone workstations, and then networked computers, have evolved into Web-distributed resources, usually licensed to institutions (universities, hospitals, group practices), and are now appearing on public health portals as well. Some examples:

Dictionary of Cell Biology. Retrieved May 30, 1999
URL: <http://www.mblab.gla.ac.uk/~julian/Dict.html>

The Dictionary of cell biology, 2nd ed, edited by J. M. Lackie and J. A. T. Dow is copyright 1995, by Academic Press Limited, London.

Merriam-Webster's Medical Desk Dictionary. Retrieved May 30, 1999
URL: <http://www.medscape.com/mw/medical.htm>

Merriam-Webster's Medical Desk Dictionary (originally published 1996) is available through Medscape. The dictionary is also available as a JavaScript addition to the **emedicine: Emergency Medicine** on-line textbook. URL: <http://www.emedicine.com/emerg/index.shtml>. Whenever a word in the textbook is highlighted a small window pops up containing the definition of the word, with links to other related definitions. This emedicine-medical dictionary linkage, which appears at first sight to be a hotbed of rampant hypertextuality, is a wonderful example of the use of Web technology.

Stedman's Medical Dictionary. Retrieved May 30, 1999
URL: <http://pdr.net/>

Stedman's Medical Dictionary is available to registered users of PDR.net.

Taber's Cyclopedic Medical Dictionary. Retrieved May 30, 1999
URL: <http://www.tabers.com/>

Taber's Online is the Internet based service offered by the F.A. Davis Company to provide access on a subscription basis to the digitized contents of *Taber's Cyclopedic Medical Dictionary* 18th ed. 1998. Available free for a limited time.

Merck Manual of Diagnosis and Therapy. Retrieved September 8, 1999
URL: <http://www.merck.com/pubs/mmanual/>

Merck Manual of Diagnosis and Therapy, 17th ed., 1999, is available in its entirety.

Merck Manual of Geriatrics. Retrieved May 30, 1999
URL: <http://www.merck.com/pubs/mm_geriatrics/home.html>

Merck Manual of Geriatrics, 2nd ed., 1995, is available in its entirety.

Merck Manual of Medical Information–Home Edition. Retrieved
May 30, 1999
URL: <http://www.merck.com/pubs/mmanual_home/>

Merck Manual of Medical Information–Home Edition, a general audience work based on the forthcoming 17th edition of the *Merck Manual of Diagnosis and Therapy*, presents the table of contents and the entire sections on gynecology and obstetrics, infections, the eye, and the heart.

There are Internet-based resources for which there is no print equivalent:

AMA Health Insight Medical Glossary. Retrieved May 30, 1999
URL: <http://www.ama-assn.org/insight/gen_hlth/glossary/index.htm>

AMA Health Insight Medical Glossary is part of the American Medical Association's consumer health site.

BioTech's Life Science Dictionary. Retrieved May 30, 1999
URL: <http://biotech.icmb.utexas.edu/pages/dictionary.html>

BioTech's Life Science Dictionary, developed by the staff and contributors to Biotech, a biology/chemistry educational resource at Indiana University Bloomington, consists of 8300+ terms that deal with biochemistry, biotechnology, botany, cell biology and genetics. Last updated: July 21, 1998.

CancerWeb On-Line Medical Dictionary. Retrieved May 30, 1999
URL: <http://www.graylab.ac.uk/omd/>

CancerWeb On-line Medical Dictionary, copyright Academic Medical Publishing & CancerWeb 1997-98. "OMD is a searchable dictionary created by Dr. Graham Dark and contains terms relating to biochemistry, cell biology, chemistry, medicine, molecular biology, physics, plant biology, radiobiology, science and technology. It includes: acronyms, jargon, theory, conventions, standards, institutions, projects, eponyms, history, in fact anything to do with medicine or science."

Dictionary of Dental Terms. Retrieved May 30, 1999
URL: <http://www.bracesinfo.com/glossary.html>

A Dictionary of Dental Terms, copyright 1999 Rich Masel, is part of a Web site devoted to orthodontics.

Dictionary of Epidemiology. Retrieved May 30, 1999
URL: <http://www.kings.cam.ac.uk/~js229/glossary.html>

The Dictionary of Epidemiology is edited by Jonathan Swinton and copyrighted by the University of Cambridge, 1998, 1999.

Glossary of Terms in Oral Physiology. Retrieved May 30, 1999
URL: <http://www.eclipse.co.uk/moordent/glossary.htm>

Glossary of Terms in Oral Physiology by R. J. C. Wilding is part of a dental Web site.

Indiana Prevention Resource Center On-Line Dictionary of Street
Drug Slang. Retrieved May 30, 1999
URL: <http://www.drugs.indiana.edu/slang/home.html>

The Indiana Prevention Resource Center On-line Dictionary of Street Drug Slang contains more than 3,000 street drug slang terms from the Indiana Prevention Resource Center files, with more than 1,200 additions from the National Drug and Crime Clearinghouse slang term list.

MedicineNet Medical Dictionary. Retrieved May 30, 1999
URL: <http://www.medicinenet.com/Script/Main/AlphaIdx.asp?li=MNI
&p=A_DICT>

MedicineNet Medical Dictionary is written by the MedicineNet editorial staff.

Multilingual Glossary of Technical and Popular Medical Terms
in Nine European Languages. Retrieved May 30, 1999
URL: <http://allserv.rug.ac.be/~rvdstich/eugloss/welcome.html>

The Multilingual Glossary of Technical and Popular Medical Terms in Nine European Languages was created by the University of Ghent Heymans Institute of Pharmacology for the European Commission to aid drug information leaflet writers as they wrote directions in the 9 languages of the European Community. Last update: December 10th, 1995.

Office of Rare Diseases Glossary. Retrieved May 30, 1999
URL: <http://rarediseases.info.nih.gov/ord/glossary_a-e.html>

The U.S. Office of Rare Diseases Glossary was "developed from glossaries prepared by (1) U.S. Congressional Office of Technology

Assessment, (2) National Institutes of Health's Understanding Gene Therapy On-line Glossary, and (3) Genetics Education Center, University of Kansas Medical Center."

PharmInfoNet Glossary. Retrieved May 30, 1999
URL: <http://pharminfo.com/pia_glos.html>

The PharmInfoNet Glossary is a dictionary of medical and pharmacological terms linked to articles in PharmInfoNet's other services, DrugDB and Disease Centers, databases of the contents of its journal, Medical Sciences Bulletin.

University of Alberta's Cognitive Science Dictionary. Retrieved May 30, 1999
URL: <http://matrix.psych.ualberta.ca/~mike/Pearl_Street/Dictionary/dictionary.html>

"This dictionary of cognitive science terms was initiated by Dr. Michael Dawson, and introduced as a class project for Psychology 560, a graduate course in memory and cognition, and Interdisciplinary Studies 554, a graduate course in cognitive science (both are offered at the University of Alberta). The project was designed to give students the opportunity to learn more about the basic concepts of cognitive science, and also to learn about the delivery of information via the World Wide Web. This page is maintained by Dr. Michael Dawson, and is protected by copyright."

There are a few medical encyclopedias on the Web, one a transcription of a printed work, the others original to the Web.

drkoop.com: Medical Encyclopedia. Retrieved June 8, 1999
URL: <http://www.drkoop.com/conditions/encyclopedia/>

An online adaptation of the printed works *World Book Medical Encyclopedia* and *World Book Illustrated Home Medical Encyclopedia*.

World Book Rush-Presbyterian St. Luke's Medical Center Medical Encyclopedia. Retrieved June 8, 1999
URL: <http://my.webmd.com/encyclopedia/>

World Book Rush-Presbyterian St. Luke's Medical Center Medical Encyclopedia serves as the encyclopedia at WebMD, which originally hosted the adam.com works.

PORTALS

The growth of Internet usage has encouraged a plethora of commercial ventures on the Web. Just as commercial entities aggregated databases for the dial-up online and CD-ROM markets, companies have begun packaging Web-based databases and sites. One of the fastest growing is "a new class of Web site that some call a health portal, which makes it easier for consumers to retrieve health information and resources over the Internet."[15]

allHealth. Retrieved June 8, 1999
URL: <http://www.allhealth.com/>

allHealth began as an America Online forum, became a service of iVillage called BetterHealth, and is now called allHealth. Includes access to MEDLINE, AIDSLINE, the Advice for the Patient portion of the United States Pharmacopeia USP Drug Database, the home oriented Healthwise Handbook, and interactive community forums devoted to consumer health.

CommuniHealth. Retrieved June 8, 1999
URL: <http://www.communihealth.com/>

CommuniHealth provides content to health care organizations and includes information from ADAM.com, Better Health, First Databank, Healthway Communications, the National Health Council, Reuters Health Information Service.

drkoop.com. Retrieved June 8, 1999
URL: <http://www.drkoop.com/>

drkoop.com is a consumer-oriented site that also sells content to healthcare organizations and corporations. A unique offering is the Personal Medical Record, "a personal, Internet health management tool that allows consumers to develop a private, lifelong health record for themselves and their family members."

Healtheon. Retrieved June 8, 1999
URL: <http://www.healtheon.com/>

Healtheon is primarily aimed at institutions, but has a consumer health segment called Solutions for You and Your Family. URL: <http://healthcenter.healtheon.com/>.

HealthGate. Retrieved May 30, 1999
URL: <http://www.healthgate.com/>

HealthGate is aimed at health care professionals. It provides access to AgeLine, AIDSDRUGS, AIDSLINE, AIDSTRIALS, BIOETHICS-LINE, CANCERLIT, CINAHL, EMBASE, HealthSTAR, MEDLINE, PsycINFO. A registered user is allowed to search all these databases, but some of them require a small fee to view full citations. In addition to the databases, HealthGate provides continuing medical education credits, and patient education materials. HealthGate also has a consumer health site called beWELL.com. URL: <http://beWELL. com/>. Free, but requires registration.

HealthLeaders.com. Retrieved June 8, 1999
URL: <http://www.healthleaders.com/>

HealthLeaders.com is "an online health leadership community."

InteliHealth. Retrieved June 8, 1999
URL: <http://www.intelihealth.com/IH/ihtIH>

InteliHealth is a joint venture between Aetna U.S. Healthcare and Johns Hopkins University and Health System. Includes access to Adult Health Advisor, AIDSDRUGS, AIDSLINE, AIDSTRIALS, CANCERLIT Drug Resource Center, MDX Health Digest (indexes over 200 peer-reviewed medical journals, newsletters, popular newspapers, popular magazines, medical school and hospital publications for articles dealing with consumer health), MedCite (a topic-driven approach to MEDLINE), MEDLINE, Webster-Medical Dictionary.

Kinetra. Retrieved June 8, 1999
URL: <http://www.kinetra.com/>

Kinetra provides information services and healthcare information to institutions.

Mayo Clinic Health Oasis. Retrieved June 8, 1999
URL: <http://www.mayohealth.org/>

Mayo Clinic Health Oasis was launched in 1995 by the Mayo Clinic as a consumer health site.

Medcast. Retrieved June 8, 1999
URL: <http://www.Medcast.com/>

Medcast is a medical news and information service started in early 1998 and aimed at institutional users.

Mediconsult.com. Retrieved June 8, 1999
URL: <http://www.mediconsult.com/>

Mediconsult.com includes consumer health information, clinical trials information, drug information, and medical news.

Medscape. Retrieved June 8, 1999
URL: <http://www.medscape.com/>

Medscape, created May 24, 1995, includes news, continuing medical education opportunities, professional conference summaries, database search, full-text journals, patient education materials, and practice guidelines. Medscape offers a sophisticated interface to MEDLINE from 1996 to the present, AIDSLINE, and TOXLINE. The MEDLINE search can be rerun against Medscape's collection of full-text journals and to its online bookstore. Free, but requires registration. Now edited by George D. Lundberg, the former editor of *JAMA: Journal of the American Medical Association*.[16]

Medsite. Retrieved June 8, 1999
URL: <http://www.medsite.com/>

Medsite is another commercial Web site providing MEDLINE access, in addition to ratings and reviews of more than 11,000 medical and health-related Internet sites.

OnHealth.com. Retrieved June 8, 1999
URL: <http://www.onhealth.com/ch1/index.asp>

OnHealth.com is a consumer health site featuring "information from the publishers of the New England Journal of Medicine, from Beth Israel Deaconess Medical Center, and from physicians who teach at Harvard, Columbia and Stanford." Includes discussion areas, a drug database, an herbal index, and an encyclopedia of diseases.

PDR.net. Retrieved June 8, 1999
URL: <http://pdr.net/>

PDR.net is a site created by the Medical Economics Company and features that publisher's products: the *Physicians Desk Reference, Stedman's Medical Dictionary*, several databases (AIDSLINE, CANCERLIT, HealthSTAR, MEDLINE), and several journals. Has separate sections for physicians, pharmacists, nurses, physician assistants, and consumers. Requires registration.

Physicians' Home Page. Retrieved June 8, 1999
URL: <http://php2.silverplatter.com/>

SilverPlatter Information, Inc.'s Physicians' Home Page features continuing medical education, databases (AIDSLINE, BioethicsLine, HealthStar, MEDLINE), Drug Information Handbook, and WebMed-Lit, a current awareness service that indexes the tables of contents of 21 major medical journals that publish content on the Web.

Physicians' Online. Retrieved June 8, 1999
URL: <http://www.po.com/>

Physicians' Online began in 1994 as a physician-only service that was one of the first to offer free MEDLINE to registrants. Features discussion groups, continuing medical education.

Thriveonline. Retrieved June 8, 1999
URL: <http://www.thriveonline.com/>

Thriveonline is a consumer oriented health portal. "Founded in 1996 as a joint venture between America Online and Time Inc., Thrive Online is now a wholly owned subsidiary of Oxygen Media."

WebMD. Retrieved June 8, 1999
URL: <http://my.webmd.com/>

WebMD has 2 sections: the free Health & Wellness Center aimed at consumers, and one called "Healthcare Professional," which requires membership. Membership benefits include continuing medical education, reference data from Intellihealth and elsewhere, and medical news. In June 1999 it was announced that WebMD and Healtheon were merging into one company.

FEDERAL DATABASES

U.S. federal health agencies have been in the forefront of producing and distributing databases.

CHID: Combined Health Information Database. Retrieved May 30, 1999 URL: <http://chid.nih.gov/>

CHID: Combined Health Information Database is a database produced by health-related agencies of the Federal Government that provides titles, abstracts, and availability information for health information and health education resources. CHID is a cooperative effort among several Federal agencies that combined their information files into one database–thus creating the Combined Health Information Database or CHID. CHID has been available to the public since 1985 and presently covers 18 topics: AIDS Education, Alzheimer's Disease, Arthritis and Musculoskeletal and Skin Diseases, Cancer Patient Education, Cancer Prevention and Control, Complementary and Alternative Medicine, Deafness and Communication Disorders, Diabetes, Digestive Diseases, Disease Prevention/Health Promotion, Epilepsy Education and Prevention, Health Promotion and Education, Kidney and Urologic Diseases, Maternal and Child Health, Medical Genetics and Rare Disorders, Oral Health, Prenatal Smoking Cessation, Weight Control. Searching CHID can yield some surprising results: from journal article citations to grey literature, obscure, limited run printed pamphlets from hospitals, medical societies, pharmaceutical corporation that are not usually indexed.

CRISP (Computer Retrieval of Information on Scientific Projects). Retrieved June 8, 1999 URL: <https://www-commons.cit.nih.gov/crisp/>

"CRISP (Computer Retrieval of Information on Scientific Projects) is a searchable database of federally funded biomedical research projects conducted at universities, hospitals, and other research institutions. The database, maintained by the Office of Extramural Research at the National Institutes of Health, includes projects funded by the National Institutes of Health (NIH), Substance Abuse and Mental Health Services (SAMSHA), Health Resources and Services Administration (HRSA), Food and Drug Administration (FDA), Centers for Disease Control and Prevention (CDCP), Agency for Health Care Policy Research (AHCPR), and Office of Assistant Secretary of Health (OASH)."

healthfinder. Retrieved June 8, 1999
URL: <http://www.healthfinder.gov/>

healthfinder is a free gateway to reliable consumer health and human services information Web site developed by the U.S. Department of Health and Human Services and launched in April 1997. healthfinder includes references to selected online publications, clearinghouses, databases, Web sites, and support and self-help groups, as well as the government agencies and not-for-profit organizations that produce reliable information for the public.

MEDLINEplus. Retrieved June 8, 1999
URL: <http://www.nlm.nih.gov/medlineplus/>

The National Library of Medicine's MEDLINEplus was launched October 22, 1998 as "a pilot project designed to increase public awareness of and access to health information via the Internet," involving "39 public library organizations with more than 200 locations in nine states" for which "NLM has developed MEDLINEplus, an easy-to-understand resource for the public which includes MEDLINE–the world's largest database of peer-reviewed information–as well as links to self-help groups, access to the NIH consumer health information, clearinghouses, health-related organizations, and clinical trials."[17] MEDLINEplus combines "canned" searches of MEDLINE with a directory of consumer-oriented health information from trusted sources (medical societies, government agencies) on the Web.

National Guideline Clearinghouse. Retrieved June 8, 1999
URL: <http://www.guidelines.gov/>

The National Guideline Clearinghouse is a public resource for evidence-based clinical practice guidelines sponsored by the U.S.

Agency for Health Care Policy and Research in partnership with the American Medical Association and the American Association of Health Plans. The clearinghouse, which first appeared December 15, 1998, makes use of NLM's Unified Medical Language System (UMLS) that was developed to map variant medical terms to the MeSH.[18]

OMIM: The Online Mendelian Inheritance in Man. Retrieved June 8, 1999
URL: <http://www3.ncbi.nlm.nih.gov/omim/>

"OMIM: the Online Mendelian Inheritance in Man is a catalog of human genes and genetic disorders authored and edited by Dr. Victor A. McKusick and his colleagues at Johns Hopkins and elsewhere, and developed for the World Wide Web by the National Center for Biotechnology Information. OMIM includes links to MEDLINE and to the many genetics and molecular biology databases curated by the National Center for Biotechnology Information."

WEB DATABASES AND CATALOGS

As Web sites providing health and medical information have proliferated, so have efforts to catalog and categorize them. Many catalogs and databases have appeared, at first mostly from educational institutions, but now increasingly from commercial entities. The first two listed below are strictly databases of health-related sites; the rest are static catalogs.

MedHunt. Retrieved June 8, 1999
URL: <http://www.hon.ch/cgi-bin/find>

The Health on the Net Foundation's MedHunt is a database populated by a site-harvesting Web crawler.[19] Search results are drawn from 2 sources: from the results of the Web crawler, and from a compendium of sites adhering to the Foundation's Code of Conduct, these having been distinguished by the addition of brief descriptions or summaries.

MedicalWorld Search. Retrieved May 30, 1999
URL: <http://www.mwsearch.com/>

MedicalWorld Search is a database and search engine that uses the Unified Medical Language System to parse retrieved Web pages and retain only those deemed of clinical significance.[20]

CISMeF: Catalogue et Index des Sites Médicaux Francophones.
Retrieved June 8, 1999
URL: <http://www.chu-rouen.fr/ssf/ssf.html>

CISMeF: Catalogue et Index des Sites Médicaux Francophones at the Rouen University Hospital Medical Library began in February 1995 and provides a thorough and frequently updated catalog of medical Web sites, particularly those written in French.[21]

CliniWeb International. Retrieved June 8, 1999
URL: <http://www.ohsu.edu/cliniweb>

The Oregon Health Sciences University CliniWeb International[22] is a database of strictly clinical information on the Internet, concentrating on anatomy and disease states. It employs the Unified Medical Language System for organization.

Hardin MD. Retrieved June 8, 1999
URL: <http://www.lib.uiowa.edu/hardin/md/index.html>

Hardin MD (Hardin Meta Directory of Internet Health Sources) from the University of Iowa Hardin Library for the Health Sciences is a directory of Web-based subject catalogs of medical resources on the Internet. An excellent feature is the regular checking of the validity of the links of each catalog and the awarding of a "Hardin Clean Bill of Health" to sites that are well maintained.

Health on the Net Foundation. Retrieved June 8, 1999
URL: <http://www.hon.ch/>

Health on the Net Foundation (HON) is a not-for-profit international organization headquartered in Geneva, Switzerland and dedicated to realizing the benefits of the Internet and related technologies in the fields of health and medicine.[23] The site was launched March 19, 1996.

HealthWeb. Retrieved June 8, 1999
URL: <http://healthweb.org/>

Premiering in 1995, HealthWeb is a collaborative project of the health sciences libraries of the Greater Midwest Region (GMR) of the National Network of Libraries of Medicine (NN/LM) and those of the Committee for Institutional Cooperation. Currently there are over twenty actively participating member libraries. This project is supported by the National Library of Medicine (NLM) under contract.[24]

Karolinska Institutet Library Diseases, Disorders and Related
Topics. Retrieved June 8, 1999
URL: <http://www.mic.ki.se/Diseases/index.html>

Karolinska Institutet Library Diseases, Disorders and Related Topics is a large database of clinical resources categorized with MeSH.

Medical Matrix. Retrieved June 8, 1999
URL: <http://www.medmatrix.org/Index.asp>

Medical Matrix, one of the oldest medical catalogs on the Web, is a peer-reviewed database devoted to items dealing with clinical medicine.

MedWeb. Retrieved June 8, 1999
URL: <http://www.medweb.emory.edu/MedWeb/>

MedWeb began April 16, 1994 as a catalog of medical Internet resources and has evolved into an extensive database maintained by the Emory University Health Sciences Library.[25] It is one of the oldest such resources on the Web.

MedWebPlus. Retrieved June 8, 1999
URL: <http://www.medwebplus.com/>

MedWebPlus, begun November 8, 1998 as an off-shoot of Med-Web, is a database of over 25,000 medical Internet sites categorized by

MeSH headings enhanced by synonym finding UMLS-based searching, reducing the need for familiarity with medical terminology.[26]

OMNI. Retrieved June 8, 1999
URL: <http://omni.ac.uk/>

Launched November 1995, OMNI: Organising Medical Networked Information is a project funded by the UK Joint Information Systems Committee Electronic Libraries' Programme.[27] It functions primarily, although not exclusively, as a gateway to British medical Internet resources. OMNI was one of the first sites to use MeSH for subject access.[28]

VIRTUAL LIBRARIES

In addition to cataloging information on the Web, academic institutions have produced a good portion of the health-related information on the Internet.

Hospital Virtual Brasileiro. Retrieved June 8, 1999
URL: <http://www.hospvirt.org.br/>

Hospital Virtual Brasileiro is a virtual library produced by the State University of Campinas Center for Biomedical Informatics in Sao Paulo, Brazil.

MD Consult. Retrieved June 8, 1999
URL: <http://www.mdconsult.com/>

MD Consult is a virtual library composed of reference books and full-text journals published by Lippincott Williams & Wilkins, Mosby-Year Book, and the W.B. Saunders Company. The MEDLINE search provides links to full-text articles in journals produced by these publishers. Includes medical news, clinical practice guidelines, patient education handouts and continuing medical education.

New York Online Access to Health (NOAH). Retrieved June 8, 1999
URL: <http://www.noah.cuny.edu/>

New York Online Access to Health (NOAH) is a project of the City University of New York, the Metropolitan New York Library Council, the New York Academy of Medicine and The New York Public Library. Begun in October 1994, NOAH is a bilingual, English and Spanish, consumer health information site that provides free full-text documents.[29]

Virtual Hospital. Retrieved June 8, 1999
URL: <http://www.vh.org/>

The Virtual Hospital, presented by the University of Iowa College of Medicine Department of Radiology Electric Differential Multimedia Laboratory, is a virtual library of 120 textbooks and booklets digitized and put on the Web. Begun as a gopher in 1992, it moved to the World Wide Web in 1993 to take advantage of that protocol's multimedia capabilities.[30]

ELECTRONIC JOURNALS

Of all the traditional medical information sources, it is the peer-reviewed journal that has changed and is changing the most. Indexes made the transition from print to electronic media fairly easily as they were already in electronic format for typesetting purposes and were more useful when searched online in their entirety. Journals, on the other hand, are produced, sold, and distributed in a myriad of ways, not all conducive to electronic distribution, for reasons of text conversion and cost recovery. For journals, the transition from paper to electronic formats, though long called for, has been a slow evolutionary process.

There has long been dissatisfaction with the dissemination of scientific information through scholarly journals: publication lags, restrictions on length and numbers and quality of illustrations, and high costs have been an issue since before 1960.[31] That dissatisfaction continues to this day.[32,33] As networked resources, particularly the World Wide Web, become more widespread, the conditions for new means of dissemination of scientific and clinical information have developed.

In the 1980s, Bibliographic Retrieval Service (BRS) added value to its online version of MEDLINE by signing contracts with many medical publishers to link bibliographic citations in its product to the full text of articles. But what was provided was literally the text of the articles, without tables or illustrative matter, a diminished electronic copy of the printed original.

Among the first biomedical journals to go online was **Psycholoquy,** which began publication in 1990 as text files made available through the Internet via FTP (file transfer protocol). URL: <http://www.princeton. edu/~harnad/psyc.html>.

In the early 1990s, there were several attempts to present collections of electronic journals. One electronic library project was Red Sage, a collaboration between AT&T Bell Laboratories, the publisher Springer-Verlag and the University of California, San Francisco. Red Sage consisted of a database of the scanned pages of 20 molecular biology and 20 radiology journals stored in 2 forms: images of the pages for display and printing and as a searchable textbase. TULIP was an electronic library experiment involving 17 universities accessing an image and text database of the contents of 42 Elsevier Science journals.[34]

In July 1992, the American Association for the Advancement of Science began publication of the *Online Journal of Current Clinical Trials* as a purely electronic peer-reviewed journal devoted to tests of therapies and procedures. Originally, the *OJCCT* relied on a graphical display technology called Guidon, developed by OCLC and accessed through the OCLC network or over the Internet.[35] The advent of Web technologies allowed the journal to be distributed in a more standard way, and OCLC continued as distributor when the American Association for the Advancement of Science ended its sponsorship and passed the journal on to a commercial publisher, Chapman and Hall. Although the *Online Journal of Current Clinical Trials* ceased publication in 1996, it established a standard followed by many electronic journals today: graphics, "instant publication" rather than a set weekly or monthly schedule, attachment of corrections and amplifications, and links to MEDLINE citations and abstracts.

Online Journal of Knowledge Synthesis for Nursing, a joint publishing venture between OCLC and the Sigma Theta Tau International nursing organization, began in November 1993. URL: <http:// www.stti.iupui.edu/library/ojksn.html>.

The World Wide Web solved a lot of the problems of electronic publishing, primarily distribution and presentation. The wide spread nature of the Internet and the graphical presentation capabilities of Web browsers allowed publishers to replicate the printed page at first and finally to enhance it by adding multimedia resources and links outside of the journal of publication.

In 1995, two U.S. federal health agencies, the National Library of Medicine and the Centers for Disease Control and Prevention (CDC), began publishing information on the World Wide Web, adding further legitimacy to the presence of health information on the Internet. In January of 1995, the CDC's National Center for Infectious Diseases began a journal, **Emerging Infectious Diseases**, which was published simultaneously online and on paper. URL: <http://www.cdc.gov/ncidod/eid/index.htm>.

Other biomedical journals that began early publishing on the Web early are: **Molecular Vision** (http://www.molvis.org/molvis/), which began in October 1995, and **Frontiers in Bioscience**: a journal and virtual library (http://www.bioscience.org/), which began in 1996.

The Stanford University Libraries began a publishing house, **High-Wire Press**, debuting with the World Wide Web version of the *Journal of Biological Chemistry* in July 1995.[36] URL: <http://www.highwire.org/>. Taking advantage of Web hypertext linking between journal articles and to the free MEDLINE access provided by PubMed, High-Wire Press attracted many traditional biomedical publishers affiliated with scientific societies (American Heart Association, American Physiological Society, American Psychiatric Press, American Society for Microbiology, BMJ Publishing Group, MIT Press, Oxford University Press, Society for General Microbiology, and others). As of August 1999, HighWire Press produces 141 journals online.

Database aggregators BioMedNet and Ovid both offer the full text of journals, enhanced by hypertext links to cited articles and to versions of MEDLINE.

Current Practice: the Internet Source for Clinical Care, a Web site based on the print journal *Current Practice*, published by Praxis Press, is an excellent example of the use of Web technologies to add value to a print publication. URL: <http://www.currentpractice.com/>. Not only a continuously updated version of its print parent, Current Practice has also transformed the journal into a database of clinical practice information, intertwined with links to NLM's PubMed and a tailored version of the commercial drug database GenRxTM produced by Mosby.

Libraries, hardest hit by journal price increases, have successfully found alternative means of distribution and storage of scholarly journals: HighWire Press, **SPARC** (Scholarly Publishing and Academic Resources Coalition) (http://www.arl.org/sparc/),[37] and **JSTOR** (http://www.jstor.org/).[38,39] Publishers have established online collections of journals to which libraries can subscribe; MCB University Press Emeraldplus (http://www.emerald-library.com/) and Elsevier Science ScienceDirect (http://www.sciencedirect.com/) are two major examples. But a proposal by the director of the U.S. National Institutes of Health to establish a pre-publication database of biomedical journal articles,[40,41] if accepted and adopted by authors and publishers, truly may help bring biomedical information sources into the 21st century.[42] The NIH proposal was put forth on May 5, 1999 and by August 30, 1999 had evolved into a combination pre-print peer-reviewed article repository: "a Web-based repository for barrier-free access to primary reports in the life sciences . . . called PubMed Central, based on its natural integration with the existing PubMed medical biomedical literature database. PubMed itself will extend its coverage of the life sciences and continue its linkage to external online journals."[43] Peer-reviewed articles will be provided by participating publishers and pre-prints by independent organizations. It has already sparked emulation by the Association of Research Libraries and the American Institute of Biological Sciences' joint effort to produce BioOne by early 2001, providing access "to a common database of leading journals in their fields–at prices and under usage terms sensitive to the interests of society publishers, institutional subscribers and users."[44]

CONCLUSION

Medical reference tools have been online in one form or another for over two decades, changing to adapt to current electronic delivery mechanisms (dial-up access, CD-ROM, Internet telnet and World Wide Web). What has changed most has been the environment of medical information, online and off: social changes involved with patients' rights have opened up access to information to consumers, and the World Wide Web, with its standards and ubiquity, has given equal footing to entities not previously considered to be publishers. The huge potential market of the healthcare industry has lured many information providers onto the Web where much of what is offered is a repackaging of other information. Venerable print resources transformed into electronic databases are repackaged by database vendors who, in turn, lease them to Internet companies which offer them as part of their services. Interest is keen for health information on the Internet. According to one company's white paper, "in 1998, over 22 million Internet users (representing 43% of adult users) accessed health-related information from one or more of over 20,000 health-related Web sites."[45] So it is not surprising that there is such a rush to establish health portals; of the commercial health portals listed above, it is unlikely that all will continue to exist in the next millennium. Indeed, Healtheon and WebMD have announced that they are merging in the fall of 1999 and will acquire MedCast. In the late summer of 1999, one of the first free MEDLINE sites and health portals changed its name and has a site that is "under construction," two sites changed their names, both drkoop.com and WebMD changed information content providers for their medical dictionaries and encyclopedias, and Mediconsult.com announced it is buying Physicians' Online. The 20 portals mentioned here are not even all the sites extant, and most of them are surprisingly, even drearily, similar: with similar aspirations, similar markets, similar appearance, and similar content.

The plethora of health-related Web sites has created not only a discovery problem, but also a problem of determining quality. In 1997 and in 1998, the U.S. Federal Trade Commission conducted "Health Claim Surf Days" during which it "identified approximately 800 World-Wide Web sites and numerous Usenet newsgroups that contain questionable promotions for products or services purporting to help cure, treat or prevent six diseases."[46] There have been many efforts to help discern the good from the dubious among medical Web sites. In July 1996, the Health on the Net Foundation, an international organization based in Geneva, issued the first public version of its Code of Conduct, now known as the HON Code.[47] The code was developed as a self-governing initiative whereby sites declare adherence to a few basic principles that essentially indicate credentials and sincerity, such as stating that medical information is provided by trained and qualified persons, guaranteeing confidentiality, declaring sources of financial support and thus potential conflicts of interest. Adherents display the HON Code logo on their sites, and the Health on the Net Foundation, after checking the site for compliance, lists the site in its database of medical Web sites. In November 1996, the Health Information Technology Institute organized a group representing academia, the pharmaceutical industry, government health care agencies, and medical, nursing, and pharmacy societies, to begin working on *Criteria for Assessing the Quality of Health Information on the Internet*, to "provide a set of criteria that can be used accurately and reliably by the general public (consumer) to assess the quality of health information on the Internet."[48] In June 1997, representatives of patient organizations, medical societies, pharmaceutical manufacturers, medical journal and other publishers, and medical schools met to form the Internet Healthcare Coalition, an outgrowth of an electronic discussion group devoted to publishing medical information on the Internet, created in reaction to U.S. Food and Drug Administration hearings on Internet use by entities it regulates.[49] The coalition attempts to educate producers and consumers of Internet medical sites as to what constitutes quality and what constitutes fraud.

The HON Code, the Health Information Technology Institute criteria, and the Internet Healthcare Coalition all suggest voluntary guidelines to help health information providers to create quality Internet sites, along with checklists to help consumers determine the quality of the information they find. There are other efforts to pinpoint quality sites on the Web: Medical Matrix (http://www.medmatrix.org/) uses an editorial board to select high quality information for clinicians. Two efforts by the U.S. National Institutes of Health consist of consumer health information sites chosen for their integrity: healthfinder (http://www.healthfinder.gov/) and the National Library of Medicine's MEDLINEplus (http://www.nlm.nih.gov/medlineplus/).

It would be no exaggeration to say that the state of medical reference tools at the turn of the century is unsettled. Traditional printed indexes to the medical literature gave way to electronic versions because they can be updated more quickly, are easier to search, and, for the most part, are easier to store. The indexed journals are trying to find their way into easily distributed, accessible, and searchable electronic media. The World Wide Web has allowed almost anyone, legitimate or dubious, to publish medical information to a wide audience, creating a need for indexes and for quality filters. Commercial concerns have attempted to become the name brand synonymous with Web-based health information by aggregating databases, dictionaries, Web-only publications, electronic bulletin boards, news services, and other enticements, hoping to capture the growing Internet market. Those seeking medical information must endure a lot of noise to find something worth hearing.

NOTES

1. Guice, Jon. "Looking backward and forward on the Internet," *Information society* 14:5 (July-September 1998): 204.

2. Quarterman, John S. "Medicine in the Matrix," *Annals of the New York Academy of Sciences* 670 (December 1992):13.

3. DeBakey, Michael E. "The National Library of Medicine: evolution of a premier information center," *JAMA* 266:9 (September 4, 1991): 1253.

4. Feinglos, Susan J. *MEDLINE: a basic guide to searching.* Chicago: Medical Library Association, 1985, 5.

5. National Library of Medicine. *MEDLINE (MEDlars onLINE).* 18 November 1998. [Online]. Retrieved June 8, 1999. URL: http://www.nlm.nih.gov/databases/medline.html

6. Feinglos, Susan J. *MEDLINE: a basic guide to searching.* Chicago: Medical Library Association, 1985, 5-6.

7. Gloucestershire Royal Hospital Library. *Dr Felix's Free MEDLINE Page.* [Online]. Retrieved June 8, 1999. URL: http://www.docnet.org.uk/drfelix/

8. Stewart, Michael G.; Moore, Aletta S. "Searching the medical literature," *Otolaryngologic clinics of North America* 31:2 (April 1998): 278-280.

9. Kurkul, Donna. "Free MEDLINE shakes up content providers: what it means for you," *Medicine on the Net* 3:9 (September 1997): 9-10.

10. Sikorkski, Robert; Peters, Richard. "Medical literature made easy: querying databases on the Internet," *JAMA* 277:12 (March 26, 1997): 959-960.

11. National Library of Medicine. *MEDLINE Journals With Links to Publisher Web Site.* 29-Mar-99. [Online]. Retrieved August 27, 1999. URL: http://www.ncbi.nlm.nih.gov/PubMed/fulltext.html

12. Jasco, Peter. "Ovid online puts on a graphical (inter)face," *Online* 20:1 (January/February 1996): 40.

13. Allen, Ace; Frisse, Mark Edwin; Osheroff, Jerome A. "The Internet in medicine: an update," *Patient care* 33:1 (January 15, 1999): 35.

14. Blanken, R. R.; Stern, B. T. "Excerpta Medica's system for automated storage and retrieval of biomedical information," *Federation proceedings* 33:6 (June 1974): 1719.

15. Menduno, Michael. "Net profits," *Hospitals & health networks* 73:3 (March 1999): 44.

16. Smith, Stephen E. "Refining your online medical searching: here's a user's guide to help you find your way around Medscape," *Information today* 16: 3 (March 1999): 22-24.

17. National Library of Medicine. *Public Library Initiative/New Consumer Health Site* (press announcement) (10/22/98) [Online]. Retrieved June 8, 1999. URL: http://www.nlm.nih.gov/news/press_releases/ medplus.html

18. Humphreys, Betsy L.; Lindberg, Donald A. B. "The UMLS project: making the conceptual connection between users and the information they need," *Bulletin of the Medical Library Association* 81:2 (April 1993): 170-177.

19. Baujard, O.; Baujard, V.; Aurel, S.; Boyer, C.; Appel, R. D. "MARVIN, multi-agent softbot to retrieve multilingual medical information on the Web," *Medical informatics* 23:3 (July-September 1998): 187-91.

20. Suarez, Humbert H.; Hao, Xiaolong; Chang, Ifay F. "Searching for information on the Internet using the UMLS and Medical World Search," *Proceedings AMIA Annual Fall Symposium* 1997: 824-828.

21. Darmoni, S. J.; Thirion, B. *Internet and Intranet Web sites at Rouen University Hospital* 15 novembre 1998. [Online]. Retrieved June 9, 1999. URL: http://www.chu-rouen.fr/dsii/html/interdefeng.html

22. Hersh, William R.; Brown, Kevin E.; Donohoe, Larry C.; Campbell, Emily M.; Horacek, Ashely, E. "CliniWeb: managing clinical information on the World Wide Web," *Journal of the American Medical Informatics Association* 3:4 (July-August 1996): 273-80.

23. Boyer, C.; Baujard, O.; Baujard, V.; Aurel, S.; Selby, M.; Appel, R. D. "Health On the Net automated database of health and medical information," *International journal of medical informatics* 47:1-2 (November 1997): 27-29.

24. Redman, Patricia M.; Aguirre, Anthony R.; Bradley, Doreen R.; Savage, Darin C. "HealthWeb: a collaborative interinstitutional Internet project," *Library hi tech* 16:61 (1998): 37-44.

25. Kogelnik, Andreas M.; Foote, Steve. "MedWeb: Biomedical Internet Resources," *Proceedings AMIA Annual Fall Symposium* (1996): 969.

26. Flory, Joyce, "MedWebPlus," *Medicine on the Net* 5:4 (April 1999): 17.

27. Norman, Frank. "OMNI: Organising Medical Networked Information," *Ariadne* 1 (January 1996). [Online]. Retrieved June 8, 1999. URL: http://www.ariadne.ac.uk/issue1/omni/

28. "Organizing medical networked information (OMNI)," *Medical informatics* 23:1 (January-March 1998): 43-51.

29. Voge, Susan. "NOAH-New York Online Access to Health: library collaboration for bilingual consumer health information on the Internet," *Bulletin of the Medical Library Association* 86:3 (October 1998): 553-563.

30. D'Allesandro, Michael P.; Glavin, Jeffrey R.; Erkonen, William E.; Choi, Teresa A.; Lacey, David L.; Colbert, Stephana I. "The Virtual Hospital: experiences in creating and sustaining a digital library," *Bulletin of the Medical Library Association* 86:4 (July 1998): 326-334.

31. Phelps, Ralph H.; Herlin, John P. "Alternative to the scientific periodical: a report and bibliography," *Unesco bulletin for libraries* 14:2 (March-April 1960): 61-62.

32. Piternick, Anne B. "Attempts to find alternatives to the scientific journal: a brief review," *Journal of academic librarianship* 15:5 (November 1989): 260.

33. Butler, Declan. "The writing is on the Web for science journals in print," *Nature* 397:6716 (January 21, 1999): 195-197.

34. Borman, Stu. "Advances in electronic publishing herald changes for sciences," *Chemical & engineering news* 71:24 (June 14, 1993):18, 21.

35. Hickey, Thomas B.; Noreault, Terry. "The Development of a Graphical User Interface for The Online Journal of Current Clinical Trials," *Public-Access Computer Systems Review* 3:2 (1992): 4-12. [Online]. Retrieved June 8, 1999. URL: http://info.lib.uh.edu/pr/v3/n2/hickey.3n2

36. Tucker, William. "Dancing on the HighWire: HighWire Press, Stanford University Libraries," *HMS Beagle* 4 (March 21, 1997). [Online]. Retrieved June 8, 1999. URL: http://www.biomednet.com/hmsbeagle/1997/04/people/profile.htm

37. Buckholtz, Alison. "SPARC: The Scholarly Publishing and Academic Resources Coalition," *Issues in science and technology librarianship* 22 (Spring 1999) [Online]. Retrieved June 8, 1999. URL: http://www.library.ucsb.edu/istl/99-spring/article2.html

38. Butler, Declan. "The writing is on the Web for science journals in print," *Nature* 397:6716 (January 21, 1999): 196-197.

39. Butler, Declan. "Preserving papers for posterity," *Nature* 397: 6716 (January 21, 1999): 198-199.

40. Delamothe, Tony. "NIH's plans for online publishing could threaten journals," *BMJ* 318: 7186 (March 20, 1999): 754.

41. Marshall, Eliot. "Varmus circulates proposal for NIH-backed online venture," *Science* 284:5415 (April 30, 1999): 718.

42. Varmus, Harold. *E-biomed: a proposal for electronic publications in the biomedical sciences.* Bethesda MD: National Institutes of Health, May 5, 1999 (DRAFT). [Online]. Retrieved June 8, 1999. URL: http://www.nih.gov/welcome/director/ ebiomed/ebi.htm

43. Varmus, Harold. *PubMed Central: an NIH-operated site for electronic distribution of life sciences research report.* Bethesda MD: National Institutes of Health, August 30, 1999 (DRAFT). [Online]. Retrieved September 8, 1999. URL: http://www.nih.gov/welcome/director/ebiomed/ebi.htm

44. Buckholtz, Alison. "Public-Private Collaboration Develops BioOne, Providing Online, Full-text Access to Aggregated Database of Bioscience Research Journals," *SPARC in the News* June 21, 1999. [Online]. Retrieved September 10, 1999. URL: http://www.arl.org/sparc/bio1/bio1.html

45. HEALTHvision. *Healthcare and the Internet: the Time Is Right.* July 15, 1999 [Online]. Retrieved August 23, 1999. URL: http://www.healthvision.com/literature/internet.htm

46. U.S. Federal Trade Commission. *"Operation Cure.all" Targets Internet Health Fraud: FTC Law Enforcement and Consumer Education Campaign Focuses on Stopping the Quacks and Supplying Consumers with Quality Information.* June 24, 1999. [Online]. Retrieved August 23, 1999. URL: http://www.ftc.gov/opa/1999/9906/opcureall.htm

47. Boyer, C.; Selby, M.; Scherrer, J. R.; Appel, R. D. "The Health On the Net Code of Conduct for medical and health Websites," *Computers in biology and medicine* 28 (1998): 603-610.

48. Health Information Technology Institute. *Criteria for Assessing the Quality of Health Information on the Internet.* Edit Date: 14 October 1997; Last updated page 4 May 1999. [Online]. Retrieved August 23, 1999. URL: http://hitiweb.mitretek.org/docs/criteria.html

49. Mack, John. "Improving the quality of health information on the Internet: the formation and rise of the Internet Healthcare Coalition," *Health care on the Internet* 2:4 (July-September 1998): 21-28.

WEBLIOGRAPHY

National Library of Medicine. (1995) *National Library of Medicine* [Online]. Bethesda, MD: National Library of Medicine. Retrieved May 30, 1999. URL: http://www.nlm.nih.gov/

National Library of Medicine. (October 22, 1998) *MEDLINEplus* [Online]. Bethesda, MD: National Library of Medicine. Retrieved June 8, 1999. URL: http://www.nlm.nih.gov/medlineplus/

National Library of Medicine. (1997) *PubMed* [Online]. Bethesda, MD: National Library of Medicine. Retrieved May 30, 1999. URL: http://www.ncbi.nlm.nih.gov/PubMed/

National Library of Medicine. (1996) *Internet Grateful Med* [Online]. Bethesda, MD: National Library of Medicine. Retrieved May 30, 1999. URL: http://igm.nlm.nih.gov/

MEDLINEs

BioMedNet. *Evaluated MEDLINE* [Online]. London: EPRESS. Retrieved May 30, 1999. URL: http://www.biomednet.com/db/medline

HealthGate. *MEDLINE* [Online]. Burlington, MA: HealthGate Data Corp. Retrieved June 8, 1999. URL: http://www.healthgate.com/medline/search-medline.shtml

Medscape. (May 24, 1995) *MEDLINE* [Online]. New York: Medscape. Retrieved May 30, 1999. URL: http://www.medscape.com/misc/FormMedline.html

National Library of Medicine. (1996) *Internet Grateful Med* [Online]. Bethesda, MD: National Library of Medicine. Retrieved May 30, 1999. URL: http://igm.nlm.nih.gov/

National Library of Medicine. (1997) *PubMed* [Online]. Bethesda, MD: National Library of Medicine. Retrieved May 30, 1999. URL: http://www.ncbi.nlm.nih.gov/PubMed/

Ovid. *MEDLINE* [Online]. New York: Ovid Technologies. Retrieved May 30, 1999. URL: http://www.ovid.com/

PaperChase. *MEDLINE* [Online]. Boston: Beth Israel Deaconess Medical Center. Retrieved May 30, 1999. URL: http://www.paperchase.com/

Database Aggregators

Dialog Corporation. *DialogWeb*[Online]. Mountain View, CA: Dialog Corporation. Retrieved May 30, 1999. URL: http://www.dialogweb.com/

EBSCO Information Services. *EBSCO Information Services* [Online]. Birmingham, AL: Ebsco Industries. Retrieved May 30, 1999. URL: http://www.ebsco.com/home/MICROMEDEX.

MICROMEDEX [Online]. Englewood, CO: MICROMEDEX. Retrieved May 30, 1999. URL http://www.micromedex.com/

OCLC. *FirstSearch* [Online]. Dublin, OH: Online Computer Library Center. Retrieved May 30, 1999. URL http://www.oclc.org/oclc/menu/fs.htm

Ovid Technologies. *Ovid Technologies* [Online]. New York: Ovid Technologies. Retrieved May 30, 1999. URL: http://www.ovid.com/

SilverPlatter. *SilverPlatter* [Online]. Norwood, MA: SilverPlatter Information, Inc. Retrieved May 30, 1999. URL:http://www.silverplatter.com/

Other Databases

American Psychological Association. *PsycINFO* [Online]. Washington, DC: American Psychological Association. Retrieved June 8, 1999. URL: http://www.apa.org/psycinfo/

CINAHLsources. *CINAHLsources* [Online]. Boston: Beth Israel Deaconess Medical Center. Retrieved May 30, 1999. URL: http://www.cinahl.com/

Excerpta Medica. *EMBASE: the Excerpta Medica Database* [Online]. Amsterdam: Elsevier Science Publishers. Retrieved June 8, 1999. URL: http://www.elsevier.nl/locate/inca/523328

Dictionaries and Other Reference Works

AMA Health Insight. (1997) *Medical Glossary* [Online]. Boston: Beth Israel Deaconess Medical Center. Retrieved May 30, 1999. URL: http://www.ama-assn.org/insight/gen_hlth/glossary/index.htm

BioTech. (1996) *Life Science Dictionary* [Online]. Austin, TX: University of Texas at Austin. Retrieved May 30, 1999. URL: http://biotech.icmb.utexas.edu/pages/dictionary.htm

CancerWeb. (1997) *On-line Medical Dictionary* [Online]. Northwood, UK: Gray Laboratory Cancer Research Trust. Retrieved May 30, 1999. URL: http://www.graylab.ac.uk/omd/

Dawson, Michael. (1996) *University of Alberta's Cognitive Science Dictionary* [Online]. Calgary, Alberta: WebMD. Retrieved June 8, 1999. URL: http://matrix.psych.ualberta.ca/~mike/Pearl_Street/Dictionary/dictionary.html

drkoop.com. (1999) *Medical Encyclopedia* [Online]. Austin, TX: drkoop.com. Retrieved June 8, 1999. URL: http://www.drkoop.com/adam/mhc/

Indiana Prevention Resource Center. (1997) *On-line Dictionary of Street Drug Slang* [Online]. Bloomington, IN: Indiana Prevention Resource Center. Retrieved May 30, 1999. URL: http://www.drugs.indiana.edu/slang/home.html

J: Merck and Co. (1999) *Merck Manual of Diagnosis and Therapy*, 17th ed. [Online]. Whitehouse Station, NJ: Merck and Co. Retrieved May 30, 1999. URL: http://www.merck.com/pubs/mmanual/

J: Merck and Co. (1995) *Merck Manual of Geriatrics*, 2nd ed. [Online]. Whitehouse Station, NJ: Merck and Co. Retrieved May 30, 1999. URL: http://www.merck.com/pubs/mm_geriatrics/home.html

J: Merck and Co. (1999) *Merck Manual of Medical Information*, Home ed. [Online]. Whitehouse Station, NJ: Merck and Co. Retrieved September 8, 1999. URL: http://www.merck.com/pubs/mmanual_home/

Lackie, J. M.; Dow, J. A. T. (1995) *Dictionary of Cell Biology* [Online]. London: Academic Press. May 30, 1999. URL: http://www.mblab.gla.ac.uk/~julian/Dict.html

Masel, Richard. (1999) *Dictionary of Dental Terms* [Online]. Champaign, IL: Richard Masel. Retrieved May 30, 1999. URL: http://www.bracesinfo.com/glossary.html

MedicineNet. (1999) *Medical Dictionary* [Online]. Foothill Ranch, CA: Medicine Network Incorporated. Retrieved May 30, 1999. URL: http://www.medicinenet.com/Script/Main/AlphaIdx.asp?li=MNI&p=A_DICT

Merriam-Webster. (1996) *Medical Desk Dictionary*, Home ed. [Online]. New York, Medscape. Retrieved May 30, 1999. URL: http://www.medscape.com/mw/medical.htm

Swinton, Jonathan. (1998) *Dictionary of Epidemiology* [Online]. Cambridge: University of Cambridge. Retrieved May 30, 1999. URL: http://www.kings.cam.ac.uk/~js229/glossary.html

Taber's Cyclopedic Medical Dictionary, Home ed. (1998) [Online]. Philadelphia, F.A. Davis. Retrieved May 30, 1999. URL: http://www.tabers.com/

U.S. Office of Rare Diseases. (1998) *Office of Rare Diseases Glossary* [Online]. Bethesda, MD: U.S. Office of Rare Diseases. Retrieved May 30, 1999. URL: http://rarediseases.info.nih.gov/ord/glossary_a-e.html

University of Ghent Heymans Institute of Pharmacology. (1995) *Multilingual Glossary of Technical and Popular Medical Terms in Nine European Languages* [Online]. Ghent, Belgium: University of Ghent Heymans Institute of Pharmacology. Retrieved May 30, 1999. URL: http://allserv.rug.ac.be/~rvdstich/eugloss/welcome.html

WebMD. (1999) *World Book Rush-Presbyterian St. Luke's Medical Center Medical Encyclopedia* [Online]. Atlanta, GA: WebMD. Retrieved June 8, 1999. URL: http://my.webmd.com/encyclopedia/

Wilding, R. J. C. (1997) *Glossary of Terms in Oral Physiology* [Online]. Exeter, England: Moorland Dentistry. Retrieved May 30, 1999. URL: http://www.eclipse.co.uk/moordent/glossary.htm

Portals

allHealth [Online]. New York, NY: iVillage. Retrieved June 8, 1999. URL: http://www.allhealth.com/

CommuniHealth (Sept. 1997) [Online]. Malvern, PA: Shared Medical Systems. Retrieved June 8, 1999. URL: http://www.communihealth.com/

drkoop.com [Online]. Austin, TX: Personal Medical Records. Retrieved June 8, 1999. URL: http://www.drkoop.com/

Healtheon [Online]. Santa Clara, CA: Healtheon Corporation. Retrieved June 8, 1999. URL: http://www.healtheon.com/

Healthgate [Online]. Burlington, MA: HealthGate Data Corp. Retrieved May 30, 1999. URL: http://www.healthgate.com/

HealthLeaders.com [Online]. Brentwood, TN: Passport Health Communications. Retrieved June 8, 1999. URL: http://www.healthleaders.com/

InteliHealth (1996) [Online]. Santa Clara, CA: Blue Bell, PA: InteliHealth. Retrieved June 8, 1999. URL: http://www.intelihealth.com/IH/ihtIH

Kinetra [Online]. Golden, CO: Integrated Medical Systems. Retrieved June 8, 1999. URL: http://www.kinetra.com/

Mayo Clinic Health Oasis (1995) [Online]. Rochester, MN: Mayo Foundation. Retrieved June 8, 1999. URL: http://www.mayohealth.org/

Medcast (1998) [Online]. Atlanta, GA: Global On Line Services. Retrieved June 8, 1999. URL: http:// www.Medcast.com/

Mediconsult.com [Online]. Hamilton, Bermuda: MEDICONSULT.COM. Retrieved June 8, 1999. URL: http://www.mediconsult.com/

Medscape (1995) [Online]. New York, NY: Medscape. Retrieved June 8, 1999. URL: http://www.medscape.com/

Medsite [Online]. New York, NY: Medsite.com. Retrieved June 8, 1999. URL: http://www.medsite.com/

OnHealth.com [Online]. Seattle, WA: OnHealth Network Company. Retrieved June 8, 1999. URL: http://www.onhealth.com/ch1/index.asp

PDR.net [Online]. Montvale, NJ: Medical Economics Company. Retrieved June 8, 1999. URL: http://pdr.net/

Physicians' Home Page [Online]. Norwood, MA: SilverPlatter Information. Retrieved June 8, 1999. URL: http://php2.silverplatter.com/

Physicians' OnLine (1994) [Online]. Tarrytown, NY: Physicans' Online. Retrieved June 8, 1999. URL: http://www.po.com/

Thriveonline (1996) [Online]. San Franciso: Thrive Partners. Retrieved June 8, 1999. URL: http://www.thriveonline.com/

Federal Databases

CHID: Combined Health Information Database [Online]. Bethesda, MD: National Institutes of Health. Retrieved May 30, 1999. URL: http://chid.nih.gov/

CRISP (Computer Retrieval of Information on Scientific Projects) [Online]. Bethesda, MD: National Institutes of Health. Retrieved June 8, 1999. URL: https:// www-commons.cit.nih.gov/crisp/

healthfinder (1997) [Online]. Washington, DC: U.S. Department of Health and Human Services. Retrieved June 8, 1999. URL: http://www.healthfinder.gov/

National Guideline Clearinghouse (1998) [Online]. Rockville, MD: Agency for Health Care Policy & Research. Retrieved June 8, 1999. URL: http://www.guidelines. gov/

OMIM: the Online Mendelian Inheritance in Man [Online]. Bethesda, MD: National Center for Biotechnology Information. Retrieved June 8, 1999. URL: http:// www3.ncbi.nlm.nih.gov/omim/

Web Databases and Catalogs

CISMeF: Catalogue et Index des Sites Médicaux Francophones (1995) [Online]. Rouen, France: Centre Hospitalier Universitaire de Rouen Bibliothèque médicale. Retrieved June 8, 1999. URL: http://www.chu-rouen.fr/ssf/ssf.htm

CliniWeb International (1996) [Online]. Portland, OR: Oregon Health Sciences University. Retrieved June 8, 1999. URL: http://www.ohsu.edu/cliniweb

Hardin MD (1997) [Online]. Iowa City, IA: University of Iowa Hardin Library for the Health Sciences. Retrieved June 8, 1999. URL: http://www.lib.uiowa.edu/ hardin/md/index.html

Health on the Net Foundation (1996) [Online]. Geneva, Switzerland: Health On the Net Foundation. Retrieved June 8, 1999. URL: http://www.hon.ch/

HealthWeb (1995) [Online]. Ann Arbor, MI: Greater Midwest Region of the National Network of Libraries of Medicine. Retrieved June 8, 1999. URL: http://healthweb. org/

Karolinska Institutet Library. Library Diseases, Disorders and Related Topics [Online]. Stockholm, Sweden: Karolinska Institutet Library. Retrieved June 8, 1999. URL: http://www.mic.ki.se/Diseases/index.html

MedHunt (1996) [Online]. Geneva, Switzerland: Health On the Net Foundation. Retrieved June 8, 1999. URL: http://www.hon.ch/cgi-bin/find

Medical Matrix (1994) [Online]. Thorofare, NJ: Medical Matrix L.L.C. Retrieved June 8, 1999. URL: http://www.medmatrix.org/Index.asp

MedicalWorld Search [Online]. Katonah, NY: Medical World Search. Retrieved June 8, 1999. URL: http://www.mwsearch.com/

MedWeb (1994) [Online]. Atlanta, GA: Emory University Health Sciences Center Library. Retrieved June 8, 1999. URL: http://www.medweb.emory.edu/MedWeb/

MedWebPlus (1998) [Online]. Atlanta, GA: y-DNA, inc. Retrieved June 8, 1999. URL: http://www.medwebplus.com/

OMNI (1995) [Online]. Nottingham, England: University of Nottingham. Retrieved June 8, 1999. URL: http://omni.ac.uk/

Virtual Libraries

Hospital Virtual Brasileiro (1997) [Online]. Campinas, Brazil: Universidade Estadual de Campinas Núcleo de Informática Biomédica. Retrieved June 8, 1999. URL: http://www.hospvirt.org.br/

MD Consult [Online]. St. Louis, MO: Medical Online. Retrieved June 8, 1999. URL: http://www.mdconsult.com/

New York Online Access to Health (NOAH) (1995) [Online]. New York, NY: City University of New York. Retrieved June 8, 1999. URL: http://www.noah.cuny. edu/

Virtual Hospital (1993) [Online]. Iowa City, IA: University of Iowa Health Care. Retrieved June 8, 1999. URL: http://www.vh.org/

Electronic Journals

HighWire Press (1995) [Online]. Stanford, CA: Stanford University Libraries and Academic Information Resources. Retrieved August 18, 1999. URL: http://ww.highwire.org/

JSTOR (1995) [Online]. New York City, NY: JSTOR. Retrieved June 8, 1999. URL: http://www.jstor.org/

SPARC (Scholarly Publishing and Academic Resources Coalition) (1997) [Online]. Washington, DC: Association of Research Libraries. Retrieved June 8, 1999. URL: http://www.arl.org/sparc/

Varmus, Harold. (1999) *E-biomed* [Online]. Bethesda, MD: National Institutes of Health. Retrieved September 8, 1999. URL: http://www.nih.gov/welcome/director/ ebiomed/ebi.htm

Current practice (1999) [Online]. Iowa City, IA: University of Iowa Health Care. Retrieved June 8, 1999. URL: http://www.currentpractice.com/

Emerging infectious diseases (1995) [Online]. Atlanta, GA: Centers for Disease Control and Prevention, National Center for Infectious Diseases. Retrieved June 8, 1999. URL: http://www.cdc.gov/ncidod/eid/index.htm

Molecular vision (1995) [Online]. Decatur, GA: Molecular Vision. Retrieved June 8, 1999. URL: http://www.molvis.org/molvis/

Frontiers in bioscience (1996) [Online]. Tampa, FL: Frontiers in Bioscience. Retrieved June 8, 1999. URL: http://www.bioscience.org/

The Web of Life:
Natural Science Information
on the Internet

Gail Clement

SUMMARY. As society has come to equate economic prosperity with the health of our living resources, national science policy has called for the development of a comprehensive digital knowledge base to support informed decision making and wise resource management. The Internet and World Wide Web demonstrate the earliest stages of this evolving virtual library of the natural world, offering an increasing array of high-quality, innovative resources and services in the natural science arena. This article discusses the leading providers of natural science information on the Internet and highlights some of the exemplary resources they are delivering online. The discussion concludes with a brief discussion of the role of the librarian in developing the Web of natural science knowledge online and provides a short Webliography of starting points for further exploration of this subject area. *[Article copies available for a fee from The Haworth Document Delivery Service: 1-800-342-9678. E-mail address: <getinfo@haworthpressinc. com> Website: <http://www.HaworthPress.com>]*

Gail Clement is a science information specialist with over 15 years' experience in research and academic settings. In her current position at the Southeast Environment Research Center, Florida International University, she manages information technology and digital library activities for the Restoration Ecology Branch of the Florida Caribbean Science Center, USGS Biological Resources Division. She is also Technical Advisor of the Library of Congress National Digital Library project, "Reclaiming the Everglades: South Florida's Natural History, 1884-1934." She has a Master of Science in Geology from the University of Oregon and a Master of Library and Information Science from the University of South Florida.

[Haworth co-indexing entry note]: "The Web of Life: Natural Science Information on the Internet." Clement, Gail. Co-published simultaneously in *Journal of Library Administration* (The Haworth Information Press, The Haworth Press, Inc.) Vol. 30, No. 3/4, 2000, pp. 271-292; and: *Academic Research on the Internet: Options for Scholars & Libraries* (ed: Helen Laurence, and William Miller) The Haworth Information Press, an imprint of The Haworth Press, Inc., 2000, pp. 271-292. Single or multiple copies of this article are available for a fee from The Haworth Document Delivery Service [1-800-342-9678, 9:00 a.m. - 5:00 p.m. (EST). E-mail address: getinfo@haworthpressinc.com].

KEYWORDS. Environmental and earth sciences, Internet research in, Internet resources in, online research in, online resources in

> *Humankind did not weave the web of life.*
>
> *We are but one strand within it.*
>
> *Whatever we do to the web,*
>
> *we do to ourselves.*
>
> *All things are bound together.*
>
> Chief Seattle (1786-1866)

INTRODUCTION

At the dawn of the 21st century, humankind is rethinking its standpoint toward the rest of nature. Society is beginning to recognize that the quality of human life is inextricably linked to the condition of the natural world. This paradigm shift is very well described by the President's science advisors. In their landmark report, *Teaming with Life: Investing in Science to Understand and Use America's Living Capital,* they observe:

> We now understand that the sustained bounty of our Nation's lands and waters and of its native plant and animal communities is the natural capital on which our economy is founded . . . In the age of biology, policies that enhance human health and wealth will be the same policies that protect the biological resources of our Nation and the world. (President's Committee of Advisors on Science and Technology, 1998)

The PCAST report recommends a national strategy that transforms society's new understanding into action. It calls on the nation to use its current store of knowledge as the basis for natural resource management and to incorporate new knowledge as it is generated. Achieving this goal, it advises, will require a coordinated network of digital information that provides the tools of discovery and the techniques of analysis needed to sustain the web of life.

The vision promoted by national science policy is, in effect, a virtual library of natural science. The mission of this library is to provide "comprehensive and comprehensible information for devising strategies, making responsible management decisions, and resolving conflicts" (PCAST, 1998). Its collections are envisioned to comprise the great diversity of electronic natural science information available today: primary data, documents, maps, tools, multimedia, biological specimens, and the catalogs and indexes used to describe them (Fenn, 1999). Its clientele includes all sectors of society: scientists, resource managers, policy makers, educators and their students, and the concerned public (Carroll and Frondorf, 1999). And its services are envisioned to include not only the collection, organization, access, and preservation of knowledge resources, but also their analysis and visualization (National Science Board, 1999).

Building the envisioned virtual library (or, in the words of PCAST, a National Biological Information Infrastructure) will be a long-term process. As a framework for this endeavor, policymakers look to the powerful capabilities of the global computer network to link people, data, and information on a worldwide scale. Though today's Internet and World Wide Web support natural science activities on a relatively modest scale, it is expected that the emergence of advanced "information theory and large capacity computational systems" will support the needs of this complex subject in the next generation (Bowker, 1999).

This article explores the ways in which today's Internet already serves the needs of the natural science community. It aims to identify the key providers of natural science information on the Internet, and assess the scope and types of information products available. The discussion of Internet resources presented in this article is designed more as a "guided tour" of representative sources than as an exhaustive review of the subject. However, to promote further exploration of this subject area, a brief Webliography of helpful starting points is provided at the conclusion of the article.

The subject focus of this article will strike most readers as somewhat "blurry." This fact reflects the current state of inquiry about the natural world, which today fuses knowledge from the established disciplines of biology, ecology, earth science, and environmental science. As interdisciplinary approaches emerge to study nature's complexity in more integrative ways (United States Geological Survey, 1999), we may gain a new vocabulary to describe the study of nature as a whole. For the purposes of this article, however, the term "natural science" has been applied for lack of a better alternative.

A WEB OF AGENCIES

National science policy calls for a cross-disciplinary, cross-sector enterprise to build a natural science knowledge base. The web of agencies involved in this effort includes federal, state, local and tribal governments, non-governmental organizations, and institutions in the private sector. Most of these agencies currently provide quality natural science information on the Internet. Key agencies are discussed below.

Several federal agencies have a mission to inventory, monitor, research, or manage some component of the natural world. These agencies include the Departments of Agriculture, Interior, and Commerce; the Environmental Protection Agency; and the National Aeronautics and Space Administration (NASA). Most notable among these federal information providers is the Department of the Interior (DOI), whose individual bureaus monitor, research, and manage most U.S. public lands and natural resources. URL: <http://www.doi.gov/>. Through its network of bureau Web sites, DOI provides extensive collections of high-quality data, scientific documents, reference resources, and tools in the natural science arena. The Fish and Wildlife Service offers authoritative information on endangered, threatened, protected, and invasive species. The National Park Service provides information directed at the general public: visitor and recreation guides, educational materials, and general interest publications on natural history and conservation. URL: <http://www.nps.gov>. The Bureau of Indian Affairs (http://www.doi.gov/bureau-indian-affairs.html), through its Office of Trust Responsibilities (http://www.doi.gov/bia/otrhome.html), provides information on mineral, energy and water resources, land use, and fish and wildlife for the trust assets of the American Indians, Indian tribes, and Alaska natives. The United States Geological Survey, or USGS, offers extensive Internet-based information concerning the environment, natural hazards, mineral, energy, water, and living resources. URL: <http://www.usgs.gov/>. As the federal government's principal natural science and information agency, the USGS has a direct responsibility to disseminate sound scientific information to resource managers and decision makers both within the Department of Interior, and nationwide. This leadership role is evident in the tremendous volume and diversity of USGS information products on-line. The bureau's Web search facility, for example, covers "over 175,000 earth science documents residing on a distributed network of 155 USGS web servers." URL: <http://search.usgs.gov/>.

Several federal agencies outside the Department of Interior provide information about biodiversity, ecosystem science, and natural resources. The Department of Commerce's National Oceanic and Atmospheric Administration provides substantive information about ocean life and processes, marine environments, and climatic trends. URL: <http://www.noaa.gov/>. The Department of Agriculture (USDA) supports research in the areas of global change, biodiversity and ecosystems, toxic substances, water resources, air quality, and sustainable agriculture. URL: <http://www.usda.gov/>. The Environmental Protection Agency (EPA) offers a variety of information resources about pollution and other environmental contaminants. URL: <http://www.epa.gov/>. The National Aeronautics and Space Administration (NASA), with a unique ability to view the planet in its entirety from space, produces information about Earth as an integrated system of land, air, water, and living organisms. NASA's Earth Science Enterprise program is well-known for its curriculum materials, scientific data sets, and earth images that inform (and inspire!) scientists and lay people alike. URL: <http://www.earth.nasa.gov/>.

Federal libraries and information centers also have much to contribute to the knowledge base of natural science. The Library of Congress, the National Archives and Records Administration, and the Smithsonian Museum of Natural History each contain significant holdings in natural history. Efforts are underway at these institutions to convert select holdings and make them freely available over the Web. The Library of Congress, for example, has added significant natural history collections to the National Digital Library, including *The Evolution of the Conservation Movement, 1850-1920* (http://memory.loc.gov/ammem/amrvhtml/conshome.html); American *Environmental Photographs, 1891-1936: Images from the University of Chicago Library* (http://memory.loc.gov/ammem/award97/icuhtml/aephome.html); and *Mapping the National Parks* (http://memory.loc.gov/ammem/gmdhtml/nphtml/nphome.html).

State and local government agencies also provide valuable content to the web of agency information. Their expertise with local ecosystems, species, and resource management issues contributes important detailed knowledge to the larger national picture. One state agency that provides significant information over the Web is the California Resources Agency. Its California Environmental Resources Evaluation System, or CERES, facilitates "access to a variety of electronic data describing California's rich and diverse environments." URL: <http://www.ceres.ca.gov/>. Web resources from other states may be found through the Environmental Council of the States (http://www.sso.org/ecos/) or the Association of American State Geologists (http://www.kgs.ukans.edu/AASG/AASG.html). Both organizations maintain online directories of agencies and contacts for the fifty states.

International organizations also have a place in the web of agencies, as they are uniquely positioned to address the many environmental issues transcending political boundaries. Leading the effort to disseminate information over the Web are the Convention on Biological Diversity (http://www.biodiv.org/); the United Nations Environmental Programme, or UNEP (http://www.unep.org); the European Environment Agency (http://www.eea.eu.int/); and the Inter-American Biodiversity Information Network (http://www.nbii.gov/iabin/).

Outside the government sector, non-governmental organizations (NGOs) are also using the Internet to disseminate quality information about biodiversity and ecosystems. The Nature Conservancy, for example, has used their expertise in conservation science to produce a detailed classification manual for the terrestrial ecological communities of the United States. This work, now freely available via the TNC Web site, has been endorsed as the standard for use by all federal agencies. URL: <http://www.tnc.org/>. Commercial publishers are using the Web to provide convenient access to electronic facsimiles of their core products. Most of these Web services are fee-based, but many provide supplementary materials or abbreviated versions of their products at no cost.

Finding information providers on the Web is made easier by the numerous locator services now online. Federal government agencies, for example, are listed in the Government Information Locator Service (GILS), a searchable catalog of federal information. URL: <http://www.access.gpo.gov/su_docs/gils/whatgils.html>. The GILS Search page at Access GPO offers searches by keyword(s) and by name of agency. GILS servers are also in place for certain state government and international agencies. URL: <http://www.access.gpo.gov/su_docs/gils/gils.html>. A listing of these is available from the GILS home page <http://www.gils.net/>. Of particular interest is the Global Environmental Locator Service (GELOS) under development by the G8 Global Information Society. GELOS, available as a prototype at the time of this writing, is intended to serve as a multinational virtual library of data and information for environment and natural resources management (Christian, 1998).

Finding the information services of non-governmental organizations on the Internet is more difficult because there is no comprehensive directory of these agencies. A good place to start may be one of the Web starting points listed in the Webliography at the end of this article.

A WEB OF PEOPLE

As long as humans have observed their surroundings, individuals have contributed to our knowledge of the natural world. The field of natural history has long depended on amateur or popular observations of natural processes and phenomena. For that reason, the Web of people engaged in natural science research includes all manner of investigators–scientists, resource managers, conservation workers, educators, students, and concerned "citizen scientists."

The Internet helps these natural scientists contribute their individual observations and expertise to a greater whole. Internet discussion groups, for example, enable individuals around the world to find each other, collaborate, and benefit from their mutual interests. Hundreds of electronic discussion groups relate to natural science, according to the *Directory of Scholarly and Professional E-Conferences* (Kovacs et al., 1999). While many of these groups function primarily as mailing lists for broadcasting of announcements, news updates, and notices of opportunities, some offer a genuine forum for exchanging ideas or seeking expertise from like-minded colleagues. The Deep Ecology discussion group, for example, affords lengthy exchanges about the natural world and humankind's place in it. It also has the usual announcements and news (archives available at URL: <http://csf.colorado.edu/forums/deep-ecology/>). Internet discussion groups are a particularly useful means of communication for individuals otherwise isolated by political, geographic, or pecuniary factors. Their contributions to global environmental issues are especially important.

Scientific societies are another place where individuals gather to exchange ideas and collaborate. Although these forums are generally geared toward professional scientists, their Web sites are typically accessible to any interested user. Societies provide valuable resources, such as news articles, career resources, educational materials, and sometimes publications over the Internet. The Ecological Society of America, for example, offers fact sheets on key scientific issues, such as "Invasive Species" and "Biodiversity." These easy-to-understand summaries of ecological issues would benefit any non-specialist. URL: <http://esa.sdsc.edu/factsheet.htm>. Nearly every society in the natural science arena maintains a Web site. Many are listed in the online directory of the *Scholarly Societies Project,* under the sections for Environmental Sciences, Earth Sciences, Geography, and Biology (Resources of Scholarly Societies–Subject Guide, URL: http://www. lib.uwaterloo.ca/society/subjects_soc.html).

Non-profit organizations provide another forum for individual observers to contribute to larger scientific research efforts. The Audubon Society, for example, has long involved bird watchers across North America to contribute their local observations to the Society's ongoing ornithological research. Their BirdSource project provides online data entry forms, reference resources for identification, and bird distribution maps showing the project data. URL: <http://birdsource.cornell. edu/>. Another project that enables individuals to participate in a natural science investigation is "Discover Life in America," where participants from all walks of life come together to study, use, conserve, and enjoy the diversity of life. URL: <http://www.discoverlife. org/>. This volunteer organization is sponsoring a comprehensive inventory of all species in Great Smoky Mountains National Park, with the aim of disseminating information that is useful in resource management, science, education, and recreation. The Internet helps to "forge a partnership among scientists, students and other citizens both to teach and to learn while doing science" (Pickering, 1999).

"Ask-A" (expert) services are another mechanism to put laypeople and scientists in touch with one another via the Internet, and a number of reputable services cover the natural science arena. The Natural Center for Ecological Analysis and Synthesis sponsors "Ask an Ecologist" and answers questions submitted through their Web form, primarily as a service to schoolchildren. URL: <http://www.nceas.ucsb.edu/nceas-web/kids/center/ask.html>. The "Ask-A-Geologist" service sponsored by USGS answers questions about maps, ground water, lakes, or rivers. URL: <http://walrus.wr.usgs.gov/ask-a-geologist/>. To find other AskA services that maintain quality standards, consult the AskA Locator service maintained by the ERIC Clearinghouse on Information & Technology. URL: <http://www.vrd.org/>.

As individuals gain new ways to communicate and collaborate online, the Web of people contributing to our natural science knowledge base is sure to grow. The biggest stumbling block to this endeavor, however, is the difficulty in locating others with whom to confer. One natural science community has addressed this problem by producing an online directory of experts in its field. The Taxonomic Resources and Expertise Directory (TRED) contains listings of individuals with expertise in naming, describing, and classifying plants and animals. Each entry provides the individual's name and contact information, areas of specialty, and the specific habitat(s) or geographic region in which he or she works. The TRED Web site offers forms for searching the directory or submitting a new entry for inclusion. URL: <http://www.nbii.gov/tred>. These types of directories are available for many other communities and projects, as well.

A WEB OF DATA

The fields of natural science produce a prolific amount of primary data. The global or long-term nature of many science problems requires extensive data collection over large geographic areas or extended time periods. Additionally, new technologies, such as remote sensing and robotic instruments, enable scientists to gather data from heretofore inaccessible study areas–space, the deep sea, or the subterranean depths of the Earth. While these developments have greatly advanced our knowledge of the natural world, they have also increased the cost of doing science. Society expects to receive the best return on its investment, so scientists are encouraged (and in many cases required) to share their data openly.

The Internet provides a relatively efficient means to share natural science data and the tools to use them. Government agencies, in particular, are using the Internet to provide public access to their data resources. As an example, the USGS National Water Information System offers daily stream flow values from thousands of stations in its national water monitoring network. Available data may be as recent as same-day, or extend as far back as 100 years. Once a desired dataset is identified, users may opt to receive the results in graphical format (for easy visualization) or in no-frills tab-delimited format for reuse. NOAA's National Climate Data Center, "the world's largest active archive of weather data," is an excellent source for historical climate data. From a user-friendly Web form, one can request information about the temperature, humidity, and other climatic parameters for any location in the U.S., and for periods extending as far back as 1893. The data is available, immediately online, in a variety of format options: as maps, plots, or in raw data files. URL: <http://www.ncdc.noaa.gov/ol/ climate/climatedata.html>.

Adding to the Web of government data on the Internet are the many university-based databases. The U.S. Long Term Ecological Research Network, for example, uses the Internet to share long-term datasets collected from twenty-one university research stations. Their proto-type Climate Database serves as a model for improving access to data scattered across many distributed sites. URL: <http://sql.lternet.edu/ climdb/climdb.html>.

Compared with the government's copious data resources, however, university-sponsored databases are not as widely available as one might expect. This circumstance may be due less to the availability of suitable technologies for collection, analysis, and storage than to so-ciological factors inhibiting open access to individual datasets. Scien-tists may recognize the benefits of data exchange, but may have many good reasons to abstain from such activity. Reasons cited for their reluctance include: fear that others may reuse the data inappropriately or without permission; concern that the data has not been cleaned up enough for public use; or unwillingness to devote precious time to an effort for which they receive no recognition. Concerned policy makers have considered several solutions to the problem, but acknowledge that this issue remains a barrier to open and free data sharing (Vogel, 1998).

Another issue complicating the use of scientific databases on the Web is the need for documentation that describes a dataset to those not involved in its original creation. Documentation about a dataset is called "metadata." Though many formats and standards for metadata exist, most natural science metadata describes the content, source, quality of the dataset, and any requirements for processing it.

The metadata format used by data providers depends largely on their institutional affiliations. Agencies of the U.S. federal government are required to document their natural science data in one of a few standard formats. Datasets referenced to a geographic location must be described according to the Content Standard for Digital Geospatial Metadata, a standard format developed by the interagency Federal Geographic Data Committee (FGDC). Datasets with an explicit biological component (e.g., species names) are documented according to the Biological Profile of the FGDC standard. Dataset descriptions entered in NASA's Global Change Master Directory follow the Directory Interchange Format (DIF). Outside the federal arena, documentation of datasets is generally a matter of local practice. Some communities, such as the Long-Term Ecological Research (LTER) network, have developed their own metadata formats to facilitate resource discovery, sharing, and reuse. Other communities are adopting one of the federal standards. Unfortunately, some communities have yet to consider the need for metadata, expecting that established researchers already know where to get data. This failure to document valuable science data limits the usefulness of these resources and ultimately hinders scientific progress (Vogel, 1998).

Datasets that are documented through standard metadata are a lot easier to find. Most data providers use metadata records to build data catalogs or clearinghouses that may be searched online. Some of the largest data search facilities are the National Geospatial Data Clearinghouse (http://130.11.52.184/), providing records from 100 spatial data servers nationwide; the National Biological Information Infrastructure Clearinghouse, providing access to the holdings of ten data centers (http://www.umesc.usgs.gov/http_data/meta_isite/nbiigateway.html); and the Global Change Master Directory (http://gcmd.nasa.gov/), a catalog of datasets from NASA and other participating agencies. Non-government data providers typically maintain a catalog of datasets as well.

A WEB OF HISTORY

The preceding discussion about the web of data has focused on "traditional" types of scientific data such as numerical or statistical values, collected through careful monitoring and measuring. A very different source of data about the natural world resides in the collections of libraries, archives, and the forgotten file folders of research centers. These historical data sources include old photographs and maps, diaries, and correspondence that describe the natural world in its undisturbed state. These historical sources thus provide critical baseline data about biodiversity and ecosystems.

Baseline data sources are particularly important in ecological restoration efforts. In South Florida, for example, historical accounts of wading bird colonies, engineering surveys, and other archival documents have helped define targets for the Everglades restoration effort. With support from the Library of Congress, a small sample of this baseline data will be digitized and made available online through "Reclaiming the Everglades: South Florida's Natural History: 1884-1934," a forthcoming collection of the National Digital Library Program (NDLP). URL: <http://everglades.fiu.edu/reclaim/>.

Other initiatives to make archives and records available online include NARA's Electronic Access Project (URL: <http://www.nara. gov/nara/nail.html>), which is providing digital reproductions of aerial photographs, engineering drawings, data files, maps and charts, satellites, and texts from government agencies; and the CalPhotos project of the University of California at Berkeley's Digital Library (URL: <http://elib.cs.berkeley.edu/>). The latter offers a well-designed search interface that enables searches of plant photographs by species, location, photographer, and even color.

A WEB OF SPECIES

The alarming rate of extinctions today (Raven, 1999) is fueling concerted efforts to discover, describe, classify, and map the world's living resources. In the past, scientists have had difficulty studying biological diversity because much of the knowledge about species and their habitats remained in the hands of the local investigators who studied them. The Internet is transforming biodiversity research by enabling scientists from around the world to weave together this local knowledge into a global picture of the biological world.

An excellent example of biodiversity information on the Internet is the Species2000 project, an international voluntary effort to create an index of all known organisms. URL: <http://www.sp2000.org/>. Users will be able to use this resource to receive brief information about the nomenclature of a given species, along with a listing of other data sources on the Web which contain information about that species. Current databases available from Species2000 cover bacteria, legumes, and fish.

Other providers of species information online are the world's biological museums, whose specimen collections represent the most detailed record of life on earth. Catalogs for these collections provide information about each species of flora or fauna and, in some cases, a photograph of a representative specimen. Museums that have made their catalogs accessible online are providing a unique reference resource for research and study.

The Mammal Species of the World database provided by the National Museum of Natural History, Smithsonian Institution, contains the names, type locality, and other information about 4,629 currently recognized species of mammals. URL: <http://www.nmnh.si.edu/msw/>. It is useful for identifying or verifying recognized scientific names and for taxonomic research. The Fairchild Tropical Garden's 'Virtual Herbarium' offers photographs and identification information for thousands of plants and trees. URL: <http://www.ftg.fiu.edu/>. An extensive listing of other biological museums on the Web is available from the Missouri Botanical Garden. URL: <http://www.keil.ukans.edu/cgi-bin/hl?museum>.

Species checklists are another source of information available from the Web sites of government agencies, museums, and university biology departments. A notable example of an online checklist is the *Species in Parks: Flora and Fauna Database,* made searchable by the Information Center of the Environment of the University of California at Davis in cooperation with the National Park Service. URL: <http://ice.ucdavis.edu/nps>. This unique resource exemplifies the benefits of cross-partnerships in making biotic information available worldwide.

A WEB OF DOCUMENTS

The array of online text resources available to natural science users represents both electronic facsimiles of printed documents and altogether new electronic publications designed to exploit the capabilities of the Web. The genres of these electronic documents include text and reference books, government reports and other grey literature sources, and the published scientific literature comprising refereed journal articles and conference papers.

An example of a Web document that parallels a printed version is the Fish and Wildlife Service's *Multispecies Recovery Plan,* "one of the most far reaching ecosystem plans developed." URL: <http://www.fws.gov/r4eao/wildlife/esvb.html>. This highly authoritative government document presents the blueprint for recovering the endangered and threatened species and natural habitats of South Florida. Though the agency produced the report in print and CD-ROM formats, it also provides a Web version in Portable Document Format (PDF). The PDF version retains the exact layout and pagination of the original, ensuring that readers can use and cite the electronic document exactly as they would the printed version. The Portable Document Format is the file format of choice for electronic publishers wishing to reproduce exactly an original paper document.

An example of an online book that does take advantage of the Web is the *Tree of Life,* an online encyclopedia about the origin and diversity of life. URL: <http://phylogeny.arizona.edu/tree/phylogeny.html>. Comprising more than 1000 pages covering all forms of life on Earth, this reference work is the collaborative effort of biologists around the world. The branching design of the *Tree of Life*'s format uses hyperlinks to follow the hierarchy of family, genus, and species for any given organism. Hyperlinks also allow the reader to move easily between text, illustrations, and references.

Journal publishers are also developing Web-based services to deliver, for a fee, both traditional and new journal products to subscribers. Elsevier's *ScienceDirect Service,* for example, provides convenient desktop access to hundreds of natural science journals with full-text, illustrations, and references. URL: <http://www.sciencedirect.com/>. Articles are available for the most recent 3-5 years. HTML versions of the articles enable automatic linkages between text, figures, tables, and cited references. PDF versions are convenient for printing articles as one linear document.

While *ScienceDirect* focuses on current issues of journals, the JSTOR (Journal Storage) service, which began with grant funding from the Mellon Foundation and now operates through the University of Michigan, specializes in back issues. The purpose of this approach is to "inject new life into materials that may seem moribund." URL: <http://www.jstor.org/about/need.html>. The growing electronic collection of more than 100 backfiles of journals includes several core titles in the field of ecology, such as *Ecology* and *Ecological Monographs* from the Ecological Society of America, and the *Journal of Ecology* from the British Ecological Society. Back issues for the latter title extend back to 1913, the first year of publication.

In contrast to the many "electronic journals" that parallel printed publications are the growing numbers of electronic-only titles that are transforming the processes of scientific publishing. An example from the natural science field is *Conservation Ecology*. An electronic, peer-reviewed journal produced by the Ecological Society of America and "devoted to rapid dissemination of current research," the journal is published continually on the Internet. URL: <http://www.consecol. org/Journal>. New articles are added to the "Issue in Progress" as they are accepted. Additionally, all reviewed articles are published along with an accumulation of commentaries that readers send in. In this way, *Conservation Ecology* transforms the one-sided process of journal publishing into an open, interactive forum for discussion.

An additional type of resource in the Web of natural science literature online are the abstracting and indexing services that add considerable value to the primary literature. These secondary publications provide coherent access to the literature as a whole by selecting, analyzing, sum-marizing, and classifying individual articles into predictable categories. Users have long relied on printed abstracting and indexing services as the primary means of identifying and evaluating articles of interest.

Cambridge Scientific Abstracts, one of the leading secondary pub-lishers in the natural science field, uses the web to provide more convenient access to its services and add value to its products. URL: <http://www.csa.com/>. Their Internet Database Service (IDS), for example, enables subscribers to search such mainstays as *Aquatic Science & Fisheries Abstracts* (ASFA) using a simple Web form, with context-sensitive help, pull-down menus, and buttons for easy access to document ordering services. An innovative element of this service is the ability to apply a given search not only to traditional sources (e.g., scientific journal articles, conference papers, etc.) but also to a batch of Web resources selected and evaluated by the company's subject specialists. This coherent integration of traditional and elec-tronic resources is an invaluable help to searchers.

A WEB OF PLACES

The recent explosion of geographic information technologies is enabling society to view and understand the natural world in entirely new ways. Global positioning systems, remote sensing satellites, and digital aerial photography provide a unique class of data that ties scientific observation and measurement to specific geographic locations. In the natural sciences, geographic information is used to investigate such questions as the location and extent of natural occurrences, the distribution of biological resources, and the patterns of large-scale phenomena. While Geographic Information Systems (GIS) are well beyond the scope of this article, the following Internet resources merit attention.

National Atlas of the United States of America

The National Atlas of the United States of America provides a map-like view into a variety of data collected by the Federal Government. URL: <http://www.nationalatlas.gov>. Produced by the USGS, this authoritative resource is an electronic version of the printed reference work by the same title. The Web version of the Atlas, however, offers capabilities not afforded in any printed resource.

The National Atlas offers several distinct products. The interactive map browser allows users to generate custom maps on demand. These maps display particular types of information for the selected geographic region. At present, users may generate a map for any portion of the United States showing such parameters as butterfly distribution or land cover. Users select the characteristics they wish to display from a graphical interface displaying all options as buttons or checklists.

The custom map is quickly generated and displayed on screen. Users may opt to print the map for their personal use. They may also download individual data layers for use in their own GIS systems.

Another unique resource offered by the National Atlas site is a collection of multimedia maps that portray natural phenomena using animation. The current selection of multimedia maps covers exotic animal species, vegetation growth, and the terrain of the U.S. All of these multimedia resources require the Shockwave plug-in.

Microsoft TerraServer

The TerraServer Web site, provided as a public service of Microsoft Corporation, makes available digital aerial photographs and satellite images of most places on Earth. The black and white images are provided by the USGS and SPIN-2 Marketing, a partnership of the Russian space agency and two private firms in the U.S.

Users request an image by entering a place name on the TerraServer search page. URL: <http://terraserver.microsoft.com/default.asp>. The server quickly returns a table of place names matching the user's query, along with the date of each image available for that locale. Clicking on any image immediately brings up a screen containing both the image, information about its scale, and a control panel for changing the size of the image, zooming in or out, or downloading the image file to one's personal computer. The control panel also provides a link to more information about the image.

The images, provided at no cost by TerraServer, are of moderate resolution (up to 896 x 600 pixels), suitable for browsing or general interest information. Users with serious research or analysis needs will find these online images inadequate. Most of the images represented in TerraServer, however, are available, for a fee, in high resolution, uncompressed formats. However, the excessive sizes of these files (48 or 151 MB) and their proprietary format require considerable technical expertise to use (USGS, 1999b).

Alexandria Digital Library Gazetteer Server

The ADL online gazetteer is a tool that translates place names into specific geographic coordinates. URL: <http://fat-albert.alexandria. ucsb.edu:8827/gazetteer/>. Its availability as a prototype is intended to demonstrate the value of gazetteers in helping users retrieve geographic information. The current version of the ADL online gazetteer is exceptionally well-designed and easy to use. Users may specify a geographic area by entering free-text or by clicking on a particular zone on a U.S. map, and they select the desired geographic feature (e.g., bridge, canal, desert, etc.) from a pull-down list of feature types. Based on the user's criteria, the gazetteer server returns a list of entries matching the request. Clicking on any one of the entries brings up a report that includes the geographic name of the feature (e.g., Aerojet Canal Number C-111), its latitude and longitude, a map displaying its location, and other reference information. The geographic data used by the Gazetteer comes from authoritative sources such as the U.S. Board on Geographic Names (BGN) and the U.S. Geological Survey (USGS).

Ultimately, tools like the Alexandria Digital Library Gazetteer Server can be developed as middleware for geo-referenced digital libraries, functioning "behind the scenes" as a translator service. URL: <http://www.dlib.org/dlib/january99/hill/01hill.html> (Hill, 1999).

A WEB OF STANDARDS

The great variety of Internet resources detailed in the preceding discussion contributes significant content to our natural science knowledge base. However, their number and diversity may also inhibit their effective use. To weave together such numerous, heterogeneous sources into a coherent whole, a technical and intellectual framework is needed. The essential building blocks of this framework are collaboratively-developed standards. Standards are the set of protocols, practices, and shared vocabularies needed to inter-operate distributed information services on the Internet and integrate the information they provide (Carroll and Frondorf, 1999). Standards for natural science services on the Internet have been evolving rapidly over recent years, and many new proposals are under consideration at the time of this writing. National policy has designated the National Information Infrastructure as the overall framework encompassing the nation's online information base. Two components of the NII govern standards for natural science information at the national level. The National Spatial Data Infrastructure (NSDI) promotes the sharing and use of geospatial data (that is, data referenced to a defined point or area on Earth) through the development of policies, standards, and procedures for all information providers to follow. The NSDI is managed by the interagency Federal Geographic Data Committee (FGDC), comprising sixteen federal agencies in cooperation with state, tribal, academic, and private-sector organizations. Part of the FGDC mission has been to develop standards for dataset documentation, such as the Content Standard for Digital Geospatial Metadata, and to maintain the National Geospatial Data Clearinghouse, a large, distributed catalog of data. Additional standards from the FGDC include a classification system for wetlands and deep-water habitats and a geographic standard for soils. (FGDC, URL: <http://www.fgdc.gov/standards/status/textstatus.html>.)

The biological component of the NSDI is the National Biological Information Infrastructure (NBII), managed by the USGS Biological Resources Division with participation of the FGDC Biological Data Working Group. The NBII maintains a clearinghouse for biological datasets, documented using the proposed Biological Data Profile of the Content Standard for Digital Geospatial Metadata. URL: <http://www.fgdc.gov/standards/status/sub5_2.html>. The NBII effort is strongly supported by science policy makers, such as the President's Committee of Advisors on Science and Technology (PCAST, 1998) and the National Science Foundation (NSF, 1999). One especially important standard proposed for the NBII is the "Biological Nomenclature and Taxonomy Data Standard," which provides a consistent reference for scientific names and classification of biological organisms. Scientific names are, in effect, the coordinate system for the biological world, much as latitude and longitude are the coordinates for the geographic arena. Having a standard nomenclature will provide a common language for those creating biological information and those searching for it. The proposed standard would be based on the Integrated Taxonomic Information System (ITIS), a Web-accessible database of scientific names and taxonomy for biota. URL: <http://www.itis.usda.gov/itis>. The highly successful development of ITIS by six federal agencies has rendered it the "de facto standard" for many information providers. Gaining status as an FGDC standard would make its use mandatory, at least for federal agencies.

CONCLUSION

The evolving web of online information about the natural world presents libraries an opportunity to help improve the quality of human life in the coming century. Integration of these resources into library collections and services will strengthen our support for research, education, and decision making. Incorporation of natural science content standards into our descriptive practices will bring coherence to the vast and heterogeneous body of knowledge now available to our clientele. And contribution of librarians' expertise and wisdom to national policy will ensure a national information investment that truly benefits all members of society. Librarians have a unique role in building the virtual library of the natural world and, in so doing, will help to sustain the Web of Life.

WEBLIOGRAPHY

California Digital Library/Library of California Environmental Information Resources [Online]. Retrieved September 15, 1999. URL: http://www.eip.cdlib.org/.

This Web site facilitates access to high-quality environmental information from diverse sources: a licensed commercial database (Cambridge Scientific's *Environmental Sciences and Pollution Management Database*), collections from institutions in the University of California system, and selected sites on the Internet. It was developed through a partnership of the California Digital Library and the Library of California. The directory is divided into topical categories, such as ecology, agriculture, climate, etc., with additional links to reference resources, image collections, and more. There is also a search capability (simple keyword or boolean). Every Web site listed in the directory includes a paragraph-long summary. Access to the commercial database is restricted to qualified California users.

The Clearinghouse Mechanism [Online]. Retrieved September 1, 1999. URL: http://www.biodiv.org/chm/.

The Clearinghouse Mechanism is an international Web directory developed to promote information exchange among the parties to the worldwide Convention on Biological Diversity (CBD). The Clearinghouse Mechanism maintains links to over 10,000 Web pages from 137 participating around the world. The Clearinghouse Mechanism also maintains the BIO-SEEK service, a search engine with an index of numerous biodiversity-related sites on the Internet. CHM menus are available in English, Spanish, and French; most of the linked sites included in the directory provide information in English.

Committee for the National Institute for the Environment (CNIE) [Online]. Retrieved August 25, 1999. URL: http://www.cnie.org/.

CNIE is a cooperative effort of scientists, policy makers, and concerned citizens promoting the development of a National Institute for the Environment (NIE) for environmental science research and education. The CNIE Web site is a rich source of readings from news, laws, meetings and conferences, publications, briefings. Other resources provided from this site include yellow pages of environmental contacts, reference tools, databases, and statistics. The only concern about this directory is its misleading title, "National Library for the Environment." Though the CNIE proposal for a National Institute for the Environment does include a library component, the current Web directory reflects little of this vision.

Ecoinformatics: an on-line data and information management resource for ecologists [Online]. Retrieved September 1, 1999. URL: http://lternet.edu/ecoinformatics/.

Developed by a team of data managers and scientists from the Long Term Ecological Research Network, this Web site provides an extensive listing of publications, such as *Data and Information Management in the Ecological Sciences: A Resource Guide* and links to other Web sites concerning ecological data management.

National Biological Information Infrastructure (NBII) [Online]. Retrieved August 25, 1999. URL: http://www.nbii.gov/.

This directory provides extensive links to biological data and information maintained by federal, state, and local government agencies; non-governmental organizations; and other information providers around the world. Maintained by the

Biological Resources Division of the U.S. Geological Survey, it is an authoritative source of information on Web sites in the areas of ecology and biodiversity. The NBII directory is divided into nine categories for easier browsing, but the variable nature of the categories (some topical, others defined by organization or intended audience) may confuse visitors unfamiliar with the site. A simple keyword search capability may be a preferable means for finding information on a particular topic from the NBII site.

The Scout Report for Science & Engineering [Online]. Retrieved September 7, 1999. URL: http://scout.cs.wisc.edu/report/sci-eng/current/index.html.

This bimonthly report is designed as a current awareness and evaluation service for science faculty, students and librarians in the sciences, and related fields such as math and engineering. It covers research sites, learning resources, news and general interest items, and data resources. Though not specifically dedicated to the natural sciences, each issue contains numerous resources in this subject area. For example, of the 50+ sites detailed in the Sept. 15, 1999 issue, more than half directly relate to natural science. This range of selected sites includes tapirs, NASA's earth observatory, ocean current data, an online exhibit devoted to the endangered tapir, the EPA Enviromapper, and much more. The Web addressed provided here links to the most current issue available, but all previous issues are also online and searchable.

REFERENCES

Bowker, Geoffrey C., Schnase, John L., Lane, Meredith A., Star, Susan Leigh, and Silberschatz, Abraham, 1999. "Teaming with Life: the PCAST Report on Biodiversity and Its Implications for Biodiversity Informatics." In *Metadiversity: the grand challenge for biodiversity information management through metadata: the call for community: proceedings of the symposium*, edited by R.T. Kaser and Victoria Cox Kaser, 1-9. Philadelphia: National Federation of Abstracting and Indexing Services.

Carroll, Bonnie and Frondorf, Anne, 1999. "National Biological Information Infrastructure Strategy for Biodiversity and Ecosystems Information Framework Document." In *Metadiversity: the grand challenge for biodiversity information management through metadata: the call for community: proceedings of the symposium* edited by R.T. Kaser and Victoria Cox Kaser, Appendix B. Philadelphia: National Federation of Abstracting and Indexing Services.

Christian, Elliott, 1999. "The Global Information Locator Service." In *Metadiversity: the grand challenge for biodiversity information management through metadata: the call for community: proceedings of the symposium* edited by R.T. Kaser and Victoria Cox Kaser, 83-87. Philadelphia: National Federation of Abstracting and Indexing Services.

Fenn, Dennis, 1999. "Metadiversity: Welcome and Charge to Participants," In *Metadiversity: the grand challenge for biodiversity information management through metadata: the call for community: proceedings of the symposium* edited by R.T. Kaser and Victoria Cox Kaser, xiii-xv. Philadelphia: National Federation of Abstracting and Indexing Services.

Hill, Linda L., Frew, James and Zheng, Qi, 1999. "Geographic names: the implementation of a gazetteer in a georeferenced digital library." *D-Lib Magazine* 5 (1). [Online]. Retrieved Sept. 1, 1999. URL: <http://www.dlig.org/dlib/january99/hill/01hill.html>.

Kovacs, Diane, Balraj, Leela, Fleming, Martha, Killeen, Mitzi, and Parsson, Molly, 1999. *14th Revision Directory of Scholarly and Professional E-Conferences.* [Online]. Retrieved September 15, 1999. URL: <http://www.n2h2.com/KOVACS/>.

National Science Board, Task Force on the Environment, 1999. *Environmental science and engineering for the 21st century: the role of the National Science Foundation.* Washington, D.C.: National Science Foundation, 80 pp.

Pickering, John, 1999. "Discover Life in America & the database needs of the All Taxa Biodiversity Inventory (ATBI) of Great Smoky Mountains National Park." In *Metadiversity: the grand challenge for biodiversity information management through metadata: the call for community: proceedings of the symposium* edited by R.T. Kaser and Victoria Cox Kaser, 51-56. Philadelphia: National Federation of Abstracting and Indexing Services.

President's Committee of Advisors on Science and Technology, 1998. *Teaming with life: investing in science to understand and use America's living capital.* Washington, D.C.: President's Committee of Advisors on Science and Technology. [Online]. Retrieved December 15, 1998. URL: <http://www.whitehouse.gov/WH/EOP/OSTP/Environment/html/teamingcover.html>.

Science Year, 1998. "An interview with Peter Raven." *World Book Online*, [Online]. Retrieved August 20, 1999. URL: <http://www.worldbook.com/fun/wbla/earth/html/ed04.htm>.

United States Geological Survey, 1999a. *Summary Report of the workshop on enhancing integrated science.* [Online]. Retrieved September 1, 1999. URL: <http://www.usgs.gov/integrated_science/summary.html>.

United States Geological Survey, 1999b. "Digital Orthophoto Quadrangles." [Online]. Retrieved September 1, 1999. URL: <http://terraserver.microsoft.com/DigitalBkyd/doqs.html>.

Vogel, Ronald L., 1998. "Why scientists have not been writing metadata." *Eos, Transactions, American Geophysical Union* 79 (31): 373, 380.

Internet Resources for Politics, Political Science, and Political Scientists

Bruce Pencek

SUMMARY. A typology of information needs for political science allows academic librarians to match local and Internet resources with materials relevant to public users, non-major undergraduates, political science majors, graduate students, and professional political scientists. Recognizing public and non-specialist users, we may distinguish needs for information about politics from that which is specifically political science information. Second, the needs of majors, graduate students, and political science professionals often fall within the bounds created by the discipline's generally recognized subfields. Finally, as academics, graduate students and professionals have functional needs for information that helps them teach, publish, and participate in professional affairs. Because the number of potentially relevant topics is singularly broad and the literature of the discipline spans two and a half millennia, this article emphasizes gateway or directory Web sites appropriate to each type of information need. *[Article copies available for a fee from The Haworth Document Delivery Service: 1-800-342-9678. E-mail address: <getinfo@haworthpressinc. com> Website: <http://www.HaworthPress.com>]*

KEYWORDS. Political science, Internet research in, Internet resources in, online research in, online resources in

Bruce Pencek received his PhD in government from Cornell University in 1988 with concentrations in political philosophy, public law and policy, and American politics. After receiving his MSLIS from the University of Illinois at Urbana-Champaign in 1998, he was invited to join the Center for Business and Economic Research at the University of Nevada, Las Vegas, as a senior research associate and information specialist.

[Haworth co-indexing entry note]: "Internet Resources for Politics, Political Science, and Political Scientists." Pencek, Bruce. Co-published simultaneously in *Journal of Library Administration* (The Haworth Information Press, an imprint of The Haworth Press, Inc.) Vol. 30, No. 3/4, 2000, pp. 293-334; and: *Academic Research on the Internet: Options for Scholars & Libraries* (ed: Helen Laurence, and William Miller) The Haworth Information Press, an imprint of The Haworth Press, Inc., 2000, pp. 293-334. Single or multiple copies of this article are available for a fee from The Haworth Document Delivery Service [1-800-342-9678, 9:00 a.m. - 5:00 p.m. (EST). E-mail address: getinfo@haworthpressinc.com].

Since at least the time of Aristotle, the profession of political science has recognized that there is very little in the course of human events that is not affected by or does not affect politics. Accordingly, it is extremely difficult to delimit and categorize what resources could *not* be included in any account of the Internet materials relevant to political science teaching and research. This article deals primarily with free Internet directories and other gateways to political information sources rather than with the innumerable unique sites that might be relevant to one or another teaching or research need.

It is written with two uses in mind: to assist subject specialists in creating Web-based resource guides that adapt globally available resources to local needs and opportunities for political science instruction, research, and professional development, and to provide non-specialist reference and instruction librarians with convenient entrees to a few types of political science information needs as well as to key Internet resources themselves. I used conventional criteria, including currency, identifiability of responsibility or sponsorship, scope, and navigability. The primary criterion was fitness of purpose in light of one of the three clusters of information need around which this essay is organized.

I write as one who spent a dozen years teaching political science in American colleges and universities before migrating to librarianship, bringing to this review some of the expectations that sympathetic teaching faculty have of libraries and librarians as resource providers and collaborators.

POLITICS OR POLITICAL SCIENCE?

The simplest, though in some respects most problematic, way of sorting out information for political science from the wealth of potentially relevant materials is to distinguish between sites about *politics* and sites about *political science*–the one a "real-world" activity about ruling and being ruled, the other a self-conscious, academic discipline, with its own methods and literature, networks and rivalries. While a political scientist may want access to the latest campaign news, it is not clear that a public user would want to deal with pointers to an online syllabus collection. Moreover, the breadth of politics and its study means that political scientists will labor in the other disciplines, from philosophy, religion, and the arts among the humanities, to history, economics, sociology, psychology in the social sciences, to biology, mathematics, and computer science in the natural sciences.

GENERAL GATEWAYS AND PORTALS

Web users who do not already have a particular resource in mind may well begin searching the Web for political information via a general-purpose portal. Given the indifferent quality of so many Web sources, it makes more sense to choose a general-purpose portal as a roadmap to a fairly well defined destination than to trust it as a guide across a trackless swamp.

Web users who do not already have a particular site in mind may well begin searching for political information via a general-purpose portal, such as the familiar *Yahoo* directory, or with more specifically politically oriented pages. These latter range from sites devoted to advocacy to ones directed at professional, academic political scientists; often they will mix both with news. Because Internet service providers, search-engine companies, and the browser makers are racing to be users' gateways to the Web, it is probably more useful to note some general characteristics about these starting points than to suppose they will start with the same one we, presumably more expert, would. By distinguishing politics and political science, we may begin to sort out the jumble students may encounter.

It takes some looking to get started in the branches and layers of general directories, and the different portals apply different connotations of politics in their classification systems, some institutionalist, others process-oriented, and some do not identify political things at all. Given the consumer orientation of most general-interest portals, it is no surprise that "politics" is not always a prominent heading.[1]

- Politics may be conjoined with society (as in *AltaVista* and *Hotbot*) or subsumed under culture (*Lycos*) or people (*Snap*).
- It may be associated with government and separate from society and culture (*Yahoo, Britannica Internet Guide*).
- In the *Argus Clearinghouse,* it is two levels down from government–on the same level as its logical child, American politics, and grandchild, John F. Kennedy.
- It is even further, improbably, from Lifestyles in *Netscape.*
- Under the topics tab at *Infoseek* there is a heading for government and politics.

- It is not to be seen on the front pages of *Netscape*, MSN, nor *LookSmart* (though AltaVista's society page bears a *LookSmart* title).

"Political science" is even more obscurely situated. It is in the second level under social science in *Yahoo*, *LookSmart*, and *Argus*, two levels down from society and social science in *Britannica*'s rich portal, and on the third level from Lifestyles in *Netscape*.

While *Yahoo* does an adequate job of laying out headings for political science, politics, government, and law, its contents are very much a mixed bag. The Berkeley Digital Library's **Librarians' Index to the Internet** is more selective, and with vastly greater credibility and quality control, than nearly all the commercial portals. URL: <http://sunsite.berkeley.edu/InternetIndex/>. Its timeliness and annotations make it a better point of departure for unassisted users. While its main page divides political information among headings for government, law, and politics, its site-specific search engine and abundant subject cross-references in each entry overcome this obstacle.

Gary Price of Georgetown University provides a valuable service in **Direct Search**, providing access to Web directories and databases that search engines cannot plumb. URL: <http://gwis2.circ.gwu.edu/~gprice/direct.htm>. It provides very good access to government data of all sorts, an especially important function as federal publications migrate to electronic-only distribution. Its business and legal resource links are also deep. The interface is inelegant and annotations laconic.

POLITICALLY ORIENTED GATEWAYS

Several notable gateway sites to political information are essentially journalistic in their orientation, counterparts in their fashion to *Facts on File* and the *CQ Researcher*. Though wide-ranging, they lack the analytical depth, data, and indexing of *National Journal* and *CQ Weekly*.[2] As such, they may be most useful to American public users and lower-level undergraduates; their lack of scholarly and primary-source materials restricts their utility as information sources for advanced research. As many explicitly journalistic enterprises on the Internet do, they offer current-awareness e-mail services but may not maintain deep archives.

U.S. Politics

Policy.com is an excellent resource for the "politics junkie," with a strong emphasis on political issues and organizations, which is updated every weekday. URL: <http://www.policy.com>. Cross-referencing and cross-linking allow relatively in-depth coverage of leading issues via wire-service stories, background information in the "Issues Library," statements by politicians and agencies, and pages of interested organizations. Access to agencies, think tanks, universities, and interest groups is arranged under the cant heading of "Community." One- or two-sentence organization descriptions are a strength. However, a two-stage (one free, the other fee-based) "Independent Content Provider" program appears to skew the inclusion, degree, and prominence of organizations.

Policy.com is strong on organizations and issues but weak as a source of news. Student and public users will need to complement it from journalistic sources, such as the major newspapers and broadcasting organizations provide. One such starting point for political coverage is **Allpolitics.com**, a portion of the CNN Interactive site that pulls together the broadcast and print resources of Time-Warner and the established political coverage and analysis of Congressional Quarterly, Inc. URL: <http://cnn.com/ALLPOLITICS>. Access to the archives of the *Allpolitics.com* stories, to *Time,* and to *Congressional Quarterly* (all arranged by date, to 1996) makes the site useful for starting research, and sidebar pointers take users to CNN multimedia files and to the print sources in the Time-Warner "Pathfinder" database.

Project Vote Smart appropriately calls itself "a voter's self-defense system," providing access to a virtual reference library relating to most levels, branches, and processes of America politics. URL: <http://www.vote-smart.org/>. The emphasis is upon people–13,000 of them–seeking or serving in public offices: biographies, issue-orientation, voting, financial disclosures, performance assessments by interest groups, and so on. The site includes presidential and congressional electoral data to 1992, state-level data to 1995. Sections on the federal executive and Congress include useful nuts-and-bolts descriptions of their principal parts, along with current events. Internal and external links abound. The "Government and Politics by Topic" page would be an excellent, general-purpose point of departure for public users and undergraduates who need to bolster their knowledge of American political institutions. URL: <http://www.vote-smart.org/other/>.

The project supports several special services for students, instructors, and journalists, and it is seeking partnerships with libraries to disseminate its information and services. This non-profit, nonpartisan site should not be confused with the similarly named **VoteSmart**, a front for a Web site design business for politicians that claims a similar mission and has from time to time been linked, mistakenly, from respectable sites. URL: <http://www.votesmart.com/>.

Though set up as "the largest online public service campaign promoting the use of the Internet in democracy" for the 1998 elections, **Web White & Blue**'s pages are still available on the Web, and the site's architecture lends itself to being an ongoing resource about voting, candidates, and issues. URL: <http://www.webwhiteblue.org/>. Even as planning proceeds for a site devoted to the 2000 elections, *WWB*'s 1,000 vetted and categorized resources remain available to savvy users (and Web designers). Most of these pointers are to ongoing sources of information, such as news organizations and public interest groups, that are likely to be useful sources of American political information across future electoral cycles.

International Politics

The Online Intelligence Project provides access to news and analyses about international relations and comparative politics, giving a wider perspective than the American public affairs news sites. Users should start with the OLIN database and "web walker" page. URL: <http://www.icg.org:80/intelweb/wilma/index.html>. The database is of country-specific information, especially news media and some U.S. government information sources. Web walker searches find university and think tank information sources as well as journalistic ones. Useful, but far too discreetly placed in a menu at the bottom of the pages, are links to topical directories. "International affairs" topics include general resources, news, commerce, security, and reference; pointers connect to government and journalistic information providers and to respectable directories, primarily university-based. "Regional news" is divided into Eastern Europe/Russia, Africa/Sahara, East Asia/Pacific, Western Europe, Americas/Canada, and Middle East/South Asia; when examined, many of the country entries included profiles from a discontinued Agence France-Presse free service.

Self-consciously a source of "alternative" news and views, **One-World Online** offers an extensive, international set of leftish, greenish resources regarding human rights, sustainable development, and environmental issues. URL: <http://www.oneworld.org/>. An umbrella site for "over 350 leading global justice organizations," it provides news (accessible by country or theme), opinion, and (in the form of "guides" to three-dozen topics) analysis.

Originally a commercial intelligence firm with roots in academic political science and the military, **Stratfor** has become a new-model Internet news agency, offering analysis and forecasting about geopolitically, militarily, and economically salient events worldwide.[3] URL: <http://www.stratfor.com>. "Delivering news at the speed of television with the depth of print," the site is updated several times a day. News and analysis, with frequent cross-referencing to Stratfor's previous articles, are arranged by theme ("Hotspots" and "Global Intelligence Updates") and region ("Intelligence Centers"). Archives are searchable. The firm's emphasis on providing immediate interpretation of events and its "open source intelligence" model of information gathering and dissemination using the Internet made it part of "the buzz" among policy makers and pundits during the Kosovo crisis. It also led to charges of shooting from the hip–which can make the site an excellent point of departure for instructors as well as cocktail party commentators.

POLITICAL SCIENCE DIRECTORY SITES

Grace York's **Political Science Resources on the Web** is a fundamental resource, both for its external links and as a model for organizing, annotating, and integrating external Web sites and Web-delivered resources on one's own campus. URL: <http://www.lib.umich.edu/libhome/Documents.center/polisci.html>. Like its majestic complement in the University of Michigan Documents Center, **Government Resources on the Web**, its scope is numbing. URL: <http://www.lib.umich.edu/libhome/Documents.center/govweb.html>. There is so much in the site that casual users (e.g., undergraduates) may be discouraged if they enter it without prior guidance. Specialists can be reasonably certain that the links they want are there–from major subfields of the discipline to writing and research guides, to indexes and reference tools, to links to guides in related disciplines.

Nonetheless, it is too bulky to be convenient for users who use existing sites as proxies for personal bookmark lists or as memory-joggers.

Users will appreciate having ready access to a simpler, complementary site. This might be a local adaptation of the Michigan site, changing the organizational principle and substituting local resources for those specific to the University of Michigan but otherwise retaining the content.

Another sprawling directory, covering even more (because interdisciplinary) territory and featuring an elaborate classification scheme, is **SOSIG, the Social Science Information Gateway**. URLs: <http://www. sosig.ac.uk/welcome.html> and, for U.S. users, <http://scout18.cs. wisc.edu/sosig_mirror/>. Based at the University of Bristol, *SOSIG* is an annotated, cross-referenced directory to Internet resources in education, management, and philosophy as well as the traditional social and behavioral sciences. It is arranged and abstracted by librarians and subject specialists.

Users will probably prefer to enter the directory via the *Yahoo*-style browsable index, which has worldwide, European, and U.K.-specific options. Resources are arranged by type: "articles/papers/reports" collections, individual documents of the same genres, bibliographic databases, bibliographies, "books/book equivalents," companies, company information, data, educational materials, frequently asked questions, government publications, governmental bodies, journal contents and abstracts, full text journals, mailing lists and discussion groups, news, organizations and societies, "other," reference materials, resource guides, and software. The arrangement of pointers by resource type and then by title jumbles together links that can be substantively quite dissimilar. The search function avoids this difficulty, but while a thesaurus is provided, searching by British spelling retrieves different records than searches by American spelling (e.g., *privatisation* vs. *privatization*).

Aiming for day-to-day usefulness rather than exhaustiveness, Bob Duval's **Poly-Cy** site at West Virginia University is among the most thoughtful and complete gateway pages for political science faculty, addressing their concerns as educators and scholars with a clean (albeit unannotated) design and a touch of humor. URL: <http://pslab11. polsci.wvu.edu/PolyCy/>. Its major sections are "The Profession," subfields and substantive policy areas, and governmental sources. The professional section is the largest, though its "Politics" subsection would also be useful to students of American politics. A unique section, "Warnings," deals with computer hoaxes and viruses and–useful for faculty but not something a library would mount on a publicly accessible site–links to term paper mills.

Michael Dartnell of Concordia University (Montréal) maintains a similar **Online Resource Guide to Political Inquiry**, with a more international flavor and an explicit claim that links are chosen for their significance rather than specious comprehensiveness. URL: <http://alcor. concordia.ca/~dartnel/index.html>.

For an undergraduate clientele, the International Political Science Association's **Guide to General Politics Resources** may be a more useful point of departure than the previously mentioned sites. URL: <http://www.ucd.ie/~ipsa/genpols.html>. The site is neatly organized by general links, subfields, "basic information" (country profiles, data), "official servers" of governments, parties, and the like, periodicals and news sources, and miscellany. Brief annotations accompany the links. In addition, the site is strong on comparative and international relations.

SUBFIELD DISTINCTIONS WITHIN THE DISCIPLINE

The politics-political science distinction is commonsensical for outsiders to the profession but too blunt an instrument effectively to connect practitioners with the information sources they want for their research and teaching. They will sometimes seek resources clustered into political science subfields, at other times by functional need.

Everyone in the discipline recognizes that there are subfields within it as well as intersections with other disciplines, though there is some disagreement about which ones "count"–as indeed there is about the appropriateness of conceiving of political science as one discipline at all (Lasco [1998]). The American Political Science Association recognizes eight subfields in its *Personnel Service Newsletter*: political theory, international relations, comparative politics, American politics, public policy, public law, public administration, and methodology. Public administration, policy, and law are frequently taught as if part of American, or, conversely, they may be offered outside political science departments. Give or take a subfield or two, these distinctions approximate conventional political science curricula and the short-hand self-identification of professionals about their specialties.[4]

Notable among the comprehensive Web directories to political science, **Political Science: A Net Station**, from Iza Laponce at the University of British Columbia Koerner Library, presents users directly with a dozen subfields rather than with a mix of subfields and professional topics. URL: <http://www.library.ubc.ca/poli/>. The directories for each subfield are quite extensive, notably in political theory, comparative politics, and international relations–often longer than *Poly-Cy*'s, though not as easy to navigate. They include useful pointers to the intersections of political science with sociology, anthropology, geography, and economics. The site index nests the political science teaching and research areas in a larger, library-centered context of social science and humanities reference materials and aids.

SUBFIELD-SPECIFIC DIRECTORIES
AND SELECTED RESOURCES

This section presents very brief, excessively general descriptions of the major subfields of political science and their use of information, followed by some significant gateways and interesting Internet resources for each. Public administration is excluded because it is the subject of another chapter in this volume. Similarly, the legal resources are included here selectively, depending on their interest to political scientists.

Political theory includes both normative theory and formal or positive theory. Normative theory (sometimes called political thought or political philosophy lest it be mistaken for positivist model-building) is concerned with the ways that people, peoples, and communities ought to live. This is the oldest and most humanistic portion of the discipline, intersecting philosophy, religion, literature, history (especially intellectual history), and the fine arts. Normative political theorists are divided, sometimes sharply, between those who work in the history of political thought and those who take a more analytical approach to political concepts, such as democracy or justice. The analytics often appear to have more in common with philosophy professors and lawyers than with the historians. Even among those who "do" the history of political thought, disagreements can be strident about the necessity of literal translations of texts and the appropriateness of setting thinkers in biographical, social, or other historical context. Textualists will demand particular translations and original-language editions not usually available on the Web and eschew the use of secondary sources by their students.[5] Positive and formal theories attempt to identify and model relationships among processes, institutions, and behavior. Their kinship with methodology, other social sciences (notably economics), and even parts of the natural sciences is arguably stronger than their affinity for normative theorists. See the methodology-resources section, below, for materials serving this clientele.

- The APSA **Foundations of Political Theory** section's site combines professional information (journals, conferences, announcements, and so on), pointers to online texts and theorist-specific Web sites, and teaching resources for political thought, including syllabi. URL: <http://www.apsanet.org/~theory/noframes.html> or–ugly and hard to navigate–<http://www.apsanet.org/~theory/index.html>.
- Maria Chiara Pievatolo, University of Pisa, in her **Political Philosophy** offers both a reference work on the history of political thought and an admirably organized directory to Web resources. It addresses the same sorts of philosophical and professional information as the APSA Foundations section site but with a more cosmopolitan selection of links, mostly in English. URL: <http://lgxserver.uniba.it/lei/filpol/filpole/homefpe.htm>. Pievatolo's "reasoned index" to political philosophy on the Web is heavily linked to appropriate full text Web sites and serious online secondary sources, such as the *Perseus Project* and the *Internet Encyclopedia of Philosophy*. URL: <http://lgxserver.uniba.it/lei/filpol/filpole/indicere.htm>.
- Martin Harrison's **Keele Guide to Political Thought and Ideology on the Internet** is a very large directory that points to sites about political thought, including online texts, and to sites that advocate or otherwise demonstrate an ideological commitment. It is arranged alphabetically under topical and thinker-specific headings. URL: <http://www.keele.ac.uk/depts/por/ptbase.htm>.[6]
- One of the more interesting attempts to create a virtual community of students of text-centered political philosophy is Lance Fletcher's **Free Lance Academy**, a set of 50 mailing lists de-

voted to "slow reading" of great works, from ancient to post-modern. URL: <http://www.freelance-academy.org/>. Fletcher's overview of his project is also a provocative meditation on the nature of political philosophizing.

International relations concerns the relations among nations and nation-like communities, including war, trade, and diplomacy, conducted by governments or non-governmental entities, whether carried out through such formal means as treaties and other expressions of international law or such relatively informal ones as tourism and commerce. Military science, diplomatic history, political economy, geography, and law are major points of intersection with other disciplines. Similarly, information needs can range from foreign communications media to intelligence reports, national and international government documents, and all manner of statistics. More so on the Web than in academic practice, "IR" and comparative resources overlap; sometimes distinguished in an umbrella site, such as the excellent Online Intelligence Project's index pages, already discussed, sometimes united under cross-cutting, topical categories.

- **WWW Virtual Library: International Affairs Resources** (formerly *International Studies Resources on the Internet*), compiled by Wayne A. Selcher of Elizabethtown College, is an excellent starting point for both international relations and comparative politics. URL: <http://www.etown.edu/home/selchewa/international_studies/firstpag.htm>. This directory includes detailed guides to international organizations, regions, and topics in international affairs.
- The **International Relations and Security Network**, maintained by the Center for Security Studies and Conflict Research, ETH Zurich, is slightly more strictly related to the relations of countries than to their comparison. URL: <http://www.isn.ethz.ch/>. Pages accessible through this site appear to be predominantly produced or supported by the world's governments, with some news media pages as well. Major sections for students and faculty alike include "current world affairs," a limited area search engine for international relations and security, an annotated links library, and a "facts and figures" database that was under construction through most of May 1999. Scholars will be interested in its conference calendar database, and teachers and publishers will be interested in its educational modules section.

- A political science directory for graduate students and professionals, **MENA: Political Science Resources** by Joseph Roberts of the University of Utah, emphasizes foreign policy and international affairs links, with particular attention to lists and other electronic media for interchange among political science teachers and researchers. URL: <http://www.cc.utah.edu/~jwr9311/MENA/Academic/Polsci.html>. This directory is part of Roberts's larger, interdisciplinary *Middle East North Africa Internet Resource Guide.* URL: <http://www.cc.utah.edu/~jwr9311/MENA.html>.
- **World Constitutions and International Treaties**, by Sandra da Conturbia and Xiaodong Li of the Texas A&M library, points to many sites compiling documents and other information relating to those corners of international law. URL: <http://library.tamu.edu/govdocs/workshop/>.

Comparative politics, broadly construed, has two major orientations: comparison of one or a few elements in different countries, systems, or regions; or comparison of different countries, systems, or regions taken as wholes. The comparative politics information resources on the Web, as with reference works in print, more readily support the traditional, formal approach to government and law rather than the less constrained, often interdisciplinary, orientation popular today.

- Somewhat smaller than the Virtual Library's *International Affairs Resources* site discussed above, but more richly annotated and hyperlinked, are the several related guides by Larry Schankman of Mansfield University of Pennsylvania. URL: <http://www.mnsfld.edu/depts/lib/country.html>. His **International and Area Studies** page is a fine starting point for comparativists that also points to Schankman's ongoing guides to current events, international statistics and international economics, and to his still-useful but no longer maintained guides to conflict resolution/international security, country studies, and foreign languages.
- Familiar in their own right, the online versions of the **CIA World Factbook** and the Library of Congress **Country Studies** come close to providing the ready reference, statistical, and directory information of the print *Europa World Year Book*. URLs: <http://www.odci.gov/cia/publications/factbook/index.html> and <http://lcweb2.loc.gov/frd/cs/cshome.html>, respectively. (The **CIA Hand-**

book of International Economic Statistics, in PDF and Microsoft Excel format, downloads so slowly that it should be treated as an electronically delivered print resource and consulted in hardcopy. URL: <http://www.odci.gov/cia/di/products/hies/hies.pdf>.)

- An easily navigated Web directory, Roberto Cicciomessere's **Political Resources on the Net** includes more than 16,000 links to parties, organizations, governments, and news media sites, arranged by country. URL: <http://www.agora.it/politic/>. The media and party links will be most useful for area-studies teaching and some research. Closely related is **Wilfried Derksen's Electoral Web Sites**. URL: <http://www.agora.stm.it/elections/home.htm>. An elaborate ready reference and Web directory, it comprises a frequently updated guide to elections around the world, a worldwide directory of national political parties, and another of international and national parliaments. All three parts are arranged by country, with links to a set of appropriate secondary sources on the Web.
  - The *Online Intelligence Project* and the *Middle East North Africa* sites already mentioned are good points of departure for area studies. Other notables include:
  - The regional resources section of T. Matthew Ciolek et al.'s **Asian Studies WWW Virtual Library**. URL: http://coombs.anu.edu.au/WWWVL-AsianStudies.html#Region.
  - The Georgetown University/Organization of American States **Political Database of the Americas**. URL: <http://www.georgetown.edu/pdba/>.
  - The Norwegian Council for Africa's **Index on Africa**. URL: <http://www.interpost.no/africaindex/index.html>.
  - The public affairs and government sections of the University of Pittsburgh **REESWeb: Russian and East Europeans Studies Internet Resources**, compiled by Karen Rondestvedt. URL: <http://www.ucis.pitt.edu/reesweb/index.html#Disc>.
  - Mirela Roznovschi's **Update to *Guide to European Legal Databases* and Guide to Foreign and International Legal Databases**. URLs: <http://www.llrx.com/features/europe2.htm> and <http://www.law.nyu.edu/library/foreign_intl/>, respectively.

The concerns of the *American politics* subfield are familiar: the behavior of officials, office-seekers, citizens, and groups, the causes and effects of government actions at all levels and branches, news media, political culture, and so on. Journalism, government publications, and the findings and methods of other social sciences are clearly relevant resource types. As done in the United States, the American politics subfield has its own subfields.

No free Internet resource can compare with the CIS/Lexis-Nexis print indexes and electronic databases as basic tools for students, teachers, and scholars of wide swaths of American politics and government.[7] In flexibility, scope, and ease of use, it is hard to beat *Congressional Universe* or *Statistical Universe*. Similarly, as reference sources, the large Congressional Quarterly guides to Congress, the Presidency, and the courts cannot be matched on the Web for scope, authoritativeness, and overall readability. They are, however, all at least two years old.

On the other hand, the sources discussed in the politics section above have the advantage of timeliness for tracking particular politicians or current legislative events and neatly complement the wealth of legislative data on federal sites, notably **THOMAS: Legislative Information on the Internet**, and the legislative, presidential, and administrative primary source materials at the **Office of the Federal Register** (along with a handy set of finding aids and research tools). URLs: <http://thomas.loc.gov/home/thomas.html>, <http://www.access. gpo.gov/nara/>, and <http://www.nara.gov/fedreg/nfrsrch.html>, respectively.

- **The Political Reference Almanac, 1999-2000** (sometimes linked as the *Almanac of Politics and Government*) is a pale approximation of the *Almanac of American Politics,* which is no longer available on the Web. URL: <http://www.polisci.com/ 1999.htm>. Very much like a hyperlinked legislative "blue book" applied to other branches and levels of American government and world governments, it lacks the narrative profiles that make the *Almanac of American Politics* and *Politics in America* useful and engaging. Even so, links to official government and party Web sites, significant political documents, lists of historical figures, and economic data make it a convenient "one-stop shop" for basic information. Absent access to *CQ Weekly,* the *Almanac* could be profitably used alongside **Congress.org** to track recent legislation and votes; the combination is less useful for tracking legislators because *Congress.org*'s "Scorecard" section draws on too few groups. URL: <http://congress.org/main.html>. The *Almanac*'s free online version reproduces the print version set in March 1999; updated and enhanced material is available only by subscription or by purchasing the book. Moreover, demographic statistics for states and districts use 1990 census data.

* **Political Junkie** offers a huge set of links to media outlets, newswires, pundits, political history pages, think tanks, and governments, but its design–four dozen unannotated lists of links–makes it most useful for its eponymous user: someone who already knows what kind of information to expect from a given source and wants to bookmark a handy gateway site. URL: <http://www.politicaljunkie.com>.

State And Local Politics, Federalism

* The Internet has made it much more convenient for researchers and teachers to gather state and local government information than has been possible in the print-only environment. There are several notable gateways to official state and local information. The main page of Piper Resources' **State and Local Government on the Net** is organized by name of the state, territory, or multistate organization. URL: <http://www.piperinfo.com/state/states.html>. It appears to be the most frequently updated state-information index site. **State Search**, from the National Association of State Information Resource Executives, conversely, is arranged under nearly three dozen topics. URL: <http://www.nasire.org/stateSearch/>. Its completeness and timeliness depend on a measure of self-reporting, and the appearance can be ragged. **Stateline.org**, from the Pew Center on the States, has a more sophisticated design and broader scope, featuring current and archived news relevant to state-level politics, background information and data on half a dozen important issues, and general profiles, data, and issues for each state. URL: <http://www.stateline.org/>. The Urban Institute's **Assessing the New Federalism** project provides abundant data and interpretation concerning state-level social welfare policies. URL: <http://newfederalism.urban.org/>. Its state database is available both as a live online database and a downloadable version using Microsoft Access.

- Along with a wealth of other data and analysis, **Dismal Scientist** is a convenient source of recent demographic and economic data, generally from federal agencies, for regions, states, and metropolitan areas. URL: <http://www.dismalscience.com/>. While member institutions have different research and publication, the member research centers of the **Association for University Business and Economic Research** are worth adding to the proverbial reference Rolodex as among the most authoritative providers of statistical information about their communities. URL: <http://www.auber.org/>. In addition to a directory of member centers, arranged by state, the AUBER Web site includes a directory of valuable links to state data sources as well as to several rather common state and federal statistical sources.[8]
- Kala Ladenheim's **Federalism in the United States** is a hypertext narrative study of American federalism from a variety of philosophical, historical, economic, and administrative perspectives; it includes abundant links and a bibliography. URL: <http://www.min.net/~kala/fed/>. It began as an alternative to a doctoral comprehensive examination and might thus be an interesting model project from the teaching standpoint.

Legislative

- **Congressional Mega Sites**, from the Library of Congress, includes government information sources and links to academic, non-profit, and commercial sites that provide directory information, news, voting records, legislative histories, interest group ratings, and the like. URL: <http://lcweb.loc.gov/global/legislative/mega.html>. *Mega Sites* is part of a larger, detailed directory of the **United States Legislative Branch** that includes more direct access to some of the same data. URL: <http://lcweb.loc.gov/global/legislative/congress.html>.
- The *Political Reference Almanac* provides basic directory information. Users interested in "dirt" or other information to outrage them may consult the resources discussed in the politics section or those generally dealing with American politics identified earlier in this section. They might also consult specialized databases maintained by activist groups.

Executive

- The Center for the Study of the Presidency's **Research Center** directories stand in contrast to the many sites of presidential biography and trivia. URL: <http://www.thepresidency.org/research. htm>. Most of the center's directories treat the presidency in the context of other institutions, such as parties, other branches of government, and think tanks and interest groups. The exceptions are the subdirectories of information about presidents (mostly biographical) and key documents (links to document sources, including presidential libraries, rather than directly to documents). Richard Jensen's good, annotated CSP **Guide to Political Research On-line**, which has been hard to reach from the center's own pages though it is a center project, includes a very extensive guide to presidential resources that features links to historical documents bearing on the institution, grouped by administration. URL: <http://home.nycap.rr.com/history/polsci.htm>.
- **White House 2000**, by Avi Bass of Northern Illinois University, emphasizes the presidency in the context of the upcoming election. URL: <http://www.niu.edu/newsplace/whitehouse.html>. The links in the sections on "The Presidency" and "Old Vote Counts" are the furthest removed from the horse-race aspect of the rest of the site. These include pointers to online spinoffs of television series, a few historical sites of marginal professional interest, and to POTUS: **Presidents of the United State**s, from the Internet Public Library, and **President**, from the University of North Carolina, the best biographical sites. URLs: <http:// www.ipl.org/ref/POTUS/> and <http://metalab.unc.edu/lia/president/ pres.html>, respectively.
- Rick Matlick's **The American Presidency: Selected Resources: An Informal Reference Guide** is a quixotic labor of love wrapped in grotesque formatting that, nonetheless, would be a handy gateway to useful resources–university research centers, presidential documents, and a long but indifferent bibliography–that professionals already know. URL: <http://www.interlink-cafe.com/ uspresidents/>. Undergraduates and public users will revel in the trivia that envelop the pointers to substantive sites.

Interest Groups, Parties, Elections

- Kathleen Fountain's **Political Advocacy Groups** is a superior starting point for profiling American interest groups. URLs: <http://
  www-new.csuchico.edu/~kcfount/index.html> and mirrored at
  <http://reinert.creighton.edu/advocacy/>. It provides descriptions,
  home page URLs, and contact information for groups, arranged
  both by area of advocacy and in a comprehensive alphabetical
  list. Unlike many commercial sites–and many produced within
  political science departments–the site also includes an account of
  the history and purpose of the guide, including a bibliography on
  interest groups. Complementing it, the Center for Responsive
  Politics maintains several databases on campaign contributions,
  lobbyists, and congressional and presidential campaigns at
  Opensecrets.org, the enhanced and regularly updated counterpart to the center's print *Open Secrets: The Encyclopedia of Congressional Money and Politics.* URL: <http://www.opensecrets.org/
  home/index.asp>. For directory information on electoral "insid-
  ers"–with postal and e-mail addresses but not URLs–Congressional
  Quarterly publishes print and Web versions of **The Political Pages**,
  1999-2000. URL: <http://www.campaignline.com/politicalpages/
  index.cfm>. It is an education in the election industry simply to
  read the headings for the services offered.
- Campaign news and poll results abound on the Web, and party
  platforms and home pages are easily found among the politics
  and political science sites already discussed. In contrast with
  Richard Scammon's familiar *America Votes* series or Congressional Quarterly's related *America at the Polls* volumes, free cross-
  sectional or longitudinal data for elections earlier than the 1990s
  are hard to locate consistently; this is especially true for data
  compiled at the local level. Much depends on the candidate, the
  race, and the jurisdiction.[9] The **NES Guide to Public Opinion
  and Electoral Behavior**, from the National Elections Studies
  project at the University of Michigan, provides a sample of the
  data collected at the University of Michigan since the late 1940s,
  with access to free downloadable datasets for presidential election years since 1952. Some foreign election datasets are also
  available. **United States Election Data: 1788-1990**, from the
  University of Virginia Geospatial and Statistical Data Center, is

an interactive database of gubernatorial, presidential, and House and Senate returns. URL: <http://fisher.lib.Virginia.EDU/elections/us.elections/>. Because it allows various comparisons of results by year and state for each office, it is handy for reference, but it does not allow comparison of simultaneous elections within any one state.

Public policy concerns the courses of action formally taken by governments, from the "there oughta be a law" stage to their implementation and side-effects, and the political activities that accompany them at every stage. Topical orientation (e.g., poverty policy, environmental policy, defense policy) is common and the occasion for political science to use the findings from many disciplines, from law to any of the natural sciences. Policy is sometimes offered as an expressly interdisciplinary program. Since policy is a large part of what bureaucrats are expected to "do," it has deep roots in public administration. Official and unofficial legislative and regulatory histories, the words and deeds of interest groups, and journalism are principal information sources.

- In addition to the standard section news and working papers, the APSA **Policy Section** includes a very complete directory of Web-based political, economic, and environmental data sources, and a solid selection of links to political science and public affairs sources; the directories are not annotated. URL: <http://www. fsu.edu/~spap/orgs/apsa.html>.
- The State University of West Georgia Ingram Library's **Online Government Publications** directory is an excellent starting point for students to look for policy-related research topics. It also provides an opportunity for political science faculty to show the relation among interest groups and government outputs and a chance for librarians to introduce students to the under-appreciated world of government publications. URL: <http://www. westga.edu/library/depts/govdoc/subaccess.html>.
- After years of being hard to get, **Congressional Research Service Reports** are finding their way onto the Web from various sources on and off Capitol Hill. The quality and utility of their analysis, presentation, and scholarly apparatus are mixed. Congressional Research Service WWW Accessible Reports, compiled by Gary Price, arranges the disparate sources under various

policy-oriented headings. URL: <http://gwis2.circ.gwu.edu/~gprice/crs.htm>.

- Despite the public administration allusion in its title, **PA Web Reference**, from the Maxwell School of Citizenship and Public Affairs at Syracuse University, includes a solid directory that is stronger in linking to sites about politics and policy than it is in providing information to public administrators or students in professional public administration programs. URL: <http://www.maxwell.syr.edu/maxpages/students/paphd/index.htm#web>.
- The Research Library of the Indiana University **Workshop in Political Theory and Policy Analysis** has a limited number of links to reference tools and other sites but a rich collection of full text primary sources, articles, and bibliographies related to the Workshop's work in normative and positive constitutional theory, institutional analysis, and resource economics. URL: <http://www.indiana.edu/~workshop/wsl/wsl.html>.

Public law deals with the formal relation of governments to natural and artificial persons, such as corporations and other governments, including rights, duties, powers, and regulations. Constitutional law and judicial decisions are the most familiar forms to Americans, though administrative law probably has more day-to-day influence on Americans' lives. Jurisprudence fits in the public law rubric, as do portions of economics and sociology. Statutes and regulations (including the paper trails leading to their adoption), and judicial reporters are core resources. Political scientists are divided among those who teach their courses as law school "lite," as in programs with an explicit pre-law track, and those who treat law as one set of institutions and ideologies among the many that social scientists address. Formal pre-law curricula and criminal justice are sometimes included within political science offerings. The related topic of judicial behavior, as its name suggests, treats law officials as political actors.

Public law resources on the Web are most useful to supplement existing print collections and course materials. Internet resources for law and politics are strongest in capturing the state of affairs today, as for reference, current-affairs projects, and cross-sectional analysis of "black-letter" law. Finding resources for longitudinal comparison and analysis is problematic. For the conventional upper-division constitutional law course sequence (government powers for one semester, civil liberties for another), most Supreme Court cases are available online, though their utility is primarily as a supplement to the casebook. Similarly, courses involving the political analysis of current statutes and regulations are well served–indeed, as governments at all levels put their various codes and legislative records online, the Internet allows better analysis and comparison across state and municipal boundaries than most academic libraries could afford with print sources. The same may be said of comparisons among appellate court jurisdictions. Faculty members whose teaching and research needs parallel those of lawyers will need the resources of a law library, or at least access to *Lexis-Nexis* or *WestLaw.*

- **FindLaw** is patterned on the *Yahoo* directory model, easy to navigate and very complete. URL: <http://www.findlaw.com/>. Political science researchers will be drawn to the case and code sections and the access to online law reviews. Pre-law students and pre-law advisors will be interested in the law school and various other professional sections.
- For users who already know something about the American legal and political system, Cornell Law School's **Legal Information Institute** is a very powerful and flexible resource for the texts of state and federal statutes, judicial opinions, administrative law. URL: <http://www.law.cornell.edu/>. It also includes current awareness and instructional materials. Topics in the "Law about . . ." section may be useful for public policy analysts. The **Cornell Legal Research Encyclopedia**, a work in progress, resembles conventional annotated webliographies of guides, primary source sites, and e-mail lists. URL: <http://www.lawschool.cornell.edu/lawlibrary/take1.html>. It includes both browsable lists of resource links and the searchable InSITE database, which includes annotations and metadata.
- The APSA **Law and Courts Section** page is an impressive point of departure, produced from a teaching-faculty standpoint. URL: <http://www.artsci.wustl.edu/~polisci/lawcourt.html>. The section-sponsored **Law and Politics Book Review** has been distributing timely book reviews for most of the 1990s. URL: <http://www.unt.edu/lpbr/>. The Web page of archived reviews is

browsable by book author and searchable as part of the University of North Texas Web site. It also provides a subscription form.

- **The Avalon Project: Documents in Law, History and Diplomacy** from Yale Law School is a lovely, full text source of important documents in public law, political thought, and diplomatic and political history. URL: <http://www.yale.edu/lawweb/avalon/avalon.htm>. The collection comprises primarily European and American documents, with some materials from the Middle East, from antiquity to today. Documents are in the public domain, reproduced from authoritative print editions or, sometimes, retagged existing online versions–source notes are very prominent–and may reproduce editorial commentary from those editions. In their statement of purpose, project co-directors William C. Fray and Lisa A. Spar say they expect to provide links among documents when the body of one refers to the other. The site is browsable by title, era, and topic (called "major collections"), and searchable. The "helpdesk" page is very clear and useful.
- **The Oyez Project**, is "the U.S. Supreme Court multimedia database" at Northwestern University. URL: <http://oyez.nwu.edu/>. Cases are accessible by title, subject, citation, and date. Abstracts are written in plain English. Links to *FindLaw* provide texts of opinions. The availability of many court arguments in RealAudio format makes the site especially distinctive.

Methodology, that is, the methods of empirical researchers rather than of the profession's students of history or philosophy, is very much an interdisciplinary concern for political scientists. It owes a great deal to sociology and economics for its ways of gathering, analyzing, and representing research findings.

- The **Society for Political Methodology and the Political Methodology Section** of the APSA maintain an elegant site notable for its online papers, selective access to articles and tables of contents to their newsletter and journal, and links to the archives of the H-PolMeth mailing list; an online list enrollment form is also available. URL: <http://polmeth.calpoly.edu>.
- The particular strength of Richard Tucker's **Political Science Research Resources** page is its extensive directories to interdisciplinary resources related to dynamic and nonlinear models,

game theory, artificial intelligence, econometrics, and data. URL: <http://php.indiana.edu/~rmtucker/polssrc.html>. These directories are generally divided into sections for teaching and research uses, with additional sections as warranted for general and partic-ular resources.[10]

FUNCTIONAL DISTINCTIONS:
THE KINDS AND USES OF POLITICAL INFORMATION

A topical or subfield approach to political science is appealing to the full range of potential users, from public users and undergraduates to research scholars. Internet resources in political science that take a mainly functional approach, dealing with the kinds of information and the uses to which it will be put, more commonly target graduate students and faculty.

Inasmuch as it permits browsing by resource type as well as disci-pline and descriptor, as well as word and phrase searching in and across disciplines and resource types, the Calvin College/Calvin Theo-logical Seminary's **AlphaSearch** directory of some 700 subject direc-tories is a hybrid of the topical and functional approaches. URL: <http://www.calvin.edu/library/as/>. It is selective and accessible in multiple ways. The list generated when one browses by discipline groups records by resource type; if a record falls under several categories, the database usefully displays it under each. Browsing within the list is impaired because the records under each heading commingle items from various subfields. Conversely, the opportu-nity to browse across disciplinary boundaries by resource type is AlphaSearch's strong suit. Unfortunately, it appears that most of the resource descriptions and links have not been updated since early 1998.

Gateways To Professional Associations

The **American Political Science Association** is the principal soci-ety of political science scholars in the United States. URL: <http://www.apsanet.org>. Its site is, accordingly, oriented toward profession-als rather than lay users. It is an appropriate, familiar, but incomplete gateway to several kinds of information that professionals and graduate students need to advance their careers and the state of knowledge within the discipline.

The APSA site is most useful as a clearinghouse of news in and about the profession, though the lack of dating on the pages is problematic. **PSOnline** provides timely notice of conferences, calls for papers, announcements, and links to related organizations, as well as selected content about teaching, professional advancement, and interpretation of political phenomena from the quarterly print edition, *PS: Political Science and Politics.* URL: <http://www.apsanet.org/PS/>. For good or ill, it does not include the print version's advertising.

The APSA sponsors nearly three dozen "organized sections" that provide insight about the interests of active members and the directions of their research needs, publication, and teaching. The **APSA Organized Sections** page includes pointers to their respective home pages. URL: <http://www.apsanet.org/Sections/>. The individual pages do not adhere to common criteria governing format, although in general the dozen or so useful ones combine section professional and section news and teaching and research resources, such as syllabi, working- and conference papers, datasets, and lists of pointers.

Two APSA online directories to members and departments are pale analogues of the association's triennial print directories.[11] The most complete Web directories to U.S. political science departments and institutes are at *Poly-Cy* (arranged by state) and Craig Leonard Brians's **Political Science Department Servers** (arranged by university name). URL: <http://www.majbill.vt.edu/polisci/brians/polsci.html>. Both sites provide pages to departments outside the United States; *Poly-Cy* is the larger.

The APSA's **Related Organizations** pointers are extensive, but it helps to know beforehand the name of the organization you seek. URL: <http://www.apsanet.org/PS/organizations/>. Conversely, the **National Political Science Associations** page from the International Political Science Association provides fewer links but uses its structure, internal links, and annotations to be more informative to the browsing user who seeks an organizational venue for his or her work. URL: <http://www.ucd.ie/~ipsa/natassoc.html>.

Because advisers and dissertation committees can be inconsistent sources of practical tips, professional socialization, and patronage, current and potential graduate students (not just those in political science) will want to consult Tucker's **Political Science Student Re-**

sources, part of his larger *Research Resources* site, for its links on practical subjects such as grants, job-searching, computing, writing, publishing, and teaching. URL: <http://php.indiana.edu/~rmtucker/instruct.html>. Unfortunately, many of its pointers are seriously out of date. The work of another recent political science grad student now teaching fulltime, Hal Bidlack's **PhD Help Center** is up to date but sparser. URL: <http://home.rmi.net/~bidlack/phd.html>. The other sections of his "Dissertation Den" site are of limited interest.

The APSA's placement service has a subscription-based online version. Free job postings in political science are available at the **H-Net Job Guide**, an umbrella site for positions in history, social sciences, and humanities at Michigan State. URL: <http://www.matrix.msu.edu/jobs/>. Rather more encompassing, Dan Knauft's **Jobs in Higher Education** political science page includes annotated links to the *H-Net* guide and the American Society for Public Administration's online job notices, as well as to several multi-purpose job notice resources, including the *Chronicle of Higher Education*. URL: <http://www.gslis.utexas.edu/~acadres/jobs/faculty/polisci.html>.

The utility of mailing lists for research is unpredictable, especially if lists do not maintain searchable archives, but they are a useful current awareness and networking service for graduate students and faculty. The Political Science List of Lists, by Gary Klass and colleagues at Illinois State University, lists nearly 350 electronic mailing lists relating to political issues, political science, and teaching. URL: <http://coyote.ils.ilstu.edu/tango/gmklass/listsrch.qry>. History and ideology are especially well represented. The list is organized by mailing list title, followed by a very brief descriptive label (or hotlink, when one exists), and the subscription address. It includes sample subscription commands for Listserv, Listproc, and Majordomo list software.

As a theme, history prevails in the 100-plus lists on the H-Net Discussion Networks home page, though it includes some of the joint history-political science efforts of the H-Net Humanities and Social Sciences Online project at Michigan State. URLs: <http://www.h-net.msu.edu/lists/> and <http://www.h-net.msu.edu/>, respectively.

Though the site promotes a list software package, the OneList site provides access to numerous "communities," including several hundred lists devoted to politics and government. URL: <http://www.onelist.com/geninfo/cat14.html>. Lists run the gamut from the strident to scholarly, with various degrees of access to current messages and archives for non-subscribers. Brief blurbs, evidently written by list owners, describe each list. These are accompanied by a standard set of notes that identify the language of the list, note the appropriateness of the list for children and teenagers, and state whether the list is moderated; often these provide links to the list's home page or create an electronic mail message to the list owner.

The news-update subscription services available from the journalistic sites already discussed will be more useful as aids to instructors than as research resources. The Internet Scout Report from the University of Wisconsin provides biweekly Internet-specific awareness services relevant to political science research, one for social sciences, the other for business and economics. URL: <http://scout.cs.wisc.edu/index.html>. These specialized reports use fairly generous criteria in determining what new and newly uncovered research, learning, current awareness, data, and news resources are relevant–an asset to browsing users with interdisciplinary inclinations. The current awareness sections are different from the sites' freestanding "current awareness metapages," though both versions provide access to full text materials and tables of contents, government and think tank reports, publishers (mainly new titles lists), data, and funding/employment sources. The social science report is usually mirrored on the Political Science Teaching and Research list. The weekly, general *Scout Report* will also have potentially relevant resources. "Signpost," a search function, including LC classes and subject headings, is available as well. URL: <http://www.signpost.org/signpost/>.

PUBLISHING IN VARIOUS FORMS

A number of the sites previously discussed provide links to online texts for teaching and research use. The resources described here are significant for political scientists concerned with placing their own work before the world.

In contrast with the APSA's useful *Getting Published in Political Science Journals: A Guide for Authors, Editors, and Librarians* (Martin and Goehlert [1997]), which provides information on the specialties, procedures, and manuscript submission and acceptance rates of more than 100 journals, the APSA's Web-based directory of journals is not comprehensive, leaving out, among other things, the subfields of political theory and public law. It also leaves out journals published by commercial American houses, conspicuously *Sage*, but includes a handful from English houses.

This journal list is neither fish nor fowl: it does not indicate whether a pointer is to a journal's home site or simply to contact information, nor does it suggest whether or to what degree a journal is available online in part (e.g., tables of contents) or full-text, nor if it is part of JSTOR, nor where it is indexed. As usual, *Poly-Cy* provides better coverage and access to publications in various formats.

Another Richard Tucker page, **Academic Journals**, is a directory to the homepages of principal journals, primarily in methodology and international relations, with shorter links to principal general, comparativist, and Americanist titles. URL: <http://php.indiana.edu/~rmtucker/pjournls.html>. The University of Michigan Library's **Electronic Journal and Newspaper List** is another directory to homepages. Its political science section ranges from scholarly and government titles to ideological tub-thumpers. This list includes some links to journal contents accessible only with OCLC, JSTOR, or other subscriptions. URL: <http://www.lib.umich.edu/libhome/ejournals/EJNLSUB.HTML#POLITISC>.

Though directed at economists, Kwan Choi's **How to Publish in Top Journals** offers lots of straightforward advice on publication and writing strategies, and tips on preparation, revision, and refereeing that are applicable to most social science writing. URL: <http://www.ag.iastate.edu/journals/rie/how.htm>.

Web-based guides to citation do not include guides to the format used by the *American Political Science Review* and various other journals, a variation on *Chicago Manual* embedded citation form. The APSA's own *Style Manual for Political Science* (1984), is available only in print, though a very abbreviated discussion of citation form appears at the *Review*'s Web site as part of the instructions to contributors submitting manuscripts. URL: <http://www.ssc.msu.edu/~apsr/instruct.html>.

The APSA Council has ruled that with the annual meeting in 2000, all papers presented at the national conference must be submitted to **PROceedings: Political Research Online**, where they will be freely available for a year. URL: <http://pro.harvard.edu/>. A project of the Harvard University Library and the APSA directed by one of the discipline's most dedicated proponents of electronic access to the literature, William J. Ball, the site currently offers only a small fraction of those in the program, but the site does reproduce the entire program—a more enduring opportunity to survey the players, topics, titles, and trends of the annual meetings than the APSA's own site yields.[12]

Authors seeking to publish in a major political science journal will not want to ruin their chance through ill-considered electronic distribution. The *American Political Science Review*'s policy, subject to revision, distinguishes between materials that have the characteristics of unvetted working papers and those that have gone through most of the traditional steps of journal publication (e.g., the forum calls itself a journal, it is run by a traditional publisher, it subjects submissions to peer review or other editorial selection, or it assumes copyright) (Finifter 1998).

Various political science sites provide links to publishers' Web sites, arranged by publisher name. Some are tilted toward providing access to publishers' catalogs for course-related book selection, some intended for authors seeking outlets. While most faculty are familiar with *Amazon.com* as the de facto standard source for identifying books, any seeking publishers would welcome knowing about Vanderbilt's AcqWeb Directory of Publishers and Vendors as well. URL: <http://www.library.vanderbilt.edu/law/acqs/pubr.html>.

R.J. Rummel's **Freedom, Democide, War** is interesting as an example of a scholar's life's work rendered in hypertext as well as an academic political science site with a political agenda. URL: <http://www2.hawaii.edu/~rummel/welcome.html>. Rummel marshals data, documents, online essays (most previously published in print by respectable academic publishers), detailed discussions of methodologies and philosophy, and a topical list of links to illuminate relationships among political freedom, war, genocide, and government-sponsored mass murder. He claims that the site includes 900 documents and the equivalent of 4,000 pages of text.

POLITICAL SCIENCE TEACHING

Teaching Politics, by Bill Ball of The College of New Jersey in association with the H-Teachpol discussion list, provides the most content-rich source of information for instructors. URL: <http://teachpol.tcnj.edu/>. The site includes conference papers on teaching, selections from the H-Teachpol list, and an archived online conference on teaching politics. A multimedia section includes materials from the APSA Conference Group on Politics and Film, information on multimedia classrooms, and a relatively short, selective, and annotated list of online resources for political science teachers.

Many APSA organized section sites include online archives of syllabi and other teaching materials. The APSA sells print syllabus collections for various subfields and standard courses that date from 1991 to 1996, along with other course materials. *Poly-Cy* and the **University of Texas World Lecture Hall** provide extensive links to Web-based courses. URL: <http://www.utexas.edu/world/lecture/pol/>. Karl Ho appears to keep his **Political Science Cyberclasses** (University of North Texas) up to date more regularly than other directories to syllabi and courses and aspires to be both advocate and clearinghouse for "cyber-education." URL: <http://www.psci.unt.edu/kho/cybercls/>.

The **SSRIC Teaching Resources Depository Home Page**, from the California State University Social Sciences Research and Instructional Council, is an extremely well thought out, interdisciplinary package of teaching modules (mainly involving California data and topics), syllabi, exercises and instruction in the SPSS statistical analysis software, and other course materials. URL: <http://www.csubak.edu/ssric/welcome.htm>. The directory to teaching resources on the Web, emphasizing the integration of computers into instruction, is an excellent, annotated selection.

Publishers' Web-based supplements to their textbooks include exercises and study guides, discussion and debate points, discussions relating news events to texts, and data and documents. Instructors and librarians could view these both as substantive resources and as models for locally developed pages. Of the major textbook publishers, Houghton Mifflin's **Political SourceNet**, which supplements its half-dozen textbooks on American national politics, is the most extensive. URL: <http://www.hmco.com/college/polisci/psn/index.html>.   W.W. Norton provides the same sort of features in a **Politics and Participation "Webbook"** to accompany *We The People, An Introduction to American Politics* by Benjamin Ginsberg, Theodore J. Lowi, and Margaret Weir. URL: <http://www.wwnorton.com/college/wtp/>. Other major textbook publishers use passwords to restrict access to their Web supplements.

Political science instructors in American politics, public law, and international and comparative politics should know about the subject guides and specialized course materials in the ALA Government Documents Roundtable **Handout Exchange**. These resources can be useful for designing their courses, preparing their own handouts and assignments, and coordinating instruction with their colleagues in the library. URL: <http://www.lib.umich.edu/libhome/Documents.center/godort.html>.

The American Political Sciences' Association's **Civic Education Network** is the profession's response to the ongoing calls by pundits and legislatures for schools to teach the principles of American liberal democracy. URL: <http://www.apsanet.org/CENnet/>. Directed at primary and secondary school teachers and teacher educators, *CENnet* offers essays relating to civic education, an annotated list of organizations that actively support citizen education and involvement, and a link to the APSA's teaching resources page. **Civnet** is a broader clearinghouse for news, opinion, studies, and course materials for promoting "civil society" around the world. URL: <http://www.civnet.org>. Notable among other civic education sites, the Claremont Institute's **Founding.com: A User's Guide to the Declaration of Independence** speaks from a very definite philosophical foundation. URL: <http://www.founding.com>.

STATISTICS AND DATASETS

For public users and undergraduates seeking quantitative evidence for their papers, University of Michigan Documents Center strikes again. **Statistical Resources on the Web** arranges annotated links under two-dozen commonsense major headings and more than 200 common topics, with the Document Center's usual comprehensiveness. URL: <http://www.lib.umich.edu/libhome/Documents.center/frames/statsfr.html>. The directory includes notes on sources that are available only in paper.

Researchers seeking datasets will find them spread throughout the Michigan directory and the data sources section of Richard Tucker's *Research Resources* project. More direct access to data sets and their underlying dictionaries and codebooks comes via the University of California, San Diego's **Social Science Data on the Net and Internet Crossroads in the Social Sciences**, from the University of Wisconsin's Data and Program Library Service; one arranged by functional resource type (data, catalog, etc.), the other by broad provenance and subject area. URLs: <http://odwin.ucsd.edu/idata/> and <http://dpls. dacc.wisc.edu/internet.html>, respectively.

The Inter-university Consortium for Political and Social Research maintains "the world's largest archive of computerized social science data." URL: <http://www.icpsr.umich.edu/>. It is a familiar resource for behavioralist researchers, which compensates for the barebones content of most of the catalogs to the data archives. Even for those datasets with access restrictions, the catalogs provide a potentially useful overview of research activity in their enumeration of study titles and principal investigators.

The Institute for Research in Social Sciences at UNC Chapel Hill claims to maintain the third-largest archive of machine-readable social science data. URL: <http://www.irss.unc.edu/irss/dataservices/dataservices. html>. Distinctive holdings include Louis Harris poll data, the National Network of State Polls, and a public opinion poll question database. The searchable catalog to data is easy to use; records are rich in metadata and hypertext links point to publicly accessible data and codebooks in various formats. The question database is searchable and freely accessible.

CONCLUSION

Given the range of topics and resources that might reasonably be used by political science students and professionals, it seems ill advised to approach free Internet resources as if they could be comprehensively located, systematically assessed, and described in the small space available. Doing so would, moreover, beg two questions. First, how would the resources discussed abstractly complement the materials already available in this or that academic library? Second, in what respects would they suit the particular needs of public users, undergraduate non-majors, upper division majors, graduate students, and faculty? We cannot think about the information without thinking about its uses and users.

To deal with the first question, I have drawn on my own training in a reasonably prestigious Ph.D. program in political science and on my experiences teaching and advising in colleges and universities that inclined toward the opposite end of the prestige and resource availability spectrum. I suggest a typology of political science information needs to help information professionals match relevant resources to local needs. To deal with the second question, I have concentrated here on resources that themselves marshal and arrange–presort, as it were–resources. If nothing else, when several observers, both political scientists and librarians, create directories to the vast gray literature that fills the Internet, they will not all miss or misidentify the same ones.

- The distinction between political science and politics recognizes that many users, particularly non-majors and public users, will be more interested in facts about the political world than in learned discourse about measuring them and their interrelation. For current events news and analysis and for basic directory information the Web is unexcelled for the price. The same is true of much government information in the United States. On the other hand, for retrieving information that is no longer current, the Web remains problematic in point of storage, indexing, and retrieval.
- Practicing political scientists, from upper-division majors to faculty, identify themselves, their needs, and their agendas in terms of several generally recognized subfields of the discipline. These may further subdivide and recombine. For each subfield, there are many Web resources that support teaching. As a research medium, the Internet is mixed: very useful where there are free electronic analogues of respectable print sources, such as U.S. government documents and primary legal materials, but problematic if the researcher needs trustworthy historical data or demands specific editions or translations of seminal texts. Additionally, the Web offers a low-cost channel for cyber-aware scholars in a subfield to keep tabs on one another.
- Across all academic disciplines, there are some shared, functional information needs. These are, bluntly, job-related: teaching materials and syllabi, specialized research materials, such as datasets, publication outlets, conference listings, want ads. The Web parallels print on this score. It could be faster, but if a professional group prints its newsletters or directories erratically, its online distribution may be no more timely. The Web gives the illusion of greater comprehensiveness, but a teacher or scholar who does not choose to share his syllabi or her data will be just as invisible electronically as in print.

NOTES

1.Needless to say, characterizations of these commercial sites made as of Independence Day, 1999, may be inconsistent with their nature as of New Year's Day, 2000.

2. Congressional Quarterly offers limited free trial subscriptions to its periodicals, teasing readers with very limited free access. URL: <http://www.cq.com/>. National Journal is much the same. URL: <http://www.nationaljournal.com/>.

3. Disclaimer: Stratfor's founder and CEO, George Friedman, was my undergraduate mentor while teaching political philosophy at Dickinson College in the mid-1970s. I discovered his affiliation with Stratfor by accident.

4. For example, textbooks introducing undergraduates to the study of politics may slice the field differently or present the discipline in terms of issues, questions, or methods that cut across subfields, arranging their bibliographies and, increasingly, webliographies accordingly. One of the most interesting attempts to draw connections across subfield and conceptual distinctions in the discipline and to illustrate them with relevant Web pages is the "Personal Politics" boxes in Magstadt and Schotten, 1999. The authors describe five political science subfields in the course of their introductory chapter on the study of politics.

5. In the print world, these fundamentally opposed approaches to the nature of political philosophy are represented by a pair of classic reference works: Strauss and Cropsey 1987, and Sabine 1993, respectively.

6. This site should not be confused with Richard Kimber's jumbled, but widely linked, **Political Thought** page, also at Keele. URL: <http://www.psr.keele.ac.uk/thought.htm>.

7. For many years, Legi-Slate has been a staple among proprietary online services. Unfortunately, I did not have access to it in the course of preparing this review.

8. A directory to U.S. member centers' Web sites, arranged by university name and arguably more complete than AUBER's own "find a member" page, is available at <http://www.nscee.edu/cber/auber.html>.

9. The Web site of the **Lijphart Elections Archive** at UC San Diego is tantalizing, for the data cover many years, in many elections, in many countries, but the access is restricted to UCSD faculty, students, and staff. URL: <http://dodgson.ucsd.edu/lij/>. Some of the data are available to member institutions of the Inter-university Consortium for Political and Social Research.

10. Sometimes showing up in directories and search engines, Tucker's **Political Methodology Research Resources** page puts a terminally cute, rather obscure front end to these directories and ought therefore to be avoided. URL: <http://php.indiana.edu/~rmtucker/frmlempr.html>.

11. The APSA's membership and department directories are also flawed inasmuch as they are perennially dated and depend on responses to surveys: American Political Science Association, *Directory of Members, 1997-99* (Washington, DC:APSA, 1997); *Graduate Faculty and Programs in Political Science, 1998-2000* (Washington, DC:APSA, 1998); *Directory of Undergraduate Political Science Faculty, 1996-98* (Washington, DC:APSA, 1996).

12. **Political Science Manuscripts**, still linked from many pages, was another of Professor Ball's projects that is still available though it comprises only 56 papers, all from 1995-97, and is no longer supported. URL: <http://www.tcnj.edu/~psm/>. It includes a directory from 1996 to other online full-text and abstract/table of contents sites, primarily journals.

WEBLIOGRAPHY

General Public Affairs News and Reference

Cable News Network. *AllPolitics.com* [Online]. Retrieved May 10, 1999. URL: http://cnn.com/ALLPOLITICS

Center for National Independence in Politics. (1992). *Project Vote Smart: a Voter's Self-Defense System* [Online]. Corvallis, OR:CNIP. Retrieved July 9, 1999. URL: http://www.votesmart.com/

Center for Responsive Politics. *Opensecrets.org: the Online Source for Money in Politics Data* [Online]. Washington, DC: Center for Responsive Politics. Retrieved May 30, 1999. URL: http://www.opensecrets.org/home/index.asp

Coakley, J. *IPSA Guide to General Politics Resources* [Online]. Dublin: International Political Science Association. Retrieved May 11, 1999. URL: http://www.ucd.ie/~ipsa/genpols.html

Hemmerle, D. *Political Index* [Online]. Mill Valley, CA: National Political Index. Retrieved May 10, 1999. URL: http://ww.politicalindex.com/

Leita, C. *Librarians' Index to the Internet* [Online]. Berkeley: Berkeley Digital Library SunSITE. Retrieved May 4, 1999. URL: http://sunsite.berkeley.edu/InternetIndex/

Markle Foundation and Kennedy School of Government. (1998) *Web White & Blue* [Online]. Washington, DC: Markle Foundation. Retrieved July 9, 1999. URL: http://www.webwhiteblue.org/

One World Broadcasting Trust. (1995) *OneWorld Online* [Online]. Chinnor, Oxon.: OneWorld Online. Retrieved May 23, 1999. URL: http://www.oneworld.org/

Policy.com [Online]. Washington, DC: VoxCap.com. Retrieved May 10, 1999. URL: http://www.policy.com

The Political Reference Almanac, 1999-2000 [Online]. Arlington, VA: Keynote Publishing. Retrieved May 22, 1999. URL: http://www.polisci.com/1999.htm

Political Junkie [Online]. Retrieved May 26, 1999. URL: http://www.politicaljunkie.com/

Treadaway. C. (1999). *Stratfor* [Online]. Retrieved August 2, 1999. URL: http://www.stratfor.com

General Political Science Directories

Calvin College Hekman Library. *AlphaSearch* [Online]. Grand Rapids, MI: Calvin College. Retrieved May 9, 1999. URL: http://www.calvin.edu/library/as

Cross, P. et al. *SOSIG, the Social Science Information Gateway* [Online] Bristol, UK: University of Bristol. Retrieved May 12, 1999. URLs: www.sosig.ac.uk/welcome. html and scout18.cs.wisc.edu/sosig_mirror/

Dartnell, M. (1997) *Online Resource Guide to Political Inquiry* [Online]. Montréal: Concordia University. Retrieved May 12, 1999. URL: http://alcor.concordia.ca/ ~dartnel/index.html

Duval, R. (1996) *Poly-Cy* [Online]. Morgantown: West Virginia University. Retrieved May 4, 1999. URL: http://pslab11.polsci.wvu.edu/PolyCy/

Jensen, R. (1999) *CSP Guide to Political Resources On-Line* [Online]. Washington, DC: Center for the Study of the Presidency. Retrieved August 16, 1999. URL: http://home.nycap.rr.com/history/polsci.htm

Internet Scout Project (1994) *Internet Scout Report* [Online]. Madison: University of Wisconsin. Retrieved May 17, 1999. URL: http://scout.cs.wisc.edu/index.html

Laponce, I. *Political Science: A Net Station* [Online]. Vancouver: University of British Columbia. Retrieved May 10, 1999. URL: http://www.library.ubc.ca/poli/

Price, G. *Direct Search* [Online]. Washington, DC: Georgetown University. Retrieved May 14, 1999. URL: http://gwis2.circ.gwu.edu/~gprice/direct.htm

Tucker, R. *Political Science Research Resources* [Online]. Retrieved May 10, 1999. URL: http://php.indiana.edu/~rmtucker/polssrc.html

York, G. *Political Science Resources on the Web* [Online]. Ann Arbor: University of Michigan. Retrieved May 10, 1999. URL: http://www.lib.umich.edu/libhome/ Documents. center/polisci.html

Resources for Subfields of Political Science

Aldrich, M. (1998) *Online Government Publications* [Online]. Carrollton: State University of West Georgia. Retrieved May 21, 1999. URL: http://www.westga.edu/ library/depts/govdoc/subaccess.html

American Political Science Association. *APSA Policy Section* [Online]. Tallahassee: Florida State University. Retrieved May 21, 1999. URL: http://www.fsu.edu/ ~spap/orgs/apsa.html

Anziger, G. (1995) *Governments on the WWW* [Online]. May 10, 1999. URL: http://www.gksoft.com/govt/en/

Association for University Business and Economic Research. *AUBER: Association for University Business and Economic Research* [Online]. Monroe: Northeast Louisiana University. Retrieved May 20, 1999. URL: http://www.auber.org/

Banducci, S.A. and Karp, J.A. *We the People: Politics and Participation WebBook* [Online]. New York: W.W. Norton. Retrieved May 19, 1999. URL: http://www. wwnorton.com/college/wtp/

Bass, Avi. *White House 2000* [Online]. DeKalb: Northern Illinois University. Retrieved May 31, 1999. URL: http://www.niu.edu/newsplace/whitehouse.html

Center for Responsive Politics. *Opensecrets.org* [Online]. Washington, DC: Center for Responsive Politics. Retrieved May 30, 1999. URL: HTTP://www.opensecrets.org/ home/index.asp

Center for Security Studies and Conflict Research. *International Relations and Security Network* [Online]. Retrieved May 22, 1999. Zurich: ETH Zurich. URL: http://www.isn.ethz.ch/

Center for the Study of the Presidency. *Research Center* [Online]. Washington, DC: Center for the Study of the Presidency. Retrieved May 31, 1999. URL: http://www.thepresidency.org/research.htm

Cicciomessere, R. (1995) *Political Resources on the Net* [Online]. May 10, 1999. URL: http://www.agora.it/politic/

Conhaim, W.W. and Noonan, D. *State and Local Government on the Net*. [Online]. Minneapolis: Piper Resources. Retrieved May 28, 1999. URL: http://www.piperinfo.com/state/states.html

Cornell Law Library. *Cornell Legal Research Encyclopedia* [Online]. Ithaca, NY: Cornell University. Retrieved May 29, 1999. URL: http://www.lawschool.cornell.edu/lawlibrary/take1.html

Cornell Law School. *Legal Information Institute* [Online]. Ithaca, NY: Cornell University. Retrieved May 29, 1999. URL: http://www.law.cornell.edu/

da Conturbia, S., and Li, X. (1999) *World Constitutions and International Treaties* [Online]. Retrieved May 22, 1999. College Station: Texas A & M General Libraries. URL: http://library.tamu.edu/govdocs/workshop/

Dedman, W. (1997). *Fair Lending: A Resource Guide* [Online]. Retrieved July 15, 1999. URL: HTTP://FairLending.com/

Derksen, W. *Electoral Web Sites* [Online]. Retrieved: May 10, 1999. URL: http://www.agora.stm.it/elections/home.htm

Dismal Sciences, Inc. *Dismal Scientist* [Online]. Retrieved May 20, 1999. URL: http://www.dismalscience.com/

Epstein, L. and Handlin, L. (1996) *Law and Courts* [Online]. St. Louis: Law and Courts Section of the American Political Science Association. Retrieved May 21, 1999. URL: http://www.artsci.wustl.edu/~polisci/lawcourt.html

FindLaw, Inc. (1996) *FindLaw* [Online]. Retrieved May 11, 1999. URL: http://www.findlaw.com/

Fletcher, L.R. (1994) *Free Lance Academy* [Online]. Jersey City: Lancelot R. Fletcher. Retrieved May 12, 1999. URL: http://www.freelance-academy.org

Fountain, K.C. (1998) *Political Advocacy Groups* [Online]. Chico, CA: California State University, Chico, and Omaha: Creighton University. Retrieved June 1, 1999. URLs: http://www-new.csuchico.edu/~kcfount/index.html and http://reinert.creighton.edu/advocacy/

Fray, W. and Spar, L. *The Avalon Project: Documents in Law, History and Diplomacy* [Online]. New Haven: Yale Law School. Retrieved May 15, 1999. URL: http://www.yale.edu/lawweb/avalon/avalon.htm

Georgetown University and Organization of American States. *Political Database of the Americas* [Online]. Washington, DC: Georgetown University and Organization of American States. Retrieved May 30, 1999. URL: http://www.georgetown.edu/pdba/

Goldman, J. (1996). *The Oyez Project* [Online]. Evanston, IL: Northwestern University. Retrieved May 15, 1999. URL: http://oyez.nwu.edu/

Harrison, M. Keele *Guide to Political Thought and Ideology on the Internet* [Online]. Keele, UK: University of Keele. Retrieved May 12, 1999. URL: http://www.keele.ac.uk/depts/por/ptbase.htm

International Institute for Democracy and Electoral Assistance (1999). *Administra-*

tion and Cost of Elections [Online]. Stockholm: International IDEA. Retrieved July 10, 1999. URL: http://www.aceproject.org/

_____ . *Voter Turnout From 1945 to 1997: a Global Report on Political Participation* [Online]. Stockholm: International IDEA. Retrieved July 10, 1999. URL: http://www.int-idea.se/Voter_turnout/index.html

_____ . *Women in Politics: Beyond Numbers* [Online]. Stockholm: International IDEA. Retrieved July 10, 1999. URL: http://www.int-idea.se/women/index.html

Houghton Mifflin Co. *Political SourceNet* [Online]. Boston: Houghton Mifflin. Retrieved May 19, 1999. URL: http://www.hmco.com/college/polisci/psn/index.html

Ladenheim, K. *Federalism in the United States* [Online]. Retrieved May 29, 1999. URL: http://www.min.net/~kala/fed/

Leadership Information Archives. *President* [Online]. Chapel Hill, NC: University of North Carolina. Retrieved May 31, 1999. URL: http://metalab.unc.edu/lia/president/pres.html

Levy, J.T. (1997) *Foundations of Political Theory* [Online]. Princeton, NJ: Foundations of Political Theory Organized Section of the APSA. Retrieved May 12, 1999. URLs: http://www.apsanet.org/~theory/noframes.html and http://www.apsanet.org/~theory/index.html

Library of Congress. *THOMAS: Legislative Information on the Internet* [Online].Washington, DC: Library of Congress. Retrieved May 22, 1999. URL: http://thomas.loc.gov/home/thomas.html

_____ . *Congressional Mega Sites* [Online]. Washington, DC: Library of Congress. Retrieved May 22, 1999. URL: http://lcweb.loc.gov/global/legislative/mega.html

_____ . *Country Studies* [Online]. Washington, DC: Library of Congress. URL: http://lcweb2.loc.gov/frd/cs/cshome.html

_____ . *United States Legislative Branch* [Online]. Retrieved May 22, 1999. URL: http://lcweb.loc.gov/global/legislative/congress.html

Matlick, R. *The American Presidency: Selected Resources: An Informal Reference Guide* [Online]. Retrieved May 31, 1999. URL: http://www.interlink-cafe.com/uspresidents/

Maxwell School of Citizenship and Public Affairs. *PA Web Reference* [Online]. Syracuse, NY: Syracuse University. Retrieved May 21, 1999. URL: http://www.maxwell.syr.edu/maxpages/students/paphd/index.htm#web

National Archives and Records Administration. *Office of the Federal Register* [Online]. Washington, DC: U.S. Government Printing Office. Retrieved May 28, 1999. URL: http://www.access.gpo.gov/nara/

National Association of State Information Resource Executives. *StateSearch* [Online]. Lexington, KY: NASIRE. Retrieved May 28, 1999 URL: http://www.nasire.org/stateSearch/

National Election Studies. (1997) *NES Guide to Public Opinion and Electoral Behavior* [Online]. Ann Arbor: University of Michigan. Retrieved May 30, 1999. URL: http://www.umich.edu/~nes/nesguide/nesguide.htm

Office of the Federal Register. *Federal Register Research Tools* [Online]. Washington, DC: National Archives and Records Administration. Retrieved May 28, 1999. URL: http://www.nara.gov/fedreg/nfrsrch.html

ONElist, Inc. *Find a Mailing List: Government* [Online]. URL: http://www. onelist.com/geninfo/cat14.html

Online Intelligence Project. *OLIN Project Database* [Online]. Retrieved May 29, 1999. URL: http://www.icg.org:80/intelweb/wilma/index.html

Pew Center on the States. *Stateline.org* [Online]. Richmond: University of Richmond. Retrieved May 28, 1999. URL: http://www.stateline.org/

Pievatolo, M. C. *Political Philosophy* [Online]. Pisa: Universita' di Pisa. Retrieved May 12, 1999. URL: http://lgxserver.uniba.it/lei/filpol/filpole/homefpe.htm

Price, G. *Congressional Research Service WWW Accessible Reports* [Online]. Washington, DC: Georgetown University. Retrieved May 14, 1999. URL: http:// gwis2.circ.gwu.edu/~gprice/crs.htm

Roberts, J. (1996) *MENA: Political Science Resources* [Online]. Salt Lake City: University of Utah. URL: http://www.cc.utah.edu/~jwr9311/MENA/Academic/ Polsci.html

Roznovschi, M. *Guide to Foreign and International Legal Databases* [Online]. New York: New York University School of Law. Retrieved May 11, 1999. URL: http://www.law.nyu.edu/library/foreign_intl/

Roznovschi, M. (1998) *Update to Guide to European Legal Databases* [Online]. Retrieved May 11, 1999. URL: http://www.llrx.com/features/europe2.htm

_____ . (1999). *Evaluating Foreign and International Legal Databases on the Internet* [Online]. Retrieved May 11, 1999. URL: http://www.llrx.com/features/ evaluating.htm.

Rummel, R. (1998). *Freedom, Democide, War* [Online]. Honolulu: University of Hawaii. Retrieved May 29, 1999. URL: http://www2.hawaii.edu/~rummel/welcome. html

Schankman, L. *International and Area Studies* [Online]. Mansfield, PA: Mansfield University. Retrieved May 21, 1999. URL: http://www.mnsfld.edu/depts/lib/country. html

Selcher, W. *WWW Virtual Library: International Affairs Resources* [Online]. Elizabethtown, PA: Elizabethtown College. URL: http://www.etown.edu/home/selchewa/ international_studies/firstpag.htm

Society for Political Methodology and the Political Methodology Section of the APSA. *PolMeth Homepage* [Online]. Retrieved May 11, 1999. San Luis Obispo: California Polytechnic State University. URL: http://polmeth.calpoly.edu/.

Summers, R.S. (1996) *POTUS: Presidents of the United States* [Online]. Ann Arbor, MI: Internet Public Library. Retrieved May 31, 1999. URL: http://www.ipl.org/ref/POTUS/

The Political Pages, 1999-2000 [Online]. Washington, DC: Congressional Quarterly. Retrieved May 30, 1999. URL: http://www.campaignline.com/politicalpages/ index.cfm

U.S. Central Intelligence Agency. *World Factbook* [Online]. Washington, DC: Central Intelligence Agency. Retrieved May 14, 1999. URL: http://www.odci.gov/cia/ publications/factbook/index.html

University of Virginia, Geospatial and Statistical Data Center. *United States Election Data: 1788-1900* [Online]. Retrieved May 31, 1999. URL: http://fisher.lib.Virginia. EDU/elections/us.elections/

Urban Institute. *Assessing the New Federalism* [Online]. Washington, DC: Urban Institute. Retrieved May 27, 1999. URL: http://newfederalism.urban.org/

Workshop in Political Theory and Policy Analysis. *Workshop Research Library* [Online]. Bloomington: Indiana University. Retrieved May 21, 1999. URL: http://www.indiana.edu/~workshop/wsl/wsl.html

York, G. *Government Resources on the Web* [Online]. Ann Arbor: University of Michigan. Retrieved May 10, 1999. URL: http://www.lib.umich.edu/libhome/Documents. center/govweb.html

_____ . *Statistical Resources on the Web* [Online]. Ann Arbor: University of Michigan. Retrieved May 10, 1999. URL: http://www.lib.umich.edu/libhome/Documents.center/frames/statsfr.html

Resources Supporting Professional Activity

American Political Science Association. *APSANet: The American Political Science Association On-Line* [Online]. Retrieved May 9, 1999. URL: http://www.apsanet.org

_____ . *Organized Sections* [Online]. Washington, DC: APSA. Retrieved May 9, 1999. URL: http://www.apsanet.org/Sections/section.html

_____ . *PSOnline* [Online]. Washington, DC: APSA. Retrieved May 9, 1999. URL: http://www.apsanet.org/PS/

_____ . *Related Organizations* [Online]. Washington, DC: APSA. Retrieved May 9, 1999. URL: http://www.apsanet.org/PS/organizations/

Brians, C.L. *Political Science Department Servers* [Online]. Blacksburg: Virginia Polytechnic Institute and State University. Retrieved May 9, 1999. URL: http://www.majbill.vt.edu/polisci/brians/polsci.html

Chronicle of Higher Education. *Career Network* [Online]. Retrieved May 29, 1999. URL: http://chronicle.com/jobs/

Coakley, J. *International Political Science Association* [Online]. Dublin: International Political Science Association. Retrieved May 11, 1999. URL: http://www.ucd.ie/~ipsa/index.html

_____ . *National Political Science Associations* [Online]. Dublin: International Political Science Association. Retrieved May 11, 1999. URL: http://www.ucd.ie/~ipsa/natassoc.html

H-Net, Humanities & Social Sciences OnLine (1995). *H-Net's Job Guide.* [Online]. East Lansing, MI: H-Net. Retrieved May 10, 1999. URL: http://www.matrix.msu.edu/jobs/

University of Michigan Library. *Electronic Journal and Newspaper List* [Online]. Ann Arbor: University of Michigan. Retrieved May 31, 1999. URL: http://www.lib.umich.edu/libhome/ejournals/EJNLSUB.HTML#POLITISC

Vanderbilt University Library. *AcqWeb Directory of Publishers and Vendors* [Online]. Nashville: Vanderbilt University. Retrieved May 15, 1999. URL: http://www.library.vanderbilt.edu/law/acqs/pubr.html

Resources for Instructors and Researchers

American Political Science Association. *Civic Education Network* [Online]. Washington, DC: APSA. Retrieved May 9, 1999. URL: http://www.apsanet.org/CENnet/

_____ . *Teaching Political Science* [Online]. Washington, DC: APSA. Retrieved May 9, 1999. URL: http://www.apsanet.org/teaching/

American Political Science Review. *Instructions to contributors* [Online]. East Lansing, MI: American Political Science Association. Retrieved May 31, 1999. URL: ttp://www.ssc.msu.edu/ ~apsr/instruct.html

Ball, W. *PROceedings: Political Research Online* [Online]. Cambridge, MA: Harvard University Library and the American Political Science Association. Retrieved May 9, 1999. URL: http://pro.harvard.edu/

_____. *Teaching Politics* [Online]. Trenton: The College of New Jersey. Retrieved May 9, 1999. URL: http://teachpol.tcnj.edu/

Bimber, B. (1998). *Government and Politics on the Net Project* [Online]. Santa Barbara: University of California. Retrieved May 31, 1999. URL: http://www.polsci.ucsb.edu/~bimber/research/

Choi, K. (1998). *How to Publish in Top Journals* [Online]. Ames: IA: Review of International Economics. Retrieved May 4, 1999. URL: http://www.ag.iastate.edu/journals/rie/how.htm

Data and Program Library Service. *Internet Crossroad in the Social Sciences* [Online]. Madison: University of Wisconsin. Retrieved May 24, 1999. URL: http://dpls.dacc.wisc.edu/internet.html

Gizzi, M. *The Political Science Classroom* [Online]. Grand Junction, CO: Mesa State College. Retrieved May 13, 1999. URL: http://mesa7.mesa.colorado.edu/~mgizzi/html/resources_1.html

H-Net, Humanities & Social Sciences OnLine. (1995) *H-Net Discussion Networks* [Online]. East Lansing, MI: H-Net. Retrieved May 10, 1999. URL: http://www.h-net.msu.edu/lists/

Ho, K. *Political Science Cyberclasses* [Online]. Denton: University of North Texas. Retrieved May 13, 1999. URL: http://www.psci.unt.edu/kho/cybercls/

Institute for Research in Social Sciences. *IRSS Data Archive Services* [Online]. Chapel Hill: University of North Carolina. Retrieved May 24, 1999. URL: http://www.irss.unc.edu/irss/dataservices/dataservices.html

Inter-university Consortium for Political and Social Research. *ICPSR Homepage* [Online]. Ann Arbor, MI: ICPSR. Retrieved May 24, 1999. URL: http://www.icpsr.umich.edu/

Klass, G. *Political Science List of Lists* [Online]. Normal: Illinois State University. Retrieved May 9, 1999. URL: http://coyote.ils.ilstu.edu/tango/gmklass/listsrch.qry

_____. (1996) *Survey of Political Science Cyberclasses* [Online]. Normal: Illinois State University. Retrieved May 13, 1999. URL: http://www.ilstu.edu/depts/polisci/apsa96/roundtab.htm

Romans, L. *GODORT Handout Exchange* [Online]. Ann Arbor, MI: Government Documents Roundtable, American Library Association. Retrieved May 13, 1999. URL: http://www.lib.umich.edu/libhome/Documents.center/godort.html

Rubinson, A. (1995) *Civnet* [Online]. New York: Civitas. Retrieved July 19, 1999. URL: http://www.civnet.org/index.htm.

Social Sciences Data Collection. *Social Science Data on the Net* [Online]. San Diego: University of California. Retrieved May 24, 1999. URL: http://odwin.ucsd.edu/idata/

Social Sciences Research and Instructional Council. *SSRIC Teaching Resources De-*

pository [Online]. Bakersfield: California State University. Retrieved May 15, 1999. URL: http://www.csubak.edu/ssric/welcome.htm

University of Texas TeamWeb. *World Lecture Hall* [Online]. Austin: University of Texas. Retrieved May 13, 1999. URL: http://www.utexas.edu/world/lecture/pol/

REFERENCES

Finifter, A. (1998). "Editor's Notes." *American Political Science Review* 92 (3) (September): vii-xii.

Lasco, J. (1998). "Whither Intellectual Diversity in American Political Science? The Case of APSA and Organized Sections." *PS: Political Science and Politics* 31(4) (December): 836-46.

Magstadt, T. and Schotten, M. (1999). *Understanding Politics: Ideas, Institutions, and Issues,* 5th. ed. New York: St Martin's/Worth.

Martin, F. and Goehlert, R. (1997). *Getting Published in Political Science Journals: A Guide for Authors, Editors, and Librarians*, 4th ed. Washington: American Political Science Association.

Sabine, George H. (1993). *A History of Political Theory,* 4th. ed. Fort Worth: Harcourt Brace College Publishers.

Scammon, R., ed. (1956-). *America Votes*, vv. 1-. Washington, DC: Congressional Quarterly.

Strauss, L., and Joseph, C. (1987). *History of Political Philosophy*, 3rd ed. Chicago: University of Chicago Press.

Internet Reference Service:
General Sources and Trends

Joseph R. Zumalt
Rebecca A. Smith

SUMMARY. Providing quality reference services is more challenging than ever. In addition to traditional print sources, the information professional now has a dazzling array of databases, both free and expensive, readily available. Internet reference service has evolved quickly over the last decade, moving from a place of last resort to a mainstream application. Librarians have responded in many innovative ways to connect their customers with information available on the Internet. However, superior Internet reference service requires substantial investments in equipment that administrators will have to consider. Staff and customer training have become pressing needs. Providing access to

Joseph R. Zumalt is Business Reference Librarian and Assistant Professor at West Campus Library, Texas A&M University. He has an MPA from the University of Missouri-Kansas City and an MALS from the University of Missouri-Columbia. He has published in *Reference & User Services Quarterly* and *The Journal of Academic Librarianship* (E-mail: jzumalt@tamu.edu).

Rebecca A. Smith is Coordinator of Reference Services and Assistant Professor at West Campus Library, Texas A&M University. She has a Master of Science in Library Science from the University of North Texas. She has published articles in *Special Libraries* and *Information Outlook* and has contributed to *Managing Business Collections in Libraries* (1996). Ms. Smith has been a speaker at Special Libraries Association conferences and currently sits on the Advisory Board for the Business & Finance Division (E-mail: rebecca-smith@tamu.edu).

The authors would like to extend a special thanks to Bob Pasicznyuk (Pikes Peak Library District), Suzanne Gyeszly (Texas A&M University), and Michael Enyart (University of Wisconsin-Madison) for their assistance on this paper.

[Haworth co-indexing entry note]: "Internet Reference Service: General Sources and Trends." Zumalt, Joseph R, and Rebecca A. Smith. Co-published simultaneously in *Journal of Library Administration* (The Haworth Information Press, an imprint of The Haworth Press, Inc.) Vol. 30, No. 3/4, 2000, pp. 335-350; and: *Academic Research on the Internet: Options for Scholars & Libraries* (ed: Helen Laurence, and William Miller) The Haworth Information Press, an imprint of The Haworth Press, Inc., 2000, pp. 335-350. Single or multiple copies of this article are available for a fee from The Haworth Document Delivery Service [1-800-342-9678, 9:00 a.m. - 5:00 p.m. (EST). E-mail address: getinfo@haworthpressinc.com].

appropriate databases and materials will become increasingly challenging. *[Article copies available for a fee from The Haworth Document Delivery Service: 1-800-342-9678. E-mail address: <getinfo@haworthpressinc.com> Website: <http://www.HaworthPress.com>]*

KEYWORDS. Library reference service, Internet resources for, online resources for, development of

INTRODUCTION

Anyone who picks up a magazine or watches television is bombarded by e-mail or URL addresses. We are in the midst of wonderful innovations, especially via the Web. From downloading music tracks by an obscure band halfway around the world to securing our own airline reservations for that once-in-a-lifetime vacation, we are doing things on the Internet not even imagined five years ago. Internet reference service has evolved quickly over the last decade, moving from a place of last resort to a mainstream application. But how have these services unfolded? How are librarians providing services in accord with their clientele's information and Internet priorities? How do reference professionals easily evaluate which Internet sources, some available for free and others for fee, are appropriate? How do reference professionals actually search the Internet to answer their customers' requests? And finally, what are the current database licensing, copyright, and technological challenges to consider when planning reference services via the Internet?

For the purposes of this paper, "electronic reference," "digital reference," "virtual reference," and "Internet reference" are all used interchangeably since reference librarians are not making great distinctions in the meaning of those terms.

Reva Basch, the author of the *Researching Online for Dummies*, commented that the Web environment has provided librarians great opportunities because users have been on the Internet and discovered it is messy.[1] However, it is important to know how Internet reference services developed and how they evolved. Maggie's Place at the Pikes Peak Library District in Colorado Springs proved to be one of the early models.

MAGGIE'S PLACE:
THE PROTOTYPE OF EARLY INTERNET REFERENCE

The driving force behind current virtual reference products and services is the World Wide Web's distributed computing environment; however, the concept is older. H.G. Wells' World Brain and Vannevar Bush's Memex both describe devices and projects with striking similarities to today's Web reference tools. But it was not until the mid-1970s that libraries became involved in building virtual reference centers. The Pikes Peak Library District's "Maggie's Place" was among the first attempts at creating a virtual reference center.

The project's aim was three-fold. First, it sought to act as a community information warehouse with files covering a number of topics of interest to the Pikes Peak region. Second, it was designed as a published-materials resource center with library catalog and reference sources available. As a third goal, "Maggie's Place" sought to become a community meeting-place and communications center, offering e-mail and discussion forums on a variety of topics.[2]

"Maggie's Place" became the emerging prototype for three types of virtual or electronic reference (e-reference) centers that have since come into being:

- guides to the wider Internet;
- conduits to a number of vendor-supplied resources;
- virtual reference desks via a combination of e-forms, links based on frequently asked questions (FAQs), and search engines.

Guides to the Internet

Electronic reference as a guide to the Internet was popularized by Yahoo! URL: <http://www.yahoo.com>. **Yahoo!** is a directory of bookmarks which provides users hierarchical lists of Internet sites so users can find sources appropriate to subject, age-group, or geographic region. A number of libraries have used the Yahoo! model to organize their bookmarks and create Web pages. Yahoo! has expanded greatly over the years; much success has been attained in answering many reference questions, as indicated by Zumalt and Pasicznyuk's Web version of their published project to study the utility of the Internet. URL: <http://library.tamu.edu/wcl/ref/facstaff/zumalt/netref.htm>.

Interface for Vendor-Supplied Databases

Another type of e-reference is commonplace to most libraries: an Internet-based interface to provide user access to vendor-supplied databases. Many general reference databases, such as InfoTrac, ProQuest, and Wilson, are now offered on the Web, either as networked CD-ROMs or as Web subscriptions. In addition, electronic journals (e-journals) are becoming an important resource for the reference librarian. While these databases are often used for general reference, subject specialists have been integrating these subscription databases with free sites to provide the user with a seamless interface for serious research needs. Depending on the organization of these library Web sites, resources may be listed by subject-matter, by database title, or both. To use this interface, some kind of validation scheme is necessary to allow only the organization's clients access to subscription resources.

Virtual Reference Desk

The third type of e-reference, the formation of a virtual reference desk, is exemplified by the **Internet Public Library** (IPL), an initiative by the University of Michigan's library school. URL: <http://www.ipl.org>. Started in 1995, it has now grown through funding from several private foundation grants. IPL's professional staff of five is assisted by student volunteers from the library school and University of Michigan library, and by other outside librarians when needed.[3] They have compiled detailed pathfinders. IPL does not claim to take the place of a real public library; rather, it provides answers to many questions by developing a virtual "form" which allows for asynchronous answering of reference questions. This means that reference questions can be answered by electronic mail as time allows. IPL was designed for those who already know how to logon to the Internet; users want just-in-time answers, rather than learning how to seek the answers themselves. IPL could prove to be the next model for public libraries as they get more involved in virtual reference.

With Maggie's Place as the prototype for electronic reference, how did Internet reference make its rapid progress in the 1990s? The next section provides the ingredients–the advent of the World Wide Web, the evolution of Internet search tools, and the use of those tools to build Web sites–needed to answer questions.

Internet Reference via World Wide Web: History, Tools, and Web Site Construction

History

Unbeknownst to the general public, the scientific community was already using Internet since the development of ARPANET. Academic librarians were first to jump on the Internet bandwagon, since the backbones originated in research universities. Reference librarians were able to obtain answers to reference questions by e-mail from other librarians either directly or through participation in listservs.[4] In 1991 there were about 110 listservs but by 1996 this number had grown to approximately 1,700.[5] LIBREF-L was one of the first listservs for reference librarians, followed by STUMPERS-L, which sought to answer the more esoteric and vexing questions.

The advent of searching capabilities offered by Thinking Machine's WAIS and University of Minnesota's Gopher (1991) was followed quickly by the birth of the World Wide Web accessible via the Mosaic browser, and its successor, Netscape (1992, 1994).[6] Before Netscape appeared, Lynx, a non-graphical user interface (GUI) browser, searched text-based Web sites. Microsoft's Internet Explorer would soon follow in 1995. All of these browser capabilities captured more than messages from listservs; they linked to the relevant data. The rich content now seen on the Web developed after only a few years of effort by countless individuals.

The Web became an increasingly successful source for the answers to basic reference questions. Chuck Koutnik, in a study of approximately 100 sample reference questions, was able to answer a little over 30 percent using Internet sources in late 1995.[7] The resources on the Web had grown enough so by 1997, Zumalt and Pasicznyuk successfully answered over 60 percent of a larger sample of actual public library reference questions.[8] This success rate was confirmed by Janes and McClure in mid-1998. A larger group of searchers representing various skill levels sought answers to a smaller group of questions, with a success rate comparing favorably to answers achieved using a strong print collection.[9]

TOOLS

The majority of reference questions are now answered using software programs known as search engines, which index various subsets of the Internet; some even claim to search the whole Web. The first search engine, AltaVista, developed by Digital Equipment Corporation, appeared in 1994. It allowed keyword access to thousands of Web pages and listed links to Web sites according to relevancy rankings. WebCrawler, Lycos, and Hotbot quickly followed AltaVista.

How does a librarian choose which search engine to use when there are now dozens? Each of them has strengths and weaknesses that must be carefully evaluated. **Search Engine Showdown** and **Search Engine Watch** are two excellent Web sites that assist librarians to keep up with search engine developments and trends. URL: <http://www.notess.com/search> and URL: <http://searchenginewatch.com>. The consensus among expert searchers is that learning a few major search engines will compensate for their individual weaknesses, akin to diversifying a stock portfolio. Meta-search engines, such as **DogPile** and **Savvy Search**, which perform simultaneous searches across several search engines, are also used by librarians.[10] URL: <http://www.dogpile.com> and URL: <http://www.savvysearch.com>.

A new Internet model has emerged within the last year: the information portal. The portal is similar to a meta-search engine; it provides access to a great deal of free information but also offers access to fee sites. The portal is designed to provide one-stop shopping. America Online (AOL), Yahoo!, **Electric Library** and **Northern Light** are good examples of portals that most consumers use. URL: <http://www.elibrary.com/> and URL: <http://www.northernlight.com>. However, Electric Library and Northern Light differ from AOL and Yahoo! in that one can search the site for free, but to get the articles one must subscribe for a monthly fee. Electric Library, now offered through consortia, contains journals, newspapers, transcripts, and images. Northern Light has similar content, but includes more business databases. Many corporate librarians have used Northern Light because of the vast number of pages indexed and the "pay as you go" structure. However, both Electric Library and Northern Light's portals, while extensive, still do not offer the full gamut in distributing fee-based information; they are very selective, based on the distribution agreements with the information suppliers.

Of the aforementioned portals, Northern Light searches the most Web pages. However, scientists have reported that Northern Light only searches about one-sixth of the entire Web.[11] Web developers are competing not only to search the maximum number of Web pages, but also to develop the "smartest" portal. One recent effort in particular stands out: **Ask Jeeves**. URL: <http://www.askjeeves.com>. It is different because it accepts natural language queries, and it will prompt for further questions or additional keyword input. Ask Jeeves' unique Question Processing Engine (QPE) technology attempts to match queries against a list of millions of known questions in its database knowledge core.[12] Ask Jeeves has the potential to outperform other engines because it closely mimics what a reference librarian would do: reframe the question by asking another question. If such systems can actually capture this type of knowledge or at least frame better queries, information professionals may be have more time to work on the tougher questions.

Serious reference work requires the acquisition of fee-based databases, not just access to "free" Internet resources. Contrary to popular belief, it is not, nor will it ever be, "all free on the Net." Fee-based databases may be the electronic equivalent of a time-tested paper source, such as the *Encyclopedia Britannica*. Other fee-based services may include indexes, such as *Library Literature*, whereby libraries pay for citation and indexing only, or they may offer full-text. Venerable search services, such as DIALOG, BRS, and Lexis/Nexis, have provided for the information needs of the customer for years but have been rather arcane to search, requiring a great deal of experience to gain proficiency.

What type of questions does the Internet truly excel at answering? The Web is ideal for locating recent events, such as local and state election results. Information about small businesses is now easier because many companies have home pages. Recent book reviews, which used to be found only in indexes, can be located on the *New York Times* Web pages. If the user wants reviews by other readers, one can click on *Amazon.com, Barnesandnoble.com* and many other large commercial online booksellers. Governmental information is often sought by the general public. The **Library of Congress** promotes many useful services of interest to libraries, such as its home page, which provides links to Web pages of all three branches of the government. URL: <http://www.loc.gov>. Users also frequently seek biographical or genealogical information. Search engines such as **Hotbot** are very successful for this type of question. URL: <http://www.hotbot.com>.

WEB SITE CONSTRUCTION FOR INTERNET REFERENCE

While search engines are helpful in finding often obscure or specific items, they may not be the best at finding general items that a traditional ready reference collection might contain. Librarians again have stepped in and sifted through millions of Web sites and provided their patrons with easy access to the most appropriate ones in the form of handy lists of good Web sites to answer their questions. They can be as simple as a one page listing of frequently used sites; another way is to have a Web page grouped by subject headings and richly annotated, as exemplified by the Kansas City, KS Public Library. URL: <http://www.kckpl.lib.ks.us/refdept/readyref.htm>.

Evaluation of Web content is an important consideration during the construction and maintenance of any library Web site. Reliability of information is paramount in providing good reference service whether it is in print or electronic format. Since most Web sites do not go through the rigorous fact checking found in the traditional publishing process, librarians have a greater responsibility in evaluating these information sources for their customers. There are many fine Web pages and bibliographies addressing this issue, including those of **Widener University's Science Division**. URL: <http://www.science. widener.edu/~withers/wbstrbib.htm>. Alexander and Tate at Widener have also written a helpful primer, regarding Web page creation and evaluation, entitled *Web Wisdom*.[13]

Pathfinders for Internet Reference pose great concerns for some administrators. The quality and authority of Web sites can be more difficult to ascertain than that of books. Recommendations for Web sites can thus pose liabilities for state entities. Moreover, librarians do not always agree on the policy of including commercial sites on library Web pages. Some sites give a few pieces of data to entice the user to the site, then ask for a credit card. Some reference librarians, aware that users expect to receive free information, will select Web sites that have a lot of free data to save research time for the user. The **University of Pennsylvania** is one library that has a Web inclusion policy on its Web site. URL: <http://www.library.upenn.edu/resources/subject/colldev_policy.html>.

The World Wide Web has enabled reference librarians to be creative and dynamic in answering more questions than their traditional collections had previously allowed. However, there are many challenges for

Internet reference: licensing for remote access, copyright, making consortial agreements for better subscription prices, keeping pace with emerging technologies, and examining the costs involved.

INTERNET REFERENCE CHALLENGES: LICENSING AND COPYRIGHT, CONSORTIA, EMERGING TECHNOLOGIES, AND COSTS

Licensing and Copyright

Electronic licensing is a critical issue that must be addressed by information professionals. With thousands or millions of dollars in the balance, great attention to detail is essential to avoid costly mistakes for an organization. Some library directors have added product managers within their organizations to develop relationships with online vendors, keeping track of these costs, negotiating contracts and implementing their installation.[14] In addition, many larger institutions employ a full-time person charged with coordinating database acquisition and licensing. Because of the liability issues involved, in-house legal counsel for public and most university libraries negotiate the final contracts. Reference librarians who deal with vendors are seeing a trend towards the development of friendlier front-ends to make searching easier for the end user. Whether or not these are truly better or are merely more window dressing to maximize return on publishers' design costs is another matter, but library administrators and reference staff alike need to address the tradeoffs of manipulation versus the quantity and quality of content. Moreover, because of the mega-mergers that have occurred over the decade, the combination of original content with newly-acquired products often creates both redundancy and glaring gaps. Help screens do not indicate how databases should be searched in different scenarios to achieve the results desired, and publishers' full-text source lists often are not accurate. Vendors need to be more accountable to deliver what they promise.

There are other concerns in libraries about paying for the convenience of end-user retrieval of full-text scholarly journals, especially those already owned by the institution. Many "leased" products do not allow for a permanent archive, so cancellation of print subscriptions to offset the price of electronic access is impossible. Many libraries have opted first for pilot programs with well-known publishers such as Elsevier before deciding to pay for the service. Pilot programs can pose problems because the user expects an ongoing service and is dumbfounded when the materials are no longer available. Related to licensing is copyright. With the extension of copyright recently passed by the 1998 Digital Millennium Copyright Act and the Sonny Bono Term Extension Act, librarians and administrators are having to rethink the meaning of "fair use" because the fallout from these complicated pieces of federal legislation is quickly evolving. It is difficult to keep abreast of the latest developments. However, the **United States Copyright Office** provides an excellent Web site that contains the latest copyright news. URL: <http://lcweb.loc.gov/copyright/>.

Consortia Building

In an effort to maximize resources, alliances between libraries are being constructed which allow better access to a wider range of databases and library materials than individual libraries could offer. These "consortia" can help libraries endure the upward spiral of acquisition costs by providing volume discounts on items such as electronic databases. Successful resource sharing can result from these agreements. How these agreements are funded varies widely, from subscription fees assessed to member libraries, to central state funding. As of late 1998, at least 14 states were providing central funding for e-resources.[15] Many successful consortial relationships have evolved. These relationships can be at the state, regional, or national level. TexShare in Texas, PALCI in Pennsylvania, and OhioLink for Ohio are just a few examples of state systems that have both public library and academic library members. In addition, there are many academic consortia, such as the Committee on Institutional Cooperation (CIC), representing 12 major research institutions in the Midwest. However, there are drawbacks: consortial agreements can be inflexible, with institutions forced to pay for electronic access to unneeded resources based on their populations. The contracts are not easy to withdraw from; sometimes the library is better off negotiating on its own.

Emerging Technologies

One innovation (borrowed from AOL) used by information professionals to enhance service is the use of online chat to answer reference questions. The University of North Texas and the Kresge Library at the University of Michigan Business School have been experimenting with this technology. However, one has to remember these chats take more time than if someone just walked in for service and asked for a book or how to use the Internet.

Two additional developments that have the potential to enhance reference service are videoconferencing and voice recognition technology, which are in their infancy now but will fully flower in the next few years. While videoconferencing classrooms have been available for some time, reasonably inexpensive, off-the-shelf videoconferencing software for consumers on the desktop has just now become available. Voice recognition software, the other emerging technology, will enable library professionals to avoid or mitigate the debilitating effects of repetitive motion injuries such as carpal tunnel syndrome. Already voice software, used in schools for the blind, can tell the user where the cursor is and point out the Web links.[16] This technology will evolve in the next few years to become a knowledge recognition system, not just identifying links on the page. However, at this writing, there is a considerable training curve, not only in terms of learning proper use of the software, but also for the software to recognize individual speech patterns. One day soon, library users may very well be able to query verbally and receive suggested information sources, as on the television series *Star Trek*.

Costs Associated with Internet Reference

There are obvious equipment and networking infrastructure costs associated with Internet reference. Beyond these immediate costs, however, administrators are grappling with the more subtle costs of providing Internet reference service. Unfortunately, very little has been written on this topic, despite the growing demand for benchmark data concerning library buildings, computer systems, and network infrastructures. While the authors were able to locate a few publications in this area, none of the results, figures, or charts will be reproduced here; instead, significant readings and Web sites are presented.

Companies can easily find estimated Web development costs on the Web. However, librarians have written very little about average costs, such as Web surfing time, writing annotations, programming in HTML, and most importantly, putting a monetary value on the time it takes to evaluate sources critically when developing in-house Web pages for their sites. Part of the reason may be because reference staff salaries are fixed and the cost would be incurred anyway.

McClure's **Internet Costs and Cost Model for Public Libraries: Final Report** lists 14 different cost models for providing Internet access based on the kind of telecommunication vehicle being employed, the kind of interface a given library seeks to provide (graphical vs. text), the type of computer hardware a library devotes to Internet access, and the number of service points that the library provides its patrons or staff users. URL: <http://istweb.syr.edu/~mcclure/nclis/Figures.html>. Whether a library provides access through one workstation with a modem link to a subscription ISP or through a dedicated telecommunications system with multiple workstations in a variety of locations, the cost of supporting Internet access outpaces the substantial price of installation.

Staff training has been cited as a necessary, but intangible cost component in the provision of Internet reference; however, it is not known what the total price tag is for training in our industry. The constant march of technology and increased competition require us continually to upgrade our skills or risk being replaced by a more technologically savvy person who may not be a librarian. Corporate libraries have been eliminated because they were considered cost centers and were replaced by an outside firm that sold its services to do database searching and Web development and management more cheaply. Periodic staff training has become the norm. With so much of library work now dependent on interaction with technology, inefficiencies and mistakes here are much more costly than the expense of timely training. The traditional library conference itself is no longer enough to keep up with the growing need for technological competence. Librarians are beginning to attend more technology-oriented conferences. Examples include: COMDEX, which showcases many new and upcoming electronic products, particularly in information technology in the marketplace; School for Scanning, hosted by the **Northeast Document Conservation Center**, where library technology experts train participants in the applications and management of digital technologies; and Internet World, an annual gathering that connects Internet vendors with their corporate customers, some of whom are librarians. URL: <http://www.nedcc.org>. Employees are expected to bring back knowledge from these conferences and share it with others in order to maximize the funds available for training and continuing education.

CONCLUSION

The current state-of-the-art in Internet reference service provides many examples of librarians in different settings serving their customers in many innovative ways. While basic, "free" Internet services are often adequate to answer a significant number of questions in a public library environment, a specialized library additionally requires access to expensive databases. As vendors proliferate and seek out new markets, more complex pricing structures will confound librarians' efforts to understand and determine fair value. Consortia have proven to be valuable tools in the pricing battles with vendors.

Connecting users to these resources presents an ongoing challenge to information professionals because of the overwhelming amount of information available to the researcher today. But reference librarians have not shied away from this great highway; they have created value-added Web sites of use to their customers, and often they have made them available to the entire Web community.

Because of the quick obsolescence of much of the equipment needed for searching of these databases, frequent updating of technology is essential and must be factored into library budgets. If Internet reference is to endure, libraries will have to keep pace with this technological new world by regularly updating machines and continually seeking quality information that is free or reasonable in cost.

NOTES

1. Reva Basch, "The New Web Order: The Changing Shape of the Information Environment." SLA 1999 Annual Conference. Minneapolis: June 8, 1999.

2. Bernard A. Margolis, "A Paradox for the Public Library," in Laverna M. Saunders, *The Evolving Virtual Library: Visions and Case Studies.* (Medford, NJ: Information Today, 1996), 31.

3. Joseph Janes, David Carter, Annette Lagace, Michael McLennen, Sara Ryan, and Schelle Simcox, *The Internet Public Library Handbook.* (New York: Neal-Schuman, 1999).

4. Sharyn J. Ladner and Hope N. Tillman, "Using the Internet for Reference," *Online* 17 (January 1993): 45-51.

5. Dru Mogge. *Directory of Electronic Journals, Newsletters and Academic Discussion Lists*. 7th ed. (Washington, DC: Association of Research Libraries, 1997).

6. Peter Clemente. *The State of the Net: the New Frontier*. (New York: McGraw-Hill, 1998): 13-18.

7. Chuck Koutnik, "The World Wide Web is Here: Is the End of Printed Reference Sources Near?" *RQ* 36 (3) (Spring 1997): 422-429.

8. Joseph R. Zumalt and Robert W. Pasicznyuk, "The Internet and Reference Services: A Real-World Test of Internet Utility," *Reference & User Services Quarterly* 38 (2) (1998): 165-172.

9. Joseph Janes and Charles R. McClure, "The Web as a Reference Tool: Comparisons with Traditional Sources," *Public Libraries* (January/February 1999): 30-39.

10. Nancy Garman, "Meta Search Engines," *Online* 23 (May/June 1999): 75.

11. Steve Lawrence and C. Lee Giles. "Accessibility of information on the web," *Nature* 400 (July 8, 1999): 107-109.

12. Reva Basch, "High AJeevers: Valet-Added Searching from Ask Jeeves," *Database* 22 (June 1999): 28-34.

13. Janet E. Alexander and Marsha Tate. *Web Wisdom: How to Evaluate and Create Information Quality on the Web*. (Mahwah, NJ: Lawrence Erlbaum Associates, 1999.)

14. Rebecca A. Smith. Product Management: A New Skill for Librarians (Unpublished Manuscript, 1999).

15. Academic Library Consortia: National Trends, Local Opportunities. Retrieved July 11, 1999. [Online] <URL: http://www.Lehigh.EDU/~inpalci/presentations/falltmg_1/sld019.htm>.

16. Pamela Mendels. "Camp Teaches Blind Students Computer Skills" Retrieved July 7, 1999 from *New York Times*. [Online] URL: <http://www.nytimes.com/library/tech/99/07/cyber/education/07education.html>.

WEBLIOGRAPHY

Nearly One-Stop Shopping

Internet Public Library. [Online]. Retrieved June 28, 1999.
   URL: http://ipl.org/
   An important starting place for online research. The growing number of pathfinders found here are first rate.
Librarians' Index to the Internet. [Online]. Retrieved June 28, 1999.
   URL: http://sunsite.berkeley.edu
   This site offers librarians subject access to assist them in their everyday work life.
Gary Price's List of Lists. [Online]. Retrieved June 28, 1999.
   URL: http://gwis2.circ.gwu.edu/~gprice/listof.htm
   This massive list contains a vast number of sites and statistics which are of great help to librarians attempting to answer those thorny requests.

Mailing Lists (Listservs)

Deja.com. [Online]. Retrieved June 30, 1999.
URL: http://www.deja.com
This site archives the often arcane world of listservs, a special world providing a focused glimpse into thousands of subjects.

Diane Kovacs. **The Directory of Scholarly and Professional E-Conferences**. [Online]. Retrieved June 28, 1999.
URL: http://www.n2h2.com/KOVACS/
This provides electronic access to the well-respected database also offered in paper.

Machine-Assisted Reference Section (MARS). A section of ALA's Reference & User Services Division. **MARS-L**. Retrieved August 6, 1999.
URL: http://ala8.ala.org/rusa/mars/
This section offers MARS-L, a scholarly listserv devoted to addressing the issues of providing quality Internet reference services.

The Scout Report. [Online]. Retrieved June 28, 1999.
URL: http://scout.cs.wisc.edu/report/sr/current/index.html
This updating service provides reference librarians with the most up-to-date topical sites they need to stay current and to construct Web pages to assist their customers.

Search Engines

Greg Notess. **Search Engine Showdown**. [Online]. Retrieved July 9, 1999.
URL: http://www.notess.com/

Search Engine Watch. [Online]. Retrieved June 28, 1999.
URL: http://searchenginewatch.com/
This premiere site provides very comprehensive, up-to-date coverage of this rapidly changing Internet segment.

Ask Jeeves. [Online]. Retrieved June 28, 1999.
URL: http://www.askjeeves.com/
A popular meta search engine. A natural language question typed into the query box returns many possible scenarios from its gigantic FAQs, which often provide further insight into what will be needed to answer the question.

Northern Light. [Online]. Retrieved June 28, 1999.
URL: http://www.northernlight.com/
At this writing, *Northern Light* covers more of the Internet than any other search engine. Integrating free and fee elements, results are given in both a relevance-ranked list and in Custom Search Folders.

Copyright

United States Copyright Office. [Online]. Retrieved July 11, 1999.
URL: http://lcweb.loc.gov/copyright/

Library Consortial Issues

Texture: A Texas Library Resource Sharing Program. [Online]. Retrieved August
  13, 1999. URL: http://www.texshare.edu
Pennsylvania Academic Library Consortium, Inc. [Online]. Retrieved July 11,
  1999.
  URL: http://www.lehigh.edu/~inpalci/
  These sites spell out in great detail initiatives started in two states, which provide
  many consortial services offering increased access to dozens of libraries in each
  state.

Demographics

Computer Industry Almanac. [Online]. Retrieved June 28, 1999.
  URL: http://www.c-i-a.com/index.htm
United States Internet Council. **State of the Internet: USIC's Report on Use &
  Threats in 1999**. [Online]. Retrieved June 28, 1999.
  URL: http://www.usic.org/usic_state_of_net99.htm

Costs

Charles McClure. **Internet Costs and Cost Models for Public Libraries: Final
  Report** *(1995)*. [Online]. Retrieved June 28, 1999.
  URL: http://istweb.syr.edu/~mcclure/nclis/FinalReport.html
  While it is a little dated now, it does offer many insights into assessing the true
  cost of offering Internet access to the public.

The Philosopher's Web

Jon Dorbolo

SUMMARY. The objective of this article is to examine some of the valuable philosophical resources available on the Internet, especially for librarians who need to determine what resources to provide to faculty, students, and staff. Some main uses of the Internet for philosophical research are: accessing texts, using search strategies to examine the texts, reading and writing electronic journal articles, accessing information from encyclopedias and dictionaries, browsing through paths of interlinked Web sites, searching the Internet for sources, and participating in online discussion forums. This article examines the Internet as a source of primary and secondary texts, journal literature, research databases, reference works, specialized limited area search engines, organizational information, and discussion lists. The article ends with a philosophical reflection on the transformative effect of information technology on the growth of knowledge. *[Article copies available for a fee from The Haworth Document Delivery Service: 1-800-342-9678. E-mail address: <getinfo@ haworthpressinc.com> Website: <http://www.HaworthPress.com>]*

Jon Dorbolo began his first Web course, *InterQuest: The Fine Art of Philosophy,* in 1993. URL: <http://osu.orst.edu/instruct/ph1201>. Since then he has given over 150 talks on distance education around the U.S. and has acted as Principal Investigator on several Web education grants. Currently he is the Distributed Learning Developer at Oregon State University, designing distance education courses. Jon was honored with the 1998 Oregon State University Extended Education Faculty Achievement Award, served as a judge for the 1998 Paul Allen Virtual Education Foundation Outstanding Online Education Award, was named 1996 MultiMedia Educator of the year by the Oregon Multi-Media Alliance, and is Editor of the American Philosophical Association *Philosophy and Computers Newsletter.*

Author note: My appreciation for comments and ideas for this paper go to Bill Uzgalis, Karyle Butcher, Flo Leibowitz, Robert Cavalier, Ron Barnette, Peter List, Mariol Wogman, Michael Scanlan, Cheryl Hills, and Quincy.

[Haworth co-indexing entry note]: "The Philosopher's Web." Dorbolo, Jon. Co-published simultaneously in *Journal of Library Administration* (The Haworth Information Press, an imprint of The Haworth Press, Inc.) Vol. 30, No. 3/4, 2000, pp. 351-378; and: *Academic Research on the Internet: Options for Scholars & Libraries* (ed: Helen Laurence, and William Miller) The Haworth Information Press, an imprint of The Haworth Press, Inc., 2000, pp. 351-378. Single or multiple copies of this article are available for a fee from The Haworth Document Delivery Service [1-800-342-9678, 9:00 a.m. - 5:00 p.m. (EST). E-mail address: getinfo@haworthpressinc.com].

KEYWORDS. Philosophy, Internet research in, Internet resources in, online research in, online resources in

RESEARCH IN PHILOSOPHY

The philosophical researcher is a writer. Occasionally philosophers (e.g., Socrates and Jesus) commit themselves to acting upon the fellow person and society without resorting to publication; the rest of us write and submit. For academic purposes, research usually aims at publishable work. The products of philosophical research include:

- Original philosophy (books, monographs, and papers)
- Dissertations
- Commentaries and critiques of other written works (secondary literature)
- Book reviews
- Biography
- Bibliography
- Textbook writing
- Exegetic and hermeneutic research
- Translation
- Historical research
- Discussion at meetings and colloquia

Recently a new genus of philosophical research has developed: computational research. Through computer modeling, simulation, multi-media authoring, and experimentation, philosophers have begun exploring new approaches to epistemology, metaphysics, and ethics. James Moor, Chair of the American Philosophical Association Committee on Philosophy and Computing, observes:

> For some philosophers computing has become an essential method of doing philosophical work. For example, only by running numerous iterations of prisoner dilemma games or models of artificial life can philosophers discover the outcome of many generations of interactions of various hypothetical entities. . . . Philosophy has taken a computational turn.[1]

An excellent anthology of the types of philosophical research being performed with computation is *The Digital Phoenix: How Computers Are Changing Philosophy.*[2]

Traditional forms of research are increasingly using computers, especially the mega-computer known as the Internet. In 1996 the American Philosophical Association conducted a survey of computer-assisted research.[3] Out of about 2,000 philosophy departments surveyed, 270 responses were received, representing 2,025 faculty. The survey results showed that 58% of the faculty were using computers for some form of research. Thirteen percent were reported to be working in computational study, such as computer modeling, artificial life, software development, etc. At the time of the survey the graphical World Wide Web was just two years old. Since then the resource and the user population have exploded, quadrupling from 55 million on-line users in 1996 to 205 million users in 1999.[4] It is likely that more academics are using the Internet more often in their research.

To be an element of research, the activity must affect the content of the work. Some main uses of the Internet for philosophical research are:

- Accessing texts
- Using search strategies to examine the texts
- Reading and writing electronic journal articles
- Accessing information from encyclopedias and dictionaries
- Browsing through paths of interlinked Web sites
- Searching the Internet for sources
- Participating in online discussion forums

Judging from the resources available online, these are some of the common uses of the Internet for research. The objective of this article is to examine some of the valuable philosophical resources available on the Internet, especially for librarians who need to determine what resources to provide to faculty, students, and staff.

PRIMARY TEXTS

The touchstones of most philosophical research are the primary texts of classic philosophers, such as Plato, Aristotle, Descartes, Kant, and de Beauvoir. Philip Ivanhoe identifies three criteria that render a text *classic*: (1) it is about something important, (2) it presents important issues in beautiful, moving and memorable ways, and (3) the text has complexity (intellectual and structural).[5] Many of these same texts are important to other disciplines (e.g., political science, psychology, religious studies, history, rhetoric, and economics, to name a few). Recent decades have occasioned revisionary criticisms of the traditional canon, even rejections of the notion of *primary texts* at all. Yet, even when opposing the traditional canon, authors must make reference to the texts that they are rejecting. Our intellectual and cultural histories are so imbued with the classics that the traditions cannot be ignored. Thus, access to well-known philosophical texts is fundamental to the discipline.

For academic uses of classic works, high quality electronic texts with strong search and sort utilities are becoming critical. For me, evidence of this came at a session on Locke's theory of slavery at the 1998 American Philosophical Association Pacific Division meeting. Vigorous discussion followed a young author's paper. A critic challenged the author's phrasing, asking "Did Locke actually ever say it in just those words? I don't recall it." The answer came in a few moments when another participant flipped open his laptop and ran a search for the phrase. Several occurrences were found and the matter was settled. That these scholars turned to an electronic text and accepted the results of a search demonstrates the potential that electronic texts and search techniques have as authoritative sources.

Past Masters®, produced by **Intelex Corporation**, is the largest collection of electronic texts in philosophy. URL: <http://www.nlx. com/homepage.htm>. **Intelex** states as an objective "to obtain the complete corpora in original language and translation of all the great philosophers."[6] Intelex has focused on developing its offerings strategically rather than for volume so that researchers are apt to use the resources as an interconnected whole, e.g., searching across multiple titles or searching selected texts comparatively. At present the Past Masters® texts are available on CD-ROM and may be installed as a Local Area Network (LAN) resource. Alternately, Past Masters® may be accessed from a server hosted by **Intelex** and delivered to participants via the Web. A new Web interface is available at present and may be demonstrated by arrangement with **Intelex** (lamb@nlx.com).

In scholarly research, philosophers need to rely on authoritative editions of texts. Many versions of a classic text may exist, especially those in translation. Texts available on the Internet as public domain often do not have the quality control required to serve as source material for research. Many philosophical historians regard *Past Mas-*

ters® texts as equivalent to the most reliable and important print editions of up-to-date translations. **Intelex** uses a proprietary editing process, including multi-passes with independent editing for each pass, that claims to surpass some print editions in accuracy, i.e., a tolerance of five character errors per million characters. This makes *Past Masters*® an appropriate tool for serious research.

The texts are generated out of a database via the Folio Views® search engine.[7] From the table of contents for a text, one selects a portion to view in the document window. The text is displayed in 20 paragraph (or equivalent) units. Each paragraph on screen has a reference line with a concordance to the source print text. Searches can be made in single texts or across multiple texts, as well as across logical text groups (e.g., footnotes, annotations). Search results may be displayed in a variety of ways that allow for finer control over the breadth and relevance of the search. Future versions of *Past Masters*® will employ advanced query syntax searching.

The Folio Views® "shadow file" is an interesting feature for the researcher. Individuals may save customized files from the document view to disk. This allows bookmarks, highlighted text, and notes to be saved without altering the database. Shadow files can be reapplied to the document view and can be shared with other users.

Past Masters® titles may be purchased on CD-ROM (in any combination of titles), installed on a Local Area Network (LAN), or accessed from the Web. Three licensing options are available: individual license for personal use, institutional license for two simultaneous users on a LAN, campus-wide license for unlimited network use on campus among faculty, staff, and students (see Figure 1). Campus-wide, the texts can be provided either from the Intelex Web server or

FIGURE 1

Philosophy Faculty	Yearly Access Fee
0-3	$300
4-9	$750
10+	$1500

mounted locally using SGML files. Not all of the databases are currently available in SGML. The yearly access fee is based on the number of philosophy faculty listed at the institution in The Directory of American Philosophers[8] or The Directory of International Philosophers.[9] (See Figure 1.) This formula sets the base rate, but not a limit on how many faculty may access the databases.

As of this review twenty-nine *Past Masters*® collections are available:

1. Anselm: Works
2. Aquinas: Works
3. Aristotle: Works
4. British Philosophy: 1600-1900
5. Berkeley: Works
6. Calvin: Works
7. Dewey: Works
8. Dewey: Correspondence
9. Economic Philosophy: From Smith to Mill
10. Hobbes: English Works
11. Hume: Works and Correspondences
12. Kant: Hauptwerke
13. Kierkegaard: Works
14. Locke-Berkeley-Hume: Philosophical Works
15. Locke: Works & Selected Correspondence
16. Luther: Sermons
17. Nietzsches Werke (in German)
18. Ockham: Work of Ninety days
19. Peirce: Collected papers
20. Peirce: Published Works
21. Plato: Collected Dialogues
22. Poinsot: Tractatus de Signis
23. Political Philosophy: Machiavelli to Mill
24. Rationalists: Descartes-Leibniz-Spinoza
25. Santayana: Works
26. Sidgwick: Works
27. The Utilitarians
28. Wittgenstein: Published Works
29. Wittgenstein: Nachlass

For a general academic population, the period collections *British Philosophy: 1600-1900, Rationalists: Descartes-Leibniz-Spinoza, The Utilitarians, Political Philosophy: Machiavelli to Mill*, and *Economic Philosophy: Smith to Mill* are sound choices. Absent are similar assorted collections of ancient, medieval, nineteenth century, and twentieth century works. Intelex offers to custom build databases. Presumably, some of these could be partly assembled on request from the available texts.

Conspicuously absent is work by women and non-Europeans. The canon of philosophy has long been determined to exclude female and non-European sources. Why this has been and what it implies for the discipline is itself a matter of academic debate. Yet, with the transition to electronic texts, the opportunity arises to improve the canon by making it representative of the genuine range of philosophical works and concerns. To miss that opportunity at this juncture will require a different explanation than any applied to past exclusions. We know too much about the past to allow its errors to circumscribe the present. Libraries and departments have the power to influence this selectivity by voicing the desire to build electronic collections inclusively. Intelex President Brad Lamb made clear the accordance of the *Past Masters*® with this inclusive aim:

> We are working to create a critical mass of the complete works and correspondence in original language and English translation of the great minds, men and women.[10]

Electronic texts are not presently suitable as substitutes for print volumes, as far as reading and printing are concerned. This may change as display technology improves. Still, *Past Masters*® texts are not designed as primary reads. They are research tools. In that role, they are becoming common accessories for researchers and graduate students, and are likely to become crucial sources.

A current limitation of note is that **Intelex** does not offer individual texts, nor does it provide for course packages. This may change with the current higher education emphasis on distance education. Having a quality source of primary texts is one of the sticking points for many distance educators. Granted, the readability problem will have to be solved before these texts can serve as the course textbook. It is also important to build quality support materials around the source texts for learners. Competent distance education on the Web is far more than text delivery. Means of interacting with, manipulating, and augmenting texts need to be developed and tested. In order to get there, we need good electronic texts to work with.

Intelex President Brad Lamb took me on a tour of the Web site that **Intelex** is building for the next generation of *Past Masters*®. Along with the texts and enhanced search tools, the user will have access to dictionaries, encyclopedias, maps, and translation software. The design will allow interface with electronic journals (see *Poiesis* below), making a seamless environment for scholarship. Lamb indicates a desire to create "a space that you do not have to leave in order to do all that you need to do with the primary and secondary texts."[11] This is an estimable goal. The results thus far are encouraging.

SECONDARY TEXTS

The exchange of academic knowledge depends on scholarly publication. Academia must move its discourse online because print publications are no longer effective for wide scale scholarly communication. The problem with print is economic. Since the 1970s libraries have spent more of their money to acquire fewer materials. Library acquisition budgets have generally decreased as a percentage of university budgets, while new book and periodical offerings have steadily increased. More devastating than budget allocation is the reduced buying power of the library budget. Book and periodical costs have climbed relentlessly. Science and technical journal subscription rates increased at 11.3 percent per year from 1970 to 1990.[12] Humanities periodical costs have risen as well, albeit at a much slower pace. Just to subscribe to *Ethics, Mind,* and *The Journal of Philosophy* cost an institution $264 in 1999. That is not terribly pricey for three top-quality journals, yet, **Episteme Links** lists 348 additional philosophy-related journals and newsletters. URL: <http://www.epistemelinks.com/Main/MainJour.asp>. It is difficult for libraries to keep pace with the volume and cost of print literature, given the need to support many areas of scholarly inquiry.

The negative impact of print economics on libraries and scholars can perhaps be solved by electronic publication. Putting journals online should reduce cost and increase access. Online journal publication (eJournals) could be a means of solving the serials crisis and offer additional benefits to the academic community. The savings that electronic publication affords, however, are generally not being realized by libraries. Mike Sosteric of **The International Consortium for Alternative Academic Publication (ICAAP)** regards this as the result of intentional profiteering. URL: <http://www.icaap.org/>.

Some commercial publishers, rather than seeing electronic publishing as an opportunity to reduce costs and bring needed relief to the academic libraries that they serve, have chosen to exploit the opportunities for increasing profit presented by the new technologies.[13]

The International Coalition of Library Consortia (ICOLC) sees publishers as passing along the costs of the research and development leading to the production of electronic publications:

> academic libraries cannot afford to commit long-term to the now-prevalent electronic journal pricing model that is premised upon a base price of "current print price plus electronic surcharge plus significant projected inflation surcharges." furthermore [sic], today's electronic information products are neither fully formed nor stable, yet libraries are being asked to support in full the cost of the research and development to bring such products to market.[14]

Whatever the cause of the current cost of inflation, it seems clear that electronic publication has potential to increase access at lower cost. Consider the delivery of all course reserve materials as pdf files by the Wallace Library at **Rochester Institute of Technology**. URL: <http://wally.rit.edu/map/1/reserve.html>. Electronically, the materials are available 24 hours and can be shared simultaneously by many students. This is an instance of the model many in academia had hoped the Internet would bring to scholarly communication. That this hope has not been answered is more a matter of economics and law than one of technology. While it is clear that technology alone will not solve problems like the serials crisis, the capacities a technology brings to bear will have strong impact on how scholars approach communication. It seems to me that economic forces will eventually have to follow the lead of the consumers (academics), be that for better or worse.

Electronic publishing will affect the pace of academic communication. Layout, printing, and shipping are centralized processes and add significant time to the publication process. It is not uncommon for more than a year to pass between an author's submission of an article and the shelving of the journal. Replies to articles can be years apart, requiring an anthology to pull the parts together into an overall presentation. There is no *prima facie* reason why increasing the pace of scholarship is desirable, and some common experience counts against it (i.e., most of us already have too much to do in too little time). Yet, bringing more immediacy into the publishing process encourages scholars to address topical issues. Electronic publishing can reduce the turn-around time significantly, especially when submissions are received in the required formats.

Electronic journals will provide strong management capabilities to individuals. The ability to search across an entire corpus of full texts, not just bibliographies and abstracts, transforms research. Electronic journals may eventually allow Internet robots to seek articles related to relevant topics and constantly update a table of contents in those areas. *Netscape* and *Yahoo* offer personalized pages in which the individual manages the sources and topics of the daily news. Applied to academic journals, this selectivity would make scholars more informed and effective.

Journals in the online media affect scholarship by transforming every article into a potential discussion. Socrates observed that texts create intellectual distance between reader and writer. He tells Phaedrus that written words "seem to talk to you as though they were intelligent, but if you ask them anything about what they say, from a desire to be instructed, they go on telling you just the same thing forever."[15] Online discussion media (email, threaded discussion) transform passive, static texts into living discourse. Every online journal and article should have comment areas in which critics, defenders, and authors may carry on the matter of the text. These contemporary *objections and replies* will have to be stylized and may become part of a new genre of academic prose. The journal editor's role should grow to include moderating the discussion on the article or review.

Making eJournals a standard for scholarship is crucial to the quality of research libraries and the health of academic conversation. Given the low cost and wide distribution, one wonders why journals have not already moved online. Two factors dominate in the reluctance to take this needed step: readability and authority.

Online text has to be fully usable to serve readers. The main deficit in the usability of online text is readability. Most people who use computers complain at some point about the difficulty of reading text from the screen (eText). Part of this may be the physical attributes of present-day computers. The ergonomics of the upright monitor are wrong; few of us are used to reading from a vertical surface. When we have high-resolution, easily held displays that can be propped on the kitchen table or read in bed, we are apt to see acceptance of the monitor as a reading source.

Functional reading display is available now as eBooks. These products are dedicated reading displays to which texts are downloaded. Four eBooks are **Everybook**® (URL: http://www.everybk.com/),

Softbook® (URL: http://www.softbook.com/), RocketBook® (URL: http://www.rocket-ebook.com/), and **Glassbook**® (URL: http://www. glassbook.com/). Unsurprisingly, these differ in approach and format. The **Open eBook Initiative** is seeking standards and compatibility among display manufacturers and publishers. URL: <http://www. openebook.org/>. These devices hold much promise for advancing the viability of academic electronic texts.

Progress in the readability of eText is appearing due to sub-pixel font rendering. This method uses the component areas of individual pixels to smooth out the edges of the lettering. Each pixel on the screen is composed of three sub-pixels: red, green, and blue. The visual system mixes these three colors in combination to form all the visible color combinations, including black and white. Each sub-pixel can be controlled to have a cumulative effect on the visible object. This method allows the production of lines and curves that have 300% more resolution than current whole-pixel rendering. This enhanced format produces a much more solid, high contrast, and readable text, although eText is still not comparable to print text. In viewing demonstrations of this technique, I find the text to be better than existing CRT output, but it appears fuzzy rather than sharp. To make the wholesale shift to eText we will need text rendering that is a virtual facsimile of the paper original. For demonstrations and explanations of this technology see Steve Gibson's pages at <http://grc.com/freeandclear. htm> and **Microsoft ClearType**™ press releases at <http://www. microsoft.com/typography/cleartype/default.htm>.

Xerox PARC is developing an imaging technology that signals the coming shift to eText. URL: <http://www.parc.xerox.com/parc-go. html>. *Electronic paper*, invented by Nick Seridon at **Xeroc PARC**, has many of the properties of paper but with an electronically produced image. The electronic paper image is generated from a matrix of solid balls with light/dark regions on them floating in an oil-filled cavity between plastic sheets. The balls are polarized and can be selectively oriented by applying an electrical current pattern. The image (words, pictures, videos, etc.) is viewed in reflected light (not backlight) and is reusable; on the order of thousands of reuses. Electronic paper is flexible, light-weight, has a large viewing angle, is writable, and (according to Xerox) is relatively inexpensive. Two sheets of electronic paper on a clipboard, with auxiliary data storage and power supply units, may be the sole retrieval medium for all of a researcher's books, papers, newspapers, Web pages, newspapers, magazines, and videos. Actually, one sheet may be sufficient for most text reading, but I am picturing research comparing multiple texts side-by-side. When the promises of electronic paper are fulfilled, the conversion from print to eText will begin in earnest, much as electronic video imaging supplanted celluloid and digital photography is succeeding paper.

The critical factor in the evolution of the eJournal is its acceptance into the formal academic process. Very important is the acknowledgment by departments and colleges of eJournal publication as legitimate research. Peer review may be a requisite factor in this acceptance. When top quality scholarship is available in only electronic form, academics will read it. We do not have the option of ignoring the work of major scholars. Researchers will go where the research is. The major force in putting quality contemporary philosophy research online in journal form is **Poiesis**.

POIESIS

Poiesis is a growing collection of online texts of major print journals in philosophy. The service is a joint venture between the Philosophy Documentation Center and the Intelex Corporation, which produces *Past Masters*® texts (see above). The list of participating journals is impressive (see below), as are the reputations of both entities for producing quality scholarly materials. **Poiesis** has the potential of adding value to any library collection and may serve as a long term solution for the serials cost crisis, at least for titles in philosophy.

Two levels of service are available to institutions: *basic subscription* and *full-text subscription*; individual subscriptions are not offered due to authentication issues. The basic subscription provides citation information (Figures 2 and 3) and is priced by number of users (Figure 1).

The full-text subscription provides complete texts of the journal articles linked from the search results and a browsable menu. The cost for each full-text description is determined by the journal publisher. A basic subscription is required in order to obtain full-text subscriptions. Moreover, the journal publishers require subscription to the print journal in order to acquire the full-text service from **Poiesis**. This is an instance of what **The International Coalition of Library Consortia**

FIGURE 2

16 The Philosophical Review

. . . are manifestations of sentient life and hence natural phenomena. [. . .

. . . party ones. But human life, with its enormously complex . . .

. . . such people in real life, nor anything like them, . . .

. . . in practice bet one's life against a penny that . . .

. . . ideas are brought to life . . . The contributors . . . bring to . . .

. . . the history of his life is the history of . . .

FIGURE 3

The Philosophical Review
    Volume 105
    Volume 105, No. 4, October 1996
    Articles
    John V. Canfield: The Community View†*
    4. Page phr.105.4.485 [article top] phr. 105.4.485.2

Sophisticated Crusoe is not a borderline case of language use or rule following, as we can see by considering his behavioral twin, a fully acculturated person who takes a vow of silence to others but who continues to engage in such one-person language-games as admonishing himself. Sophisticated Crusoe is so close to the paradigmatic instances that we have little hesitation in granting him the status of a rule-follower or language user. Simple Crusoe on the other hand is a borderline case of language use. He and the monologuists of §243 are extreme cases, ones at the edge of our conceptual world. We do not encounter such people in real life, nor anything like them, and our everyday concepts of language and rule following are not geared to deal with them. Wittgenstein holds that even in the case of a fully acculturated person we grant rule-following status in the one-person case only by analogy.

(ICOLC) calls the "current print price plus electronic surcharge plus significant projected inflation surcharges" pricing model.[16]

A basic subscription allows for running searches across the full texts of participating journals. The search results return up to one paragraph of the text surrounding each hit. A basic subscription search of *The Philosophical Review* in the demonstration area of the **Poiesis** Website, URL: <http://www.nlx.com/posp/pospdemo.htm>, for the keyword "life" gave the results in Figure 2.[17]

The results are hyperlinked so that selecting any line retrieves the article information. Selecting the third of the sixteen listed in Figure 2 returned the following (Figure 3).[18]

This is ample context for a researcher to determine the relevance of the article to their investigation.

Given the range of important journals included in **Poiesis** (e.g., *Mind* and *The Journal of Philosophy*) this service is valuable to all professional philosophers and scholars in other disciplines as well. Another search tool, the **Philosopher's Index** (see below), covers all of the journals that **Poiesis** maintains and many other sources as well. Yet, **Poiesis** offers a capacity that other referencing tools do not: full-text subscription for some participating journals.

A *full-text subscription* is the second level of service available from **Poiesis**. A full-text subscription provides links to the entire text of the articles cited. Eighteen of the 30 current titles are available as full-text. Twelve of the 32 forthcoming titles are planning full-text service. Even with only one-half of the titles in full-text, this aspect of **Poiesis** is attractive for the philosophy researcher. The last 50 years of the *Review of Metaphysics*, one of the most important philosophy journals, is available as full-text subscription and can be purchased on CD-ROM.[19] Some other current full-text titles are *American Philosophical Quarterly, Business Ethics Quarterly, Philosophical Review, Philosophy and Phenomenological Research, Philosophy and Theology, Southern Journal of Philosophy*, and *Teaching Philosophy*. Under construction as forthcoming full-text titles are *Asian Philosophy, Hypatia*, and *International Studies in the Philosophy of Science*. All of these are mainstay periodicals in the well-stocked library collection.

The true value of **Poiesis** depends upon which and how many of the publications will be available as full-text. *The Journal of Philosophy, Mind, Monist, The Philosophical Quarterly, Metaphilosophy, Philosophical Investigations, Philosophical Topics*, and *Philosophy* are among those offered for searching but not as full-text subscriptions. If these became available as full-text subscriptions on the Web (and if *Ethics* joined the titles), **Poiesis** would be counted as an essential service for philosophical research. The prospects are excellent, especially since Intelex also offers *Past Masters®*, full electronic editions of classic philosophy titles (see above). Intelex President Brad Lamb makes clear his vision to integrate Poiesis with *Past Masters®* to create a Web-based environment with immediate access to core texts, current and prior secondary literature, and sophisticated search and management tools. The only deficit in sight with all this is that serious researchers may never want to leave their offices! At least until wireless mobility is a commonplace.

Full-text subscriptions can be purchased by institutions that have print subscriptions and the basic subscription. Thus, **Poiesis** is not designed as an electronic alternative to print periodicals. It is an excellent addition to them. Full-text subscriptions of available journals are priced by the individual journal publishers. **Poiesis** suggests an additional subscription fee of 30% over the print subscription fee. This would add between $6 and $18 to the subscription costs of individual journals.

Basic subscription for an institution is based upon the number of philosophy faculty listed in *The Directory of American Philosophers*[20] or *The Directory of International Philosophers*.[21]

Consortium and satellite campus pricing is available, as well as pro-rated subscription periods to accord with the institution's fiscal year.

ICAAP

Poiesis is setting the standard for Internet access to traditional print journals in philosophy. Yet, provision needs to be made for access to startup and smaller publications. Academic philosophy is in a continual process of redefinition as theories and schools rise and fall. Startup journals and newsletters play an important role in this process, as factions and talents seek to gain visibility. The problem is how to keep track of this tumult and present it in a form usable by the philosophical community. A promising approach to this problem is found in journal consortiums. **The International Consortium for Alternative Academic Publication (ICAAP)** is a non-profit collective of libraries, individual scholars, editors, programmers, and university officials dedicated to the viability of cost effective and research quality electronic journals. URL: <http://www.icaap.org>. **ICAAP** provides services useful to eJournals, including archiving, advanced search capabilities, site management, conferencing, email list services, and secure server space. Providing these basic services as a package greatly simplifies the task of eJournal start up. **ICAAP's** objective is to host about 30 eJournals and provide them as a unified resource to libraries, institutions, and individuals. The motive is to demonstrate how strategic uses of information technology can reduce costs, speed up production, and enhance eJournals compared to their print relatives.

ICAAP lists seven journals related to philosophy. URL: <http://www.icaap.org/database/philosophy.shtml>. These journals originate from Spain, Canada, Finland, and the United States. **ICAAP** encourages multilingual publication. The journals are:

- *A Parte Rei. Revisita de Filosophia*; Spanish, General philosophy topics.
- *Animus: A Philosophical Journal for Our Time*; English, Social Criticism.
- *Basileus*; English, Philosophy of Law.
- *Negations: An Interdisciplinary Journal of Social Thought*; English, Social-Political.
- *Other Voices*; English, Cultural Criticism.
- *Smarandache Notions Journal*; Vanity publication by the author, F. *Smarandache*.
- *The Trumpeter*; English, Environmental Philosophy.

None of these is peer-reviewed, which lessens the research value of the sources to academic researchers. **ICAAP** services are free for journal editors and the journals are free for all Web users. However, in order to support the project, institutions and individuals are asked to purchase memberships. Membership for large institutional libraries is $300/yr and smaller specialty or faculty support libraries is $100/yr. Given the impact of serials costs on library budgets, supporting viable projects to advance electronic publication solutions is a worthy investment. **ICAAP** appears to be such a viable project.

A unique item among the periodicals is **The Philosopher's Web Magazine**, the online companion to the print edition of *The Philosopher's Magazine*. URL: <http://www.philosophers.co.uk>. This publication is directed to the general public rather than specialized academic readers and resembles *Psychology Today* in the way it reaches the non-academic public with news and ideas from psychology. Still, the news and events covered in recent issues will be of interest to all philosophers.

RESEARCH DATABASES

Since 1966 **The Philosopher's Index** has been the staple of literature reviews for philosophical research. The resource provides annual
indexing and abstracts from over 300 journals, contributions to anthologies, and philosophy books. The addition, over a decade ago, of **The
Philosopher's Index from 1940** was a substantial gain for researchers.
This resource collected together over 20 years of scholarship references
into a single indexed volume. The introduction several years ago of all
the published volumes on CD-ROM enhanced the value of the resource
again. Now, the publication of **The Philosopher's Index** on the Web
promises even greater advantages to scholars.

SilverPlatter Information Ltd. acquired **The Philosopher's Index** in the summer of 1999. URL: <http://www.silverplatter.com>.
The database includes major articles from anthologies and books written in English, Spanish, German, Italian, and French, as well about
480 journals adding up to over 213,000 bibliographic citations with
author abstracts. Recent features of **The Philosopher's Index** include:

- Journal names instead of abbreviations
- Browsable indices of full journal names, authors, descriptors,
  and persons discussed in the document
- A pseudo-field to enable searching both descriptors and persons
  simultaneously
- Backward navigation for changing some search terms without re-
  starting the entire search
- ISSNs in the journal article records

Annual licenses are based on the number of users. The single user
rate is $995 per year; the rate for two to four users is $1,493; the
unlimited license campus wide access (five users and up) is $2,239 per
year. The licenses include the full database which extends back to
1940 to the present year.

Reference Works

Encyclopedias and dictionaries have been part of the philosopher's
research repertoire since Bayle's *Dictionnaire Historique et Critique*
(1697) and Diderot's *Encyclopédie* (1771). In the later twentieth century, the major large-scale reference work has been the 1967 *Macmil-*

lian Encyclopedia of Philosophy, edited by Paul Edwards. In 1998 the *Routledge Encyclopedia of Philosophy* edited by Edward Craig was released.[22] The thirty years between these volumes created gaps in the literature. As John Perry and Ed Zalta of Stanford University observe:

> By the mid to late 1970s, a student might go to an encyclopedia looking for information about the Kripke/Donnellan theory of reference, the Lewis and Armstrong identity theories of mind, Putnam's functionalist theory of mind, or Rawls's theory of justice and find nothing of value in the *Macmillan Encyclopedia.* So the philosophy community went for 20-25 years before the recent handbooks and dictionaries attempted to fill the gap.[23]

In response to the gap between academic developments and reference documentation, the Center for the Study of Language and Information (CLSI) is producing the **Stanford Encyclopedia of Philosophy**: Principal Editor: Edward N. Zalta, CSLI/Stanford University; Associate Editor: Colin Allen, Philosophy/Texas A&M University; Assistant Editor: Uri Nodelman, Computer Science/Stanford University. URL: <http://plato.stanford.edu>. This work is entirely on the Web with no print equivalent. Two years into the project, the encyclopedia is about 40% complete with 444 entries assigned (written or in process) out of 1,138 entries in its planned table of contents. The intended value of this work, however, is that it will never be complete. It will be a dynamic and continually revised work that grows and changes with developments in the discipline and criticisms of the contents. Four times per year the entire content is frozen and archived, thus allowing for author and editor revisions. The archived versions are all available. This ambitious project is likely to advance knowledge concerning the nature of reference works online as well as producing a body of first-rate commentary on a wide range of philosophic topics.[24] The submitted articles are peer-reviewed for quality control. The resource is free for all to access and belongs in every set of philosophy reference Web links.

Another source is **The Internet Encyclopedia of Philosophy** edited by James Fieser with Bradley Dowden as Science and Logic editor. URL: <http://www.utm.edu/research/iep>. Most of the 428 entries are modified from public domain sources or from professor Fieser's class notes. Other articles, notably the biographical, are from other philosophers. Thirty-two such original articles are in production at present. While this resource lacks the scope and authority of the **Stanford Encyclopedia of Philosophy**, it may serve nicely as an additional resource for courses. It is interesting to note that by surface appearance alone it is hard to tell the important differences between these two encyclopedias. Yet, the difference in editorial standards is major. The **Stanford Encyclopedia of Philosophy** has a core editorial board of three and fifty-eight subject-specific editors. URL: <http://plato.stanford.edu/info.html>. The **Internet Encyclopedia of Philosophy** has two editors, making this resource a remarkable accomplishment. As a resources for class use, it is unparalleled on the Web. The authoritative talent available to the **Stanford Encyclopedia of Philosophy** makes it most valuable to researchers.

The Catholic Encyclopedia is an online version of the 1913 edition published by Robert Appleton Company and found in many university libraries. URL: <http://www.newadvent.org/cathen>. This is a valuable reference work for philosophers as it covers topics in church history and scholarship not found elsewhere. There are, however, later editions of **The Catholic Encyclopedia**. The 1913 edition was chosen because it is in the public domain while more recent editions remain copyright protected.[25] The electronic version is being transcribed autonomously by a multitude of volunteers. While volunteerism is a poweful force, it leaves the product open to uncontrolled error. Assuming that one objective of a reference collection is to provide up-to-date sources produced under reliable editorial controls, the value of this resource to the researcher is questionable (compared to the print editions). Still, **The Catholic Encyclopedia** provides philosophy resources that neither the **Stanford Encyclopedia of Philosophy** nor the **Internet Encyclopedia of Philosophy** presently provides, such as an extensive article on Socrates.

Philosophical dictionaries typically have briefer entries than the encyclopedias. Two Internet resources of this sort are **A Dictionary of Philosophical Terms and Names** edited by Garth Kemerling (URL: http://people.delphi.com/gkemerling/dy) and **Dictionary of Philosophy of Mind**, edited by Chris Eliasmith (URL: http://www.artsci. wustl.edu/~philos/MindDict/). **The Encyclopedia of Philosophy of Education,** edited by Michael A. Peters and Paulo Ghiraldelli Jr., is an international effort that has produced a small collection of articles useful to educators. URL: <http://www.educacao.pro.br>.

Search

The Internet contains a huge base of resources that is continually growing and changing. The ability to search that base effectively and organize it strategically is a distinct advantage to the researcher. General use search engines, such as **AltaVista** and **Google,** are valuable, especially if one has strong search strategy skills. Limited Area Search Engines (LASE) build bases of selected items deemed relevant to the intended users. Consequently, searches yield highly relevant results and allow for more refined search strategies across the selective base.

Such a LASE for philosophers is Noesis. URL: <http://noesis. evansville.edu>. It currently indexes about 8,500 essays, lectures and other course materials, images, graphs, charts, book and article reviews, primary texts, bibliographies, chronologies, and glossaries. The sources in the base are moderated by an editorial board, resulting in a search base from the Internet that is akin to a juried journal. Anthony Beavers is the General Editor, with two associate editors and eleven topic editors on the board.

Another philosophy LASE is **Hippias**, which covers a much wider range than **Noesis**. URL: <http://hippias.evansville.edu>. For instance, Noesis does not include links to pages of **The American Philosophical Association** while Hippias does. The aim of **Hippias** is to include in the search area resources that are likely to be of interest to academic philosophers, while excluding links that belong to the more popular sense of "philosophy" (e.g., New Age ideas, Astrology sites, vanity opinion pages).

> Hippias searches a small set of associate sites and all the pages they link to, with the exception of a few pages that Hippias is told to avoid, such as personal homepages and the major search engines discussed above. This procedure, in turn, passes Hippias' editorial control over to the experts that manage the associate sites. By simply linking their index to a page, these editors are also instructing Hippias to include it in the search window.[26]

A companion and predecessor to **Hippias** is **Argos**, which uses the same system of peer-review that Hippias uses to limit the data set to ancient and medieval resources. URL: <http://argos.evansville.edu>.

Perseus is a major research tool for scholars of antiquity. URL: <http://www.perseus.tufts.edu>. It provides a top rate set of searchable primary texts, secondary sources, and resources limited to the area of the Archaic and Classical Greek world. Researchers will find here the standard Greek editions of works by Plato and Aristotle, English Index to the Database, Greek Word Search of Primary Texts, English Word Search of the Liddell, Scott and Jones Greek Lexicon, and an engine for all primary texts (Greek and English), reference texts to Greek and Latin grammar and syntax, a pictorial guide to Greek architecture, a Perseus Encyclopedia, and more. Perseus 2.0 is available for the Macintosh (only) on four CD-ROMs, or in a concise version on one CD-ROM. It appears that the CD-ROMs contain sources that the Web site lacks.

The International Directory of On-Line Philosophy Papers is edited by Joe Lau. URL: <http://www.hku.hk/philodep/directory>. Individual authors submit papers to the site, which currently contains about 500 entries. Only work by professional philosophers working at academic institutions is accepted. Searches may be performed by keyword or by selecting from 16 pre-defined topic areas.

Internet Indices

Web indices, or *link-sites*, organize sets of links to Web sites by topic. These are edited by self-initiated individuals or with boards of editors. The following are some of the most comprehensive, well organized, and up-to-date portals to philosophy resources on the Internet:

- **EpistemeLinks.com** edited by Tom Stone. URL: <http://www. epistemelinks.com>.
- **Guide to Philosophy on the Internet** edited by Peter Suber. URL: <http://www.earlham.edu/~peters/gpi>.
- **Philosophy in Cyberspace** edited by Dey Alexander. URL: <http://www-personal.monash.edu.au/~dey>.
- **Yahoo! Guide to Philosophy**. URL: <http://dir.yahoo.com/ humanities/ philosophy>.
- **Ethics Updates** edited by Larry Hinman. URL: <http://ethics. acusd.edu:80>. A strong collection of ethics-related links, texts, and multimedia (e.g., streaming videos).
- **Great Voyages** edited by Bill Uzgalis. URL: <http://ucs.orst. edu/~uzgalisw/302>. A collection of Modern Philosophy links

and resources including *Women in Modern Philosophy* and sources on Bartolome Las Casas, "the father of anti-racism."

ORGANIZATIONS

The **American Philosophical Association** is the American national professional association for philosophers, with over 5,000 members. URL: <http://www.udel.edu/apa>. The Web site provides information about, from, and for professional philosophers. The **Computers and Philosophy Conference** is an annual meeting held at Carnegie Mellon University and organized by Robert Cavalier. URL: <http://caae. phil.cmu.edu/CAAE/CAP/CAPpage.html>. CAP has shared sessions across the continent (e.g., with Oregon State University in 1999) by teleconference and plans to start Webcasting (live video multicast on the Web) conference sessions in the 2000 meeting. Web-accessible live conferences will be a major advance for researchers. The **Philosophy Documentation Center** is a non-profit organization at Bowling Green State University, offering publications, multimedia titles, software, and information services of value to philosophers. URL: <http://www.bgsu.edu/pdc/index.html>.

LISTS

The power of the Internet to facilitate communication across space and time for sizable groups adds much value to philosophical research. Email lists, newsgroups, and threaded Web boards provide venues for ongoing discussion among scholars. **Philosophy in Cyberspac**e lists 302 philosophy related online discussion groups.[27] Not all of these are still active, but some are impressive. JDEWEY-L is an email list for discussion of John Dewey's philosophy moderated by Tom Burke (subscribe: listserve@vm.sc.edu). In the six months that I received the list, participation was constant with between 5 and 20 messages posted each day. Most of the posts fall squarely in the realm of scholarly inquiry. Philosophers need to be made aware of these discussion forums and the potential to create new topic forums as needed.

PHILOSOPHICAL REFLECTION

Michael Heim raises an important issue about the effect of search processes on the growth of knowledge.[28] The method of the logical keyword search structures our inquiry in fundamental ways. Searches operate with Boolean logic. Boolean logic breaks our language into discrete, binary units and transforms it according to a rigid system of categories and rules. Neither everyday language nor academic conversation accord rigorously with those categories and rules; language and thought proceed partly intuitively. Connections between ideas may be made loosely, by association, by analogy, by chance, and by metaphor. Heim is interested in how our mechanisms of information retrieval may shape our approaches to knowledge and inquiry.

The Boolean search shows the characteristic way we put questions to the world of information. When we pose a question to the Boolean world, we use keywords, buzzwords, thought bits to scan the vast store of knowledge. Keeping an abstract, cybernetic distance from the sources of knowledge, we set up tiny funnels to capture the onrush of data. The funnels sift out the "hits" triggered by our keywords. Through minute logical apertures, we observe the world much like a robot rapidly surveying the surface of things. We cover an enormous amount of material in an incredibly short time, but what we see comes though narrow thought channels.[29]

Whether information technology transforms language and thought, as Heim suggests, is open to question. Conducting searches and browsing the Web need not be rigidly systematic. But Heim's epistemological point is strong. The means by which we gather and organize information has a profound impact upon which questions get asked, answered, or discarded. Computer search and sorting techniques pose a hazard because they are relatively primitive and because many computer-using academics may not see how primitive they are. The common view of computers and the Internet is that they are highly advanced forms of technology. Thus, it is easy to assume that operators, like search engines, are similarly advanced. They are not, however, advanced compared to the capacities of the intelligent human researcher. It may be easy to conceal and forget this crucial distinction. If that happens, then Arthur C. Clarke's Third Law obtains; "Any sufficiently advanced technology is indistinguishable from magic."[30] Were we to move from intellectual rigor to magical thinking in the academic conversation, we will have lost significant ground in the growth of knowledge. The Internet is a wonderful and powerful tool for philosophical research. It is even more worthy as the *subject* of such investigation.

NOTES

1. Moor, J. 1997. "The Computational Turn." *American Philosophical Association Philosophy and Computers Newsletter.* Fall 1997, 97(1): p. 28.

2. Bynum, T.W. and Moor, J.H. 1998. *The Digital Phoenix: How Computers are Changing Philosophy.* Blackwell Publishers, Ltd. Oxford.

3. Cavalier, R. 1998. "Using Computing Technology for Philosophical Research: An APA Report." In *The Digital Phoenix: How Computers are Changing Philosophy.* Edited by Bynum, T.W. and Moor, J. Blackwell Publishers, Ltd. Oxford. pp. 338-392.

4. *How Many Online?* NUA Internet Surveys. [Online]. Retrieved August 12, 1999. URL: <http://www.nua.ie/surveys/how_many_online/index.html>.

5. Ivanhoe, P.J. 1996. "What Makes a Classic?" *The Stanford Daily* Volume 210a. [Online]. Retrieved June 7, 1999. URL: <http://daily.stanford.org/7-11-96/OPINIONS/index.html>.

6. *Past Masters*R Frequently Asked Questions. [Online]. Retrieved July 8, 1999. URL: <http://www.nlx.com/pstm/pstmfaq.htm>.

7. Folio Views® is a product of OpenMarket, Inc. URL: <http://www.openmarket.com>.

8. *Directory of American Philosophers, 1998-1999, Nineteenth Edition.* Archie J. Bahm, Founding Editor. Bowling Green: Philosophy Documentation Center. URL: <http://www.bgsu.edu/offices/phildoc/ad98-99.html>.

9. *International Directory of Philosophy and Philosophers, 1999-2000,* Eleventh Edition. Edited by Ramona Cormier. Bowling Green: Philosophy Documentation Center. URL: <http://www.bgsu.edu/offices/phildoc/id99-00.html>

10. Lamb, B. August 10, 1999. Telephone interview conducted by Jon Dorbolo. Oregon State University.

11. Lamb, B. August 10, 1999. Telephone interview conducted by Jon Dorbolo. Oregon State University.

12. Okerson, A. 1996. *University Libraries and Scholarly Communication.* Scholarly Publishing: The Electronic Frontier. Ed. Peck, R. and Newby G. B. The MIT Press. Cambridge, Massachusets. p.189.

13. Solsteric, M. 1998. "At the Speed of Thought: Pursuing Non-Commercial Alternatives to Scholarly Communication." *Association of Research Libraries Newsletter,* October 1998, Issue 200. [Online]. Retrieved August 15, 1999. URL: <http://www.arl.org/newsltr/200/sosteric.html>.

14. International Coalition of Library Consortia (ICOLC). 1998. *Statement of Current Perspective and Preferred Practices for the Selection and Purchase of Electronic Information.* [Online]. Retrieved August 15, 1999. URL: <http://www.library.yale.edu/consortia/statement.html>.

15. Plato, *Phaedrus*, 521d.

16. *Op. Cit.*

17. Search performed August 21, 1999. URL: <http://poiesis.nlx.com/cgi-bin/folioisa.dll/dphilrev.nfo/query=?realquerydlg> and results retrieved at <http://poiesis.nlx.com/cgi-bin/folioisa.dll/dphilrev.nfo/query=+life+/hit_headings/words=4?realquerydlg>.

18. Results retrieved August 21, 1999. URL: <http://poiesis.nlx.com/cgi-bin/folioisa.dll/dphilrev.nfo/query'+life+/doc/{t127}/h it_headings/words'4?>.

19. The *Fifty Years of the Review of Metaphysics* CD-ROM costs $1,500 for a campus-wide license, $750 for a 2-person LAN license, and $300 for the individual subscriber. Updates to the CD-ROM collection are scheduled for every five years.

20. *Directory of American Philosophers, 1998-1999, Nineteenth Edition.* Archie J. Bahm, Founding Editor. Bowling Green: Philosophy Documentation Center. [Online]. URL: <http://www.bgsu.edu/offices/phildoc/ad98-99.html>.

21. *International Directory of Philosophy and Philosophers, 1999-2000,* Eleventh Edition. Edited by Ramona Cormier. Bowling Green: Philosophy Documentation Center. [Online]. URL: <http://www.bgsu.edu/offices/phildoc/id99-00.html>.

22. The Routledge Encyclopedia of Philosophy is available for £1,995/$2,995 in the 10 volume print format only; £1,995/$2,995 for the CD-ROM with a licence for up to 10 simultaneous users across a LAN; £2,295/$3,495 for the print/CD-ROM package. URL: <http://www.rep.routledge.com/>.

23. Perry, J. and Zalta, E.N. *Why Philosophy Needs a "Dynamic" Encyclopedia of Philosophy.* [Online]. Retrieved May 17, 1999. URL: <http://plato.stanford.edu/why.html>.

24. Hammer, E.M. and Zalta, E.N. 1997. "A Solution to the Problem of Updating Encyclopedias." *Computers and the Humanities* 31 (1): pp. 47-60.

25. Dittman, M and Drake, T. 1997. *Byte by Byte, Catholic Encyclopedia Launched into Cyberspace.* [Online]. Retrieved May 17, 1999. URL: <http://www.newadvent.org/cathen/00002a.htm>.

26. *About Hippias.* 1997. [Online]. Retrieved June 12, 1999. URL: <http://hippias.evansville.edu/about.htm>.

27. Philosophy in Cyberspace, Section 4: Discussion Groups. [Online]. Retrieved June 12, 1999. URL: <http://www-personal.monash.edu.au/~dey/phil/section4.htm>.

28. Heim, M. 1993. *The Metaphysics of Virtual Reality.* New York: Oxford University Press.

29. Heim, M. 1999. "Computer Search Logic." *The American Philosophical Association Newsletter on Philosophy and Computers.* 98 (2), Spring 1999, p. 59.

30. The Arthur C. Clarke Foundation. [Online]. Retrieved June 13, 1999. URL: <http://www.acclarke.co.uk/a6.html>.

WEBLIOGRAPHY

Internet Research and Libraries

How Many Online? NUA Internet Surveys. http://www.nua.ie/surveys/how_many_online/index.html

The International Coalition of Library Consortia (ICOLC). http://www.library.yale.edu/consortia/statement.html

At the Speed of Thought: Pursuing Non-Commercial Alternatives to Scholarly Communication. Solsteric, M http://www.arl.org/newsltr/200

The International Consortium for Alternative Academic Publication (ICAAP). http://www.icaap.org

Rochester Institute of Technology. http://wally.rit.edu/map/1/reserve.html

eTexts

Everybook® URL: http://www.everybk.com/
Softbook® URL: http://www.softbook.com/
RocketBook® URL: http://www.rocket-ebook.com/
Glassbook® URL: http://www.glassbook.com/.
Open eBook Initiative is seeking standards and compatibility among display
  manufacturers and publishers. URL: http://www.openebook.org/
Steve Gibson's pages. URL: http://grc.com/freeandclear.htm
Microsoft ClearType ™ press releases at http://www.microsoft.com/typography/cleartype/
  default.htm.
Xerox PARC is developing an imaging technology that signals the coming shift to
  eText. URL: http://www.parc.xerox.com/parc-go.html.

Primary Texts

What Makes a Classic? Ivanhoe, P.J. http://daily.stanford.org/7-11-96/OPINIONS/
  index.html
Past Masters®. http://www.nlx.com/homepage.html
Past Masters® **Frequently Asked Questions.** http://www.nlx.com/pstm/pstmfaq.
  htm 8/8/99
Directory of American Philosophers, *1998-1999, Nineteenth Edition.* Archie J.
  Bahm http://www.bgsu.edu/offices/phildoc/ad98-99.html
Directory of International Philosophers, *1998-1999, Nineteenth Edition.* Archie J.
  Bahm, Founding Editor. http://www.bgsu.edu/offices/phildoc/ad98-99.html

Secondary Texts

Poesis. http://www.nlx.com/posp
Episteme Links. http://www.epistemelinks.com
ICAAP lists seven journals related to philosophy. URL: http://www.icaap.org/database/
  philosophy.shtml.
The Philosopher's Web Magazine. http://www.philosophers.co.uk

Research Databases

The Philosopher's Index. http://products.dialog.com/products/oddatas/philo.html
Folio Views®. http://www.openmarket.com

Reference Works

Why Philosophy Needs a 'Dynamic' Encyclopedia of Philosophy. Perry, J. and
  Zalta, E.N. http://plato.stanford.edu/why.html

Stanford Encyclopedia of Philosophy editied by Edward Zalta. http://plato.stanford. edu.

The Internet Encyclopedia of Philosophy edited by James Fieser with Bradley Dowden. http://www.utm.edu/research/iep

The Catholic Encyclopedia is an online version of the 1913 edition published by Robert Appleton Company and found in many university libraries. http://www.newadvent. org/cathen

A Dictionary of Philosophical Terms and Names edited by Garth Kemerling http://people.delphi.com/gkemerling/dy

Dictionary of Philosophy of Mind edited by Chris Eliasmith http://www.artsci. wustl.edu/~philos/MindDict

The Encyclopedia of Philosophy of Education edited by Michael A. Peters and Paulo Ghiraldelli Jr. http://www.educacao.pro.br

The Routledge Encyclopedia of Philosophy. http://www.rep.routledge.com

Search

Noesis edited by Anthony Beavers. http://noesis.evansville.edu

Hippias edited by Anthony Beavers. http://hippias.evansville.edu

The International Directory of On-Line Philosophy Papers edited by Joe Lau. http://www.hku.hk/philodep/directory

Argos edited by Anthony Beavers. http://argos.evansville.edu.

Perseus. http://www.perseus.tufts.edu

Indices

EpistemeLinks.com edited by Tom Stone. http://www.epistemelinks.com

Guide to Philosophy on the Internet edited by Peter Suber. http://www.earlham.edu/~ peters/gpi

Philosophy in Cyberspace edited by Dey Alexander. http://www-personal.monash. edu.au/~dey

Yahoo! Guide to Philosophy. http://dir.yahoo.com/humanities/philosophy

Ethics Updates edited by Larry Hinman. http://ethics.acusd.edu:80

Great Voyages edited by Bill Uzgalis. http://ucs.orst.edu/~uzgalisw/302

Organizations

American Philosophical Association is the American national professional association for philosophers, with over 5,000 members. URL: http://www.udel.edu/apa

Computers and Philosophy Conference is an annual meeting held at Carnegie Mellon University and organized by Robert Cavalier. URL: http://caae. phil.cmu.edu/CAAE/CAP/CAPpage.html

Philosophy Documentation Center http://www.bgsu.edu/pdc/index.html

Philosophical Reflection

Philosophy in Cyberspace: Discussion Groups.
http://www-personal.monash.edu.au/~dey/phil/section4.htm

The Metaphysics of Virtual Reality. Michael Heim. http://www.mheim.com/
The Arthur C. Clarke Foundation. Retrieved from the World Wide Web June 13,
   1999: http://www.acclarke.co.uk/a6.html

Index

Abraham, T., 223
Allason-Jones, L., 20
Allen, C., 368
Allied health sciences research
    resources and tools. *See*
    Medical research resources
    and tools
American and English literature
    research resources and tools.
    See English and American
    literature research resources
    and tools
Anderson, R.E., 16
Anglo-American legal research
    resources and tools. *See*
    Legal research resources and
    tools
Anthropology research resources and
    tools
    cyberculture, study of, 30-32
    disciplines on the Internet, 16-19
    e-publications, 28-30
    forums for communication and
        exchange, 19-20
    full text versions of print
        publications, 23-25
    importance of, 32-33
    indexes and abstracts, 21-23
    Internet as educational environment
        and, 30-32
    introduction to, 15-16,20,32-33
    online catalogs, 20-21
    primary resources, 26-28
    research about, 35-37
    web directories, 25-26
    webliography of, 34-35
Architecture research resources and
    tools. *See* Art and
    architecture research
    resources and tools

Art and architecture research resources
    and tools
    history research resources and
        tools. *See* History research
        resources and tools
    image web sites, 48-52
    importance of, 60-61
    introduction to, 39-43
    research about, 62
    research resources
        reference works, 44-48
        research databases, 52-60
    webliography of, 61-62
Aversa, E., 41

Ball, B., 321-322
Ball, W.J., 321
Basch, R., 336
Bass, A., 310
Bates, M.E., 9-14,41
Bell, S.J., 5-6,74-104
Berinstein, P., 48-49
Bidlack, H., 318
Biology research resources and tools
    importance of, 71-72
    introduction to, 63-64
    medical research resources and
        tools. *See* Medical research
        resources and tools
    natural science research resources
        and tools. *See* Natural
        science research resources
        and tools
    web sites
        citation web sites, 64-65
        clearinghouse web sites, 65-68
        information web sites, 68-71
    webliography of, 72-73
Blazek, R., 41-43
Boaz, F., 28

Leadership in Academic Libraries: Proceedings of the W. Porter Kellam Conference, The University of Georgia, May 7, 1991, edited by William Gray Potter (Vol. 17, No. 4, 1993). *"Will be of interest to those concerned with the history of American academic libraries." (Australian Library Review)*

Collection Assessment and Acquisitions Budgets, edited by Sul H. Lee (Vol. 17, No. 2, 1993). *Contains timely information about the assessment of academic library collections and the relationship of collection assessment to acquisition budgets.*

Developing Library Staff for the 21st Century, edited by Maureen Sullivan (Vol. 17, No. 1, 1992). *"I found myself enthralled with this highly readable publication. It is one of those rare compilations that manages to successfully integrate current general management operational thinking in the context of academic library management." (Bimonthly Review of Law Books)*

Vendor Evaluation and Acquisition Budgets, edited by Sul H. Lee (Vol. 16, No. 3, 1992). *"The title doesn't do justice to the true scope of this excellent collection of papers delivered at the sixth annual conference on library acquisitions sponsored by the University of Oklahoma Libraries." (Kent K. Hendrickson, BS, MALS, Dean of Libraries, University of Nebraska-Lincoln) Find insight discussions on the impact of rising costs on library budgets and management in this groundbreaking book.*

The Management of Library and Information Studies Education, edited by Herman L. Totten, PhD, MLS (Vol. 16, No. 1/2, 1992). *"Offers something of interest to everyone connected with LIS education–the undergraduate contemplating a master's degree, the doctoral student struggling with courses and career choices, the new faculty member aghast at conflicting responsibilities, the experienced but stressed LIS professor, and directors of LIS Schools." (Education Libraries)*

Library Management in the Information Technology Environment: Issues, Policies, and Practice for Administrators, edited by Brice G. Hobrock, PhD, MLS (Vol. 15, No. 3/4, 1992). *"A road map to identify some of the alternative routes to the electronic library." (Stephen Rollins, Associate Dean for Library Services, General Library, University of New Mexico)*

Managing Technical Services in the 90's, edited by Drew Racine (Vol. 15, No. 1/2, 1991). *"Presents an eclectic overview of the challenges currently facing all library technical services efforts. . . . Recommended to library administrators and interested practitioners." (Library Journal)*

Budgets for Acquisitions: Strategies for Serials, Monographs, and Electronic Formats, edited by Sul H. Lee (Vol. 14, No. 3, 1991). *"Much more than a series of handy tips for the careful shopper. This [book] is a most useful one–well-informed, thought-provoking, and authoritative." (Australian Library Review)*

Creative Planning for Library Administration: Leadership for the Future, edited by Kent Hendrickson, MALS (Vol. 14, No. 2, 1991). *"Provides some essential information on the planning process, and the mix of opinions and methodologies, as well as examples relevant to every library manager, resulting in a very readable foray into a topic too long avoided by many of us." (Canadian Library Journal)*

Strategic Planning in Higher Education: Implementing New Roles for the Academic Library, edited by James F. Williams, II, MLS (Vol. 13, No. 3/4, 1991). *"A welcome addition to the sparse literature on strategic planning in university libraries. Academic librarians considering strategic planning for their libraries will learn a great deal from this work." (Canadian Library Journal)*

Personnel Administration in an Automated Environment, edited by Philip E. Leinbach, MLS (Vol. 13, No. 1/2, 1990). *"An interesting and worthwhile volume, recommended to university library administrators and to others interested in thought-provoking discussion of the personnel implications of automation." (Canadian Library Journal)*

Library Development: A Future Imperative, edited by Dwight F. Burlingame, PhD (Vol. 12, No. 4, 1990). *"This volume provides an excellent overview of fundraising with special application to libraries. . . . A useful book that is highly recommended for all libraries." (Library Journal)*

Library Material Costs and Access to Information, edited by Sul H. Lee (Vol. 12, No. 3, 1991). *"A cohesive treatment of the issue. Although the book's contributors possess a research library perspective, the data and the ideas presented are of interest and benefit to the entire profession, especially academic librarians." (Library Resources and Technical Services)*

Training Issues and Strategies in Libraries, edited by Paul M. Gherman, MALS, and Frances O. Painter, MLS, MBA (Vol. 12, No. 2, 1990). *"There are . . . useful chapters, all by different authors, each with a preliminary summary of the content–a device that saves much time in deciding whether to read the whole chapter or merely skim through it. Many of the chapters are essentially practical without too much emphasis on theory. This book is a good investment." (Library Association Record)*

Library Education and Employer Expectations, edited by E. Dale Cluff, PhD, MLS (Vol. 11, No. 3/4, 1990). *"Useful to library-school students and faculty interested in employment problems and employer perspectives. Librarians concerned with recruitment practices will also be interested." (Information Technology and Libraries)*

Managing Public Libraries in the 21st Century, edited by Pat Woodrum, MLS (Vol. 11, No. 1/2, 1989). *"A broad-based collection of topics that explores the management problems and possibilities public libraries will be facing in the 21st century." (Robert Swisher, PhD, Director, School of Library and Information Studies, University of Oklahoma)*

Human Resources Management in Libraries, edited by Gisela M. Webb, MLS, MPA (Vol. 10, No. 4, 1989). *"Thought provoking and enjoyable reading. . . . Provides valuable insights for the effective information manager." (Special Libraries)*

Creativity, Innovation, and Entrepreneurship in Libraries, edited by Donald E. Riggs, EdD, MLS (Vol. 10, No. 2/3, 1989). *"The volume is well worth reading as a whole. . . . There is very little repetition, and it should stimulate thought." (Australian Library Review)*

The Impact of Rising Costs of Serials and Monographs on Library Services and Programs, edited by Sul H. Lee (Vol. 10, No. 1, 1989). *". . . Sul Lee hit a winner here." (Serials Review)*

Computing, Electronic Publishing, and Information Technology: Their Impact on Academic Libraries, edited by Robin N. Downes (Vol. 9, No. 4, 1989). *"For a relatively short and easily digestible discussion of these issues, this book can be recommended, not only to those in academic libraries, but also to those in similar types of library or information unit, and to academics and educators in the field." (Journal of Documentation)*

Library Management and Technical Services: The Changing Role of Technical Services in Library Organizations, edited by Jennifer Cargill, MSLS, MSed (Vol. 9, No. 1, 1988). *"As a practical and instructive guide to issues such as automation, personnel matters, education, management techniques and liaison with other services, senior library managers with a sincere interest in evaluating the role of their technical services should find this a timely publication." (Library Association Record)*

Management Issues in the Networking Environment, edited by Edward R. Johnson, PhD (Vol. 8, No. 3/4, 1989). *"Particularly useful for librarians/information specialists contemplating establishing a local network." (Australian Library Review)*

Acquisitions, Budgets, and Material Costs: Issues and Approaches, edited by Sul H. Lee (Supp. #2, 1988). *"The advice of these library practitioners is sensible and their insights illuminating for librarians in academic libraries." (American Reference Books Annual)*

Pricing and Costs of Monographs and Serials: National and International Issues, edited by Sul H. Lee (Supp. #1, 1987). *"Eminently readable. There is a good balance of chapters on serials and monographs and the perspective of suppliers, publishers, and library practitioners are presented. A book well worth reading." (Australasian College Libraries)*

Legal Issues for Library and Information Managers, edited by William Z. Nasri, JD, PhD (Vol. 7, No. 4, 1987). *"Useful to any librarian looking for protection or wondering where responsibilities end and liabilities begin. Recommended." (Academic Library Book Review)*

Archives and Library Administration: Divergent Traditions and Common Concerns, edited by Lawrence J. McCrank, PhD, MLS (Vol. 7, No. 2/3, 1986). *"A forward-looking view of archives and libraries. . . . Recommend[ed] to students, teachers, and practitioners alike of archival and library science. It is readable, thought-provoking, and provides a summary of the major areas of divergence and convergence." (Association of Canadian Map Libraries and Archives)*

Excellence in Library Management, edited by Charlotte Georgi, MLS, and Robert Bellanti, MLS, MBA (Vol. 6, No. 3, 1985). *"Most beneficial for library administrators . . . for anyone interested in either library/information science or management." (Special Libraries)*

Marketing and the Library, edited by Gary T. Ford (Vol. 4, No. 4, 1984). *Discover the latest methods for more effective information dissemination and learn to develop successful programs for specific target areas.*

Finance Planning for Libraries, edited by Murray S. Martin (Vol. 3, No. 3/4, 1983). *Stresses the need for libraries to weed out expenditures which do not contribute to their basic role–the collection and organization of information–when planning where and when to spend money.*